The Ghosts of
Johns Hopkins

The Ghosts of Johns Hopkins

The Life and Legacy that Shaped an American City

Antero Pietila

ROWMAN & LITTLEFIELD
Lanham • Boulder • New York • London

Published by Rowman & Littlefield
An imprint of The Rowman & Littlefield Publishing Group, Inc.
4501 Forbes Boulevard, Suite 200, Lanham, Maryland 20706
www.rowman.com

Unit A, Whitacre Mews, 26-34 Stannary Street, London SE11 4AB

Distributed by NATIONAL BOOK NETWORK

British Library Cataloguing in Publication Information Available

Library of Congress Cataloging-in-Publication Data Available

978-1-5381-1603-6 (hardcover)
978-1-5381-1604-3 (e-book)

∞™ The paper used in this publication meets the minimum requirements of American National Standard for Information Sciences—Permanence of Paper for Printed Library Materials, ANSI/NISO Z39.48-1992.

Printed in the United States of America

For Marva

Contents

Author's Note

My Baltimore Story Quilt

Johns Hopkins destroyed his private papers so thoroughly that no real biography exists of the Baltimore Quaker titan.[1] *The Ghosts of Johns Hopkins* uses scraps of history to quilt a fully documented reconstruction of the magnate's life and career as a railroad tycoon, venture capitalist, and merchant in the times of the Industrial Revolution, America's westward movement, and the Civil War. It analyzes how his legacy—the university, hospital, and medical school—became the defining factors that they are today, the largest private-sector employers in the city and the state, with a robust worldwide reach.

My 2010 social history, *Not in My Neighborhood: How Bigotry Shaped a Great American City*, scrutinized real estate industry sales practices in the aftermath of Baltimore's 1910 imposition of mandatory residential segregation, the first such law in the nation. This stand-alone companion volume follows ethnic and class rotations in The Basin (today's Inner Harbor), the city hall area, and the east side home of Hopkins Hospital. It tells the stories of the Germans, Irish, Jews, Bohemians, Poles, and Italians who passed through before the African American influx, which is described in detail. The narrative errs on the side of readability and will not overdose the reader with irrelevant minutia or an excessive listing of the cast of characters.

The book consists of three parts. "The Pragmatic Opportunist" explores Johns Hopkins's family origins, his religious and racial beliefs, and how he operated his businesses, becoming one of America's wealthiest men. It scrutinizes his peculiar role in the Civil War, and discusses how his health problems inspired him to create his educational and medical legacies, and the challenges those institutions faced. One chapter examines how medical schools acquired cadavers for dissection. The chapter title says it all—"Doctors Rob Graves."

The second part deals with "The Racial Dynamics of Modern Baltimore" and the role of Daniel Coit Gilman, the first Hopkins president, in their creation. The city took initial steps toward formal segregation in 1899, when it set in motion the first "Negro removal." Thousands of blacks were evicted from their homes around city hall in the name of municipal rebuilding, along with the community's most important institutions: schools, churches, the *Afro-American* newspaper, Masonic halls, and lawyers' and doctors' offices. Strivers headed for the west side, where they replaced white Christians and coexisted with Jews; ordinary folk ended up on the east side, where Hopkins Hospital had opened a decade earlier. These events created the racial dynamics that continue to this day.

The third part, "Pushing Out the Lumpenproletariat," discusses Hopkins Hospital's crisis in the 1960s, after the neighborhood became black. In the middle of menial employees' unionization drive, the hospital and medical school contemplated moving out of the Broadway campus altogether. "A hostile black community, constantly reminded of past expansion, limits future enlargement of the site," a 1970 assessment stated. "The characteristics of the neighborhood make the area uncongenial for employees, staff and students." The move never happened. Instead, Hopkins adopted a diversification strategy that led to partnerships and acquisitions of other hospitals. It also diverted routine patients away from the hospital on Broadway so that doctors there could concentrate on medically challenging cases. I document the giant demolition and rebuilding effort that, after several ethnic and class rotations, is reconstituting the hospital area.

A main goal of this book is to help the reader understand the idiosyncrasies and complexities of Baltimore, the closest "real" American city to Washington and therefore a place where foreign media keep flocking. I branch out far beyond Hopkins. I tell the story of 1950s nightlife and organized crime, including a time when the city police commissioner was in the pocket of the Mob. All this is relevant. Later, I delve deeper into the corruption in the police department. Such reconstructions help put today's headlines in perspective. I tell the stories of Federal Hill, Fells Point and Canton, examine the longtime mayor and governor William Donald Schaefer and profile his successors, Clarence "Du" Burns, the city's first African American mayor, and Kurt L. Schmoke. I dissect various social activist movements and show that neighborhoods do not belong to any specific ethnic group, race, religion, or class. Instead, they are living organisms, mutated over time by economic, social, and political forces.[2]

The Hopkins legacy straddles two realities. His pathfinding First World institutions are islands of excellence in a city that rewards mediocrity and increasingly exhibits Third World dysfunctions. Killing and drug addiction are out of control, bureaucracies are faltering amid corruption and falling tax revenues, and kids drop out of school, or are graduated without being able to read or write.

LIFE IN *THE SUN*

I first saw America's shores in May 1964 from the deck of the MS *Finntrader*. I was a twenty-year-old aspiring journalist from Finland, wanting so badly to spend that summer in the United States—the summer of Lyndon B. Johnson's reelection campaign, civil rights strife, and of the New York World's Fair—that I worked my way across on freighters. I came from a country so homogeneous that eye and hair color marked the chief differences among its four and a half million people. No blacks lived in Finland in those days, and only fifteen hundred Jews.

New York's polyglot metropolis stunned me. While reporting one day in Harlem, I found myself naked and sweating in an old Finnish steam bath operated by an immigrant from Jamaica. It had been a popular gathering spot among residents of the Finnish community, which thrived in Harlem from the 1910s until the 1950s. Few traces of that population of several thousand survived. Rival socialist halls, including one with an indoor swimming pool and bowling alley, were long gone, as were Finnish churches. One vestige still remaining was a hat shop on 125th Street belonging to an elderly Finnish woman, who had stayed after other whites ran. Another relic was the steam bath, with its black owner, a professional masseur, at Madison Avenue and 122nd Street. Among the thinning ranks of his Finnish customers was an Olympic gold medalist.

The phenomenon of changing neighborhoods fascinated me. In 1969, after receiving my MA degree in journalism from Southern Illinois University-Carbondale, I found an urban observatory in Baltimore, a declining but still-great city trying to recover from the 1968 riots that followed the assassination of the Reverend Martin Luther King Jr. The city was in a defeatist funk. Racial tensions flared, white flight to the suburbs continued; smokestack industries kept shutting down. I witnessed civil rights protests, reported on two Ku Klux Klan cross burnings, covered school desegregation, antiwar actions, religion, community organizing, city hall, and Baltimore County, a separate jurisdiction that was overtaking the city. I even joined a ragtag army of mercenaries that the Congress of Racial Equality was recruiting for a civil war in Angola. I never quite figured out what CORE's motive was in this effort that quickly flopped. My black fellow recruits, though, had a clear game plan. Once in Africa, they confided, they would frag the officers and loot diamond mines.

Making this journalistic enterprise possible was *The Sun*, Baltimore's venerable newspaper of record, founded in 1837. Owned by establishment families, the company also published *The Evening Sun*, the paper of H. L. Mencken, and a Sunday edition. It was a mighty peculiar institution. A mural in its Calvert Street lobby depicted a slavery-time Baltimore scene at the flagship paper's founding. (It was later covered with a false wall.) Into the sixties, the paper's real estate sale and rental ads were listed according to "white" and "colored." "Restricted" meant that no Jews or blacks could live in the neighborhood.

I had been eleven years on the paper when, in 1980, I was chosen to establish a bureau in Johannesburg. South Africa was full of bizarre stories. The most profound and thought-provoking, I discovered in Kliptown, near Soweto, the official dumping ground for people whom the authorities found impossible to classify racially. None would have qualified as white, but the government was petrified that it might mistakenly give a black the limited property and legal rights that "coloreds" and Asians enjoyed but blacks did not. Better avoid mistakes. As a result, hundreds of Kliptown residents had no race at all. Without a race classification, they could not go to school, work, or marry. They were known as "Twilight People."

In the surreal world of Kliptown, one denizen was a black woman who had married a colored man, an act that violated the immorality laws that banned intercourse among the country's four racial groups. When they divorced, a domestic court judge gave her the real estate, except that in South Africa blacks could not own real estate. Another resident was a white woman who had married a black policeman. The government came down on her like a ton of bricks. She was ready. Having been reared among Africans on a white farm, she came to court wearing a Zulu tribal outfit and carrying a baby in a bundle on her back, as was the custom among rural Africans. She spoke only Zulu and claimed to understand no Afrikaans or English. For the case to proceed, the government would have had to prove that she was white. Embarrassed to acknowledge that she belonged to the master race, the government dropped the charges, took away her constitutional rights, and banished her to Kliptown.

Because apartheid-ruled South Africa was a pariah nation in much of black Africa, I used two Finnish passports. One contained South African immigration and customs stamps, the other did not. This puzzled one official at the Johannesburg airport, a white man dressed in the tribal summer uniform of bureaucrats—khaki shorts and a matching short-sleeved, open-collared khaki shirt, with an obligatory comb stuck into one of his knee-high white socks. He went through my passport, stared at me, leafed through the passport again, and shook his head. "Mynheer," he remarked, "you are a most interesting man. You always leave but you never arrive."

I may use that on my gravestone yet.

A note on geography: Baltimore is often called a city of neighborhoods. In fact, many of today's neighborhood names are recent inventions. Among the city's regentrification successes is Charles Village, near the Hopkins University's Homewood campus. In the exciting 1960s, its huge Victorian row houses attracted young professionals, long on ambition but short of money. In 1967 *Evening Sun* copy editor Grace Darin, who lived there, came up with the current name that replaced the old one, Peabody Heights. In general, people usually referred to their area by its ward number, or some religious institution. Also, neighborhood borders keep changing. Much of what today is referred to as Federal Hill was simply called South Baltimore in pregentrification days. Similarly, before someone came up with Sandtown, it was just part of West Baltimore. I consistently use the Sandtown name in this book, instead of the planners' Sandtown-Winchester, because my book deals with neighborhoods east of Fulton Avenue. The Winchester part is several hundred yards away to the west, where the armory is, and can be reached only by bridges across a vast expanse of railroad tracks.

I strive for simple clarity. Thus I have effectively merged the old Jonestown area with Old Town, a commercial center that saw rotations from German to Irish to Jewish to black. Old Town borders are debatable. At one time the combined area was understood to stretch from Pratt Street past Green Mount Cemetery (where Johns Hopkins is buried) to the old city line at North Avenue. It was a bastion of the Irish, who succeeded Germans and were followed by Jews and blacks. I also chronicle Little Bohemia, the next neighborhood to the east. Its Czechs were the hospital's nearest neighbors.

In the quilt of America every city has stories to offer. These are Baltimore's.

Acknowledgments

Writing This Book

Johns Hopkins was a private man who left behind very little personal documentation. I had to get around that to primary sources from each period. As a sole researcher, I never could have achieved this goal without the Internet and Google Books.

The Internet enabled searches of the most unusual kind and of great specificity. Such searches led to Margaret Cook's 1781 diary that described how torn about slavery were the Quakers farming tobacco in Anne Arundel County—including Johns Hopkins's grandfather. Google's digitization of some fifty million books, in turn, included Dr. Horatio Gates Jameson's remarkable eyewitness account of the 1832 cholera epidemic that infected Johns Hopkins. Another find was the Virginia slave Noah Davis's 1859 volume about how the white Southern Baptist Convention bought his freedom, and sent him to Baltimore as a missionary.[1] However, the resource that I ended up using the most was ProQuest. That commercial database has stored facsimile copies of major newspapers from their first issues onward, and I could access it from home free of charge through local libraries.

The Enoch Pratt Free Library's Maryland room, the University of Baltimore's special collections, and the Maryland Historical Society offered documentation, including oral recollections, about bygone days. Andrew Harrison helped at the Alan Mason Chesney Medical Archives. Two Hopkins authorities, retired vice president Ross Jones and senior research archivist James Stimpert, read the whole manuscript. As to the city's history since the 1968 riots, I had reported on much of it. I knew the scene, I knew the players.

Gene Raynor was a particularly important resource. We were friends for more than three decades; he was William Donald Schaefer's buddy and confidante. As first city and then state elections chief, Raynor knew every politician and hanger-on, and he sure knew where the bodies were buried.

He spent countless hours with me, sharing secrets that enhance this book, particularly chapter 8. One morning, he looked up from his crossword puzzle at Vaccaro's, a Little Italy pastry shop, and said, "There's young Gambino. He doesn't know anything about the business."

The mention of a famous Mafia family name got my attention. It jogged Raynor's memory, too, because presently he began rambling about a long-ago murder near Little Italy involving a boxing figure who disrespected the Gambino family. Despite my over four decades in Baltimore, I had never heard about that particular murder, which opens chapter 8. It was a big story for a few days in 1952 and then was forgotten by nearly all, except for Raynor, whose father was of Irish origin and mother an Italian who spoke the lingo. When the parents separated, he became a denizen of Little Italy.

He was thirteen when he began mixing cement for Carl Julio, a big contractor. Two years later, he became a gofer for "Old Tommy," Mayor Thomas J. D'Alesandro Jr. Raynor saw a lot and heard even more. He graduated from Patterson High School, the alma mater of the bakery magnate John Paterakis, a close friend, and Peter Angelos, the asbestos litigator and Orioles owner. He once drove Old Tommy to a row house where police and firefighters were trying to convince a D'Alesandro kin, naked and raving mad, not to jump off the tarred roof. He witnessed a kitchen argument over the schooling of the mayor's daughter, the future Nancy Pelosi, the first woman Speaker of the House of Representatives. It started with D'Alesandro's wife, Anunciata, announcing that she agreed with Nancy's choice of a school out of state.

"Over my dead body," grunted the mayor.

"That can be arranged," she shot back.

Raynor was a short, rotund man, who rode to work on a rickety bicycle with fat tires and a shopping basket at the handlebars. He obtained a law degree from the University of Baltimore, and clerked for an attorney who belonged to the D'Alesandro family. When state senator Joseph Bertorelli was paralyzed in a car accident, Raynor became like a second son to the east side politician, who had previously served in the city council and the House of Delegates. Besides politics and strategy, Raynor knew plenty about the tentacles of the underworld—his uncle was Leo DaLesio, the Teamster boss ruling over all Maryland locals. (A federal probe convicted both DaLesio and Harry Raynor Jr., Gene's brother, of misuse of Teamster union funds.)[2]

In the chapter about Charles Street nightlife in the 1950s, I am indebted to Sidney Weinberg, who spent an afternoon with me in 2005 at Miller's Delicatessen in Pikesville. Milton Bates, a common friend and an erstwhile organizer for the Progressive Party, connected us and then left us alone. Weinberg had worked as an accountant for the original Club Charles and kept the books for several gambling figures on The Block. The second time we met, he was scared. On the advice of a son, a lawyer, he wanted to take back everything he told me.

I thank Stanley Sugarman, a real estate broker. He guided me in researching *Not in My Neighborhood*; this time he helped me with Sam Boltansky. I had met the international wholesaler of pornography who said our chance meeting would be the last because I was a journalist. Stanley had played handball with Sam at the old Monument Street Y, and he put a good word in for me. Sam had many irons in the fire. He was a real estate bottom-fisher. He owned the old Hendler's ice cream fortress on Baltimore Street, which had a stage and auditorium on the second floor and an expensively paneled boardroom that he donated to the Jewish Museum of Maryland, around the corner. He was the landlord of legendary Jack's Corned Beef on Lombard Street, where politicians and bureaucrats met and where a stock ticker let customers find out how they were doing on the market. He showed me his warehouses—the size of a football field in the Jones Falls Valley, now converted into apartments—where dozens of employees sorted out and stored "books." He catered to all tastes—big breasts, washboards, fat women, hairy women, women with one or both legs missing. Prisoners were his biggest customers, he told me, showing stacks of State of Illinois checks from inmates.

Among my Pennsylvania Avenue guides was Walter R. Carr Sr. He was a dapper, reefer-smoking old dude with a goatee whom I met at Left Bank Jazz Society. He published *Nightlifer,* available at bar counters, which mixed entertainment advertising with political diatribes. WMAR's George Collins, a former *Afro* city editor, took me to the Sphinx Club, a select membership club catering to doctors, lawyers, educators, and entrepreneurs. Once I met Charles Tilghman, the founder, there.

I thank Michael Olesker for providing me a copy of the Maryland Senate report on its hearings about police commissioner Donald Pomerleau, when state archives were unable to locate one. (They later did.) I thank Roger Twigg, an ace police reporter, with whom I worked closely when I was a rewrite man. How he ever got into the Marine Corps was beyond me—he was color-blind!

My journalistic adventures would not have been possible without Scott Sullivan, who hired me for *The Sun*; William F. Schmick 3rd, Gil Watson, Steve Luxenberg, Richard O'Mara, James Houck, and countless colleagues whose reporting strengthened this book. David Ettlin and Mark Reutter read the entire manuscript, saving me from embarrassments, as did Ralph Moore, Hal Riedl, Arnold Sherman, and Michael Seipp. I thank Bill Henry Sr., James H. Bready, David Cramer, Stacy Spaulding, Jay Brodie, Martin Millspaugh, Edgar P. Silver, Walter Sondheim, Samuel Hopkins, C. Fraser Smith, Gilbert Sandler, Neil Grauer, Edward C. Papenfuse, Garrett Power, William

L. Adams, Charles T. Burns, A. Robert Kaufman, Troy Brailey, Kenny Webster, Joe Nawrozki, Stuart Wechsler, Clarence Logan, Robert B. Moore, Philip Berrigan, Morton Pollack, Verda F. Welcome, Richard Lidinsky, Eva Slezak, Wolodymyr C. Sushko, Joe Tropea, Van Smith, James Crockett, J. Joseph Clarke, Jack Lapides, Jo-Ann Meyer Orlinsky, Joan and Gunther Wertheimer, Stephen H. Sachs, Joseph Sterne, Barry Rascovar, Jacqueline Thomas, Rafael Alvarez, Amy Davis, Frank P. L. Somerville, Judy Cooper, William Grigsby, Ed Kane, Bob Keith, and Charlie Duff. Speakers and participants at invaluable Baltimore City Historical Society programs inspired me; thank you, Mike Franch. Dozens of others helped me in important ways. This is their book too.

Robert Cronan did the dynamic maps. Bonnie Schupp made me look good in author's photos. Thank you. My agent, Marva Regina Harris-Watson, put order into my chaotic life and made sure I stayed focused. The book is dedicated to her. At Rowman & Littlefield, my thanks go to Jon Sisk, Kate Powers, and Alexander Bordelon.

The Ghosts of Johns Hopkins and *Not in My Neighborhood* are the culmination of my "American Experience," as a brass plaque describes my Baltimore years at an oak tree I donated decades ago next to the Shot Tower. When the thin-skinned Schaefer was mayor and we had our ups and downs, I checked the tree occasionally—just to make sure he had not cut it down out of spite!

anteropietila.com

Part I

THE PRAGMATIC OPPORTUNIST

Chapter One

Johnsie's Baltimore

Johnsie Hopkins, as family called the blue-eyed, long-legged seventeen-year-old, encountered a city divided by race, class, religion, national origin, and gender when he arrived in Baltimore in 1812. Born on a tobacco plantation in nearby Anne Arundel County, he hoped to make his mark in the nation's third-largest city, a noisy and sooty Industrial Revolution boomtown. His timing could not have been better. The rough-hewn youth witnessed the dawn of new transportation technologies that opened up the West. He grew up with an expansionist vision, and the will to pursue his goals. In time, he built such a fortune as a merchant, banker, and venture capitalist that a book published in 1996, 123 years after his death, ranked him as no. 69 among the hundred richest Americans up to that point. He shared the roster with Benjamin Franklin—and Bill Gates.[1]

Baltimore traced its origins to a 1729 port settlement in the Patapsco River marshlands that bordered the Chesapeake Bay and thus accessed the Atlantic. The *incorporated* city, however, was no older than Johnsie himself. Run by Anglo-Saxon Protestant grandees, it attracted enterprising newcomers from Europe, notably Protestants from Northern Ireland's Ulster, and a blend of Lutherans, Catholics, and Jews from Teutonic lands. Along with penniless strivers came men of accomplishments and substance, who all vied for recognition in the New World, challenging boundaries and testing social conventions. Since no federal taxation existed, huge fortunes could be quickly made, inherited, or married. Then there were the people of African blood, roughly a quarter of the population. Most were free, giving Baltimore the highest free black population in the nation. Counteracting that distinction was another. After federal law banned direct imports of African slaves in 1808, the city became the busiest Atlantic coast transfer point for slaves in domestic interstate transit from the Chesapeake to expanding cotton plantations in

Louisiana and in southwestern lands being stolen from Native Americans. In some early morning hours, slavers' cracking whips and barking dogs herded wretched men, wailing women, and bewildered children on Pratt Street to today's Inner Harbor and Fells Point where ships awaited.[2] The chattel, bound in chains, tied with ropes, and clothed in rags, had been sold South. An 1845 city directory listed "Slave Dealers" between "Silversmiths" and "Soap." Human trafficking remained perfectly legal in Maryland until one year after the Civil War.[3]

Johnsie would grow to oppose slavery, but he was born into the slaveholding tradition. His paternal grandfather, the first Johns Hopkins—whose given name in turn honored Johnsie's great-grandmother's family—owned a hundred captive men, women, and children on the family plantation, Whitehall, thirty miles south of Baltimore. Some slaves the grandfather bought, others he received as dowry. Or inherited, the way he inherited his faith from Puritan ancestors who converted after George Fox, the Quaker movement founder, sojourned in Anne Arundel County in 1672.[4] Fox was a dissenter who bolted out of the Church of England, taking thousands of followers with him. His Society of Friends rejected baptism, the doctrine of the trinity, and all sacraments, forms, and ceremonies. It was a contemplative faith, and if believers felt the spirit, they might quake. In many colonies, the authorities took a dim view of Friends, because they opposed wars and expressed eccentric behavior, such as refusing to take oaths—which a Maryland law required until 1899 to be done by kissing the Bible—and failing to uncover their heads indoors. In Massachusetts, forty-five Quaker women walked naked on streets, witnessing.[5] Quakers "represented, on their best side, the most vigorous effort of the Reformation to return to the spirituality and the simplicity of early Christians," wrote the Philadelphia essayist Sydney George Fish.[6]

Fox taught that God is in everyone, that each of us has the capacity to be inhabited by Christ's light, but each of us also has an "ocean of darkness" within. Each of us. He recognized the prophetic role of women.[7] He preached respect for our common humanity—including captive Native Americans and blacks. He urged kindness toward slaves, and freedom. However, even as he advocated abolition, faster sailing ships kept bringing in more slaves from Africa. The Chesapeake region's Quaker planters eagerly bought such captives; there were even slave traders who were Friends. Then, beginning in the 1770s, abolitionist fervor gripped Quakers throughout the Atlantic seaboard. Silence was not an option. Or as the abolitionist poet James Russell Lowell wrote, "They are slaves who fear to speak for the fallen and the weak." Activists also quoted Cyprian, the third-century Christian thinker from North Africa: "Both religion and humanity make it a duty for us to work for the deliverance of the captive. They are sanctuaries of Jesus Christ, who have fallen in the hands of the infidel."[8] Many Chesapeake planters disagreed, arguing that slaves were not human in the ways that whites were. Hadn't they warned Fox that even "making the negroes Christians would make them rebel?"[9]

The congregation that grandfather Johns Hopkins attended near Annapolis, West River Meeting, split over slavery. Incredibly, a Quaker minister visiting in February, 1781, was present to record this "trying time." Margaret Cook, of Maryland's Talbot County, describes in her journal how distressed she was after having supper with the important Montgomery County planter Roger Brooke, whose three-year-old grandson, Roger Brooke Taney, would rise to become the chief justice of the United States and rule, in *Dred Scott* in 1857, that blacks—free or slave—were not American citizens, nor could be. The Quaker grandfather owned more than a hundred slaves, and made no apologies. He "would not hear (or seem to hear) anything but his own opinion," Cook noted. "I believe the light in him is become darkness, and how great is that darkness!" She recorded that a "ranting spirit" possessed him, which he demonstrated in challenging Friends to expel him. "Nothing is better for him, I believe, than to answer him with silence, and thereby starve that spirit which rails against Friends. We left them, and I did pity him, but more his tender wife and children, who appeared like prisoners; but the hand that opened the prison door for the apostles can in his own time open it for this poor afflicted woman."

Cook and her horseback-riding traveling companions then spent a day in more satisfying conversations with John Cowman, another Quaker: "After we went to bed he signed a manumission for nine negroes, whom we had to sit with us in the morning." She also met with several members of the Thomas family. Evan Thomas, the patriarch, eventually "freed his slaves, over 200 in number, and gave them small allotments to cultivate."[10] Next day they rode to Johns Hopkins's. "As I walked up and down the little black children came about me, and I looked at them with a belief that they would not always be slaves."[11]

If it only had been that simple! It seems that grandfather Hopkins had to be shamed into his decision. Because of his slave ownership, fellow Quakers eased him out as the overseer of Indian Spring Meeting, a position of honor. He tried to make amends but his manumission offer was rejected because the ages of slaves "when to be free, being not agreeable to the advice of our Yearly Meeting."[12] Subsequently, he struck an acceptable deal, "manumitted 42 negroes and retained his membership with Friends."[13] Manumissions usually specified that freedom would come only after a set time period of additional service, so slaves remained at the Whitehall plantation. When grandfather Hopkins died, he still had fourteen slaves. Thus he never fully abandoned his belief in the institution of slavery even though he took measures to placate his coreligionists.

All of grandfather Johns Hopkins's eleven children were obligated to work on the five hundred-acre plantation. When Samuel, the eldest son, inherited the acreage and fourteen slaves, he, too, sired eleven offspring and worked them once they became old enough. Thus the schooling of his second-born son, the future philanthropist Johns Hopkins, ended at the age of twelve. Johnsie was quick-witted and quite the reader, capable of self-study under the guidance of an occasional tutor. Five years later his mother declared him ready for the world. "Thee has business ability and thee must go where the money is," she commanded. Thus at the age of seventeen he was apprenticed to an uncle, Gerard Hopkins, a substantial wholesale merchant in Baltimore and a leader of the city's small, tight-knit, thrifty, and influential Quaker community of merchants and industrialists. The youth showed aptitude. In 1814, two years into the apprenticeship, with his uncle on horseback travels for the Quakers in faraway Ohio, he ran the whole business unaided for several months without a hitch, actually growing it—just before the British Navy's bombardment of Fort McHenry. He lodged with his uncle's family and fell in love with his first cousin, Elizabeth Hopkins. She was ten years old when Johnsie moved in; he saw her blossom from a child to a young maiden. Elizabeth, too, was in love. But when Johnsie made known their intention to marry, the uncle said no. A Quaker supervisor of considerable authority, he forbade Johnsie to defy the laws of God and Nature. Johnsie didn't. He left the household and his uncle's employ; neither he nor Elizabeth ever married.

Johnsie wanted to launch a grocery and commission operation of his own. He had $800 in savings, a tidy sum but not enough to start a wholesale house. "That will make no difference," Uncle Gerard answered, offering to back him with $10,000. "I will endorse for thee, and this will give thee good credit, and in a short time thee will make a capital; thee has been faithful to my interests, and I will start thee in business," Hopkins reported the uncle as saying. That was not the only backing he got. Another $10,000 came from his mother, and an equal amount from her brother, John Janney, one of Virginia's richest and most powerful men. Thus well-capitalized, "I took a warehouse near [Uncle Gerard], and, with his endorsements and assistance, the first year I sold $200,000 worth of goods." Johnsie was off and running, for a period in partnerships, including with three of his brothers, all minors.[14]

He was clever and crafty, an imaginative dealmaker and a prudent risk-taker. He knew that farmers were only too eager to buy from him but did not have cash because of frequent money crises. There was no national currency, only notes issued by local banks, but not recognized by other banks that insisted on payment in silver, not paper. So he was ready to barter with his customers. But what could farmers trade? Grain was too difficult to transport in covered Conestoga wagons—not to say anything about livestock—but liquid corn was not. So he accepted home-distilled whiskey in payment for his goods. The barrels were loaded onto wagons, brought to Baltimore, blended, bottled, branded, and sold as "Hopkins Best." He became the talk of the town, a Quaker upstart peddling demon rum. In 1826 Quaker brethren reported that "he avows his determination to continue the practice of trading in distilled spirituous liquors" and disowned him "from having a right of membership with us."[15]

He was a pragmatic opportunist on his way to join the grandees—a contradictory entrepreneur living in transformational times.

ROYAL BLOOD

Johns Hopkins was born in 1795 during George Washington's second term. He came from the planter aristocracy. According to a family tree scripted on his mother's Bible—and confirmed by genealogists—he descended from William the Conqueror, the duke from Normandy who overran England in 1066.[16] His Welsh forebears arrived in America soon after the colonization. Of six Hopkins brothers, two settled in Rhode Island, one in Maryland's Harford County next to today's U.S. Army Aberdeen Proving Ground, another in Baltimore's Govanstown, and two in the Annapolis area of Southern Maryland, in the middle of today's Crofton. That land was a gift from the King of England, who granted them prime acreage between the scenic Severn and West Rivers. They planted leafy tobacco.

Sotweed, as it was commonly called, was the colony's early chief export, much in demand in Europe. To grow the trade, the Maryland legislature in 1706 designated a tiny settlement at Whetstone Point (today's Locust Point) as a port of entry for exports and imports. In 1729 Baltimore was born on the opposite bank. "A Town is much wanting on the North Side of Patapsco River," the legislature decreed, naming it in honor of Cecilius Calvert, Lord Baltimore and proprietor of the Maryland colony. The Calverts were an Irish line of peerage. Indeed, the name of Baltimore paid homage to the Gaelic name of a settlement in County Cork, Baile an Tí Mhóir, the "town of the big house." Cole's Harbour (today's Inner Harbor) was chosen as the site of the new town. The settlement soon eclipsed Annapolis: the state capital lacked the advantage that Baltimore had, the Jones Falls stream. There is nothing remarkable about the trickle today, but in those days its current was strong enough to power grain, textile, and lumber mills. The effluents emptied into the harbor. The Jones Falls provided drinking water; it was also a sewer.[17]

So central was tobacco to colonial Maryland's life that taxes could be paid either in English pounds or the equivalent amount of sotweed. The basic tobacco unit was a very large barrel called a hogshead. Packed full of air-cured leaves, each weighed about nine hundred pounds. Barrels were hitched to oxen, which "rolled" them down local pathways. One of those, Rolling Road, still remains, running from now-suburbanized Baltimore County highlands to a river in Elkridge that is no longer navigable.[18]

Tobacco growers depended on slave labor. Rhode Island money men, including Quakers who founded Brown University, largely bankrolled the shipping of slaves from Africa. Baltimore played a key role, thanks to Fells Point shipwrights. In the 1780s, they introduced two-masted top-sail schooners of a design that became known all over the world as Baltimore clippers. Record-fast and sleek, these "skimmers of the seas" were equipped with shipboard cannons and were widely used in privateering—officially sanctioned piracy for profit, directed toward enemy ships, real or imagined. As freebooting boomed, Fells Point thrived. Shipyards refitted clippers with chains and irons so that slaves could be imported on a large scale from Africa to the United States, Brazil, and the West Indies. Clippers brought immigrants from Europe, and rounded Cape Horn, the treacherous tip of Argentina and Chile, to transport miners to the California gold rush.[19] From China they carried tea and coolies, free or indentured laborers. The Far East trade was vital to Captain John O'Donnell, a Baltimore shipowner involved in addicting China to opium from Turkey.[20] In remembrance of the ports around Hong Kong, he gave the name Canton to his twenty-three hundred acres of industrial waterfront east of Fells Point. Illicit love was involved in this tribute. "On one of his visits he fell in love with a Chinese lady, whom he married, and her father gave him her weight in gold as her marriage dower." He showed good judgment by not bringing her to Baltimore, where he already had a wife.[21]

Like Rome, Baltimore was built on seven hills. That's what early painters depicted on their canvases, and hills remain part of the landscape. Much excavation and leveling has been done, but Saratoga Street near Mercy Medical Center is still far too steep for the weak or frail to climb. Other defining natural features have largely disappeared from view. The streams of the old landscape are an example. Except for the Jones Falls, totally obscured now are numerous rivulets and runs that used to meander from the highlands to the harbor. Many still exist, but underground. Harford Run is tunneled under asphalted Central Avenue, originally called Canal Street. Such was the ancient penetration of the harbor that Harris Creek cut through today's Patterson Park, all the way to Baltimore and Linwood Streets.[22] Other early streets included Fish (now Saratoga), Queen (Pratt), Market (Baltimore), and Forest (Charles). Red-brick row houses became the favored building tradition because good-quality clay was plentiful. Federal Hill, for example, is honeycombed with tunnels where brick makers dug clay. The city's growth can be measured by how kilns kept moving farther out.

Johns Hopkins tried most anything that promised to make money. He had substantial interests in railroads, coal mining, smelting, manufacturing, and real estate, often as a silent partner. His maritime investments were considerable. He held a big stake in Merchants' & Miners' Transportation Company, whose ships—including the SS *Johns Hopkins*—carried freight and passengers up and down the East Coast, from Boston to Florida.[23] His copper refinery in Canton employed more than a thousand people. He was president of the Merchants' Bank, a board member of the First National, Mechanics' Central, National Union, Citizens,' and Farmers' and Planters' Banks. That's a partial list.

Hopkins was also in the fertilizer business, importing tons of guano, urine-soaked feces of seabirds, cave-dwelling bats, penguins, and seals.[24] The very first stinking guano arrived in Baltimore from South America in 1832 in two casks consigned to the editor of *American Farmer*, who was scrambling to find ways to revitalize soil depleted by uninterrupted tobacco cultivation. Soil exhaustion was the bane of Hopkins's native Southern Maryland, which had grown tobacco since colonial times. As chemical fertilizers had not yet been invented, guano was as good a nutrient as could be found to replenish tobacco soil in preparation for rotation to wheat growing. Some two hundred pounds an acre were mixed with ashes, ground bones, and animal dung. "After preparing the ground with ploy and harrow, I sow wheat and guano together, and plow them in with a gang-plow which covers to a depth, on an average, of three inches," wrote the landscape architect Frederick Law Olmsted, who farmed in Staten Island, New York.[25]

Clippers carried guano all the way from Peru, where mountains of nitrogen-rich droppings had accumulated on rocky Pacific cliffs from birds and pelicans feasting on plentiful fish. Guano exports were a government monopoly, and Peru operated a guano trading post in Fells Point. Sea captains hated guano. Casks containing the yellowish excrement posed a fire hazard. Dust filled every crevice of the hold, releasing an odor of ammonia that dried out noses and irritated eyes. So toxic was the stench that crew members handling guano could not stay in the hold longer than five minutes at a time. "The only upside was that it killed rats on the ship, but it was equally hard on the ship's cat," writes the marine historian Peter Lesher.[26]

Johns Hopkins could smell the acrid stench of guano on the waterfront from his ornate headquarters. His "counting rooms" were on the edge of The Basin, today's Inner Harbor, on a meandering thoroughfare named after its surveyor, Nicholas Ruxton Gay. Gay Street was the fast-beating heart of America's third-largest city, the first place where all things important arrived—ships carrying mail and news about triumphs and calamities that affected financial markets; notable personages, imports. Ships were the easiest way to travel in those days, often the only one. The port cities of Norfolk, Charleston, and Savannah regarded Baltimore as the commercial and industrial capital of the upper South and maintained strong links. But The Basin was more than that. Gay Street was also the starting point of a road to Philadelphia, and an eastern terminus of growing overland traffic to Ohio and the expanding West.

No moneyman more than Hopkins proclaimed self-worth in ambitious architecture. He was a defining downtown developer, a fact that is obscured because the Great Fire of 1904 destroyed all of his buildings. He collected teardowns. His wreckers got rid of Patrick Reilly's livery stable, when it ceased to be a terminus of stagecoaches. On vacant lots he built modern "warehouses," mixed-used properties that contained shops and stockrooms and accommodated commercial and retail emporiums of all sorts. After the Civil War alone, Hopkins constructed some twenty important mixed-use warehouses, adding them to his portfolio of roughly fifty other major buildings in The Basin. "The enterprise of Mr. Hopkins has entirely changed the aspect of the neighborhood, as in each case old dilapidated buildings were removed," *The Sun* wrote at the peak of his redevelopment activity in 1869.

Hopkins's headquarters, built in 1846 of white granite, "is remarkable for its neat proportions, and the cast-iron caps ornamenting the windows of the second and third stories add much to the general effect. We observe that the ornaments on those of the second story had the trident of Neptune and the Roman spade, emblematic of commerce and agriculture, while ethels and flowers on those of the third story are also emblematic of the scientific and gayer purposes for which the large lecture hall and ball room will be used."[27] His sense of esthetics was evident. When Commodore Hugh Purviance, the hero of naval battles, built three four-story warehouses, "the fronts were uniform with those at the opposite corner belonging to Mr. Hopkins, and all are finished in the same substantial and complete manner, the iron for the lower fronts also having been furnished by Messrs. Armstrong, Cunningham and Co." in Canton.

The Basin's grandest landmark preceded him. It was the Merchants' Exchange, a three-story Greco-Roman temple of commerce, the largest domed edifice in America when it opened in 1820. Located at Gay and Water Streets (where the U.S. Customs House now stands), it was designed by Maximilian Godefroy and Benjamin Henry Latrobe, and later modified by the partnership of John Rudolf Niernsee and James Crawford Neilson, all legendary architects. The Exchange, as it was called, hosted a variety of activities over the years, including the U.S. Customs, the Bank of the United States, the Bank of Baltimore, and the post office, even city hall. Hopkins was a stakeholder in The

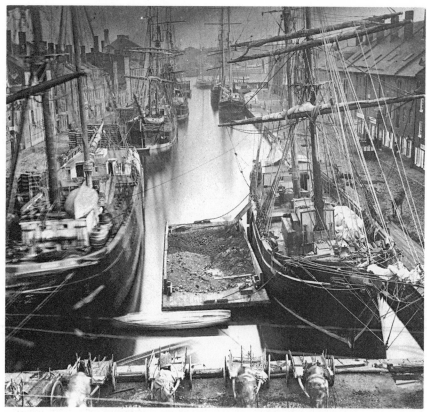

Gay Street Dock photographed from Pratt Street in 1875.
Courtesy of the Maryland Historical Society, Image #CC 2851

Exchange, but he saw growing demand for additional prime space. In 1869 he hired his old friends Niernsee and Neilson to design the Rialto building for him, at Water and Holliday Streets. Constructed of marble, it had two floors of offices, which housed the board of trade and the guano exchange. The top floor consisted of a meeting hall, which hosted a variety of events, ranging from Grand Army reunions to B'nai B'rith meetings. The National Board of Trade held its convention at the Rialto three weeks after Hopkins's death.[28] When the Baltimore Stock Exchange opened in 1876, the Rialto was its home too. Around the corner was *The Sun*'s graceful five-story Iron Building, an early demonstration of techniques that would make skyscrapers possible. The city's newspaper of record was run by his friend and neighbor Arunah S. Abell.

City hall (the early one, built in 1814, still surviving at 225 North Holliday Street as the Peale Center), Zion Church (also surviving), and the courthouse were within a short walk. Johns Hopkins was a walker. He sauntered on streets where cobblestones were being replaced by uniform quarried "Belgian blocks" that came to Baltimore as ships' ballast. He walked past a hodge-podge of workshops and factories, theaters, schools, curiosity museums, taverns, churches, shops, and halls—all indiscriminately mixed with residences and rooming houses in an age that knew no zoning. He might stroll by the Maryland Institute ("for the Promotion of the Mechanic Arts"), where auctions of all kinds were often held and among whose benefactors he was.[29] For a time that predecessor of today's Maryland Institute College of Art occupied part of the Atheneum, the city's premier cultural institution. The landmark building at Lexington and St. Paul Streets contained concert and lecture halls as well as two subscription-based lending libraries.

Many passersby recognized Hopkins, a gaunt man in ordinary clothes. Writes an 1885 profiler, Laura Carter Holloway: "Mr. Hopkins was not a handsome man; there was nothing in his appearance or manners to recommend him to the *beau monde*; brought up in faith of the Friends he was very apt, when he did speak, to express the plain truth in a way not always acceptable to 'ears polite.' But he was honest through and through, and much of what he did, which his contemporaries looked upon as mere selfish schemes for his own aggrandizement, was really done for one of the noblest motives—the desire to benefit the city of Baltimore."

Seekers of favors accosted him sometimes. He could identify the most eager from the nervousness of their approach and how they were dressed to impress. He once humbled one overdressed supplicant (whom he knew as a promising, hardworking man) by sending him back home to change clothes, then days later surprised him by granting a favor. He could be a mentor when he wanted to, but first and foremost he was a hard-nosed businessman. He was well-organized, and suffered no fools. "He was brief in his conversation, but to the point," the *New York Times* wrote. "He was of quick mind and temperament, and when he came to a determination it was difficult to get him to change it. He was honest, industrious, generous and liberal."[30] His curiosity knew no bounds, and he saw possibilities in ventures that others rejected. "His methods were bold and self-reliant, often high-handed; yet he invariably carried his point, sometimes leaving others to see the wisdom of it later," writes his grandniece Helen Hopkins Thom.[31] He was flexible, broadminded, and tolerant on many issues. He followed his own compass and allowed others to do the same. His felt strong duty toward his kin. This could be seen from the substantial bequests he gave nephews and nieces. His mother lived with him for her last years, and a widowed sister kept house for him.[32]

Plenty of Hopkins Best whiskey was consumed in waterfront grog shops. The Basin district was what Les Halles was to Paris, a never-sleeping beehive of human activity, driven by all kinds of markets along the waterfront. At the site of the old Fish Market (today Port Discovery) was Centre Market, also known as Marsh Market because swamps surrounded it in the early days. Among its 270 stalls were thirty-five belonging to fishmongers and eighty-eight to butchers. "Oh what a quality of superb beef, lamb, veal and all sorts of fowl—hogsheads full of wild ducks, geese, pheasants, partridges; and then on the other side of the market house . . . a line of wagons and carts, groaning under the loads of country productions," U.S. attorney general William Wirt reported to a daughter after visiting in 1822.[33]

The Basin itself was a nauseating cesspool of ghastly debris that floated boats of all descriptions, marking their waterline with sickly-yellow stripes and washing the shoreline from Fells Point to Federal Hill. Animal parts and carcasses drifted among rotting fruits, vegetables, and other trash. An overpowering stink greeted arriving passengers several miles downriver, making some retch. Not to worry. It was just thriving Baltimore, reeking all the money that men like Johns Hopkins were making.

The port provisioned the city. From oceangoing ships came exotic fruits: oranges and lemons from South Carolina, bananas and pineapples from Jamaica, coffee from Brazil and Java. From Chesapeake Bay came flatboats and skipjacks loaded with crabs, clams, fish of a great variety, turtles, geese, muskrats, corn, cantaloupes, watermelons. At the water's edge, much of the stock was transferred onto wagons garishly painted red and yellow that were pulled by horses and donkeys, with colorful harnesses decorated with chiming bells. The animals belonged to "a-rabbers," African American peddlers who operated regular delivery routes, selling produce, fruit, vegetables, fish, and eggs at customers' front steps. Until the tradition disappeared in the 1970s—a casualty of motorization, refrigeration, supermarkets, and neighborhood upheavals—housewives distinguished vendors from their hollers, raps delivered in nearly incomprehensibly rhythmic singsong where words melded together. Among early a-rabbers no one was more famous than "Old Moses," a burly, white-aproned coal-dark son of West Africa's Dahomey wearing a ropy red wig on his head. His trademark whistle was powerful, his mixture of calls and songs ever-changing and inimitable. "Poor old Moses!" he cried, "poor old fellah! Jist a-coming' roun' onct moah to commerdate de ladies and gentlum wid de elegint nice oysters! Oysh, oysh, shock oy—sh! Oh, my charmin' oysters! my 'lightful fresh oysters!"[34] A-rabbers peddled anything from "wah duh mil yun" (watermelon) to such "feesh" as sturgeon steaks which were incongruously promoted as "Albanyyyyyy beeeeef / Won't tangle to yo' teeeeef."[35]

The a-rabbers' seeming efficiency was deceptive; distribution in those days was a headache, and long-distance hauling on land a curse. Johns Hopkins, if anyone, knew this. His men transported merchandise deep into the Shenandoah Valley, North Carolina, and Ohio, usually with a team of six horses pulling a single covered Conestoga wagon on journeys that could take a month, one way. Sometimes wheels struck a rock, and "away went the wagon, horses and all down the hill, rolling and smashing barrels of rum, hogsheads of sugar, sacks of salt, boxes of dry-goods."[36,37] In 1804 Uncle Gerard ventured out on horseback to the wilderness of Western Maryland. "It is not unusual to meet a packer having with him half a dozen loaded horses, loaded with merchandise," he reported.[38] Ten years later, he attended an important Quaker meeting in Ohio. He rode horses with his wife and several other believers; whatever they carried had to fit saddle bags. "They all traveled on horseback and a great part of their way led through a wilderness country with no safe roads, only the Indian paths to travel and many rivers to ford," Johns Hopkins told a cousin. "It was thought to be a great undertaking, but they performed the long journey and returned after an absence of several months in safety and in good health."

THE IRON HORSE COMETH

Over his lifespan of seventy-eight years, Johns Hopkins witnessed the dawn of the transportation revolution that made today's world possible. He grasped its transformative nature, and seized the investment opportunities that came his way. His eyes were fixed on the unlimited opportunities in the expanding West, although that to him meant Ohio. His timing was perfect. About the time he arrived in Baltimore, the federal government commenced the serious westward push by beginning to construct the National Road, the embryo of today's interstate highway system. Crossing the Blue Ridge Mountains, the road linked Cumberland, in Maryland, through Virginia (still a unitary state) and Pennsylvania to Ohio, which had been admitted to statehood seven years earlier. The route had been traveled before, of course. Ancient buffalo spoors intersected with Native American trails and traces that General Edward Braddock opened during the French and Indian wars in 1755 to move some 2,000 troops, 29 pieces of artillery, 407 wagons, and 900 horses over the mountains from Fort Cumberland to the vicinity of today's Pittsburgh. That was an incredible undertaking in those primitive times. Now from Baltimore toll roads, called turnpikes, fed to the National Road. "The goods and produce carried over this road in early days was immense," writes Colonel J. Thomas Scharf, the historian. "The large Conestoga wagons, so familiar to denizens of the West as 'schooners of the desert,' passed each other, hundreds in a day, on their way to and from Pittsburgh and Baltimore, and the jingling of bells, the cracking of whips, the horses gayly caparisoned, and the drivers in picturesque costumes."[39]

With its thirty-three-foot roadbed, the National Road was an engineering marvel, and became known as Main Street in towns that formed along its route. But heavy use quickly eroded its surface. Sectional politics hampered maintenance: Congressmen from southern states cut funding. Slavery was the reason—the road tied Ohio and the rest of the Western Territory to Pennsylvania, the sentry of the abolitionist North. The congested road fell into disrepair. It had existed for some twenty-five years in 1838, when Daniel Barcus and a team of six horses spent a month hauling a Conestoga wagon containing eighty-three hundred pounds of Johns Hopkins's merchandise from Light and Pratt Streets in Baltimore to Mount Vernon, Ohio, a distance of 397 miles. Barcus then reloaded with seventy-two hundred pounds of Ohio tobacco and headed back on the National Road on another month-long trek.

Not everyone moved at such a leisurely pace. The coach companies Good Intent, June Bug Line, Landlords' Line, and Pilot Line promised to take travelers to Wheeling, on the Ohio River, in seventy-two hours, seating three abreast in three rows. In the 1820s coaches departed Baltimore and Washington at 2 a.m. on Sundays, Tuesdays, and Thursdays. The teams of six horses were changed four times over the journey.[40] Passengers carried their own bedrolls, overnighting in "ordinaries," inns where at the conclusion of bar business the floor was cleared and dozens of men snored the night away—merchants, drovers, and roustabouts democratically sharing the planks. Smaller quarters accommodated women, when needed. When winter came, service was halted. Everything could wait until the snows melted because there was no choice. At the Baltimore end, the Conestoga trade concentrated on Light and Pratt Streets, where the White Swan, Black Horse, and Golden Lamb provided chat and chew for lodging teamsters, while their horses rested in huge courtyards. Hopkins owned a dozen warehouses on adjoining blocks.[41]

Aware of the limitations of roads, many politicians and commercial interests promoted canals as alternatives. They triumphed in 1825 when the Erie Canal was dug—a 363-mile shortcut from the Hudson River to the Great Lakes. The very next year, the addition of the 108-mile Delaware-Hudson Canal enabled barges to travel from Philadelphia to New York and back. Close to home, the Chesapeake and Delaware Canal opened in 1829. An array of other blueprints suggested that engineered waterways would threaten the prominence of Baltimore's port. This was a true calamity, and many Maryland decision makers lost sleep over it. For all these years the nation's third largest city had bragged that it was nearly two hundred miles closer to the West than New York and one hundred miles closer than Philadelphia.

Canals now changed that calculus, threatening Baltimore's gateway status just as foreign immigration was speeding up and the West was being won. There was more bad news—recently introduced steamships had little use for Fells Point and Canton shipyards, experts in building and refitting wooden sailing ships. In the nearby Jones Falls valley, a dozen mills spun cotton duck for ships' sails. What was their future? What was Baltimore's future?

George Brown sounded the alarm. He was one of the four sons of Alexander Brown, a wealthy Scots-Irish linen merchant from Belfast, who in 1800 moved to Baltimore and established Alex. Brown & Sons, America's first investment banking house. The firm provided a range of financial and trading services, and at one point exported more tobacco and cotton on its ships than any other company in the country. The eldest son, William, eventually returned to England to open an Alex. Brown branch in Liverpool; he became a Liberal member of Parliament and was knighted. Facilitators like him were a godsend because the Industrial Revolution in England was the key source of capital for U.S. ventures, along with a steady stream of inventions that America craved to adopt and adapt.

Rail was one such invention. Ancient Greeks had been familiar with the concept. But they only knew the muscles of men as a power source. It took two millennia to advance to steam. In 1825 the banker Evan Thomas created a sensation at a dinner Colonel John Eager Howard hosted at his estate, Belvedere. A relative of Hopkins, Thomas reported how at a coal mine in England he had seen pony-sized steam engines pull empty cars up one side of a hill and then descend on the other side, fully loaded with coal. This curious intelligence triggered much comment. None of this was new to George Brown because he had received blueprints from his brother in Liverpool. He grasped that railroads would revolutionize transportation and offer a chance to revitalize Baltimore's port. He shared the thoughts with his father, who agreed to invest. George Brown then invited Evan Thomas and twenty-three leading merchants to his home in February 1827 to "take into consideration the best means of restoring to the City of Baltimore that portion of the western trade which has lately been diverted from it." The next meeting resolved to "construct a double railroad between the city of Baltimore and some suitable point on the Ohio River by the most eligible and direct route." The vision was set; detail and practicalities were murky. No route had been plotted, no surveys made, or land acquired. "The idea seems to have been that if we could soonest reach the vast Western trade by the shortest route, we should *command* it; and that Baltimore would be re-established, and advance to continental supremacy," writes Colonel Scharf.

Johns Hopkins, over time, would become the largest individual stockholder in the Baltimore & Ohio. Curiously, his name is missing from the list of the early organizers of the first railroad chartered in America. It seems that he felt an investment was one thing, but his precious time was quite another. He chose to concentrate on his bread-and-butter businesses in trading and financing; the highly speculative start-up was just a money gamble he took. His interests were well taken care of, however. A Quaker kinsman also originally from Anne Arundel County, Philip E. Thomas, became president. He had been on the board of the Chesapeake & Ohio Canal, but shifted his enthusiasm to railroads after Evan, his brother, sent him excited letters about steam trains he saw in England. Thomas Ellicott was another Quaker kin on the board; he owned a mill town now known as Ellicott City. George Brown was elected treasurer, and Alex. Brown one of the members. The illustrious Charles Carroll of Carrollton, the last living signer of the Declaration of Independence, also was on the board. He donated sixty acres from his vast Mount Clare slave plantation to establish the railroad's works and depot.[42]

A rail fever gripped the city. The initial public offering was snapped up. Even though the shares sold for a hundred dollars each, the issue was oversubscribed. "Everybody wanted stock," remembered John H. B. Latrobe, the railroad's chief engineer and counsel. "Parents subscribed in the names of their children."[43] The City of Baltimore and the State of Maryland were the start-up's largest investors. The gamble with taxpayers' money was extraordinary. Aside from buying stock, the city of Baltimore gave the railroad a $5 million loan and otherwise subsidized the railroad. "The first support was in the form of a $500,000 subscription to the Baltimore & Ohio. That was not all. Beginning in 1827, and for nearly sixty years thereafter, municipal authorities invested $20 million in internal improvements, more than any other city in the United States, save Cincinnati," the railroad historian Albert J. Churella writes.[44]

On the Fourth of July in 1828, Charles Carroll of Carrolton broke the ground for the first track at the site of Mount Clare Roundhouse, today's railroad museum. Thousands came to witness this historic moment. There were flags and bunting galore, speeches, floats, bands, and choirs—and Masonic rites, including the grandmaster scattering corn and pouring wine and oil for good luck. President John Quincy Adams sent his regrets, opting instead to speak at the groundbreaking of the Chesapeake & Ohio Canal. That event happened the same day, the culmination of a seemingly quixotic quest that began with the first canal company's incorporation in 1784. For decades, the project limped along, too costly to begin. According to one early survey, 398 locks needed to be constructed, as well as a four-mile tunnel. Only when Congress jumped in and funded part of the canal did it become a reality. This happened just as the B&O was being set up, without any funding from the federal government.[45] "Railroads were then not thought of. Canals were the means relied upon," remembered Latrobe. A choir sang:

O we're all full of life, fun and jollity,
We're all crazy here in Baltimore.
Here's a road to be made
With the Pick and the Spade
This to reach Ohio, for the benefit of trade;
Here are mountains to be level'd,
Here are valleys to be filled.
Here are rocks to be blown, and bridges too to build.
And we're all hopping, skipping, jumping,
And we are all crazy here in Baltimore.[46]

For the first two years, rails were little more than a smooth path where horses and mules pulled wheeled cars. That was the state of technology. Other power alternatives were tested. In one experiment, two dogs trotted off an attached car with six passengers. Evan Thomas was more bold. He constructed a boat-shaped rail car with a cotton-duck sail and called it Aeolus, after the Greek mythology's ruler of the wind. Russians liked the crazy idea, and a model of the sailing car was sent to St. Petersburg, the czarist capital on the Neva River known for its strong and shifting winds. Joyriders got a thrill from cruising at twenty miles an hour, with wind gusts rocking the car and once nearly overturning it.

America's railroad age truly began on August 28, 1830, when the New York and Baltimore entrepreneur Peter Cooper invited the B&O board of directors to test-ride a one-horsepower steam engine he had constructed in his workshops in Canton. "The machine was not larger than the hand cars used by [rail] workers to transfer themselves from place to place," remembered Latrobe, who was there. With its protruding barrel-shaped boiler, the Tom Thumb, as it was later nicknamed, looked like a moonshine still on wheels. More than two dozen guests filled the attached car, but the most adventurous risked their lives by riding in the locomotive despite the constant danger of explosion; such things did happen with steam. They made a successful journey along the banks of the Patapsco River from the Mount Clare depot to Ellicott's Mills; the twelve-mile trip took one hour and twelve minutes. On the way back the iron horse met a real-life horse wagon belonging to Stockton and Stokes, the city's biggest operator of stage coaches. A race began on parallel tracks, probably a prearranged stunt. The coal-fired Tom Thumb huffed and puffed, produced clouds of threatening smoke and menacing steam, gathered speed, ran past the horse-drawn railcar, distanced itself, and then suddenly coughed to a halt. A cord had slipped off a pulley; the horse won. Never mind. The B&O directors had seen what they came to see; they replaced horses within two years.[47] The decision was momentous. The C&O Canal certainly saw the steam locomotive as a game-changer. The canal company sought repeated injunctions against B&O, claiming that locomotives scared draught horses working on the canal. For a time, the canal company, by a court order, stopped B&O from laying tracks in Maryland's Frederick, Washington, and Allegany Counties altogether.[48]

Railroads truly changed everything. They knitted America together into a nation. They altered the sense of time and place. Timetables required coordinated times and zones; up to that time the town clock of each locality kept the local time. New hotels sprang up near train stations, creating overnight cities along the tracks. Through experimentation and expansion, mergers and acquisitions, B&O found its stride. It acquired a 50 percent ownership stake in the Bremen-based North German Lloyd, which operated steamships between Europe and U.S. East Coast ports. Immigrants arriving in Baltimore took advantage of a package deal: Atlantic crossings were sold with a transfer ticket to B&O trains that departed from the immigration pier in Locust Point. This made it easy for the newcomers, mostly from northern and central Europe, to continue to the expanding West.

The Locust Point peninsula has Fort McHenry at the tip. Just outside the fort was the immigration pier, from where trains began long journeys. Some cars were put on ferries that transported them across the harbor to Fells Point. The railroad's headquarters was Camden Station a couple of miles away, near today's Orioles Park baseball stadium. A few hundred yards to the west were B&O's Mount Clare works that eventually occupied some fifty buildings— from forges to foundries to machine shops. Narrow two-story red brick row houses lined nearby alleys, sheltering "gandy dancers." Those Irish immigrant railroad workers were among an army of enablers who grew the Mount Clare industries into a smokestack precursor of Silicon Valley, generating inventions and cutting-edge technology that changed the world.

B&O stretched tracks to Frederick in 1831; Point of Rocks in 1832; Harpers Ferry in 1834; and Cumberland in 1844. That latter year, Samuel F. B. Morse came calling, asking B&O for permission to bury a copper cable, wrapped in tarred rope yarn, along the rail bed, and also string wires between wooden poles. What on earth was that all about? After meeting the professor, B&O president Louis McLane dismissed him as a "crazy man who believed that he could send messages from Baltimore to Washington." But Latrobe, the company's chief engineer, urged reconsideration. "The day when you and I are dead and forgotten, this man will be remembered," he predicted.[49] With the aid of federal and city allocations, Morse built his experimental telegraph line. From Baltimore to the Supreme Court in Washington, the inventor tapped a coded message: "What hath God wrought?" What indeed. These were the first impulses of an electronic communications revolution that is still unfolding. Telegraph lines soon followed wherever railroads went, ultimately

Building the B&O Railroad:
Baltimore to Wheeling, 1828 – 1852

OHIO

WHEELING
1852

PENNSYLVANIA

CUMBERLAND
1842

FREDERICK
1831

GRAFTON
1852

HARPERS
FERRY
1834

BALTIMORE
1828

WEST VIRGINIA

(SECEDED FROM VIRGINIA IN 1861)

WASHINGTON
1835

MARYLAND

VIRGINIA

Chesapeake Bay

0   30 MILES

LUCIDITY INFORMATION DESIGN, LLC   SOURCE: B&O MUSEUM

This map chronicles the advance of the B&O main line toward Ohio. Also indicated is the branch line to Washington, D.C.
Robert Cronan. Lucidity Information Design, LLC

coast to coast. B&O was a pioneer: It created a commercial telegraph subsidiary but had to sell it to Western Union amid financial difficulties in 1887.

The goal of reaching the Ohio River proved elusive due to the natural obstructions of the mountains and political wrangling with Virginia and Pennsylvania legislatures. Thomas Swann, the B&O president, who would become mayor, governor, and U.S. congressman, tapped Johns Hopkins to help resolve the problems. Hopkins was fifty-two, and recently retired from his other businesses, when he joined the B&O "board of direction" in 1847. He became a full-time director, assigned to a seven-member "select committee to cooperate with the President in devising means for extension of the Main Stem of the Road to the Ohio River" and Pennsylvania's rich coal fields. That destination was reached in 1852 in Wheeling, a city that became an important B&O stockholder in order to secure the rail line. Hopkins's clout kept increasing. Three years later he became the B&O's priorities man, chairman of the finance committee. Another three years later, he staged a coup. After using his wealth to save the railroad from ruin during a terrible national economic downturn in 1857, he engineered the election of a fellow board member, John W. Garrett, thirty-eight, to the railroad's presidency. It was a hard-won victory for Hopkins, who lobbied cannily on Garrett's behalf and

A. Aubrey Bodine's artistry in light and shadows depicting a train yard in Baltimore in 1946.
Courtesy of the Maryland Historical Society, Image #B1373

produced a two-vote plurality that ousted Chauncey Brooks, the incumbent president. Brooks's management style was cautious. Garrett, by contrast, was a brash expansionist, even if that meant relentless borrowing. He was a risk-taker. Johns Hopkins liked the younger man's confidence.[50]

The Garretts descended from a Scots-Irish Presbyterian immigrant from the Belfast region who took his family to America in 1790, only to die during the Atlantic crossing at the age of forty. Relatives in Pennsylvania took the survivors under their wings. One son, Robert Garrett, proved particularly

Johns Hopkins at the peak of his powers. He was a farm boy with little formal schooling who became one of America's richest men.
Courtesy of Ferdinand Hamburger Archives, Sheridan Libraries, Johns Hopkins University

energetic. He was John Garrett's father, and met Hopkins when both were newcomers to Baltimore. Theirs turned into a lifelong friendship and mutually advantageous web of business arrangements. In his boyhood, the senior Garrett was a drover, meaning that he had to know how to repair wagons and wheels, in addition to steering teams of horses pulling Conestoga wagons. Many a rocky road he traveled suggested commercial possibilities. After his first wife died, he married nineteen-year-old Elizabeth Stouffer, a daughter of a wealthy merchant and member of the Baltimore City Council and began operating trading posts along the National Road. Eventually he and his family companies were involved in pretty much everything.[51]

They represented George Peabody, a one-time Baltimorean who headquartered his international finance house in London. They imported guano; their mines dug coal; and they dominated the movement of pigs and cattle from the West on the National Road. Besides B&O, "they were heavy stockholders in the Canton Company, the Union Manufacturing Company (a cotton factory), the Baltimore Water Company, and the Baltimore Gas-Light Company; their other investments included the Merchants' Shot Tower Company, the Merchants' Fire Insurance Company, the Susquehanna & Tide Water Canal, and the Ocean Mutual Insurance Company," writes the historian Bruce Catton in his master's thesis.[52] So vast was their ownership of the wilderness along Maryland's West Virginia border that the legislature carved out a county and named it after them.

It was in cooperation with the Garrett family that Johns Hopkins made most of his millions. He was a man on a mission. Holloway summed it up, italics and all: "Many noted persons have had curious superstitions as to their own destiny; some who, like Alexander and Napoleon, believed their star led them on as the conquerors of kings, and the destroyers of empires; others have fancied themselves preordained to the work of instructing mankind, or saving souls, like Gautima, Buddha, and Francis Xavier; but Johns Hopkins held, we believe, the unique idea that he was *divinely commissioned to make money!*"[53]

Chapter Two

The Civil War: Blue and Gray

Maryland was a slave state so overwhelmingly Southern by identification, values, customs, and culture that Abraham Lincoln polled just 2 percent of votes cast in the 1860 election. Yet after he became president (without being on the ballot in ten southern states), there was no scramble in Maryland to join the rebelling Confederate States of America. Instead, Johns Hopkins, John W. Garrett, and other potentates of wealth and power engaged in an attempt to opt out of the Civil War altogether. They wanted Maryland to stay with Lincoln but sit out the fratricide as a neutral bystander. Governor Thomas H. Hicks and Mayor George William Brown conveyed the message to Lincoln: Maryland will protect the property of the United States, but it will not get involved in the war, nor authorize any deployment or transfer of troops. "It is my solemn duty to inform you that it is not possible for more soldiers to pass through Baltimore unless they fight their way at each step," the mayor told the president.[1]

This noninvolvement policy's unmistakable aim was to save B&O investors' skin. The very economic stability of Maryland hung in the balance because the state and city had so recklessly gambled on the railroad as original start-up backers, ending up with even more stock than Hopkins and Garrett. There was also that outstanding $5 million loan the city wanted repaid. All that money now was threatened. Three-fourths of the railroad's 379-mile main stem from Baltimore to Wheeling lay in secessionist Virginia (at the outset of the war still a unitary state), which vowed to confiscate B&O property and tracks if the company transported Union troops.[2] Lincoln, on the other hand, demanded unlimited troop transfers to quell the rebellion. After sharpening tensions, the president, in a face-to-face meeting, assured Mayor Brown that no more federal soldiers would transfer through Baltimore. A municipal militia, the City Guard, was formed to enforce the ban on troop

The Sixth Regiment of the Massachusetts Volunteers firing into the people in Pratt Street, while attempting to pass through Baltimore en route for Washington, April 19, 1861.
Courtesy of Library of Congress Online Prints and Photographs Division, LC-USZ62-132929

movements. Nevertheless, on April 19, 1861, seven days after the surrender of Fort Sumter and the day after Virginia seceded, the Sixth Massachusetts Regiment showed up on its way to Washington, just over an hour south by train. Crowds of excited citizens took to the streets, passions running high.

Brawling street "mobs" were a Baltimore tradition. Some were sponsored by volunteer fire companies involved in insurance and protection rackets, others worked as enforcers for political parties. "Many of the city's most violent roughs often served on the police force and the night watch," notes Tracy Matthew Melton, who wrote a book about those mobs. "The mayor appointed them as compensation for their political support."[3] In the 1856 mayoral election five people were killed when Rip Raps clashed with the Democratic roughs of the New Market Fire Company at Lexington Market, and nativist Plug Uglies fought with Democrats in the Eighth Ward, popularly known as "Limerick" because of its large Irish population. In one Gay Street clash a cannon was used.[4] John Russell Bartlett, the pioneering lexicographer, made the Mobtown tag official in his *Dictionary of Americanisms*: "Mobtown—A name given long ago to the city of Baltimore, and which the lawless character of a portion of its inhabitants renders a not unfitting appellation at the present day."

Now, as seven hundred Massachusetts soldiers transferred by horse-drawn streetcars and on foot from President Street Station to B&O's Camden Station, a distance of about one mile, noisy mobs blocked them at Pratt and Gay Streets. Just around the corner from Hopkins's headquarters they erected all kinds of obstructions, using heaps of anchors and quarried street paving blocks.[5] The first nine streetcars full of soldiers made it through. But the subsequent cars and marching soldiers came under attacks. Ruffians bombarded the troops with whatever they could grab. On that day, twelve civilians and four soldiers were killed—the first blood of the Civil War, since none was shed at Fort Sumter. Thirty-six wounded soldiers were left behind. It was a bloody day. It was also remembered as the day when the Baltimore police did everything to protect the federal troops, escorted through by Mayor Brown himself. A military report said the mayor "seized a musket from the hands of one of the men and killed a man therewith." (Brown denied that, claiming that "a boy run forward handed to me a discharged musket that had fallen from one of the soldiers" and someone misconstrued what happened.)[6]

Within hours, the official attitude shifted, and the authorities designated the North as the menace to the city's neutrality. In the wee hours of the morning, the mayor and the police chief, Marshal George P. Kane, personally participated in the wrecking of railroad bridges going north. At 2:30 a.m. they led a company of seventy mounted City Guard members and a fifteen-man squad of police to destroy the bridges across the Gunpowder and Bush Rivers and Harris Creek. Eager civilian volunteers tagged along. Other posses of police and Guardsmen torched bridges in Cockeysville and Relay, a key railroad and telegraph junction near the old tobacco port of Elkridge where teams of draught horses used to be changed. They also cut off telegraph wires. "I asked what they were doing," a watchman recounted. "They said it was none of my business."[7] As the sun rose that Saturday morning, a large Confederate flag was unfurled from the headquarters of a State's Rights Club on Fayette Street, near Calvert. In the afternoon, according to Brown, "the Minute Men, a Union club, whose headquarters were on Baltimore street, gave a most significant indication of the strength of the wave of feeling which swept over our people by hauling down the National colors and running up in their stead the State flag of Maryland, amid the cheers of the crowd. Everywhere on the streets men and boys, demonstrating for the Southern cause, wore badges with miniature Confederate flags," writes Brown.

Brown ordered all United States flags taken down. The police took control of B&O's telegraph office; any messages sent to Washington had to be approved by Marshal Kane. Johns Hopkins, General Columbus O'Donnell, a War of 1812 hero and the eldest son of the Canton founder, and another banker, John Clark, donated $500,000 for the strengthening of the city's defenses, worth untold millions of dollars in today's money. Thousands of citizens donated muskets, pistols, Bowie knives, axes, pikes, pitchforks, swords, and clubs to the City Guard. The weaponry was stored in Hopkins's warehouses. Mobs tried to seize the arms but were repulsed. However, some four thousand muskets and swords were stolen from another owner's warehouse on the wharf. The authorities raided gun stores and appropriated the stock. Horses that normally pulled streetcars were commandeered to haul men and ammunition.[8]

Hopkins and more than one hundred other merchants contributed to the purchase of a centrifugal machine gun. "The gun is something like a steam engine and will throw three hundred balls per minute," reported *The Sun*. "It is the intention of the authorities to plant the gun at the head of the street up which the invading troops attempt to march" and "sweep the ranks." In words and deeds, the city was divided.[9] "At City Hall, Judge Benjamin C. Presstman threatened to cut off the nose and ears of Judge Hugh Lennox Bond, a Unionist," writes the historian Frank Towers.[10] Meanwhile Ross Winans was perfecting a steam-powered artillery piece of his own, which he pledged to donate to the Confederates. Winans was a true railroad pioneer. He began as a horse trader, acquiring draught horses for the B&O, and then helped Peter Cooper construct the Tom Thumb. He went on to invent breakthrough railroad equipment, eventually cornering the Russian market with his sons, who built the first railroad between St. Petersburg and Moscow.

Despite B&O trading with both sides early in the war, Johns Hopkins declared himself to be the president's "servant+friend."[11] That he was. He had met Lincoln and wholeheartedly supported emancipation and Reconstruction—rare qualities among the slave-owning men who dominated the railroad's board.[12] But business was business. Garrett was a similar pragmatist. He was a native of Baltimore, which he interpreted to mean that he was a Southerner. He repeatedly expressed Southern sympathies in private life as well as in running the railroad. Amid sharpening sectional tensions in 1860, he declared that as a matter of corporate policy B&O "is a *Southern line*" [italics in the original]. He added: "And if ever necessity should require—which heaven forbid!—it will prove the great bulwark of the border, and a sure agency for home defense. It has the ability, sir, with its equipment of 4,000 locomotives, and cars, to transport daily 10,000 troops and with its disciplined force of 3,500 men has always in its service the nucleus of an army. During a period when agitation, alarm and uncertainty prevail, is it not right, is it not becoming, that Baltimore should declare her position in the 'irrepressible conflict' threatened and urged by Northern fanaticism?"[13]

In physique Garrett "towered above his fellow men with Bismarckian proportions," the railroad historian Festus P. Summers writes. "His forehead was high, his jaw heavy, his face sometimes stern. While his business upbringing conduced to suavity of manner, his heavy tread and ponderous fist marked him as a man of direct action."[14] He was a factor in Washington. In 1859 he gave the White House the first news about John Brown's abolitionist revolt in Harpers Ferry, a strategic river crossing, rail junction, and gun manufacturing town along the Potomac where Maryland meets the Virginias. He took charge, arranging trains full of troops and material to crush the insurrection. In the process, he became friends with the top federal commander, Colonel Robert E. Lee, who had spent three years in Baltimore designing and building Fort Carroll in the harbor. Not surprisingly, Garrett joined other leading railroads in urging Congress to approve the Crittenden compromise, which called for peace through the permanent division of the United States into slave and free states, with unrestricted slave trade and no interference by the federal government.

After the Pratt Street mob attack, secessionist militia companies began arriving from counties, expecting a clash with the North. From Frederick County came a company of seventy men under Captain Bradley T. Johnson, who was to rise to brigadier general in the Confederate army. Two cavalry companies galloped in from Baltimore County. From Anne Arundel rode the Patapsco Dragoons, some thirty men. Two companies from Talbot came by steamboat, and more armed secessionists were on their way from Harford, Cecil, Carroll, and Prince George's Counties.[15] They itched for action. Rather than let the situation escalate, Mayor Brown thanked the outsiders at city hall and sent them back home. As they departed, he heard a bugler's catchy melody. It was called "Dixie," he said he was told, "the first time I heard that tune." Soon most everyone on the streets was humming it.

B&O's forty-mile single-track branch line from Baltimore to Washington provided the government its only telegraph and transportation link to the industrial and financial centers of the North. Without B&O, the capital could not survive for long. Yet in the hours after the Pratt Street mob attack, Garrett halted further troop transfers. He explained that the state's and the city's neutrality policies gave him no choice. Instead, troops from the North had to be carried by boats from Perryville to Annapolis, where a different railroad transported the soldiers onward. That could take days because secessionists repeatedly tore up rails. Close to home, the situation was dicey as well. The Pratt Street clash took place a mile east of the railroad's headquarters, Camden Station, which housed the telegraph operation. Nearby was Mount Clare depot and its irreplaceable locomotive and metal works. Those could be the next targets for secessionists; restless rowdies were already reported milling outside the station. Saboteurs repeatedly barricaded or ripped up rails.[16]

The City Guard, Baltimore's neutrality force, swelled to fifteen thousand men. It was commanded by Colonel Isaac R. Trimble, who soon switched sides and rose to become a major general in the Confederate army. He was a civil engineer, and had worked for B&O. Aside from the Guard, Baltimore was protected by 398 policemen. Some carried revolvers but many relied only on a traditional espantoon, a nightstick of heavy wood construction capable of doing lethal damage; it was not discarded until 1994. Federal troops garrisoned at Fort McHenry were not numerous enough to quell a popular uprising.

On May 5, 1861, Lincoln acted. He sent troops to secure Relay. Then, a week later, one thousand men of the Eighth Massachusetts Regiment marched on Baltimore in driving rain, and occupied the city under the cover of darkness. The Union command took over the supervision of the railroad and telegraph, and instituted censorship. Bluecoats occupied Baltimore. They rounded up Brown, Kane, police commissioners, the city council, and Ross Winans, as well as some merchants and secessionist newspaper editors, banishing them to the dungeons of Fort McHenry. Federal Hill was fortified, cannons trained on city hall and the exclusive Maryland Club, reputed hotbeds of secession. Mortars were placed in Monument Square on Calvert Street near city hall, Exchange Place near Hopkins's headquarters, and at Camden Station. Half a dozen Union encampments were erected to protect the Mount Clare works, with many others scattered in other parts of the city.[17]

A thunderbolt event two weeks later finally brought B&O to the Union fold. Up to that point trains had routinely crossed from Maryland to Virginia and back without being "molested"; they were simply inspected on both sides of the border. But on May 20, 1861, General Thomas J. "Stonewall" Jackson sprang a trap. Using various subterfuges, he created a backlog of trains at the Harpers Ferry crossing point. His soldiers then captured the equipment,

During the Civil War, Federal Hill cannons were trained on city hall. Photograph from circa 1865.
Courtesy of the Maryland Historical Society, Image #CC 987

stealing fifty-six B&O locomotives and more than four hundred freight cars.[18] The purpose was simply to remove the rolling stock from Union use; most equipment was abandoned and destroyed because the Confederate rail gauge was different. Garrett took the theft hard. He saw it as a breach of honor, and a personal betrayal. He declared himself an unequivocal supporter of the Union and ran the railroad that way. Nevertheless, he had to fight allegations of disloyalty because of his previous utterances and actions, and his friendship with General Lee. Hopkins vouched for Garrett and delivered B&O's corporate support to the Union.[19]

The single-track main line zigzagged from Baltimore through valleys and river banks first to Frederick, then into Virginia and today's West Virginia and through Pennsylvania to the Ohio River. It gave the Union side rail access to many Civil War battlefields—and a connection to the branch line running between Baltimore and Washington. The main line was so important that a Union regiment protected the tracks from Ellicott's Mills to Monocacy Junction, near Frederick. Garrett, for his part, ingratiated himself with the highest levels of the Lincoln government by sharing information gleaned from an intelligence network he operated for the benefit of the company. In the summer of 1864, he alerted Washington to conductors' reports about Confederate troop movements in Shenandoah Valley. Indeed, within two weeks, rebels under Lieutenant General Jubal A. Early, attacked B&O's Monocacy Junction switching installation and captured it. However, the battle lasted long enough to mess up Early's timetable, giving Lincoln time to beef up the defenses of Washington. With B&O carrying men and material, a Confederate attack on the nation's capital was repulsed July 12. Being on the government's side was profitable business. Charging the government regular rates, the railroad made so much money that it paid hefty dividends throughout the Civil War, even though Garrett declared that B&O alone would bear the reconstruction costs of destroyed bridges and equipment without asking for government handouts.[20]

HOPKINS IN CONTROL

In investing in B&O at the start-up stage, the State of Maryland drove a hard bargain, and so did the city. Even though they held two-fifths of the capital stock, the state had ten seats on the railroad's board of direction, and the City of Baltimore eight, a total of eighteen. By contrast, private stockowners had to contend with only twelve directors, even though the plurality of shares was in their hands. Hopkins and Garrett increasingly found themselves at odds with the governments' interests. The two wanted to expand the company aggressively and use borrowed money to fatten dividends. The state and the city, for their part, demanded that B&O reduce its soaring debt overhang. The face-off came when Hopkins—against the city's and the state's wishes and two years before Garrett took over as president—rammed through a 30 percent bonus dividend, all tax free. It is instructive to detail the artful way in which that was done because it offers an unusual peek into Johns Hopkins as a powerbroker.

The matter began as a city director's resolution to disburse to shareholders more than $3 million of accumulated profits, a phenomenal sum at the time. The board unanimously approved the dividend in October 1856, but without specifying how or when the disbursement should be made. Two months later, two city and two private directors called for "the redemption of the oft repeated, but long deferred promises made to your Stockholders." They urged an immediate disbursement by the board. "If not now—when?" they demanded to know. "The profits of the Road belong to the Stockholders—you have used their money—you have acknowledged the debt—you are not called upon to pay a doubtful claim, but one for which you have, time and again, freely and voluntarily confessed."[21] B&O minutes do not make clear who spoke, or what they said. But the idea of fixing the bonus dividend at 30 percent came from Garrett, whose resolution was approved by a vote of seventeen to twelve. This was the most spectacular payout issued by the company, which routinely granted tax-free dividends of between 6 and 10 percent.

Hopkins and Garrett took no chances. Before the heated B&O board meeting, Hopkins chaired a caucus with the private directors in the office of one of them, General Columbus O'Donnell. Hopkins chaired several caucuses each year in advance of important meetings. After all, these were his votes. At Garrett's urging, members pledged to support the divided, but only in bonds carrying a further 6 percent interest because Baltimore City could demand four more board seats if additional shares were distributed. Garrett opposed increasing the city's clout. Already, he complained, the city kept pressuring B&O to lower tariffs on coal and other cargo that moved through the port. Hopkins concurred. "I won't go in for any proposition that will give the City an increased Direction," he whispered to a director sitting next to him at the meeting of the full B&O board. We know all this from sworn testimony given after the city sued the board, arguing that profits should instead be used to retire the company's crushing debt. It was a nasty dispute that took two years to litigate. In the end, Hopkins and Garrett won. On his caucus directors Hopkins imposed stern discipline. Anyone diverting from the previously agreed-upon position was required to resign from the B&O board. The rule was enforced. Whenever that happened, Hopkins filled the vacancies by simply notifying the full board of a change in his appointees.

The state sued separately. As arguments increased, it became clear to Hopkins and Garrett that if B&O was to stay competitive, the company's governance had to change. A year before the Civil War, they proposed to shift control of the board to private stockholders. When legislation was introduced in Annapolis, public resentment fairly exploded. B&O had a reputation as a predatory and high-handed company. For example, its tariff structure forced Marylanders to subsidize cheap rates extended to out-of-state shippers, whether they were in New York, Philadelphia, or Ohio. Hopkins and Garrett and other rich men became lightning rods. "Less than a dozen men in Baltimore now control a majority of all the private stock that was ever represented at any election of directors. Give these dozen men the power to choose twenty-five directors, and you establish in our midst an oligarchy as dangerous, odious and irresponsible as any that ever ruled or ruined a people," wrote "Tocsin" in *The Sun*. The bill was defeated in Annapolis. Legislators feared that any change in B&O's governance would put it in the hands of "Northern interests." Geographically and politically.[22]

HOPKINS AND RACE

Johns Hopkins tried to get along. Without making a fuss about it, he held onto his antislavery principles but tolerated differing opinions and convictions. His three personal household servants were manumitted from Whitehall, but he routinely dealt with rich men who owned slaves without that being an issue. A case in point was his friend John Garrett, whose "body servant" was a slave. Hopkins's own loyalties were clear. He contributed financially to the antislavery cause, and was friendly with Henry Ward Beecher, the abolitionist brother of Harriet Beecher Stowe, who wrote the classic *Uncle Tom's Cabin*. Together, the men served as trustees of Myrtilla Miner's Normal School for Colored Girls in Washington, one of the institutions that eventually evolved into today's University of the District of Columbia.[23]

Most white male Marylanders—the only ones who counted in law and politics—supported the "state's right" to slavery, either for life or a set period. The "peculiar institution" only grew stronger in the run-up to the Civil War. After some sixty whites were killed in Nat Turner's 1831 slave revolt in neighboring Virginia—and more than two hundred blacks lost their lives in revenge—Maryland passed laws that prohibited any free black from moving to the state and obligated all slaves to depart upon being freed, and never return.[24] Anyone violating the law was fined. Those who were unable to pay could be sold out of state to the highest bidder, although an 1862 revision changed that penalty into whipping and two-year bound servitude in Maryland. (The law was finally revoked in 1865.)[25]

Slaves were the backbone of the Southern economic system at a time when no national currency existed. They were collateral property and could be mortgaged. After John Brown's 1859 revolt in Harpers Ferry, Maryland prohibited all further manumissions, and an Eastern Shore planter-delegate, Colonel Curtis W. Jacobs, proposed the re-enslavement of all free blacks. That did not happen but the legislature did authorize boards of white commissioners to regulate free blacks in St. Mary's, Calvert, Howard, Kent, Baltimore, Worcester, Caroline, Charles, Somerset, Prince George's, and Talbot Counties.[26] That year, the U.S. Census recorded 3.2 million slaves in various parts of a country of 31.5 million people. In Maryland the 87,189 slaves kept by 13,783 owners outnumbered free blacks, even though in Baltimore—a city of 212,418 residents—the African American population of 27,898 included only 2,218 slaves.[27]

Because white households included blacks in servant positions, many Baltimore residential areas were effectively racially mixed. A minimum of five servants, free or slave, was said to be necessary to run a respectable family's big house, "but families of modest means supported at least one servant."[28] By and large, systematic formal segregation had not yet begun; blacks just knew their place. There was some mingling, particularly around markets, where the races worked together and congregated around banjo players. Slaves brought that string instrument, carved out of a gourd, from West Africa. In the 1830s, Baltimore craftsmen modified it for T. D. Rice, a white minstrel singer and dancer, who made it hugely popular through his farcical blackface character, Jim Crow. After a few years of caricaturing the simpleton ways of "the Cuffees and Sambos of 'old Ferginny'" to sold-out houses in Baltimore, Rice took Jim Crow for a two-year run in London. He saw himself as an evangelist of segregation. "Before I went to England, the British people were excessively ignorant regarding 'our free institutions,'" he declared from a Baltimore stage after his return. "They were under the impression that negroes were naturally equal to the whites, and their degraded condition was consequent entirely upon our 'Institutions'; but I effectually proved that negroes are essentially an inferior species of the human family, and that they ought to remain slaves."[29]

Jim Crow became the symbol of segregation.

Country slaves were easy to recognize. Most wore ill-fitting potato-sack outfits made of coarse gray woolen "negro cloth" that was spun in Baltimore and sold throughout the South. City slaves, by contrast, often were undistinguishable from free blacks. Writes Frederick Douglass: "A city slave is almost a freeman, compared with a slave on the plantation. He is much better fed and clothed, and enjoys privilege altogether unknown to the slave on the plantation." Douglass knew. A country slave, he made the transition into a city slave himself.[30]

Maryland was full of sunset towns, where blacks, free or enslaved, were required to be off the streets by 9 p.m. in winter, and 10 p.m. in summer, or face arrest. This custom apparently was so satisfactory that an 1859 bill to legally establish a statewide curfew was not passed. Any white man could confront a black and demand documents by simply asking: "Whose Negro are you?" Money could be made through such inquiries. Baltimore Life, New York Life, Aetna, and AIG were among companies that insured slaves and paid rewards for recaptured runaways.[31] That put blacks of all ages at risk, regardless of status. "Many children, specifically those between the ages of six and twelve, were often targets of kidnappers in Baltimore," Ralph Clayton writes in *Cash for Blood: The Baltimore to New Orleans Domestic Slave Trade.* "It was a great deal easier to kidnap a child from the streets of the city, falsify ownership papers, and sell the victim to a trader than it was to kidnap an adult (although those kidnappings succeeded on occasion)."[32]

Even free blacks found their situation precarious. Laws were confusing, their administration inconsistent. No black could testify against whites. In his study of slave laws, *The Negro in Maryland*, Jeffrey R. Brackett makes it clear that promised manumissions could be revoked at any time. Many a widow canceled a dead husband's manumission promises by arguing that she needed the slaves as assets to satisfy creditors, or maintain her lifestyle. There were instances of courts overturning already granted manumissions because of widows' pleas.[33]

Between 1821 and 1845 some 2,350 slaves were manumitted in Maryland. Writes Brackett: "Of these, eleven hundred were freed forthwith; one hundred and seventy were manumitted to be free on some condition, such as emigrating to Africa; the rest, after service for stated terms. From 1845 to 1850, some eighteen hundred and fifty additional manumissions were reported."[34] Those spans coincided with the peak of the Maryland Colonization Society's efforts to ship blacks to Liberia, West Africa, instead of abolition at home. Financed with an annual $10,000 allocation from the State of Maryland, the resettlement drive had mixed motivations, including a pious declaration that removal of blacks from the United States "will not only promote their own temporal freedom and happiness, but be the means of spreading the light of civilization and the Gospel in Africa." However, "there can be little doubt that [colonization] was owing, in great measure, to Nat Turner's slave revolt in 1831," writes the effort's historian, John H. B. Latrobe, the same man who was B&O's legal counsel and chief engineer. The very next year, Maryland enacted a law to provide "for the appointment of three commissioners, members of the Maryland State Colonization Society, whose duty it is to remove from the State the people of color now free, or such as shall become so, to Liberia, or such other place, without the State, as they may approve." The same law prescribed continued slavery to those rejecting deportation. "Up to this time there had been a growing feeling in favor of emancipation in Maryland, Virginia, Kentucky.

Now there was a strong reaction, and stringent laws affecting slavery and free negroes were enacted in these States."[35]

It seems that Johns Hopkins, except for a recorded ten-dollar donation, did not get involved in the colonization cause, and neither did his identifiable Quaker peers.[36] Perhaps they felt that blacks had earned the right to pursue happiness in America, instead of being banished to a continent many had never seen? We don't know. Hopkins destroyed his personal papers; nothing should be assumed. The tenor of many emancipators was freedom *and* deportation from the United States. President Lincoln himself toyed with the expulsion of freed blacks to Belize in Central America; that project collapsed by 1864.[37] One thing is clear: The Maryland Colonization Society was no liberal organization. It functioned according to the state's dictates, with the deportation of blacks as its overriding goal. At society meetings, the races were seated separately and decisions were made by whites.[38] "One should not assume that Maryland's colonization movement under Latrobe's guidance had any sympathy with the policies of abolitionists. Instead, colonization, as seen by Latrobe, was a distinct movement reflecting his belief that two free races could not coexist in the republic," Eugene S. Van Sickle writes in a dissertation.[39]

From three African kings, the society acquired "Maryland in Liberia," a hot and steamy thirty-five-mile coastal strip today known as Maryland County. The black settlers transplanted a red, white, and blue flag (with one star and six stripes), a constitution based on America's, and the mentality of slave masters. They built elaborate antebellum mansions and imposing Masonic temples, and subjugated the indigenous people, whom they called "natives" and "aborigines."[40] One Americo-Liberian monument I saw in Maryland County praised the "Pilgrim Fathers" for coming to "tame and civilize this wild continent." The capital, Harper, honors a white-supremacist U.S. senator from Maryland (and a South Carolina congressman), Robert Goodloe Harper; the main streets still are Maryland Avenue and Baltimore Street. In fact, many settlers came from coastal South Carolina; their influence may still be heard in the Gullah-like English many Liberians speak.[41]

Once direct African imports of captives were outlawed in 1808, Chesapeake Bay slave owners controlled the nation's only sources of surplus slaves. After every harvest, they culled their work force. "Hands" from Virginia and Maryland commanded a premium. Baltimore, along with the Potomac River ports of Georgetown and Alexandria (both at the time part of the District of Columbia), served as transit points in interstate slave transfers to the cotton-based Southern market. They served the Louisiana and Mississippi slave auction houses of New Orleans and Natchez, which supplied growing demand in the southwest territories that were being populated with the aid of slaves and converted into cotton growing. For slave transfers, Baltimore wharves jutting into The Basin at the end of Gay Street were favored, along with Fells Point.

A three-week-long transfer by ship was faster than any other transport alternative and likely delivered slaves in better condition. But mass transfers were also conducted in railroad freight cars, by wagons, and by foot. Chained captives trudged for seven weeks on the National Road to Wheeling, from where Ohio River boats took them to the Mississippi. Such human trains were called coffles and sometimes consisted of more than forty men, women, and children chained and tied to one another. Many a coffle slogged some twenty miles a day in scorching heat or rain. At sunset they camped wherever they happened to be, with white overseers and slaves sleeping on the ground, regardless of weather.

The slave commerce operated in the open even though acquiring and selling slaves was as disreputable as horse trading. Private jails charged owners twenty-five cents a day to stable a slave, the same as a horse; indeed many a trader dealt in both humans and animals. A handful of slave dealers kept dungeons in that corner of the Inner Harbor environs where the Convention Center is now located and the Orioles and Ravens play. It was a convenient location, close to B&O's Camden Station and the harbor, which in those days before massive landfilling penetrated deep inland. Other traders operated in Old Town and near the Philadelphia, Wilmington, and Baltimore Railroad's President Street Station in today's Harbor East, buying and selling slaves or renting them out as laborers. The State of Maryland actively participated. The law required the penitentiary to sell all black repeat convicts out of state. In 1857 a free black was sold into slavery for thirty years for recruiting slaves to escape. Indeed, one trader was located "in a white house" near Gallows Hill, just outside the state penitentiary. "Auction & Negro Sales," declared another's shop sign.[42]

While no slave farm could profitably exist on breeding alone, many bred as a sideline and had a "stockman" to impregnate women from puberty onward. Fecund women were advertised as "breeders," their fertility a desirable quality that promised profits for the new owner. One stockman claimed to have fathered fifty-six children. He was six feet four inches tall, and weighed nearly 250 pounds.[43] Other studs claimed even more offspring. White owners and straw bosses fornicated with captive women, in competition with slave husbands and boyfriends. It was copulation for profit. Each pregnant woman produced a slave offspring whose value at birth was $200 and grew the more adulthood approached.[44] The architect Frederick Law Olmsted, traveling through Southern slave states, cited a 5 percent annual natural increase as normal. Documents show that high numbers of children were shipped out of

Baltimore, including a four-day-old infant boy, George. Some were undoubt-edly offspring of owners.

For a time, Austin Woolfolk was the big man to see. The Georgia native worked with half a dozen family members and sold 53 percent of the 4,304 slaves shipped from Baltimore to New Orleans and Natchez between 1819 and 1831. "200 negroes for the New Orleans market," he advertised. He scoured the Eastern Shore. One Woolfolk conducted business in Salisbury, a partner in Princess Anne, and an agent in Snow Hill. Affiliate traders op-erated in Easton, Cambridge, and Centreville.[45] Woolfolk tentacles reached to Tidewater Virginia as well; those acquisitions, too, were first shipped to Baltimore. His agents "were sent into every town and county in Maryland, announcing their arrival through the papers, and on flaming 'hand-bills,' headed CASH FOR NEGROES," Frederick Douglass writes. "These men were generally well dressed men, and very captivating in their manners; ever ready to drink, to treat, and to gamble. The fate of many a slave has depended upon the turn of a single card; and many a child has been snatched from the arms of its mother by bargains arranged in a state of brutal drunkenness." Frederick Douglass himself lived in fear of the Woolfolk name. Separated from his mother at an early age and sold to slavery, the future abolitionist often woke up in Fells Point to "the dead heavy footsteps, and the piteous cries of the chained gangs that passed our door."[46]

While assembling a full gang to ship, Woolfolk detained his purchases in his Pratt Street jail, not far from today's Oriole baseball park. He then trans-ferred them in the bowels of ships to New Orleans, with white passengers sometimes traveling on upper decks, along with their personal slaves.[47] Con-tentions that slavery had no future in Maryland increased such exportation. "The market for slaves, in the recently settled cotton and sugar states, is the only case that makes the slaves of Maryland, Virginia, Kentucky and Tennes-see, worth holding as property," one observer wrote. "The value of slaves in Maryland depends entirely on their value at New-Orleans. Shut up the south-ern market and the Maryland slave-holder is richer without his slaves than with them, so that his pecuniary interest is on the side of emancipation."[48]

When Benjamin Lundy's abolitionist newspaper *The Genius of Universal Emancipation* called Woolfolk "a monster in human shape" and "a soul seller," the slaver nearly beat the editor to death in January 1827. He was prosecuted for attempted murder, trying to bust the editor's skull by kicking and stomping. At the trial, Chief Judge Nicholas Brice found him guilty and sentenced him to pay one dollar in damages. But it was the editor, a Quaker, that the judge held at fault: Lundy provoked the attack through his harangues. The judge said the editor had no right to reproach Woolfolk for being "en-gaged in a trade sanctioned by the state—for the trade itself was beneficial to the state, as it removed a great many rogues and vagabonds who were a nuisance in the state."[49]

Hope H. Slatter, another native of Georgia, succeeded Woolfolk as the city's leading slave trader. He built a two-story brick jail at the corner of Howard and Market (today's Baltimore) Streets, and connected it to The Basin with an underground passage.[50] Slatter told two enquiring Quakers that he was in favor of "compensated emancipation, and utterly opposed to the sale of children." That was nonsense; he left behind a record of trafficking minors for sexual purposes. He advertised "particularly to purchase several seamstresses and small fancy girls for nurses."[51] Fancy girls was a term readily understood, describing light-skinned underage females being trained to be owners' bedmates or prostitutes. His asking price was $250 for a "sprightly, bright mulatto girl only 7 years old, as fine a servant as I saw, who can intelligently run errands and small articles by herself." Iron bars covered the windows and air holes of Slatter's jail.[52] The brick-paved yard contained a few benches, a water pump, numerous wash tubs and clothes lines. On one side was the auction block, where the fate of humans was decided.

Lincoln's Emancipation Proclamation, on January 1, 1863, did not free Maryland blacks because it only applied to slaves in the Confederacy, and Maryland was a Union state. After the battle of Gettysburg, a Union colonel, lieutenant, and sergeant stormed Slatter's jail, now run by a successor, looking for able-bodied slaves who could be drafted to the army. "In this place I found 26 men, 1 boy, 29 women and 3 infants," reported Colonel William Birnie, a white commander of the U.S. Colored Troops. "Sixteen of the men were shackled and one had his legs chained together by ingeniously contrived locks connected by chains suspended to his waist." Among those imprisoned was a four-month-old born in the jail and a twenty-four-month-old who had spent all of his life behind the bars while his mother was used for breeding.[53]

THE MASQUERADE IS OVER

Maryland voters in 1864 approved a new constitution that abolished slavery. The vote may have been rigged. The margin of victory—just 375 votes out of a total of 59,973—was provided by Union soldiers amid war conditions. Various sources suggest that supporters of slavery were kept from the polls. "The test oaths and intimidation tactics employed by the military and the politicians that stood behind it disfranchised three-fourths of the white male citizens of Maryland," wrote Frank R. Kent, a leading political journalist and author of *The Story of Maryland Politics* (1911). He also wrote *The Great Game of Politics: An Effort to Present the Elementary Human*

Facts about Politics, Politicians, and Political Machines, Candidates and Their Ways (1923).

During the war, many Democrats escaped the authorities' harassment by hiding in the ranks of the Union Party, which Lincoln's national government created to broaden support for the war in border states. Robert Jefferson Breckinridge, an educator from divided Kentucky, explained the rationale: "As a Union party I will follow you to the ends of the earth, and to the gates of death. But as an Abolition party, as a Republican party, as a Whig party, as a Democratic party, as an American [Know-Nothing] party, I will not follow you one foot." Lincoln, in turn, had to keep his coalition happy. In Maryland, he appointed at least one postmaster who owned slaves. The wartime governor Augustus W. Bradford, for his part, pardoned a free black who had been imprisoned for having a copy of *Uncle Tom's Cabin.* The governor imposed a condition: The prisoner had to leave Maryland and never return. "The preservation of the Union was one thing, the abolition of slavery, even, was another," writes Brackett.

Democrats in hiding took off the masks in 1866, six months after the provost marshal's office closed and the military control ended. Johns Hopkins was among a bevy of honorary vice presidents at a huge Union Party rally at Calvert and Fayette Streets, where the Mitchell Courthouse now stands. He was an *Unconditional* Unionist, a Republican, who supported the Lincoln-inspired Reconstruction that President Andrew Johnson was rolling back in favor of state's rights on civil liberties and black voting. Garrett, another honorary vice president, also was there. He was a *Conditional* Unionist, a Democrat in disguise. That night these two capitalist pals—an abolitionist and a recent slave owner—witnessed how clandestine Democrats hijacked the Union Party rally attended by thousands, including commanding generals with military bands. Featured speakers declared that the war had settled the slavery issue, and the fight now was about whether Congress should be allowed to trample on state's rights and give blacks the vote.

"This Congress wishes to treat these States as Territories, and give the right of suffrage and the offices to the niggers and those so-called Southern loyalists," declared Kentucky Governor Thomas E. Bramlette, according to *The Sun*'s stenographer. "If those Southern loyalists cannot demean themselves so as to live peacefully down South, let them and their niggers travel elsewhere. We will find a place somewhere that will hold them. Not here so help me God; I will never consent that they will remain." Alabama's Union-appointed provisional governor, Lewis Parsons, a native of New York, also advocated continued suppression of blacks. Congress had failed to do so, he charged, and was responsible for "restrictive and intolerant laws and the elevation of the negro on the backs of white men." President Johnson was now trying to right things, but encountered opposition among politicians. Signs spotted among the crowd declared: "Sustain Congress and you support the black man. Sustain the President and you support the white man." Seen among placards was a depiction of a huge woodpile with the legend: "No niggers in the woodpile." Also spotted was an anti-Semitic drawing.[54]

Within months, Conditional Unionists quit the party altogether. Like Garrett, they again became Democrats, whose platform demanded an end to "radical" Reconstruction, opposed voting rights for blacks, and advocated the enshrinement of white supremacy in life and law. The Democrats gained the upper hand—which they have historically largely maintained—after Governor Swann bolted from the Union Party to Democratic ranks over "forced negro suffrage." He was a one-time Know Nothing mayor, who as company president had recruited Johns Hopkins to the B&O board. Brackett writes: "The radical wing of the old Union party became a minority; as the Republican party of Maryland; while the conservatives and all those who again became voters, on a lenient use of the old war test oaths, with those who came from the South, took control of the State" as Democrats. Theirs was the party of white domination. Governor Swann spearheaded Maryland's refusal to ratify the Fourteenth Amendment which gave blacks citizenship rights, and the Fifteenth, which gave them the vote. (Maryland ratified the former amendment only in 1959 and the latter in 1973.) To Swann, Reconstruction meant returning the vote to those whites who lost it for siding with the Confederacy.

Johns Hopkins did not like Swann's politics. Despite their shared history at the B&O, the philanthropist was upset that the governor kept moving Maryland further away from the spirit and practice of Lincoln's ideals. He was so worried about Swann's intentions that he sought an injunction to block an 1867 convention to draft a new constitution. When that failed, he and other like-minded individuals took the matter to the court of appeals, which rejected the plea as well.[55] At stake was the constitution's ban on "rebel suffrage," which Swann wanted to lift. Hopkins called Confederates "traitors" and did not want to give them the vote.[56] The state constitution, crafted mainly by Unionists, also "expressly and emphatically" prohibited "negro suffrage"—after declaring that all men were "created equally free."[57]

As strange as it may seem, some Maryland blacks had the right to vote as early as in the first decade of the 1800s. Among requirements were that they be property owners and freeborn, not manumitted later.[58] Once their numbers so increased as to pose a perceived threat to white supremacy, they lost the suffrage. That seems to have been fine by Hopkins. He belonged to the Unconditional Unionists' organization, which demanded continued exclusion of both former Confederates and blacks, although individual views varied widely. Hopkins's beliefs on black voting rights are hard to pin down because no records exist. The only direct testimony comes from Judge J. Thomson Mason, a former U.S. congressman, who said that Hopkins did not deign to "confer the right of suffrage on the negro, nor place him on a footing of social equality with the whites." Nevertheless, said Mason, Hopkins felt that "the negro claims our benevolence and charity—he is a part of the great human family, and is entitled to the same mercy and charity as that bestowed on the white man."[59]

NO OVERCOAT

As Christmas approached in 1873, the country was in an economic freefall. Failures of New York banks created a domino of collapsing financial institutions, prompting Johns Hopkins to exclaim in horror: "This is a tornado." But rather than wring his hands, he intervened, using his fortune to stabilize Baltimore's banks. He was successful—"the only single man who could have done it," according to Colonel Scharf. But bad times did not go away. Instead, the nation fell into one of history's deepest depressions. Putting uninterrupted dividends first, B&O discharged a thousand of thirty-five hundred workers in the machinery and car shops; the city's fifty packing houses, which employed ten thousand, laid off seven thousand. Many sugar refineries and furnaces in the port closed, and hundreds of paupers gathered at police stations every night, looking for shelter.

During the first week of December, mild weather unexpectedly changed into frost. Johns Hopkins caught a cold. But after temperatures turned mild again, he disregarded doctors' orders and left his bed so as to attend to grave matters at hand. He had never in his life owned an overcoat and did not wear one when the temperature plunged again. No winter boots protected his feet.[60] Soon he had an even worse cold, punctuated with asthma attacks, and was fading fast. His in-town mansion, a handsome two-story, white-granite edifice was located on an elevated perch at 81 West Saratoga Street, near where the Old St. Paul's Church rectory still stands. Today, that site has been excavated into a level parking lot, and high-rises block the view. But in 1873 Johns Hopkins could see a rapidly growing city from his windows. He died of pneumonia on December 24, aged seventy-eight. His dog, Zeno, was stretched on the floor at the foot of the bed.[61]

Chapter Three

A Brush with Death

The initial spark that inspired Johns Hopkins to create a university, hospital, and medical school may have come from his brush with death, when he was thirty-seven years old. Malaria was rampant, and typhus and yellow fever frequent around The Basin, the smelly waterfront business district where he was headquartered. Then in August of 1832, in the middle of heat and wet-blanket mugginess, Baltimoreans began turning blue and dying from attacks of uncontrollable diarrhea, spasmodic vomiting, violent stomach cramps, and hellish convulsions—all evidence that dreaded epidemic cholera had reached the nation's third largest city. Within the next two months, 853 succumbed to a painful death from the intestinal infection. The randomness of cholera caused panic, and so did its ability to kill swiftly. A person could be perfectly healthy in the morning and dead in the afternoon. Those able to flee escaped the city, including dozens of unfortunates at the almshouse where 133 died.[1]

Johns Hopkins was among the thousands who fell seriously ill. Opiates were legal and a common remedy in those days. His doctors treated him with some variation of this noxious cocktail of poisons: mercury chloride and opium, mercury and potassium nitrate, saline mixture, opium and aloes, sassafras oil, mercurial frictions with melted lard, and plaster made of ground mustard. "If the bowels are constipated rhubarb should be preferred, if the least lax, lead and opium, or calomel and opium, with rest in bed," one doctor advised. Bloodletting was routine, through a surgical incision to a vein.[2]

No record exists of Hopkins's case beyond a mere mention in *A Silhouette*, a biography based on family lore by his great-niece Helen Hopkins Thom. "His health had never been the same since an attack of cholera, contracted in 1832, had resulted in a very severe illness," she writes. "He did not sleep for nearly two weeks at that time, and his doctor said that if this continued he would die. Although this contingency was averted, insomnia became one of the things that he had to fight against the rest of his life."[3] The absence of details is not surprising; cholera was regarded as God's revenge for wrongful living. After the first cases were confirmed, a number of physicians met with Mayor Jesse Hunt, demanding that he deny cholera's presence. "The meeting, by a small margin, decided that the cholera to some extent did exist in the city," recorded Dr. Horatio Gates Jameson, the city's consulting physician.[4] The issue was touchy. "Asiatic cholera was a disease not only of the sinner but of the poor," writes Harvard medical historian Charles E. Rosenberg. "Neither poverty nor wealth seemed to be an accidental condition, and many well-to-do Americans saw in their riches visible testimony to the regularity of their habits. The vices—intemperance, immorality, impiety—which doomed a man to poverty were the same ones which predisposed him to cholera. The Irish and Negroes, the most filthy, intemperate, and imprudent portion of the population and hence the poorest of Americans, were, not surprisingly, the most frequent victims of cholera."[5] Jameson concurred: "A very great majority of those who died were of the most worthless; but a few of our respectable citizens fell victim to this scourge of humanity."[6]

Johns Hopkins may have contracted the disease from eating a tainted peach, apple, or watermelon. That's how people got sick. Jameson recounted how a black man sitting on the stoops and spitting watermelon seeds with a chum joked that they were feasting on a "mess of cholera." They guffawed and had a merry old time. Both got sick and died within a day. Watermelon almost killed three white teenagers from a "respectable" family who disobeyed their mother's warning not to eat any. All fruits and vegetables were suspect. That's why a physician, Dr. John Cromwell, astonished friends when he declared that peaches were "wholly innocent." To demonstrate this, the thirty-three-year-old University of Maryland alumnus—and nephew of Jameson—bought a peach and ate it. He was dead within a few hours, the only degreed physician to die in the epidemic.[7]

Lewis G. Wells also died. A "carter," a wagon-and-buggy man by trade, and a deacon at his church, Wells had "devoted several years to the study of medicine," likely under Jameson, "and had become a busy practitioner among our colored people."[8] He collapsed on a street at midnight after a busy day of attending to the sick and dying. He was carried home. "The pulse was gone; skin and tongue as cold as marble; though still sensible, he was prostrated," recorded Jameson, who gave Wells a large dose of laudanum, a sedative tincture of opium. "He coolly, and with a degree of indifference which, we think, was common in such cases, desired us to take charge of some pecuniary concerns of his. His sufferings were heart-rending."[9] Two nuns from the Sisters of Charity also perished: Mary Frances and Mary George, both aged nineteen. They were among nine nuns who came to treat cholera patients whom others feared to care for.

All this is based on Jameson's remarkable eyewitness account of the 1832 epidemic, *A Treatise on Epidemic Cholera*.[10] Aside from painful deaths, he documented miraculous recoveries. On the Fells Point waterfront, he encountered a "stout muscular [presumably African American] man rolling over the pavement, with his mouth wide open, his limbs contorted, his pulse very tense, but slow, and his groans and shrieks were heart-rending, and had attracted a large crowd of people around him. He had not been drinking." Jameson bled the man on the spot. After drawing thirty ounces, he noticed that black blood was turning into florid purple. He took that as a good sign. After a while the sick man stood up and simply walked away, "reached his stopping-place, his wife being a slave, some squares [blocks] off; he soon regained good health without any medical aid."[11]

In 1832 Baltimore's 80,625 inhabitants were served by some 120 recognized white physicians, many without a medical degree, and an unknown number of black and white medicine men and women, including midwives. Regardless of training, everyone's knowledge was shockingly deficient by contemporary standards. For example, they all kept purging cholera victims without realizing that rehydration was essential to compensate for lost fluids. That single mistake cost countless lives.

Jameson, fifty-four, was the cholera authority. He was an 1813 graduate of the University of Maryland medical school, which had opened eight years earlier at Lombard and Greene Streets, where it is still located. A native of York, Pennsylvania, he came from a long line of Scots-Irish medical practitioners in this country and in the old one. He studied medicine under his father and began to practice at seventeen. During the War of 1812, he was surgeon to the troops at Fort McHenry. He was a dapper man with a heap of snow-white hair, full of energy; he fathered nine children. He edited *Maryland Medical Recorder*, was a frequent contributor to scholarly journals, and authored a popular 557-page compendium, *The American Domestick Medicine, Or, Medical Admonisher*. In 1829 he took away nearly the entire upper jaw of a patient, the first such surgery in the world. In 1831, searching for a more potent smallpox vaccine, he extracted cowpox serum from an infected cow, then used it to vaccinate four humans.[12] "Two of the patients took the disease very handsomely," he reports without saying anything about the other two. He performed Baltimore's first tracheotomy, puncturing the windpipe of a patient who could not breathe, and attempted to remove an ovary but failed, all without the benefit of modern-day anesthesia. His expertise was wide. He was the first American to read a paper on latest discoveries at a yellow fever conference in Hamburg, Germany.

This man was singlehandedly responsible for Baltimore being prepared when the cholera epidemic struck. "Few men did so much to give credit to early American surgery as Dr. Horatio Gates Jameson, who from 1820 to 1840 carried the fame of Baltimore, as a seat of medical and surgical research, to all parts of the civilized world," writes an admiring profiler.[13]

Corresponding with medical colleagues in Europe, Jameson tracked the epidemic's progression from India, where hundreds of thousands died in the 1820s, including ten thousand British colonial soldiers and administrators. Previously limited to the Ganges valley, cholera then began migrating. It penetrated the Russian Empire, then in February 1832, surfaced in Hamburg. As soon as he heard about that, Jameson warned the mayor that it was only a matter of time before cholera appeared in Baltimore. The mayor heeded the advice and ordered preventive measures. The number of sweep superintendents was doubled, and they were ordered to inspect "twice a week every street, lane, or alley, public or private, and have them scraped and swept, and filth and dirt be immediately removed." Whenever necessary, cellars were whitewashed with a stain of lime and water. Pools of stagnant water were eliminated, privies treated with lime. From hog pens to lumber yards, sites were inspected so as to remove insect and rodent breeding grounds. No one quite understood what cholera was or how it spread, but stepped-up sanitation was recognized as key to fighting it. That went only so far, though; open gutters doubled as Baltimore's sewers.[14]

Two months before the first cholera cases were detected, Jameson persuaded the mayor to put a hospital on standby to "make preparation for cholera patients by preparing bedding, &c., and also fit up as many houses within the city as may be thought necessary." A plan was proposed to create twelve cholera hospitals, but Jameson opposed the idea; in the end, only three were opened. Instead, physicians were appointed for each ward to make house calls.[15] Also, an apothecary was opened "in each ward, where medicines could be had, at all hours, for sick of cholera, at the city expense." All ships coming from any foreign country or infected U.S. ports were ordered to stay at anchor in the Patapsco River, quarantined for a minimum of fourteen days.

Thus Baltimore was quite ready, when the American ship *Brenda* arrived from Liverpool June 7, 1832. It was a coffin ship. When it left England, it carried 123 passengers, along with a cargo of salt, crates, dry goods, and hardware. But during the miserable forty-two-day Atlantic crossing fourteen passengers died from cholera and five from other causes. By the time the *Brenda* reported at the Lazaretto Point quarantine station (which was located in Canton, across from Fort McHenry), "the disease had entirely disappeared from the ship," reported Dr. Samuel B. Martin, the city's health officer. As a precaution, the passengers and crew were isolated in the pesthouse, as Lazaretto Point was known, where they were disinfected and quarantined at city expense for a fortnight. They were housed in dormitories with open windows so as to take advantage of fresh air and breezes. "All the children and others requiring it" were vaccinated against smallpox because widespread vaccinations had proven successful in curbing that disease and might aid combating other diseases as well, or so it was thought.[16] Belongings were stored and "ventilated."[17] None of the remaining passengers was infected, nor was a single case of cholera detected among the 11,827 other passengers who were quarantined during the epidemic.[18]

A month later, deaths began. The first recorded cholera fatality occurred on August 4, 1832: a seven-year-old white girl "of respectable parentage, and in a neighborhood where cholera was not likely, from appearance, to show itself, being a very respectable neighborhood." The location was at Liberty and Baltimore Streets. Long since landfilled, that stretch of "clean and airy buildings" bordered the alluvial edge of The Basin. Fecal bacteria spread the virus. Overflowing cesspools and privy pits poisoned wells. Cholera did not discriminate among black or white, rich or poor, virtuous or not.[19]

JOHNS HOPKINS BUYS A HOSPITAL

It is not known whether Hopkins ever met Jameson, who became an outspoken critic of the way the University of Maryland medical school and the affiliated hospital were run. Jameson was not the only critic. During prolonged faculty strife and administration upheavals, he and a number of others quit the university and organized a rival medical school. When he went to charter it, the state rejected his application at the request of the University of Maryland. There were also attempts to destroy his professional reputation by scurrilous leafleting. A resultant criminal trial fined one of his accusers, Dr. Frederick F. B. Hintze, while vindicating Jameson. "The whole thing originated in the jealousy over Jameson's rising reputation as a surgeon and his efforts to found a new school in Baltimore," *The Medical Annals of Maryland* concluded. As to the medical school, he found a crafty solution, nearly unique in academic annals. In 1827 he opened it under the out-of-state charter of Washington College of Washington, Pennsylvania. The school operated until 1851, but lost Jameson when he moved to Cincinnati in 1835.[20]

Three years earlier, in preparation for the cholera epidemic, Jameson designated Maryland Hospital as the first infirmary to provide treatment. That hospital had been created in 1793 as one of the first acts of the city health department, the oldest such continuing bureaucracy in the nation. The hospital was described as "a temporary retreat for the strangers and sea-faring people." That quaint portrayal was accurate. In those days, such infirmaries that existed offered only disadvantages over treatment at home by a doctor and care by family members or friends. Those who had neither languished in almshouses. Of the thousands who fell sick in 1832, only 387 were taken to the three cholera hospitals: 217 were cured, 170 died.[21]

After the epidemic, Maryland Hospital became an asylum for the "lunatics and insane," a use well-suited for its isolated location at Broadway and Old Philadelphia Road (today's Monument Street), roughly one mile uphill from the Fells Point waterfront and a similar distance from city hall. The terrain to the east was twitter country. Truly. Before the telegraph was invented, that's where *The Sun* kept its aviary of some five hundred Antwerp homing pigeons. These trained birds flew between Baltimore, Washington, New York, and Philadelphia, with urgent messages or newspaper clippings attached to their legs. They couriered news beats and financial information from ships to shore. Until the telegraph was introduced in the 1840s, such pigeons were the fastest means of news transmission.[22]

Things were moving fast. All around the asylum site Johns Hopkins saw evidence of development about to burst.[23] In 1870 he bought the hospital's thirteen-acre grounds, pledging to demolish the asylum buildings. The acquisition gave the public the first inkling about how one of America's richest men planned to spend his fortune. The man whose own formal schooling ended at twelve was going to create the finest charity hospital that money could buy. And he was going to endow a medical school. Newspapers and leading citizens praised him for his generosity. But the announcement also created racial stir. The asylum's two hundred lunatics, male and female, were all white. Now Johns Hopkins wanted to have a four hundred-bed hospital built that also treated blacks. Or as his will put it: "The indigent sick of this city and its environs, without regard to sex, age, or color, who require surgical or medical treatment, and who can be received into the hospital without peril to other inmates, and the poor of the city and State, of all races, who are stricken down by any casualty, shall be received into the hospital without charge, for such periods of time and under such regulations as you may prescribe."

The hospital site was within the semirural Loudenslager's Hill district that included today's Hampstead Hill, Washington Hill, Butchers Hill, and Patterson Park sections. Within those borders already operated tanneries and slaughterhouses—nuisances that were evicted as health hazards from more populated areas. Four other hospitals existed in the district. One was the predecessor of today's Sinai Hospital. The Hebrew Hospital and Asylum was at Monument Street and Rutland Avenue, across from the Hopkins Hospital site. St. Joseph, catering to German Catholics, was at Caroline and Oliver Streets. Then there was an infirmary dating back to Jameson's old medical school. Its cupolaed main building still stands at Broadway and Fairmount

Avenue, the old Episcopalian Church Home and Infirmary, now in use by the Johns Hopkins University. The fourth hospital was located on Greenmount Avenue across from the Green Mount Cemetery near today's Station North. It would change names a couple of times and move crosstown, ultimately becoming St. Agnes Hospital on Caton Avenue.

Arguing that their turf was already oversaturated with nuisances, a group of influential citizens mobilized to stop Hopkins's hospital plan. City councilman Andrew J. Saulsbury declared at a crowded meeting that he and his constituents did not want "a hospital of any kind and particularly one for the use of colored persons." The convener was General William H. Neilson, of the Maryland Militia, who was a big shot in Freemasonry, a potent civic force at the time.[24] A previous meeting had tasked him to find out more about Johns Hopkins's racial thinking. He and a delegation had done so. According to *The Sun*, they were told that a "brick wall" would separate white patients from blacks.[25]

Naval surgeon Charles H. White then stood up. Whatever was going on, he suspected skullduggery in Hopkins's acquisition. He recalled that two years earlier Dr. Richard Stewart, the president of the Maryland Hospital board, combed the neighborhood and "secured the signatures of nearly all property holders" in support of a petition to move the hospital to the Spring Grove in Catonsville. After the legislature granted the request, the hospital board over a ninety-day period invited sealed bids on the Broadway property. The minimum for the thirteen acres was set at $200,000, the naval surgeon said. Yet Hopkins paid only $123,000 for the land and buildings. Something fishy was going on. At the next meeting, General Neilson said he, too, was suspicious. A letter was read from a Somerset County state senator, who protested the sale to the legislature. Meanwhile, opponents appeared before the city council, hoping to block Hopkins's construction footprint because it required the demolition of existing houses and the permanent closure of streets.

In contrast to protesting whites, the African American leadership hailed the hospital as a breakthrough in race relations. "Johns Hopkins will ever be regarded as the friend of the colored race in that we will teach our children to do honor for his memory," declared a resolution passed at a mass meeting. His "noble liberality of spirit" was praised, as was "the comprehensiveness of mind characterizing his conduct in recognizing our race as being entitled to equal consideration and treatment." [26]

HOPKINS GAINS EXPERIENCE

Johns Hopkins, in fact, did have an inside track in acquiring the mental asylum. He served as a member of its board of visitors from 1852 onward and signed reports that recommended the abandonment of Broadway in favor of rural Catonsville.[27] After he retired from his mercantile endeavors to devote his energy to B&O Railroad, he began educating himself about hospitals. He joined the board of trustees setting up the new Union Protestant Infirmary, and remained a member until his death.[28] That predecessor of today's Union Memorial Hospital opened a twenty-bed sickroom in a rented corner row house (still extant) at Baltimore and Stricker Streets, welcomed by a community that donated "an overwhelming number of Bibles, 100 cotton bats, 6 flatirons, 2 spittoons, an invalid's chair, a basket of grapes, 15 bananas."[29] The infirmary's charter commanded that "the major affairs of the Hospital shall be entirely in the hands of women." An all-woman board of managers indeed ran the sickroom, but the board of trustees consisted of men. Hopkins must have found the nonsectarian nature of the infirmary attractive. Although largely inspired by two Episcopal parishes, Emmanuel and St. Peter's, a fund-raising appeal described Union Protestant as "a society in which sects and parties—those pests of religion—are not known; in which the long lost word 'brother' is reinstituted in the vocabulary of disciples of Jesus, and love—love to man—that philanthropy of when Jesus was the first teacher and perfect embodiment—is rethroned over the heart."[30]

Brotherhood did not include blacks. Not far from B&O's Mount Clare works, the sickroom neighborhood boasted a mansion, Garrett Park, another estate owned by the railroad president. Imposing residences of brick or brownstone surrounded nearby Franklin, Union, and Lafayette Squares, where flowers bloomed and fountains bubbled behind Victorian iron fencing. People of African bloodlines lived in alleys behind the homes of whites, but Union Protestant did not treat them, in that it was no different from other infirmaries, which only took care of whites. This may have fostered Johns Hopkins's repeated insistence on nondiscriminatory medical care at the hospital he willed. He knew that poor blacks had it tough if they fell ill. When he himself got sick with cholera, he received the best available care by leading doctors living next door who treated him at home, with his own servants providing nursing care. But while he rested and recovered in his own bed, eating the food of his mansion kitchen, black cholera victims, if they were lucky, lay on cots in tents erected outdoors on infirmary grounds because they were not wanted inside, and the hovels where they lived didn't have space.

His will distributed more than $1 million to relatives and friends.[31] But the bulk of his fortune—$7 million—he divided between the university and hospital, in equal amounts. It was the largest donation to American education up to that day. Each had a separate board, but with so much overlap that ten of the twelve original trustees served on both boards.[32] He sketched no grand vision, nor issued any overarching mission statement. Aside from financial stipulations, he hardly mentioned the university, giving the trust-

The architectural majesty of Johns Hopkins Hospital, circa 1920.
Courtesy of the Maryland Historical Society, Image #CC1009

ees a free hand. The medical school, while adjoining the hospital, was to be part of the university.[33]

Much of Hopkins's attention went to the hospital. He wanted it to be a showpiece. It was to be an innovator in medicine and care, and it had to look the part. "It is my wish," he wrote, that the hospital's architectural design "will permit symmetrical additions to the buildings which will be first constructed, in order that you may ultimately be able to receive four hundred patients, and that it shall provide for an hospital which shall in construction and arrangement compare favorably with any other institution of like character in this country or in Europe." His aesthetic instructions to the hospital trustees were detailed: "I wish the large grounds surrounding the hospital to be properly enclosed by iron railings, and to be so laid out and planted with trees and flowers as to afford solace to the sick and be an ornament to the section of the city in which the grounds are located. I desire that you should, in due season, provide for a site and buildings of such and at such distance from the city as your judgment shall approve, for the reception of convalescent patients. You will be able in this way to hasten the recovery of the sick, and to have always rooms in the main hospital building for other sick persons requiring immediate medical or surgical treatment." He also wanted the hospital to operate "a training school for female nurses."

CLIFTON

Broadway began as a wide market street on the Fells Point waterfront, then climbed past the hospital site and continued uphill, dead-ending at Boundary Avenue (today's North Avenue), which at the time marked the city line. Clifton, Hopkins's 330-acre estate, was a few hundred yards farther, occupying a high hill, with the harbor visible in the distance. Hopkins wanted the university built at Clifton and he commanded his trustees to extend Broadway there. That way the boulevard would connect the university, the hospital, and the medical school. Esthetics mattered to him. That could be seen from the attention, care, and expense that he devoted to Clifton, located in a part of the town favored by grandees. Neighbors included the ironmonger-tycoon Enoch Pratt; A. S. Abell, founder of *The Sun*, and William T. Walters, the art collector who bequeathed a museum. Next to Clifton, John W. Garrett bought the five hundred-acre Montebello estate, which he nearly tripled in size through acquisitions.[34]

Hopkins acquired Clifton at a distress sale from the heirs of Captain Henry Thompson who, despite his birth as an Englishman, was an American patriot. Thompson's militia, the First Baltimore Horse Artillery, was at the ready when the British sailed to attack Baltimore in September 1814 after burning Washington, including the White House. (He put the troops under the command of General Sam Smith, his neighbor who owned the Montebello estate.) Thompson was a capitalist. His dozen or more ships transported goods up and down the Atlantic coast and to New Orleans. His largest ship, *Clifton*, was built in a local Harris Creek shipyard. He invested in B&O; both he and Hopkins were board members of the Merchants' Exchange, and both were involved in restabilizing banking when bank scandals and panics were afoot. He was a member of the Poppleton Commission, which laid out the street grid that Baltimore still largely follows.[35]

Thompson's Clifton was known for extensive orchards, prize Devon cattle, and Merino sheep, all cared for by slaves as well as indentured servants and paid trades people. Hopkins employed no slaves. A gardener from Scotland, William Fowler, supervised some sixty-six acres of meticulous gardens, glasshouses, graperies, orangeries, ponds, lawns, and tree plantings. Hopkins, a country boy at heart, involved himself in many agricultural activities. In 1858 the Maryland State Agricultural Society gave him a three-dollar first prize for the "best specimens of eating grapes" and one dollar for the second place.

When Hopkins acquired Clifton, along came a panhandler who had long stationed himself at a tollhouse of Thompson's privately owned Harford Road turnpike. Hopkins wanted to get rid of the nuisance. Friends advised him to resort to bribery. "Pay him money!" he shrieked, "God forbid! If I should once do that, there would be a hundred instead of one." He also rejected a recommendation to simply kick the tramp off the property. "No, no, no." He said he felt like the Bible's rich man condemned to eternal damnation for shunning Lazarus, a beggar pockmarked with sores. "Would you have me do like him and burn in hell forever?" He said he was not afraid of the beggar, "but I'm afraid of God." The vagrant stayed, but Hopkins built a gatehouse closer to the city so that he and his guests did not have to deal with the panhandler.[36]

Thompson had been content with a substantial manor house, a stone mansion in the Georgian style with two stories and attic and full basement, completed in 1803 and enlarged later. Hopkins, for his part, hired Niernsee and Neilson, the celebrated local architects who had designed important public buildings, including B&O's Camden Station. They refashioned the old house into a vaguely Tuscan villa, complete with an observation tower. Hopkins often climbed eighty-four steps to the top, where he could spend time with his telescope, following ships in the harbor. (The view was even better from his city mansion on Saratoga Street, where he could read flags on Federal Hill's signal tower, which announced the approach of ships.) A frugal man, he retained much of the Thompson interior woodwork and windows even though he radically redecorated the walls and ceilings and added six rooms to the first and second floors and the wraparound porch. He converted the attic into a third floor, where his butler and housekeepers made residence.

Unlike contemporaries of similar wealth and recognition, Hopkins did not go to Europe or travel widely at home. Instead, he worked, only periodically journeying to Delaware's beaches. He read voraciously as an antidote to insomnia. His interests were wide-ranging, innovations intrigued him. He eagerly quizzed knowledgeable visitors about faraway places, beliefs, and customs. His table was praised, and so were his wines (he seldom drank, but favored champagne). He had never seen Italy, but visitors entering from the covered entrance drive were greeted with a huge wall painting of the Naples harbor, with Mount Vesuvius billowing volcanic smoke in the background. He wanted to project a certain degree of worldliness.[37]

In writing his will, Johns Hopkins assumed that the hospital would open first, before the university. That did not happen. Instead, the university was assembled from scratch in just three years. It opened in 1876 with fifty-four graduate students and twenty-three undergraduates, initially occupying two remodeled rental houses and a newly constructed annex near Howard and

Centre Streets. The founder's handpicked trustees worked hard to achieve the fast-track feat. With Cornell University president Andrew D. White as their guide, they consulted leading educators at home and also toured Europe. Money was no object. Presidents Charles W. Eliot, of Harvard, and James B. Angell, of the University of Michigan, traveled to Baltimore to meet with the trustees. All those presidents were old friends, trained in Germany. For the job as Hopkins's founding president they recommended another from their midst, Daniel Coit Gilman. Andrew White made it unanimous by adding his voice in support of Gilman, a Yale PhD who had gone to head the University of California, only to find himself there embroiled in ugly confrontations with legislators who wanted the university to remain a cow school.

Gilman was far more ambitious than that. He was a truly remarkable find. Like the presidents who recommended him, he believed that American education would benefit from the rigorous approach of Germany's best universities. He had been a diplomat with the American Legation in St. Petersburg, where he spent his time studying the Russian education system. A crazy American, czarist officials decided. He seemed interested in everything. He was current on all aspects of education, of course, and quite knowledgeable about medicine, ready for the job the moment he arrived in Baltimore. He was an organizational wizard. In addition to the university, the trustees soon—and without additional pay—put him in charge of the much-delayed hospital. He troubleshooted and saw to its successful opening. He was a consummate networker, a cofounder of the trust behind Skull and Bones, the Yale secret society. He was so slick that his behind-the-back nickname was "Oily Dan."[38]

The university's Howard Street location put it within a few blocks of an adult education institute George Peabody had built on Mount Vernon Place. He was a Unitarian born in Massachusetts, who lived in Baltimore for two decades before moving to London where he based his important finance house, now known by the name of a successor, J. P. Morgan.[39] The university depended on Peabody's 120,000-volume library, a cathedral of books inside an architectural wonder that borrowed elements from baroque, rococo, and even gothic. The centerpiece, much in favor for weddings nowadays, was pure magic—a huge atrium lit from above with skylights soaring sixty-one feet above a patterned marble floor and flanked by gold-leafed classical columns attached to five tiers of cast-iron galleries full of books.[40] Not far away, the Maryland Historical Society offered another substantial library. Hopkins had been a board member during a period when the society practically ran Peabody. Across from the university was the new home of City College, a public high school for high-achieving boys that was planning a four-year curriculum leading to a baccalaureate degree. When that did not happen, every City students' dream was to win a competitive scholarship to go to Hopkins.[41]

Johns Hopkins in the autumn of his life
Courtesy of Ferdinand Hamburger Archives, Sheridan Libraries, Johns Hopkins University

The hospital was another story. It finally opened in 1889, after twelve years of delays. One reason for the delays was Hopkins's command that the hospital should be fully funded from interest income. Another reason was that the trustees had relied on Niernsee, now without a partner, to design it. He had remodeled Clifton, and when Maryland Hospital moved from Broadway to Catonsville, he designed the architecture of the successor, the Spring Grove mental hospital. He was also the architect when the Union Protestant Infirmary, on whose board Hopkins served, relocated in 1859 to a new building at 1514 Division Street, a bequest of the financier George Brown. (After the neighborhood changed racially, Union Protestant renamed itself and, in

1923, opened as Union Memorial at its current location on 33rd Street. The old edifice was taken over by Provident Hospital, a now-defunct hospital owned by blacks.)

Niernsee produced a plan for Johns Hopkins Hospital, but then asked to be relieved because of other commitments. A Boston firm, Cabot and Chandler, completed the design. Dr. John Shaw Billings, who had a knack for architecture, made important modifications and alternative designs. He was Gilman's primary advisor, whose wide-ranging interests perfectly complemented the president. The two were different in demeanor and style. Gilman was solicitous, political, Oily Dan; Billings was brilliant and brash. Before joining Hopkins, he was a medical doctor on the U.S. surgeon general's staff and created today's National Library of Medicine; he eventually became the first director of the New York Public Library.

He and Gilman picked many of the hospital's early luminaries. Beyond that, he was a disciple of Florence Nightingale, the Crimean War nurse and creator of modern nursing, who wrote: "The very first canon of nursing, the first and the last thing upon which a nurse's attention must be fixed, the first essential to a patient, without which all the rest you can do for him is as nothing, with which I had almost said you may leave all the rest alone, is this: TO KEEP THE AIR HE BREATHES AS PURE AS EXTERNAL AIR, WITHOUT CHILLING HIM."[42] This is what Billings set to deliver. "The temperature in Baltimore may vary from 103 degrees in the shade to 17 below zero, hence its perfect hospital must be one which would answer for the tropics or for northern Russia," he wrote. He designed each building with double walls, with air spaces; the flow could be regulated, enabling a patient in one part of the ward to rest in 70-degree temperature while another part was ten degrees cooler. Billings systemized his considerable knowledge in *Principles of Ventilation and Heating*, an important 244-page book that came out the same year Johns Hopkins Hospital opened. He also believed in the restorative power of light. "Light is a powerful tonic and stimulant agent, with peculiar powers and modes of action, which as yet cannot be said to be well understood," he wrote.[43]

FAMOUS ALL OVER THE WORLD

The hospital's medical operations were headed by a team that became known as The Big Four—pathologist William Henry Welch, surgeon William Stewart Halsted, internist William Osler, and gynecologist Howard Kelly. They exuded ambition, encouraged research, and promoted youth, attracting acolytes whose discoveries the Johns Hopkins Press and the university's grow-ing number of journals spread. One such eager-beaver researcher was Jesse William Lazear, who was a ten-year-old local lad when he took this 1876 letter in *The Sun* as a personal challenge: "We to-day know no more about the nature and origins of malarial, typhus, yellow fever and cholera poisons than Hottentots of Southern Africa; all we know is that such diseases do appar-ently, causelessly and suddenly spring into widespread existence and deadly activity."[44] Lazear vowed to defeat yellow fever.

Yellow Jack, as it was also called, was a scourge. A 1793 epidemic killed five thousand in Philadelphia, the U.S. capital at the time. President George Washington and the whole U.S. government fled the city, joining some sev-enteen thousand panic-stricken residents on the run—roughly one-third of the population. Baltimore, about a hundred miles away, terminated all contacts with Philadelphia, hoping to prevent the epidemic from spreading. Travelers from Philadelphia were stopped and screened, and shipments detained. ("All persons thence, required to stop at Merry's tavern and undergo the inspection of Dr. Jos. Way," read the order.)[45] Isolation, it turned out, was the correct action. Some people did get sick with yellow fever that year and in others, but Baltimore experienced nothing comparable to Philadelphia or the devasta-tions in New Orleans and Shreveport, Louisiana; Charleston, South Carolina; and several towns along the Mississippi River, where untold thousands died.

No one knew how yellow fever was contracted, or cured. Medical practition-ers were left to their own devices. Medicine had progressed, somewhat, since 1797, when *Federal Gazette* reported that a Baltimore physician (name de-leted) took "one hundred and thirty ounces of blood, [gave] three hundred and thirty-six grains of mercury and rubbed in twelve ounces mercurial ointment in the same patient," hoping to halt indescribable suffering—jaundice that turned skin yellow, endless black vomit, high fever, and hemorrhage. Another doctor prescribed ipecac, rhubarb, magnesia, camphor, and saltpeter. Some physicians favored arsenic. Lime, ashes, and lye were used as disinfectants.[46]

Jesse Lazear obtained his Bachelor of Arts in 1889 from Hopkins and his PhD in medicine from Columbia University. He came from an elite family. His grandfather was a general, who had represented Pennsylvania in Con-gress, and who owned the Baltimore & Powhatan Railroad, a short line that served his Windsor Hill estate, Garrett's Uplands (today's Edmondson Vil-lage), the mill town of Dickeyville, and other communities in the northwest. For Jesse, being well-born had its advantages. Chaperoned by his mother, this handsome, curious, intense doctor, with a neatly trimmed beard, could afford to spend a year in Paris, where he studied at the institute of Louis Pasteur, the medical biologist doing trailblazing research. During those travels proper introductions were made and he met a San Francisco girl, whom he married. In 1900 he reported to duty as a U.S. Army assistant surgeon at Columbia Barracks, near Havana.

By that time, yellow fever epidemics at home had been largely curtailed, thanks to improved cleanliness and better sanitation. By contrast, the killer fever kept cursing the empire that the United States had acquired two years earlier when it defeated Spain: Cuba, Puerto Rico, the Philippines, and Guam. Yellow fever particularly prevented the United States from exercising hemispheric hegemony in the Americas. Nothing underscored the nation's impotence more distressingly than what was happening in Panama. With no end in sight, three decades of efforts to dig a canal limped along in infested jungle camps, where much of the workforce got sick and many died.

For the United States, building a shortcut from the Caribbean to the Pacific was a matter of national interest and a trade necessity. That much had become painfully obvious in 1870, when the French attempted to gain control of the strategic isthmus. Ferdinand de Lesseps, fresh from the triumphal opening of his Suez Canal, began excavating. After a decade he was bankrupt, having been defeated by epidemics of malaria and yellow fever, and the limits of the available excavation technology. Subsequent American investors fared no better. Their thirty-eight-mile shortcut plan, with locks, proved to be a bottomless money pit, and the project fell further behind schedule. Thus, Cuba, now run by the United States, became a staging area for the Panama digging effort. Except that Cuba, just like Panama, was a yellow fever epicenter. Natives often acquired a degree of immunity, but hundreds of unacclimatized recent immigrants from Spain had not been so lucky. Casualties among U.S. occupation troops, too, were alarming.

Lazear became a junior member of an army medical commission whose mission was to defeat yellow fever and malaria. The commission's composition was a tribute to the influence that Johns Hopkins had quickly gained. Commission members knew The Big Four personally and had worked with them, Major Walter Reed in particular. He was a veteran of dusty army outposts of the American West, where he treated Geronimo, the famous Apache leader. Conditions in the bush were primitive. To brush up, Reed completed advanced coursework in pathology and bacteriology at Johns Hopkins. Lazear had been the first director of the clinical laboratory at the Hopkins medical school. He knew another commission member, Dr. Aristides Agramonte, a Cuban-born aristocrat; the two had been fast friends since their days at the Columbia University College of Physicians and Surgeons, which was also the alma mater of U.S. surgeon general George M. Sternberg, who had done lots of research at Hopkins and, again, knew The Big Four. Although Sternberg mostly stayed in Washington and was not a member, he was the undeniable taskmaster. He was an expert on yellow fever, having served in Cuba on a previous commission. Another Reed commission member was British-born Dr. James Carroll, who received his medical degree from the University of Maryland and also knew the Hopkins notables.

Such interconnections did not prevent rifts from developing. Personal rivalries aside, commission members disagreed about a crucial medical matter: How was yellow fever transmitted? Their arguments underscored how little was known about communicable diseases in 1900. Did mosquito bites transfer infections to healthy persons? Dr. Carlos Juan Finlay, an American-educated Cuban physician, theorized so in his research in 1881, eight decades after physicians fighting a yellow fever epidemic in Philadelphia first raised that possibility. But Sternberg and Reed rejected Finlay's theory. The surgeon general's view was particularly authoritative: He had worked for three months in Havana with Finlay, contracted yellow fever—and survived to tell the tale. As for Lazear, the junior member was impressed with recent malaria research conducted in India and Sierra Leone by Sir Ronald Ross, a British major general. If mosquitoes spread malaria, surely they could also transmit yellow fever, Lazear speculated. He became a man possessed, harvesting mosquito eggs and also relying on a stash received from Finlay. He recruited volunteers from among U.S. Army soldiers. He pressed a test tube containing a mosquito on a volunteer's arm, inviting it to sting. The Baltimorean hoped that someone would get yellow fever and prove that mosquitoes indeed transmitted the disease to human bloodstreams.

Neither he nor Finlay understood that not every type of mosquito was a carrier. Instead, only infected females from the common house mosquito species *Aedes aegypti* were capable of circulating the yellow fever virus, and transmittals depended on incubation periods and feeding patterns.[47] Still, Lazear kept experimenting. Seven months into his stay in Cuba, he played another round of his bizarre tropical version of Russian roulette. Attending to a yellow fever patient, he allowed a stray mosquito to land on his own arm and bite him. He watched as the small, dark mosquito, with white lyre-shaped markings unsheathed six sharp hypodermic needles, pierced his skin and sucked, its banded legs bowing further under the weight of a belly filling up with the darkness of his blood. How many humans had that particular mosquito bitten? Anyone with yellow fever? Would an infection be transmitted? So many questions. Only after the mosquito flew away did Lazear feel the sting. "I rather think I am on the track of the real germ," he wrote that night to his wife who was in the United States, pregnant with their second child. A week later he fell ill. He died at thirty-four.

Lazear's death in 1900 marked a turning point. Now that the mosquito link had been proven, aggressive campaigns began around the world to stamp out breeding grounds, and yellow fever gradually disappeared. So did Lazear's notes on the research project. Reed took them, and that was the last anyone heard of them. Reed got the credit for defeating yellow fever and had an army hospital named after him in Washington. That's where presidents went. Lazear receded into a footnote, but Johns Hopkins medicine basked in glory. The public and professional recognition was particularly sweet because the medical school nearly did not happen.[48]

Chapter Four

America's Richest Spinster

Johns Hopkins left to the hospital most of his real estate, including dozens of commercial buildings in The Basin. By contrast, the separately governed university received its $3.5 million share largely in Baltimore & Ohio stock. The railroad had greatly enriched Hopkins, but some of the early going was rough and at least twice he bailed out the company with his own riches. Still, he figured that with the company thriving, his 15,057 shares would provide sufficient steady dividend income to cover the transformation of Clifton into the university's permanent home; he did not want the capital touched. Also to be financed from that income was the medical school. However, when John W. Garrett retired and died in 1884, the already stultified B&O fell into disarray. Dividends disappeared. In 1896, twenty-three years after Johns Hopkins's death, the railroad went into receivership and, in a secret deal, was acquired by Pennsylvania Railroad. The situation was grave and embarrassing: Johns Hopkins University, an institution with a growing national and international reputation for excellence, could not afford to open the medical school that the founder's will mandated. All money went just into keeping the university afloat.[1]

An unexpected angel appeared: Mary Elizabeth Garrett. Newspapers snickered that the railroad president's thirty-year-old daughter was America's richest spinster, because the Old Man left a $17 million stash for her to share with two brothers.[2] The bulk of her inheritance, too, consisted of troubled B&O stock, which she was prohibited from selling for twenty years. Yet she was one wealthy spinster, owning plenty of land and other investments. "To this lady, more than any other single person, save only Johns Hopkins himself, does the School of Medicine owe its being," writes the medical historian, Dr. Alan M. Chesney, the medical historian.[3]

Women's medical colleges had existed since 1848, but coeducation was rare. Mary believed that true first-rate medical education could only be obtained if the best of men's colleges admitted women. She spearheaded a nationwide campaign, the Women's Fund for the Medical School of the Johns Hopkins University, to pursue that goal. She kicked off the drive on May Day, 1891, by presenting the trustees of the financially strapped Hopkins University a $111,300 check. The deposit was extortion for a good cause, an alluring come-on to persuade the trustees to admit women on equal terms with men. She was single-minded, convincing, and comforting, making it clear to the trustees—old men who were her late father's friends—that as long as women were admitted to the medical school, the rest of the university could remain all-male. It did for a long time; the first undergraduate freshman class that admitted women came in 1970.

Fifteen regional committees were formed to advance fund-raising. From the White House, Mrs. Benjamin Harrison endorsed the drive. The First Lady, the women's right activist Caroline Harrison, also inspected the hospital, talked about plans for the medical school and underscored the need for woman doctors. Mrs. John Quincy Adams, another First Lady, was involved in Boston. That was how married women identified themselves in those days—by the husband's name and position. The Baltimore committee was headed by Mrs. Henry Winter Davis. Her husband was an Episcopalian clergyman and former Maryland congressman, a radical Republican gadfly espousing egalitarian causes. Among committee members was the former Jessie Nathan, wife of Mendes Cohen, a celebrated railroad engineer connected with B&O, an officer in the Maryland Historical Society and one of the founders of the Jewish Historical Society.[4]

On Christmas Eve in 1891, the university trustees were summoned to Mamie Gwinn's house. Her father would later become state attorney general. Now, as a university trustee, Charles J. M. Gwinn read a letter from the absent Mary, another piece of his handiwork. The facts were harsh. Despite its consciousness-raising success, the eight-month-long Women's Fund drive had collected only an additional $81,723 toward the pledged $500,000. Nevertheless, Mary Garrett had decided to donate the missing $306,977 out of her own pocket so that the goal could be met. But not a penny more. Her letter spelled out the conditions. In addition to women being admitted on equal terms with men, entering medical students were required to have a bachelor's degree and proof of completed courses in physics, chemistry, and biology, and a "good reading knowledge of French and German." The trustees acceded to her demands that night. The coming days brought buyer's remorse. University president Gilman not only opposed coeducation but also argued that no school could succeed with such demanding admission standards, the nation's strictest. At the hospital, Osler quipped to Welch: "We were fortunate to get in as professors; we would never have made it as students."

Mary was in charge. She rebuffed all efforts to modify the terms or the language. She pointed out that her offer would be withdrawn "in the event of any violations of any or all of the aforesaid stipulations." The trustees surrendered. The medical school opened next to the hospital in 1893, the twentieth anniversary of the founder's death. Three women and fifteen men graduated in the first class. The only credit she wanted was a tribute to the Women's Fund. Indeed, for a while a sign on one building honored those pioneering enablers. When the building was demolished, the sign vanished and their story slid into obscurity.[5]

In a more enlightened age Mary might have been an important executive. But she was born in 1854, wore leg braces until fourteen, and grew up in the Victorian era that offered limited choices to members of her gender, however rich and connected. Her mind was acute but she flunked a college entrance examination, and that first try was the last one. She was pudgy and unattractive in her formative years. Doomed to a life as a rich wallflower, she became "Papa's secretary," effectively the B&O president's chief of staff. The Old Man headed the railroad for twenty-six years. He could be generous in philanthropy, but in business he was a regular son of a bitch, always wanting to squeeze more profit. He cut workers' pay by 20 percent within one depression year—but kept paying dividends to shareholders. When a railroad strike crippled B&O and then spread nationwide in 1877, he tried to buy machine guns. The Gatling Company regretted that "calls made upon us during the existence of the riots were too sudden to be promptly met," but assured him: "One Gatling, with a full supply of ammunition, can clear a street or track, and keep it clear."[6]

Accounting and management historians hail B&O as a trendsetter corporation. Not only was it America's first common-carrier railroad, but it was also a publicly held joint stock company at a time when that form of ownership was being introduced. In order to satisfy shareholders, it established financial reporting standards and disclosures that much of the industry adopted.[7] Mary witnessed the Old Man's creative accounting. She also saw how her father became set in his ways. For example, for far too long he stuck to iron rail—which were cheap but brittle—instead of the more durable steel that competitors adopted. With breakages, the railroad's costs rose and its reliability suffered. In later years he became sickly and absented himself to European spas for long periods. Mary was always at his side, running the company remotely by telegraph and mail. This was unheard of for a woman in the 1870s and 1880s. "Her knowledge of the road and its management gives her a position in the councils of that corporation not possessed by any other individual," the *New York Times* observed.[8] As to the Old Man, he had one regret: "I wish Mary had been a boy."

Mary was a tomboy and became a skillful equestrian to compensate for an ankle injury she received soon after birth and leg burns when she was seven. There were suitors—one said to have been a professor—but her father did not encourage them, wanting to keep her at his side. Her intimate friends consisted of a set of young women who came together when Mary was twenty-three: M. Carey Thomas, Mamie Gwinn, Elizabeth (Bessie) King, and Julia Rogers. This was her Friday Night circle that continued to meet for two decades. They read poetry and discussed everything under the sun, from romantic love to sexuality to women's rights. All pledged not to marry. Except for Mary, who was Reformed, they were all modest daughters of wealthy Quakers, whom Johns Hopkins included in his will and put on the boards of both the university and the hospital (with the exception of Julia's, whose father was dead). The young Quaker women were all cousins of some sort, thanks to intermarriages among the Thomas, Carey, Ellicott, Poultney, Hopkins, and Tyson clans. They stood in awe of the regal Garrett lifestyle of opulent mansions, foreign travel, and special trains that each season moved the household to palatial summer homes. At gala dinners, Garrett guests sipped wine from Venetian goblets and ate from golden dishes. At one such bash, ninety terrapins were used for the soup course alone.[9]

Carey Thomas was the most dominant of the group. Committed to women's enlightenment, she was determined to get an education equal to that of any man. She was thirteen when she captured a mouse and experimented with it. "Why, why did Carey have to cut up that mouse?" a scandalized relative lamented. "If she wanted to see its internal organs, very well, but why did she have to talk about it. All Baltimore has heard the story and is shocked by her lack of modesty."[10] Instead of medicine, she ended up studying literature. Her father, Dr. James Carey Thomas, a physician who served on the Hopkins board, "was dreadfully shocked" when she chose to get her Bachelor of Arts degree at Cornell. Its founder, Ezra Cornell, was a Quaker, but was kicked out for marrying outside of the faith to a "world's woman," Mary Ann Wood, a Methodist. Carey then applied to Harvard, but was rejected. At home, Hopkins admitted only men. Her father being a trustee, courtesies were extended: She could study Greek and audit classes there but not for a degree. Instead, she went to Leipzig, Germany, then completed her PhD degree summa cum laude at Zurich University in Switzerland. That latter institution had a long record of educating women—but not granting them degrees. Carey made history by getting a PhD. Her dissertation was on *Sir Gawain and the Green Knight,* a medieval English poem about King Arthur's Round Table in Camelot. She also submitted a thesis on Algernon Charles Swinburne, the great lyricist of Victorian England. Gwinn ghostwrote it for her and was very possessive: Carey was "not to change her words or the order in which she placed them," Helen Lefkowitz Horowitz writes.[11]

Gwinn, who spent the time preoccupied with independent literary studies, was Carey's companion during the four-year stay. Early Quaker history contains examples of women cohabiting in loving relationships, but Thomas's parents seem to have had difficulties with the situation, just as they were distressed that the two women would go unchaperoned to decadent Germany. There Carey and Mamie kept pretty much to themselves, not going out at night and always making sure that their encounters with male professors were chaperoned. Carey's youngest sister, Helen Thomas Flexner, wrote that "the longer she and Gwinn remained abroad the greater the scandal." The "Boston marriage" between them—as such arrangements were called—lasted for twenty-four years. But Carey was also attracted to Mary Garrett, who reciprocated. Mary became Carey's patron in private life as well as promoter of her professional career. Her money helped to launch Baltimore's Bryn Mawr School, first on Eutaw Street near City College. She then custom-built a new school on Cathedral Street, often visiting the construction site on unannounced inspections. The school's amenities were the envy of all: an indoor swimming pool, a large and well-equipped gymnasium, showers and locker rooms, first-rate laboratory, excellent library, and well-aired classrooms. The combination of yellow-brick outer walls, ornamentation, and sharply sloping roof gave the building a vaguely Teutonic look. After the school moved to its current location in Roland Park, local German organizations bought the edifice in 1938, turning it into their *Deutsches Haus*, where choirs practiced, poetry was read, and tankards raised to the beat of oompah bands. The landmark was torn down for the construction of the Meyerhoff Symphony Hall.[12]

After Carey joined the faculty of Bryn Mawr College near Philadelphia, Mary became a rainmaker for that Quaker institution as well. The clout helped. Carey was promoted to dean, the first in any women's college to have a PhD. Her leadership qualities persuaded Bryn Mawr (on whose board her father sat, along with two other relatives) to make her president in 1894, the year after the Johns Hopkins medical school opened. Bryn Mawr quickly became nicknamed "The Miss Johns Hopkins," because the Baltimore university served as its inspiration and sent there promising scholars as professors, including Woodrow Wilson.[13] She was a stickler, a headstrong and blunt woman, who forged a large reputation as an educator. "One of her main objectives was to wake us up and to get us to cast aside the upper middle class chains of congeniality and respectability," a student recalled. "She told us that the happiest moment in her life was when she no longer believed in Hell Fire."[14]

Not everyone loved her. The faculty revolted against her bossy behavior, and a Philadelphia newspaper called her a "deceiving tyrant." She continued to keep house with Mamie, who succeeded her as dean of the college. Then a snake wiggled into Eden in the person of a young English professor, Alfred Hodder, whom Carey hired. One day, Mamie eloped with the charmer, who left behind a wife, or so it was thought until it turned out that they had been living in sin. It was steamy stuff for its time, too steamy. Gertrude Stein turned it into a lame short story in 1905. She placed the Quaker college in New Jersey and did some other camouflaging. In *Fernhurst*, the names are different but the characters are recognizable. With Mamie gone, Mary moved in to live with Carey. At her death in 1915, she willed everything to Carey. Her siblings and other relatives managed to overturn part of the will on a technicality.

HEARTFELT STIPULATIONS

Johns Hopkins wanted his hospital to care for the indigent poor regardless of gender or race. He left it to his handpicked trustees to interpret the words of his will and the intent of codicils. In one instance he was very specific. He commanded the hospital to build and operate an orphan asylum for "colored" children. It was to be located away from Broadway, but funded by the hospital. "I direct you to provide accommodation for three or four hundred children of this class, colored children who have lost one parent only, and in exceptional cases to receive colored children who are not orphans, but may be in such circumstance as to require the aid of charity." Just to be on the safe side, he added a codicil two months before his death: "I do further declare that it is my wish that the trustees of 'The Johns Hopkins Hospital' shall apply to the Legislature of Maryland for such additional authority as they may require to enable them to educate the orphan and destitute colored children by them received into their charge." The trustees were further commanded to seek authority "to provide proper and respectable employment for such orphan and destitute colored children so by them received and cared for, when such children shall arrive at a suitable age." Then came the kicker: His will told the trustees to spend whatever was reasonable—up to "one-fourth part" of the hospital's budget—for the establishment and operation of the asylum. This was a heartfelt bequest.

The Johns Hopkins Orphan Asylum was quickly set up, with newspapers adding "Colored" to the name. It was a sham. The trustees simply took over a charity Johns Hopkins himself had supported since the Civil War, a Quaker-run orphanage that began in 1862 as a shelter for daughters of escaped slaves, "contraband negroes."[15] This shortcut clearly went against the founder's wishes, as he left that orphanage a separate allocation. The rest of the stipulation the trustees simply ignored. Instead of caring for boys as well, as the founder wished in his gender-neutral wording, they limited the home to a small number of girls. "Boys can better be cared for and educated at a farm school," the trustees rationalized, shirking responsibility.[16] In 1927 the trustees abandoned the founder's wish altogether and closed the home. Nothing was created in its place. By that time, men of new generations acted as trustees, men with a hazy knowledge about the founder, few links to his values, and no understanding of the abolitionist's wish to provide education and advancement for black orphans. In time, Johns Hopkins, the man, became a ghost. As time elapsed and there were no sightings, the ghost's beliefs mattered less and less; institutional concerns took over, reflecting imperatives in shifting social and political conditions.

In the earliest years, the trustees tried to read the founder's mind. In 1887 they admitted a black student, Kelly Miller, a slave's son from South Carolina. After two years of graduate studies in mathematics, physics, and astronomy, he ran out of money and dropped out when Hopkins's financial straits led to the doubling of its tuitions. He became a significant intellectual force at Howard University. The Hopkins trustees then did not admit a single African American student until after World War II. Thus, the tradition of exclusion was established under the very men whom the founder himself appointed but who likely viewed Baltimore very differently from him.

When the hospital opened in 1889, white and black patients shared common wards, but whites complained. "The matter seems to have given the Trustees some concern," Chesney writes. A colored ward was set up, then "a separate building was erected for colored patients only." There was nothing unusual about this; segregation was being stepped up throughout the city, and Hopkins was the only local hospital that at least treated blacks. When Enoch Pratt created Baltimore's public library system, he commanded that it "shall be for all, rich and poor without distinction of race or color, who, when properly accredited, can take out the books if they will handle them carefully and return them." Pratt trustees took that to mean that while they operated three branches for blacks, the Pratt employed no black librarians.

What happened? America happened.

After the end of Reconstruction in the late 1870s, the country grew steadily more polarized in questions of race and place of origin, class, and religion. This turned the Johns Hopkins Orphan Asylum into a hostage. Just months before Republicans came to power at city hall in 1895, the asylum left a black slum on Biddle Street, moving to a three-story redbrick manor house overlooking the Jones Falls Valley at Remington Avenue and 31st

Street, next to the United States Marine Hospital. Governor Pinkney Whyte had erected that substantial stone house as his country home before the Civil War. But then the U.S. Supreme Court's landmark *Plessy v. Ferguson* ruling established segregation as the law of the land in 1896. In Baltimore white backlash against Republicans who had rewarded blacks with city jobs led to Democrats recapturing city hall under the slogan, "This is a White Man's City." The asylum's "75 pickaninnies," as *The Sun* put it, became an issue. Girls entered the institution at ages ranging from five to ten and at eighteen were "sent out to occupy positions as seamstresses, laundresses or as servants" to fine families.[17]

After Baltimore mandated citywide residential segregation in 1910, the colored orphan asylum suddenly found itself in a "white" area where it was not supposed to be at all, a point made every day when orphans crossed white neighborhoods to reach the nearest black school. To lower the asylum's visibility, the trustees converted it into a home for a small number of bedridden crippled children who were seldom seen around.[18]

The orphanage also had a new neighbor—Johns Hopkins University itself. Pressed by financial needs, the trustees, in 1895, sold Clifton after the city offered $1 million—two-thirds more than what the site was worth, according to the city solicitor. John W. Garrett fought the sale ferociously on the university board, but in vain. He saw it as a betrayal of Johns Hopkins's wishes because the founder left no doubt that he wanted the university built at Clifton. (Of course, the change in plans also reduced the redevelopment value of the fourteen hundred acres that he had accumulated along Harford Road, from Montebello to Hamilton.)[19] In truth, the trustees never much liked Clifton, and neither did the faculty. It was in the boondocks; the sparse population did not even warrant a horse-drawn streetcar line. Hopkins student athletes did use Clifton fields for practice, making the long trek from Howard Street in an omnibus operated by the university and hauled by a team of four horses. President Gilman was only too familiar with that mode of travel. In California, he had overseen the state university's relocation from Oakland to Berkeley, a dusty distance of five miles he rode in a horse carriage. He was not keen to repeat that ordeal.

Now that Clifton was no longer a consideration, industrialists William Keyser—after whom Keyser, West Virginia, is named—and his cousin, William Wyman, purchased the Homewood estate and additional land and donated it for the university's permanent home, obligating some of the 140 acres to be allocated to the Baltimore Museum of Art and Wyman Park. Both men had been friends and business partners of the founder, so this was their tribute. Hopkins trustee R. Brent Keyser (William's son) paid the cost of the architectural plan of buildings, dormitories, athletic grounds, and other structures.

Homewood appeared perfect for Hopkins. Charles Carroll of Carrollton, the signer of the Declaration of Independence, had so liked its varied vistas that he gave the estate to his son as a wedding gift. The scion built Homewood House, a stately federal-style edifice of red brick and white marble on a hillside overlooking today's Charles Street. Much Maryland history was made there, including this: Homewood House served as the first home of the Country School for Boys. Renamed Gilman School in honor of the first Hopkins president, it soon moved to Roland Park. That nearby garden suburb under development was among the most discerning in America, ready to welcome professors, as long as they were not Jewish. That was the new thing—restrictions based on race, class, and religion, which many neighborhoods and institutions adopted. In a quest for bragging rights for exclusivity, Roland Park, a mile away from the campus, in early 1910 banned blacks, other than live-in servants. Three years later, its development company stringently enforced a policy that prohibited any further sales to Jews. Like blacks, Jews hurt property values and had to be kept out, the Roland Park Company argued. Half a dozen high-profile Jewish families lived among Roland Park's white Anglo-Saxon Protestants; when they moved, they had to sell to a non-Jew screened by the development company.[20]

In Roland Park, Gilman School for boys joined the Roland Park Country School for girls in excluding Jews. In this setting, Carey Thomas's Bryn Mawr, still on Cathedral Street, became a battleground. Because it was a Quaker school, it scrutinized applicants' religious affiliation. When Sadie Szold, a daughter of Temple Oheb Shalom's rabbi, applied, Carey said no to the younger sister of Henrietta Szold, founder of Hadassah, the Women's Zionist Organization of America. Mary Garrett overruled her, prompting this outburst from Carey: "*Cannot* your action be withdrawn: We should not risk all that we care for in the success of the school." She described Jews as "the most terrible set of people to my thinking. . . . I wish us escape from them at all hazards. It is so important."[21]

Mary at least knew a number of prominent Jews: the Mendes Cohen family, of course, and a handful of other big investors in B&O, such as the Etting heirs. Carey, by contrast, did not know any. She went to Germany curious about Jews, but became infected with the antisemitism around her. Her prejudices hardened.[22] In the academic setting and everyday life she gravitated toward a white-supremacist social philosophy known as eugenics that became the rage of American campuses between the 1900s and 1930s. Eugenics regarded blacks as mentally and biologically inferior, and so did she. After attending a 1902 dinner with the educator Booker T. Washington, she wrote to Mary: "Washington was disappointing, very, although he tells admirable stories, but he is like a Negro in the way his mind works, and he relapses into Negro pronunciations."[23]

Inspired in the 1880s by Sir Francis Galton, a half cousin of Charles Darwin, the eugenics movement first studied inheritance traits in plants and animals, then shifted to improving human stock. Eugenics ranked all races and nationalities according to their presumed biological worth. The goal was to produce a master race through selective breeding. A pyramid assigned Anglo-Saxons, preferably Episcopalians, to the top, followed by Germans and Scandinavians. The Irish presented a dilemma. Protestants from the north were viewed really as wayward Scotsmen because of their predominantly Presbyterian religion and because only a narrow sound separated the two island nations. Those Scotch-Irish were regarded as worthy. Catholics from the south were a different matter entirely. According to the important eugenicist Charles Benedict Davenport, they exhibited "alcoholism, considerable mental defectiveness and a tendency to tuberculosis," qualities that had to be taken into consideration in overall rankings. Midway through the pyramid were Jews, admired for their guile but otherwise rejected by many as racially dubious Christ killers. Blacks occupied the lowest rank. Their intellectual potential was low, contended eugenicists, who got away with calling black males of any age "boy" in accordance with the 1787 U.S. Constitution's clause that said each black should be counted as three-fifths of a white.

Aside from favoring Anglo-Saxons and northern Europeans, eugenicists wanted to halt the immigration of largely Jewish or Catholic east and south Europeans, segregate races, ethnicities, and classes, incarcerate criminals, isolate tuberculosis patients, and sequester the feeble minded and mentally ill. Stratification through segregation was key to everything, it seemed. Eugenics influence peaked in 1920 and 1924 under presidents Warren G. Harding and Calvin Coolidge, when an open-door immigration policy was scrapped and replaced with eugenically desirable nationality quotas. Largely Protestant northern Europeans were favored over eastern and southern Europeans. Asian immigration was restricted; there was no quota for Africa. The goal was to keep America's ethnic tribes separate. As vice president, Coolidge famously declared that "Nordics deteriorate when mixed with other races." (Nearly a century later, Donald Trump caused a ruckus by favoring a similar immigration policy for the United States.) National origin and religion vouched for a person. "You, the students of Bryn Mawr have the best intellectual inheritance the world affords," Carey told the student body: "Overwhelmingly English, Scotch, Irish, Welsh and other admixtures of French, German, Dutch. . . . All other strains are negligible."[24]

The eugenics movement began in England. It matured in Germany, where Hitler began the *Lebenborn* ("Spring of Life") program to create a master race. Men and women handpicked for their Aryan characteristics bred about six thousand babies before the Third Reich collapsed. Eugenics peaked in

America, bankrolled by the industrialist Andrew Carnegie; Mary Harriman, wife of the railroad magnate; the cornflakes inventor John Kellogg; and oil baron John D. Rockefeller. One eugenicist, the Planned Parenthood founder, Margaret Sanger, promoted birth control to prevent the procreation of "undesirables" of all races. Castration, forced sterilization, and euthanasia were among methods practiced to weed out the "unfit."

The eugenics worldview influenced many Hopkins University luminaries. In 1910, when the Eugenics Record Office was opened at Cold Spring Harbor, New York, Welch and Dr. Lewellys F. Barker, the Hopkins chief physician, became vice chairmen under Alexander Graham Bell, inventor of the telephone. Another notable Hopkins eugenicist was Dr. William Howell, who prescribed sterilization to prevent the propagation of "worthlessness." He played a defining role at the School of Hygiene and Public Health. Eugenics studies could be serious or spurious. In 1911 Johns Hopkins staff physicians examined eleven-year-old Luella Loftridge as part of a lawsuit to determine her race. Blood drawn from her indicated "scientifically" that she was white, the *New York Times* reported. But "a black line [ran] across one of the girl's fingernails, just around the arc known as the 'half-moon.' The presence of the black line, according to the doctors, is not conclusive, but only raises a suspicion as to the ancestry of the child."[25]

JEWISH QUOTA

By rating ethnic groups in terms of perceived biological worth, eugenics contributed to antisemitism on many campuses. Harvard, Yale, and Princeton adopted quotas in the 1920s to limit Jewish undergraduate admissions. Hopkins did not and, in 1935, Jews represented 17.58 percent of its four thousand students. Then, during World War II, when other universities began phasing out overt discrimination, Hopkins reversed direction. It instituted quotas on Jewish undergraduate admissions for the first time in its history. This was done "to protect the cosmopolitan character of the Hopkins, including the prevention of dominance by any one religious group," an official put it.[26] The ceiling on Jewish undergraduate admissions was set at about 10 percent, later raised to 14 percent, and then to 17 percent. The medical school's quota was similar.

The admission ceilings were the doing of two eugenics elitists who ran the university—Isaiah Bowman, president from 1935 to 1948, and Carlyle Barton, president of the university's trustees for eighteen years, from 1941 to 1958. Their overlapping terms covered both World War II and the Cold War between the United States and the Soviet Union. Under Bowman and Barton, the university firmed up links to the federal government. The Applied

Physics Laboratory was formed and became an important military research contractor. Bowman's training was in geography. At the end of World War I, President Woodrow Wilson tapped him as a territorial expert for the Versailles Peace Conference; during and after World War II, Presidents Franklin D. Roosevelt and Harry S Truman relied on his expertise on resettlement of refugees and displaced persons. Since he was a eugenicist, "racial differences were facts of nature for Bowman, and no social liberalism could alter that scientifically derived conclusion," writes his biographer, Neil Smith.[27]

The Canadian-born Bowman was an anti-Semite. In January 1944 he wrote to First Lady Eleanor Roosevelt about "the resemblance of Zionism to Hitler's policies." His opinion was that "help given to the Jew because of political pressure in time of stress would only increase the anti-Semitism that had risen in America. . . . It would flare up and be in the end disastrous for the Jew here and elsewhere."[28] As to the university, he once said, "Jews don't come to Hopkins to make the world better or anything like that. They come for two things: to make money and to marry non-Jewish women." Remarkably, Baltimore's Jewish community tolerated his bigotry and the quotas he enforced. "In contrast to the implementation of antisemitic policies at Columbia, the University of Maryland, and elsewhere in the United States, the organized Jewish community did not fight back despite support from non-Jews in important positions and even colluded with the university administration," Hebrew Union College professor Jason Kalman concluded after scrutinizing the record.[29]

The German-Jewish elite's special relationship with Hopkins was as old as the university. As early as 1884 Mendes Israel Cohen donated priceless antiquities from his Middle East excavations in the Nile Valley; the lifelong bachelor was a banker and sponsor of legal lotteries. The elite embraced the university, seeing it not only as a gateway to first-rate education but also as a helpful introduction to the larger, non-Jewish community. As years went by, sons of prominent German Jews graduated from Hopkins and became communal opinion leaders, allies of their alma mater. If they felt forced to criticize the university, they were respectful, muted, and avoided doing so in public. An example was lawyer Leon Sachs, the founding executive director of the Baltimore Jewish Council from 1941 to 1975 and son of a wealthy Latvian-born grocer. A Hopkins graduate, Sachs believed that the quota primarily intended to screen out applicants from the lower classes. He remarked to G. Wilson Shaffer, the dean of the Homewood schools: "We know what you mean Wilson. You're not against Jews. You just don't want kikes from New Jersey."[30] But there was another reason for the communal lack of protest: fear. Bowman continued to be an influential voice in governmental decisions affecting resettlement, a key Jewish priority after the Holocaust. He was not a man to cross.

Sachs said he was told that 75 percent of Hopkins applicants were City College students seeking pre-med slots, Hopkins worried that unless that tide was curbed, the school would be branded as Jewish. Columbia instituted admission quotas after a popular doggerel suggested:

> Oh, Harvard's run by millionaires,
> And Yale is run by booze,
> Cornell is run by farmers' sons,
> Columbia's run by Jews.

In 1951 Hopkins, in an effort to stem the Jewish influx, negotiated a deal with the Baltimore Jewish Council. The university agreed to drop religion from application forms, a question that helped screen out Jews. The council, for its part, "with resignation and concern," pledged to "try to disperse the Jewish pre-med applications from City College" to other institutions.[31] That public high school's graduates itched to go to Hopkins. City, then all male, was a vehicle of social upward mobility for generations of different groups, including, eventually, African Americans and girls. The high school was so ambitious that in early years its athletes competed against colleges instead of other high schools. In 1895 its football team played a sixteen-game schedule against such college opponents as St. John's, St. Mary's, Washington, University of Maryland, and Gallaudet. The Naval Academy trounced City 42–0.[32]

The quotas also put curbs on a main source of nonlocal Jewish students: returning World War II veterans, who applied because the government paid their tuition. The GI Bill was a ladder up for many previously marginalized white ethnic groups—Jews, Italians, Irish—whom the most extreme eugenicists regarded as not fully white.[33] In 1936 such nationalities were given the federal government's stamp of approval, when Social Security legislation recognized them as fully white by covering them, whereas many blacks were not since farmworkers and domestics were excluded. To serve veterans and other nontraditional students, Hopkins established a separately named evening division, McCoy College. After less than a decade it was folded into the regular Hopkins.

James J. Sylvester, the first Hopkins mathematics professor, was an example of how attitudes toward Jews changed over time. A Jewish Londoner, he encountered discrimination in his native land, where Cambridge denied degrees he had earned because he was not a member of the Church of England, as required. After Gilman hired him in London, he was able to live across from Garrett family mansions on Mount Vernon Place, in a hotel "noted for its table, wine cellars and the quiet tone of its patronage." He was a renaissance man. His knowledge ranged from law to poetry, and Florence Nightingale was among his pupils. He read and translated works from the original French, German, Italian, Latin, and Greek, and he was not averse to inserting quotes from classical poetry in his mathematical papers. He also wrote *Laws of Verse or Principles of Versification Exemplified in Metrical Translations*, which attempted to develop mathematical laws for rhythm and sound in poetry.[34]

That was Sylvester. By contrast, many subsequent professors of Jewish descent experienced trouble in finding suitable housing. Neighborhoods surrounding the Homewood campus had either covenants or a custom of excluding Jews. Indeed, until the early 1970s Baltimore had segregated real estate markets for whites and blacks, and a separate multiple list contained properties for sale or rent in suburbs open to the Jews. Advertising in *The Sun* and in *The Evening Sun* reflected those realities. "Housing-Colored" and "Housing-Restricted" were among the classifications.[35] Everyone understood that "restricted" meant no blacks, no Jews. Three real estate agents effectively controlled the entire Bolton Hill market, and Roland Park listings were similarly handled by the developers' authorized agents who did the screening.[36]

Many professors asked the university to help them gain access to housing in today's Charles Village and Roland Park. Hopkins intervened on behalf of Abel Wolman, enabling the pioneer in sanitary engineering to acquire a Charles Street house facing the campus. Such intercessions were rare, however, and anti-Semitism drove away the German-born physicist, Nobel laureate James Franck; Simon Kuznets, a political economist who later won a Nobel; and the historian Eric F. Goldman. There were others: Jewishness disqualified the historian Richard Hofstadter from getting an associate professorship. The geographer Henry J. Bruman was considered only after Bowman satisfied himself that "Bruman is not a Jew."

Hopkins's admission ban against blacks continued. It had been reaffirmed in 1939 when the university rejected the graduate school application of Edward S. Lewis, secretary of the Baltimore Urban League. Bowman contended that race had nothing to do with the rejection of Lewis, who had a BA from the University of Chicago and an MA from the University of Pennsylvania. The *Afro-American* newspaper did not believe Bowman. "It will be recalled," it wrote, "that Dr. Broadus Mitchell, Hopkins professor of economics who pushed for Mr. Lewis's acceptance, was forced to resign from Hopkins."[37] (Mitchell was a well-known socialist who had made an unsuccessful bid for governor in 1932; his running mate was Elizabeth Gilman, the founding president's daughter).[38] In 1945 an enterprising Frederick Scott became the first black admitted to undergraduate studies at Hopkins. He applied "on a lark" after friends believed he would be rejected on the basis of his race. He asked a Hopkins official if the university "accepted Negroes in here." The registrar sent him an application and told him to try his luck. He scored high on the entrance exam, and entered as a freshman February 1, 1945, the day he graduated from Douglass High School He was the first black to graduate from Hopkins. He was among the founders of Beta Sigma Tau, the first interracial fraternity in Baltimore, and built bridges to students at Loyola College and the historically black Morgan.

A belief in WASP values and a confidence in the superiority of the white race was an unwritten Hopkins behavior norm. Few dared to violate it. Thus it was no embarrassment for the university to have the trustees headed by men who actively campaigned for segregation. When R. Brent Keyser presided over the trustees, 1904–1927, he fought for the exclusion of blacks from the prestigious Eutaw Place where he lived.[39] Later, a neighbor, Carlyle Barton, took an even more activist stance while heading the trustees. A local establishment figure, and the chancellor of the Episcopal diocese, he filed a brief in the U.S. Supreme Court in 1947, together with another Baltimore lawyer, Thomas F. Cadwalader, who at the time ran the Maryland campaign of Senator Strom Thurmond, the segregationist States' Rights Democratic Party's presidential candidate. The case involved the legality of restrictive covenants. The Baltimoreans advocated the exclusion of blacks (and Jews and other minorities) as essential for neighborhood stability. "Prejudices cannot be eradicated by law," they wrote. "This is specially true of certain so-called prejudices, which many people feel are not prejudices at all but a mere recognition of the facts of life and nature."[40]

The two freely admitted that they wanted to keep blacks out of white neighborhoods, particularly Bolton Hill where they both lived and which was popular with Hopkins faculty. Compliance was enforced by block captains and lieutenants. "The restriction has been kept in force, and attempted violations have been quashed by threatened suits or by injections obtained from local equity courts, with the result that the properties covered by the covenant have been completely restricted in fact to occupancy by white people."[41] The next year, the Supreme Court went against the Baltimoreans. In *Shelley v. Kraemer*, it ruled that while such restrictions were perfectly legal as private contracts among willing parties, courts could not legally enforce them. The edifice of separation began to crumble. Change took time. For years afterward, nearly all apartment buildings in the off-campus row-house area now called Charles Village refused to rent to Jews, even those whose owners were Jewish.

Chapter Five

Doctors Rob Graves

To many working-class neighbors, the hospital remained an enigma. Occasional whiffs of disinfectants and anesthetic gases deepened mystery, fueling rumors about unspeakable experiments going on inside, and how, when all that medical sorcery failed, bodies were cut up in ghoulish defiance of God's words and wishes. Cut up! Hadn't Paul the Apostle taught the Corinthians that the human body was "a temple of the Holy Spirit," sacred and never to be tampered with? And where did all those cadavers come from, anyway? Generations of East Baltimore mothers thought they knew the answer, admonishing their wards to be sure to be back home before streetlights were turned on. Otherwise, "a John' Hopkin' doctor man will catch you and cut you up."

Cultures and religions dealt with vivisection in different ways at various times. The ancient Egyptians embalmed mummies but did not dissect. The classic Greeks abhorred dismembering but allowed it in the conquered realm of cosmopolitan Alexandria, Egypt. To the Hebrews the dead were unclean. ("He that toucheth the dead body of any man shall be unclean seven days.") The Romans prohibited dissection of humans. So did the Quran. The Christian position evolved amid controversies about heresy. Most believers condemned cutting up the dead, and so when dissection spread among breakthrough medical practitioners of medieval Europe, most anyone engaged in it did so at his own peril. The fate of Andreus Vesalius, the father of modern anatomy, exemplified the hazards. In 1565, writes Alan F. Guttmacher, "he was dissecting, with the full consent of the relatives, the body of a Spanish grandee, and as he cut into the heart, the muscle gave a feeble contraction when it was divided by the knife (which is not uncommon in those recently dead). This was reported to the court of the Inquisition, and Vesalius was sentenced to a cruel death, which, however, through the influence of the

Spanish king, was mitigated to a pilgrimage to Palestine. En route, Vesalius was shipwrecked and died from exposure."[1]

Most Marylanders, regardless of religion, opposed dissection. In 1788 Dr. Charles F. Wiesenthal, a German Lutheran, was dismembering two criminals hanged for murdering a ship's captain, when a mob broke in and took off with the bodies. Wiesenthal, a former physician to Frederick the Great of Prussia, was a seminal figure in the professionalization of Maryland medicine. His private lecture room at Gay and Fayette Streets constituted the first medical school. In 1807 violence again erupted, just before the founding of what became the University of Maryland. A mob tore down a lecturing hall and dissecting room that Dr. John B. Davidge had built at personal expense next to his house at Saratoga and Liberty Streets. Six years later he erected a surgical operating theater on the university's grounds at Lombard and Greene Streets. The cupolaed landmark, Davidge Hall, still stands. It is the oldest such building in continuous medical use in the country.

To satisfy anatomy education's growing demand for dissection material, some European states assigned unclaimed bodies to medical schools; England, Scotland, and the United States did not.[2] Instead, Anglo-Saxon anatomy schools ended up training physicians with bodies frequently stolen from graveyards. The need to advance science trumped all ethical concerns. Baltimore became "a central point" in the "traffic of human bodies." Grave diggers supplied corpses for medical schools near and far between the 1820s and 1899, when the anatomical board was created to distribute cadavers, and grave robberies ebbed. Medical school faculty doctors themselves resorted to shovels if they needed corpses to dissect. Such pillaging was technically a misdemeanor, but seldom prosecuted. Politicians protected the racket in the name of common good, and the police looked the other way, unless forced to take action. Lawyers argued that because the previous occupant had vacated the body, its ownership was in doubt. Why bother? There was no victim, or so lawyers contended, unless a cemetery sued, which never happened because many were in cahoots with "resurrectionists," as grave robbers preferred to be called.

A fabled early practitioner was "Frank," the University of Maryland's resident grave robber. "A better one never lifted a spade," wrote an admiring professor of surgery, Dr. Nathan Ryno Smith, a next-door neighbor of Johns Hopkins's on Saratoga Street, who treated the philanthropist during his final illness. Thanks to Frank's talents, the medical school advertised that human "subjects are in great abundance."[3]

Other grave robbers solicited out-of-town medical schools and dug up bodies whenever an order came in. They then packed the human carcasses into barrels, usually filled with whiskey to mask the odor, and shipped the corpses by rail to out-of-town customers.[4] At the destination, a medical school took the corpse, and the rotgut whiskey was sold to students as "stiff drinks."[5] Demand for corpses was heavy. "We consume over one hundred in the course of a winter," wrote Dr. W. J. Herdman from the University of Michigan in Ann Arbor to the Baltimore resurrectionist Wiggo Jensen in 1880. Jensen was a forty-five-year-old medical student at the University of Maryland, a stocky, whiskered native of Denmark, who dug up corpses on order and shipped them as far west as St. Louis. "I never secured a body except in the interest of science," he told *The Sun*. "I came to Baltimore and matriculated at Maryland University, my ultimate design being to locate in the West as a practicing physician."[6] He told the *Washington Post* that he had previously been "connected" with the Georgetown University in the District of Columbia as an assistant anatomy demonstrator. He took advance orders for winter deliveries— "as a merchant contracts for pork and other goods," one critic said—when the ground froze in the north. He struck when needed. One winter "when bodies were said to be unusually scarce," he shipped twenty-five barrels by rail from the District of Columbia to Baltimore's College of Physicians and Surgeons. Each contained a doubled-up body. Another time he resurrected seven bodies in Ellicott City and brought them to the city by wagon.[7] Among his eager customers was Dr. William Perrin Nicolson, of Atlanta's Georgia Eclectic Medical College. "Ship me two models as soon as possible," commanded a telegram from Nicolson, president of the Atlanta Society of Medicine and vice president of the Southern Surgical and Gynecological Association. The doctor was impatient. "Can you fill my order? Have telegraphed twice, answer immediately." Yet another of his missives read: "We must have some material between the dates mentioned, no matter where it comes from."[8] Even the Yale medical school corresponded with Jensen. It had no current need, wrote Dr. Charles A. Lindsey, who was in charge of dissecting, but "we may be short in the winter, and perhaps would like to negotiate with you then." He gave a price range Yale was willing to pay.

Among grave robbers' favorite haunts was Baltimore Cemetery, a still-existing hundred-acre necropolis near Clifton at Gay Street and North Avenue that was already there in Johns Hopkins's days. This was cemetery territory. Among nearby cemeteries was the Baltimore Hebrew Congregation's, opened in 1830, and the twenty-eight-acre "colored" Laurel Cemetery, which the now-defunct Two Guys discount chain bought in 1962 and developed into a shopping center. This is how resurrectionists did the plunder. They dug at the head of a freshly buried coffin, broke the lid with a shovel, placed a hook around the deceased's neck or armpit and, with the help of a rope, eased the body out of the cavity. Among cemeteries they raided were St. Alphonsus's at Biddle Street and Edison Highway, and Holy Cross, at North and Broadway, which was used by the St. Patrick, St. Ignatius, and St. John the Evangelist churches.[9] "No grave, no matter how sacred or how greatly reverenced was safe from these impious ravages," *The Sun* wrote.[10]

Potter's fields for the poor and forgotten were among other preferred marauding destinations, as was the Bayview Asylum, a one-time almshouse that now is a satellite medical campus of Hopkins. There, in a section in the woods, simple pine boxes were laid out in open pits under a thin veil of earth cover until a section filled up. Only then were the graves packed and sodded. Such was the lure of easy pickings that resurrectionists raided Bayview day and night, once in the middle of the asylum's board meeting. At nearby "colored" Evergreen Cemetery, caretaker James Greenwood said he used his gun to keep marauders away.[11] Among the interlopers was Dr. Randolph Winslow, a medical demonstrator at Maryland. He had previously relied on Jensen's services but when that source dried up, he began digging himself. He was apprehended at 5:30 p.m. one October afternoon in 1883, with a "colored" helper, shovels, and bags.[12] A Quaker from a slave-owning North Carolina plantation family, Winslow went on to an illustrious career as an eye, and ear, nose, and throat specialist at the University of Maryland, becoming president of the American Surgical Association, the Southern Surgical and Gynecological Association, the Medical and Chirurgical Faculty of Maryland and the Baltimore Medical Association. His papers are archived at the Smithsonian's Museum of American History and include material about grave robbing.[13]

Dr. William T. Cathell Jr., an assistant demonstrator of anatomy at the Baltimore University medical school, was caught at 10:35 p.m. one June night in 1887. He and three medical students were on a joyride of sorts, headed back for the dissecting room with a dead young black woman. Drinking was involved. "The doctor and his companions had playfully stuck a pipe in the mouth of the corpse, which appeared to be enjoying a smoke," *The Sun* reported. Cathell, "arrayed in a pair of high rubber boots and a hunting cap jauntily on his head," drove "a large dayton wagon, drawn by a handsome pair of bay horses." He said he needed a "subject" for his anatomy class.[14]

In several other incidents, medical students got arrested when they stopped for a drink, leaving protruding corpses hanging from horse carts outside a tavern.

Desecration of graves ordinarily attracted scant newspaper attention. However, the circumstances of an 1880 dissection in Davidge Hall brought Baltimore's body-snatching racket into the headlines for a time, highlighting the state university's central role. The case was a curious one. Mrs. Elizabeth Joiner had a bad dream. Her niece, Jane Smith, had been buried earlier that evening and the more the Federal Hill matron tossed and turned, the more she became convinced that grave robbers had stolen the body afterward. In the morning, the "handsomely attired lady" from a "wealthy and respectable family" went to Baltimore Cemetery. There in disturbed earth, she found the crucifix that Jane had worn to the grave when she was laid to rest next to her mother, who had died six months earlier. Now both graves had been pillaged.

Joiner's search for her relatives' remains seemed futile. Dr. L. McLane Tiffany, the medical dean at Maryland, stated that "so far as his personal knowledge goes" no corpses of the description had been taken there. The College of Physicians and Surgeons also denied any knowledge. Then an anonymous postcard surfaced, saying that "two colored men" had taken Jane's body to Davidge Hall. Students there had already witnessed her naked nubility. They gasped. Whoever the freckle-faced young woman was on the dissecting slab, she was nothing like the ravaged wretches that came from the potter's fields. Even with her hair shorn, Jane Smith exuded "refinement and character," *The Sun* wrote.

It was the medical school janitors' task to procure cadavers.[15] Night had fallen when four robbers arrived at Baltimore Cemetery to snatch Jane's body. So much fresh soil had been scattered around during the burial that in the darkness they first opened her mother's grave by mistake. Reburying would take too much time, so they took her putrid remains along; the school used her skeleton.[16] The robbers also took Jane's clothing—to sell. Supervising this expedition was "Professor Jensen," the medical student who dug up and sold corpses to make money.

A grand jury indicted Jensen, along with Emil A. Runge, a white janitor at the University of Maryland medical school, and two "colored" dissecting room helpers, William Warren and Ezekiel Williams. The medical school dean, Tiffany, bailed them out. To defend them, the university provided one of the state's most influential lawyers, John P. Poe. He was the law dean (soon to be attorney general), a highly politicized white-supremacist Democrat who would expel black students from the university and impose segregation for decades. Now he defended grave robbers. Judge Campbell W. Pinkney, without a jury, found the accused men innocent. "The testimony implicated Jensen in the affair, but it was not such as to warrant a verdict of guilty," he ruled.[17]

Another sensational case occurred six years later, the only known incident of "burking" in the United States. The term commemorates Edward Burke, who killed at least sixteen people and sold their bodies to medical schools in Edinburgh, Scotland. He was hanged in 1829.[18] In the Baltimore case, a twenty-eight-year-old black man named John T. Ross murdered his mother's white boarder, Ellen Brown, sixty, and sold the corpse for fifteen dollars at the instigation of the mother's live-in lover, a Maryland medical school dissecting room attendant. Newspapers treated the crime as a morality play.

Ellen Brown was a wilted Southern belle from the Eastern Shore, where a brother owned the *Easton Ledger* newspaper. She drifted to Baltimore at the age of fifty, working as a dressmaker. She ran with the wrong crowd, became a rummy, then became addicted to morphine and opium. She panhandled around Lexington Market and roomed with blacks in a house on Pig Alley in a section near the university still called Pigtown because it was a slaughterhouse district. She was a deadbeat, owing back rent. For that, Ross killed her in the house in which they all lived. He confessed: "I waited until I got a good aim and hit her [with a brick]. She fell to the floor and then I jumped on her, and hit her again. Then I stabbed her."

Some nine hundred curious came to gawk at Ross's hanging. An hour before the noose and black hood were placed on him, he expressed his sentiments in a verse that a fellow inmate penned for him:

> I've no excuse to offer,
> My guilt I freely own,
> But does it look like justice
> I must suffer all alone?
> Is it fair, kind Christians,
> In this land of liberty,
> That I alone must suffer,
> And the other two go free?[19]

Indeed, the instigator of the murder, Anderson Perry, went free, and so did Albert Hawkins, another participant in the killing. The sixty-year-old "Uncle Perry" never doubted the outcome. "The doctors will clear me," he declared from the get-go. Yet he was nervous. Wrote a reporter: "Perry, who is a thickset man, almost black, with a large head, deep-set eyes, high cheek bones, heavy jaws, prominent mouth and thin black whiskers, sat in the dock with his hands clasped between his knees and a restive manner, glancing from one object to another. His bearing in the dock was just the opposite of that exhibited by Ross, who coolly chewed tobacco and occasionally smiled during the proceedings."[20] Perry's lawyers took a gamble with an all-white jury, and it paid off. They argued that Perry was deficient of mind, too dense to do anything as complicated as organizing a grave robbery. "He is known to those who come in contact with him as an exceptionally stupid man," lawyer John E. Bennett declared. "We shall show that he is not capable of conniving a scheme of such intricacy as killing this woman." Meanwhile, doctors worked the angles. One witness, Louisa Lipp, a widow who operated a junk store, said a doctor offered to provide a carriage ride and pay two dollars for her testimony.[21, 22]

Evidence showed that it was Perry who recruited Ross to do the killing, and then had Hawkins take the body in a wheelbarrow (which overturned) to the Davidge Hall dissecting room, where it was received by Emil Runge, the janitor acquitted in the theft of Jane Smith. Uncle Perry took over the shaving and preparation of the body. But a doctor refused to handle the corpse, pointing out that it was badly bloodied and still warm. Uncle Perry tried to allay the doctor's concerns. "The head might have been wounded in taking the body out of the grave and they bury people at Bayview while they are warm," he suggested. Indeed, said another voice around the dissecting table, bodies stayed warm for up to twelve hours. After police became involved, Uncle Perry and Hawkins quickly fingered Ross, one of eighteen children of Mary Bloxson (or Blockson or Bloxsom; spellings vary). She was treated as an accomplice, but was not charged. Twice married before, she had planned to wed Uncle Perry the following week. Life went on. In the dissecting room, Ellen Brown's nose and ear were eaten by rats, "of which there are plenty at the University."[23]

So serious was the shortage of cadavers that two years before the Johns Hopkins medical school opened, the trustees proposed to city hall a solution that would have eradicated grave robberies and taken care of the university's anatomy needs. The trustees offered, for free, to store unclaimed corpses. These were among the conditions:

1. The post-mortem examinations at the morgue shall be made by a physician designated and appointed by the trustees of the Johns Hopkins Hospital, and appointed, without salary, by the city for that purpose.
2. Post-mortem examinations shall be permitted in all cases where deemed necessary by this physician.
3. The transport and burial of the bodies are to be provided for by the city.

Rival schools greeted this proposal with howls of protests, accusing Hopkins of trying to gain a cadaver monopoly. "It would be in effect saying that only the Hopkins Medical University shall teach anatomy," protested Dr. James Aloysius Steuart, the health commissioner. Nothing came of the deal Hopkins offered. The hospital's neighbors did not want a corpse storehouse, and went to see Mayor James Hodges at city hall.[24] Two years earlier, the College of Physicians and Surgeons had tried to corner the cadaver market with a similar proposal, proposing a morgue location near city hall, but that, too, got nowhere. Instead, in cooperation with the Sisters of Mercy, the college built what today is Mercy Medical Center, on St. Paul Street, across from Preston Gardens.[25]

Predictably, a cadaver crunch hit Johns Hopkins when the medical school opened in 1893. That year, twelve hundred students in Baltimore's seven medical schools received only a total of forty-nine cadavers from legal sources, according to Dr. Franklin P. Mall, a famous anatomist. Grave robbers filled the need. Hopkins had promised hands-on anatomy training. But when the inaugural dissection came November 15, no human "subject" could be found. "Recourse had to be made to irregular sources of supply," a scholar reported.[26] Mall himself notes that "we postponed the work until the 16th and then the 17th, and late in the evening a subject was mysteriously left in the basement. The next day, one came from the state, and a few days later, another appeared in the basement."

Subsequently, a Hopkins janitor was put in charge of supply. Nicknamed "King Bill," William Hartley had a stable in the basement of the anatomy building, where he and his wife kept a sorrel mare, carriage, sleigh, picks, and shovels to procure cadavers. Hopkins soon had twenty cadavers stored in an icebox built to hold five.[27] Among the "irregular sources" used was the city morgue. That shelter had inadequate capacity and was open only sporadically, resulting in a dozen or more corpses sometimes being left outside unattended overnight.[28] Just about anything could happen.[29] And did. At 7:30 a.m. just before Christmas in 1899, an unknown white man was struck by a streetcar. He was taken to City Hospitals, where he died that afternoon. The corpse was sent to the morgue to await identification. At that point someone saw an opportunity to make quick Christmas cash because the corpse next turned up in a box in Sioux City, Iowa![30]

All this time, Mall experimented with embalming dogs with carbolic acid and applying his knowledge to humans. With the creation of the state Anatomy Board, grave robberies ended. The board was headed by Mall, who established procedures for the distribution of cadavers. Bodies that could not be used immediately were kept in cold storage at Hopkins. Any school in good reputation was entitled to them. In 1906 this was the distribution: Baltimore Medical College, 29; Baltimore University, 2; College of Physicians and Surgeons, 237; Homeopathic College, 11; Johns Hopkins University, 329; Maryland Medical School, 3; Medical and Chirurgical College,1; University of Maryland, 115, and Woman's Medical College, 1.[31] For Mall, anatomy was a career as well as a hobby. He dedicated himself to collecting human embryos, eventually amassing thousands of specimens.[32]

THE HIPPOCRATIC OATH

Around 450 BCE, Hippocrates the Greek introduced the physicians' basic law: Do no harm. He established the sanctity of doctor-patient confidentiality, and drew a professional distinction between physicians and surgeons. In early days, the Hippocratic Oath was taken this way:

I swear by Apollo Physician and Asclepius and Hygieia and Panaceia and all the gods and goddesses, making them my witnesses, that I will fulfill according to my ability and judgment this oath and this covenant.

I will apply dietetic measures for the benefit of the sick according to my ability and judgment; I will keep them from harm and injustice.

I will neither give a deadly drug to anybody who asked for it, nor will I make a suggestion to this effect. Similarly I will not give to a woman an abortive remedy. In purity and holiness I will guard my life and my art.

I will not use the knife, not even on sufferers from stone, but will withdraw in favor of such men as are engaged in this work.

Whatever houses I may visit, I will come for the benefit of the sick, remaining free of all intentional injustice, of all mischief and in particular of sexual relations with both female and male persons, be they free or slaves.

What I may see or hear in the course of the treatment or even outside of the treatment in regard to the life of men, which on no account one must spread abroad, I will keep to myself, holding such things shameful to be spoken about.

If I fulfill this oath and do not violate it, may it be granted to me to enjoy life and art, being honored with fame among all men for all time to come; if I transgress it and swear falsely, may the opposite of all this be my lot.[33]

Individual physicians at various times have interpreted the Hippocratic Oath in different ways. Take the case of Dr. James Marion Sims. Widely regarded as the father of American gynecology, he was honored with a bronze statue atop an elaborate marble monument in Central Park in New York where in 1855 he founded America's first hospital for women, a predecessor of today's St. Luke's–Roosevelt Hospital Center.[34] He became the toast of the surgical world, with practices in London and Paris. He treated royals and received France's highest award, the Legion of Honor, for his troubles. At his death he was president of the American Medical Association. This career he built on the basis of experimentation with slave women. "Marion Sims epitomizes the two faces—one benign, one malevolent—of American medical research," Harriet A. Washington writes in her incisive *Medical Apartheid: The Dark History of Medical Experimentation on Black Americans from Colonial Times to the Present.*[35]

Sims's own 471-page autobiography, *The Story of My Life*, gives a revealing look at his career. He was a poor South Carolinian, who got his degree from Jefferson Medical College in Philadelphia, then hung out his shingle in Montgomery, Alabama. "I had to begin at the very bottom," he writes. "The first people who took me up were 'free niggers.' Finally, I became physician to the Jewish population of the town, of which there were several families." Slave owners sought his services. One sent him a young woman whose uterus had been so torn in obstructed childbirth that she leaked urine uncontrollably. She had a hole in the bladder, vesicovaginal fistula: "It may be no larger than a pipe-stem, or it may be as large as two or three inches in diameter; but, whether big or little, the urine runs all the time; it makes no odds what position she is in, whether asleep or awake, walking or standing, sitting or lying down. The case is absolutely incurable."[36]

Soon another slave came with more female trouble. Sims had no interest in treating women in general and certainly not stinking outcasts. But before he could send the slaves back to their owners, he was interrupted. "Just as I was starting off, and was about to get into my buggy, a little nigger came running to the office and said, 'Massa doctor, Mrs. Merrill done been throwed from her pony, and is mighty badly hurt, and you must go down there right off to see her, just as soon as you can get there.'" Merrill was a white woman, "about forty-six years of age, stout and fat, and weighed nearly two hundred pounds."[37] In landing on her butt, she broke no bones but had "great pain in her back, and a sense of tenesmus in both the bladder and rectum."[38] She had dislocated her uterus; it was "half turned upside down," Sims writes. Struggling to recall what he had learned in medical school a decade earlier, he placed her on all fours and stuck two fingers in her vagina. In school, he had been instructed to put a finger in the rectum as well, but he did not dare to do so because a few days earlier a white male patient had made quite a ruckus about such penetration. Pumping his fingers in and out, Sims kept increasing air pressure until a flatulence-like pop was heard. The woman profusely apologized. Sims smiled and explained that air pressure had popped the uterus back to its proper position.

He had never experienced a rush of discovery like this. Propriety and common decency prevented him from experimenting with white women. No such restrictions applied to slaves. He could not wait to learn more. Disregarding other patients on his list of calls that day, he hurried back home to experiment with the two slave women whom owners had sent to him. Anarcha was seventeen, Betsey, eighteen, both married, both suffering from uncontrollable bladders due to obstructed childbirth. He inserted a shiny silver spoon into their uteruses. In its reflection, "I saw everything as no man had ever seen before. I felt like an explorer in medicine who first views a new and important territory." Because of their condition, the women had lost their economic value. "I made this proposition to the owners of the negroes: If you will give me Anarcha and Betsey for experiment, I agree to perform no experiment or operation on either of them to endanger their lives, and will not charge a cent for keeping them, but you must pay their taxes and clothe them." He built a makeshift ward in his backyard in Montgomery. It grew to accommodate seventeen slaves, his subjects who took care of the premises.

Anarcha not only leaked urine but feces as well. Sims operated on her more than thirty times, always without anesthesia. Ether was known in those days and Sims was an early advocate, but he chose to use it only on white patients.

He shared a widespread belief of the time that blacks did not experience pain the way whites did. For several weeks *after* each procedure, however, he gave morphine to the slaves involved in experiments. Many became addicted, begging for more experiments. His most significant work was to develop a surgical technique for the repair of a fistula. In the process, he invented surgical instruments that advanced gynecology. He was clever. When his early surgeries failed because of infections caused by silk, cotton, and flax sutures, he had an artisan fashion suture wire out of silver, which did not harbor pathogens. Success at last.

Throughout history, various governments sponsored horrendous experimentation. From the late 1920s onward, the leading lights of Germany's eugenic medicine weeded out "undesirables"—mentally and physically disabled, Roma, homosexuals, communists, and other dissidents. Bedridden old-age-home residents were given "sweet soup" that plunged them into eternal slumber. This was just one thrust of Hitler's medical establishment, which backed the Final Solution, the annihilation of Jews at concentration camps and through medical experiments. All this was detailed at the seven-month Nuremberg doctors' trial in 1947; twenty of the twenty-three defendants had taken the Hippocratic Oath. Seven were acquitted and another seven received death sentences; the remainder were imprisoned from ten years to life. One escaped: Josef Mengele fled to South America, and was never apprehended. Known at Auschwitz as Dr. Death, he oversaw the separation of inmates. Those able to work were admitted to the camp; those deemed unfit for labor were herded to the gas chambers.

Meanwhile, inhuman experimentation was going on in many other countries. During the U.S. Public Health Service's Tuskegee Institute syphilis studies (1932–1972), poor black males in Alabama were kept in the dark about what ailed them and denied treatment so that doctors could observe the disease's progression. In the 1940s Johns Hopkins was involved in similar syphilis research in Guatemala, intentionally infecting various age groups. (A $1 billion class action suit filed by offspring and relatives was still being litigated in 2018.)[39] At San Quentin Prison, between 1913 and 1951, the chief surgeon took testicles from executed prisoners and surgically implanted them into old and senile inmates. This kind of experimentation continues up to this day, according to Public Citizen's Health Group, often by First World doctors using as their subjects the poor and defenseless in Third World countries.[40]

BLACK FEARS OF MEDICINE

Blacks had feared the white man's medicine ever since slavery times. In Africa they had relied on *muti*—herbalists and traditional healers, whose mysterious powers they respected. Once brought to America, the captives were at the mercy of slave owners' doctors, strange white men who spoke an alien language and attacked indigenous cures—plants, animal parts, and African spirituality—as superstition and witchcraft. What were those strangers up to? Since they were property, slaves could not legally consent; only their owners could. As a result, fearful slaves routinely hid ailments from overseers; they did not want to end up in medical experiments. Even after slavery was abolished, this distrust toward Western medicine persisted, and continues among African Americans today. "Black iatrophobia is the fear of medicine," Harriet Washington writes, combining the Greek words iatros ("healer") and phobia ("fear").[41] Doctors are viewed with suspicion; hospitals are best avoided, because once admitted, all bets are off for the patient.

Until desegregation, Hopkins was the only white Baltimore hospital that treated African Americans. A teaching hospital focused on research; it provided the best care available in a setup that was so strictly segregated that blood from blacks and whites was kept separately and only administered to the specified race. This "was deemed best" for sensitivity reasons, even though there was "no valid objection on biological or physiological grounds for transfusing patients of one race with blood from another," wrote the blood bank director, Dr. Mark Ravitch.[42] (The American Red Cross also segregated blood during World War II.)

In 1937 the iconoclast Henry L. Mencken wrote a twenty-part series about Hopkins Hospital. His final piece showered praise on medical care and research but bemoaned the influx of strangers to the city. "First, came the machine-line automata attracted by some of the new factories and assembling plants. Next, set in motion by the depression, came a rush of Negro yokels from Virginia, the Carolinas and beyond. Finally, there has been a movement of anthropoid mountain whites from Appalachia. All classes make heavy demands on the Johns Hopkins. Wards and dispensaries are burdened with the whites and blacks who flocked to Baltimore to go on the dole."[43]

Mencken cherished his German roots and believed in the superiority of northern European-descended nationalities. He claimed that eugenics was "mostly blather," but writing about the hospital, he sounded like a eugenicist. "The influx of unclean and shiftless barbarians from the Southern swamps has created whole areas of new Negro slums (some of them under the very shadow of Johns Hopkins), and definitely put back the clock of Negro progress," he wrote. He advocated sterilization of "the hordes of worthless wretches, white and black, who were born useless, are useless all of their days, and practice as their chief and only industry the wholesale reproduction of their useless kind. What of the thousands of nitwits and wastrels who are sent out annually to provide more grist for the mill of disease and misery?"

He lamented that Maryland had not adopted sterilization. "It is now ten years since the Supreme Court of the United States (274 U.S., 200) agreed with Mr. Justice Holmes that the principle that sustains compulsory vaccination is broad enough to cover cutting the Fallopian tubes; three generations of imbeciles is enough."[44]

Because indigent blacks were treated free of charge at Hopkins, many doctors felt it was only a fair payback that they agree to experimentation in order to advance medicine. One example was Henrietta Lacks. She was a poor World War II transplant from Virginia's tobacco country to Turner Station, a black township in the shadows of Bethlehem Steel's Sparrows Point steel mills. In 1951 she was pregnant with her sixth child when she felt a "knot" in her womb. It turned out to be cancerous. She never consented to have doctors harvest her unique cells, but they did, and in their enthusiasm gave out her cells free of charge to colleagues. Soon her cells were commercialized, with companies selling billions. Her cells became essential tools in medicine, vital for developing the polio vaccine, cloning, gene mapping, in vitro fertilization, and so on. She died in obscurity, not making a penny from her cells but leaving behind a brood mired in poverty of means and minds. Rebecca Skloot, in 2010, pieced together her gripping story in *The Immortal Life of Henrietta Lacks*. "Hopkins, with its large indigent black population, had no dearth of clinical material," remarked Dr. Howard Jones, the gynecological surgeon who examined Henrietta Lacks before Dr. George Otto Gey took over.

Blacks had always been clinical material. The provenance of the early cadavers acquired for dissection underscored this point. "There was a predatory dimension to anatomical dissection, in part because the cadavers sent to Johns Hopkins belonged disproportionately to the poor black, and downtrodden," writes the medical anthropologist Lynn Morgan. "In the nine years between October 1895 and October 1904, the anatomist Franklin Mall catalogued 1,655 adult bodies received at Hopkins for dissection. The total number of bodies was overwhelmingly 'negro' (64.5 percent), at a time when only 16 percent of the total population of Baltimore was black." More than two-thirds of the cadavers were male. "White females were least likely to be subject to dissection: only one in twenty bodies in the anatomy laboratory at Johns Hopkins was that of a white female, while one in three of the 'negroes' sent for dissection was female."

Blacks may have accounted for the bulk of clinical material, but the medical profession commonly excluded them, regarding them as biologically and mentally inferior. That was in keeping with the eugenic core argument of white supremacy. So if blacks were employed at medical institutions at all, they worked as janitors or in other menial jobs. Few medical schools thought blacks were capable of becoming doctors. In 1907, when the educator

W.E.B. Du Bois sent queries to all medical schools in the country, Hopkins informed him it had never had a black student. So did the Baltimore Medical College. "One such pupil would, I am sure, do a great injury to our class on entering," an official wrote. Baltimore's College of Physicians and Surgeons was as uncompromising, saying it "does not, never has, and never will admit Negroes to its lecture halls and work." Schools further south were more blunt. "There are no niggers in this school and there never will be as long as one stone of its buildings remains upon another," declared the Medical Department of the University of Georgia. From the Central University of Louisville, Kentucky, came this statement: "The Hospital College of Medicine has never matriculated a 'coon' in all its history and never will so long as I am Dean."[45] In various parts of the country, physicians of color established medical colleges of their own. Among them was Baltimore's Medico-Chirurgical, Theological College and Law School of Christ's Institution, which existed in Old Town for eight years beginning in 1900.[46] Dr. G. Milton Linthicum, president of the Medical and Chirurgical Faculty of Maryland, disparaged it as being "run by illiterate negroes whose incorporation papers were signed by a cross mark."[47]

VIVIEN THOMAS

Against this backdrop, the arrival of Vivien Thomas at Hopkins during World War II was extraordinary. He came there because Dr. Alfred Blalock would not move to Baltimore to become chairman of the Department of Surgery in 1941 without his surgical assistant, who was black. Hopkins hired Thomas as a janitor.

Thomas was a high school graduate working as a carpenter in Nashville during the Depression, hoping to raise enough money to go to Meharry or Howard, the only two black medical schools at the time. In 1930 he learned that Blalock, a Vanderbilt professor reputedly being "'hell' to get along with," needed a helper. Although "to me the job was a stopgap measure to get me through the cold winter months," this was the beginning of an extraordinary professional partnership that lasted for decades. Blalock, looking "more like a college senior or a medical student," recognized Thomas's unusual skills, taught him to carry out complex vascular and thoracic operations on laboratory animals, including chemical determinations needed for experiments, and keeping records and protocols. "Within three days, he was administering anesthesia and performing arterial punctures on laboratory dogs. Within months, he was performing delicate and complex procedures with the ease of a master."[48] He helped Blalock with groundbreaking research into traumatic shock and high blood pressure in humans, the first African American medi-cal professional at Hopkins, five years before Ralph Young became the first physician to receive hospital privileges.

The first time Thomas walked from one Hopkins building to another on Monument Street, the traffic stopped as white motorists rubbernecked in amazement. "There were no colored people working around Hopkins," except for housekeeping staff wearing blue uniforms. "A Negro with a long white coat? Something unseen and unheard of at Hopkins," he writes in his meticulous autobiography, *Partners of the Heart: Vivien Thomas and His Work with Alfred Blalock.* "There were constant reminders of race through-out the hospital complex, especially the restrooms along the corridors, which were plainly marked for race and sex," he writes. "I knew I was something of a curiosity or oddity around Hopkins."

With Blalock as his mentor, Thomas soon effectively ran the old Hunt-erian Laboratory. Continuing projects they had started at Vanderbilt, the two ceaselessly worked on techniques to correct cardiovascular defects. Thomas demonstrated his inventiveness by devising a pioneering positive-pressure respirator that inflated the lungs of dogs under anesthesia. In 1943 Dr. Helen Brooke Taussig, a Hopkins pediatric cardiologist, asked for their help in treating "blue babies" born with deficient blood flow to the lungs. By this time they had performed hundreds of challenging cardiac procedures on dogs. Now they spent months in preparation for the first operation on a hu-man, sixteen-month-old Eileen Saxon. Thomas worked out the final details of the surgical plan, but when the time came to operate he was nowhere to be found. Surrounded by a surgical team that included foremost physicians and researchers, Blalock refused to begin without Thomas. When the assistant was located—in the laboratory—Blalock positioned him on a stool above his right shoulder. That vantage point gave Thomas a better view of the totality than anyone at the operating table, and from there he directed Blalock. "It was extremely difficult to tell if Dr. Blalock had the original idea for a particular technique or if it was Vivien Thomas, they worked so smoothly together," observed Dr. Alan C. Woods Jr., a professor of surgery.

After Blalock died in 1964, Thomas continued at Hopkins. But instead of operating he taught medical students, who in 1971 honored him by commis-sioning his portrait that was unveiled in the foyer of the Blalock building. A further honor came five years later. In March 1976 a University of Maryland vice chancellor, the historian George H. Calcott, informed Thomas by letter that College Park would award him an honorary doctor of science degree. A few weeks later, Calcott, with "great personal embarrassment," withdrew the notification. For four days Thomas was at a loss, wondering what had happened. Then the Johns Hopkins University trustees informed him that

Hopkins would grant him an honorary degree; academic politics. He retired in 1979, and died six years later.

By that time several blacks had graduated from the Hopkins medical school, following in the footsteps of Robert Lee Gamble, the first, who was awarded his MD degree in 1967. When Gamble began classes, Hopkins was still so segregated that the emergency room had a "white" entrance and the "colored" entrance, remembered a fellow student, Dr. Lewis Goldfrank, who found the treatment of Gamble appalling. "This young black guy, every time there was a class he was called to the front, we'd all get called to the blackboard to point out things and he'd be brought up and harassed and abused. . . . There was tremendous racial hostility." Hopkins had always been a medical school favored by Southerners. "A lot of these guys from the deep South had never met or worked with a black guy. The goal was clear to flunk this guy out. Several other guys and myself were trying to protect him, and then we had been there in school for three months when Kennedy was killed and there were parties in the dormitory."[49]

Gamble persisted because he wanted to live up to his role model—his grandfather, Dr. Henry Floyd Gamble. This ancestor was a son of an Irishman who in the Virginia mountains married a daughter of a white master and a slave. He wanted to become a physician but the collapse of a local bank wiped out his family's savings. He learned the elementals of medicine from a white medical student, the son of a professor of medicine at the University of Virginia, until a stop was put to such tutoring. He toiled to finance his studies. He got his bachelor's degree from Lincoln University in Pennsylvania and then, in 1891, became the sixth black in Yale University's history to receive an MD. He was a friend of Booker T. Washington, knew German and Hebrew, and was president of the National Medical Association. Many generations of his extended family chose medical careers.[50]

His grandson, the first black Hopkins medical graduate, became a rising neurosurgeon and clinical instructor at the Georgetown University medical school in Washington. A captain in the U.S. Army medical reserves, he lived in turbulent times. In 1971 he adopted the Muslim faith and changed his name to Dr. Abdur-Rahman Yusuf Ibn-Tamas. His suave ways and good looks hid a troubled man who experienced flashes of violent anger and beat women in his life. In 1976 his second wife, a nurse who was pregnant with their second child, shot him dead at their Washington home after he struck her repeatedly and threatened to kill her. He was thirty-five. A jury sentenced her to one year in prison. She appealed, using a then-novel defense: the battered-wife syndrome. She lost.[51]

Part II

THE RACIAL DYNAMICS
OF MODERN BALTIMORE

Chapter Six

The Monumental City

Daniel Coit Gilman's biographers dutifully record his triumphs as Johns Hopkins University's first president. They list his many outside professional accomplishments, including presidency of the American Social Science Association, and the books he wrote. Yet they overlook his civic engagement in Baltimore. It was astonishing. As busy as he was, he championed good government causes as a cofounder of the nonpartisan Reform League, a progressive anti-bossism group that was at the peak of its powers. He was also an initiator of a pioneering philanthropic coordination body, the Charity Organization Society, and of the Civil Service Reform Association of Maryland (serving as president of the national organization). He singlehandedly revamped the city public school system and then implemented far-reaching decisions as a school board member. "Within a couple of weeks he was the real boss of the whole school system," remembered H. L. Mencken. But Gilman's lasting impact was as a cofounder of the Municipal Art Society, the most consequential civic organization in Baltimore's history. As its first president he became an important architect of the city, including its racial geography.[1]

He was sixty-eight in 1899, when he became president of the newly formed brain trust of the city's ruling WASP elite. His energy was intact. His local clout had never been greater, thanks to his having rebuffed New York City's repeated attempts to lure him away to be its superintendent of public schools. In those days governmental planning and zoning did not exist in Baltimore or anywhere else. Under Gilman, the Municipal Art Society commissioned plans not only for downtown but for areas the city annexed from Baltimore and Anne Arundel Counties, including stream valleys.

Gilman's interest in development issues was natural; at Yale he had been a professor of physical and political geography. His peer group looked to

Paris for inspiration. There annexation enabled Georges-Eugène Haussmann to demolish teeming central city slums at the behest of Napoleon III between 1853 and 1870, and replace them with the great Arc de Triomphe, which radiated smart boulevards, leafy parks, and elegant squares flanked with Beaux-Arts edifices. More inspiration came from Chicago's World's Fair in 1893. Its centerpiece was the White City, a planned semi-utopia, whose architect, Daniel H. Burnham, became the leading light of the City Beautiful movement of neoclassical and baroque architecture of uniform height and design. Much of today's Washington around the Mall reflects his principles, for he was the man tapped to realize Pierre L'Enfant's unfinished plans for the Federal City.

Under Gilman, the society began planning for Baltimore that culminated in blueprints from the Olmsted Brothers and other leading architects, such as John Carrère and Arnold Brunner. The public parks the society created and the art and sculptures it sponsored fostered Baltimore's reputation as the Monumental City, a name bestowed as early as the 1820s, magnified with the erection of four mighty monuments celebrating the Confederate lost cause.[2] By contrast, only one was dedicated to the Union.

The earliest of the white-supremacist monuments was the 1887 sculpture honoring Supreme Court Chief Justice Taney, a Maryland native, who ruled that African Americans could not be citizens of the United States. It was donated by the art collector Henry T. Walters, who lived on Mount Vernon Place and sited it across from the Peabody Conservatory. A monument to Confederate women was erected in 1917 on University Parkway, between Guilford and the Hopkins Homewood campus, followed by a bronze equestrian statue of Robert E. Lee and Stonewall Jackson, unveiled in 1948 near the Baltimore Museum of Art. Three years earlier, Elizabeth B. Garrett White, wife of Robert Garrett, a grandson of John W. Garrett and chairman of the city recreation commission, left a bequest that was used to honor Robert E. Lee with a monument and memorial park. The city removed the statues in 2017 and renamed the park Lake Roland Park.

These monuments mirrored the city elite's sentiments in the decades after the Civil War. They also evidenced the embrace of the City Beautiful ideas espoused by the Municipal Art Society. Within the first year the society had more than 540 paying members working to bring art to classrooms, including ornamentation of school buildings.[3] The society also dealt with urgent problems. It lobbied for the construction of a sanitary sewer system, with the support of such Hopkins luminaries as Welch and Osler. The sewer system was finally inaugurated in 1915; until then Baltimore was the nation's largest city without one. The society's consultants also conceptualized the Loch Raven reservoir to provide the region with piped drinking water, and created a number of landscaped thoroughfares, including University Parkway, Thirty-Third

The John Eager Howard equestrian statue on Mount Vernon Place lived up to Baltimore's reputation as the Monumental City.

Courtesy of the Maryland Historical Society, Image #MC2901-3

Street, The Alameda, Gwynns Falls Parkway, and Fallsway, a tree-lined boulevard across from city hall that now is mostly reduced to a ramp to I-83.[4]

The American Architect called such makeovers "architectural eugenics."[5] Gilman moved easily in eugenics circles. After he left Hopkins, his friend Andrew Carnegie invited him to serve from 1902 to 1904 as the inaugural president of the newly established Carnegie Institution, which would soon become a key funder of eugenics research. Gilman shared the Progressives' prevailing view of white supremacy as a civilizing gift. "In this country, the black man is receiving or has received through the white man three great benefits—political freedom, the Christian religion and the opportunity to acquire knowledge," he declared at the Hampton Institute in Virginia.

Gilman was patronizing at that school which the American Missionary Association opened after the Civil War to educate freed slaves. "What does this assembly represent?" he asked the predominantly black audience, and then responded: "On the one hand, those who stand for the best that the white race has produced, the fruit of many generations, developed under the sunshine of freedom, religion and education; and, on the other hand, those who represent the capacity, the hopes, and the prospects of races but lately emerging from bondage of barbarism, error and illiteracy. The light-bearers are here, ready to hand to the light-seekers the torch which shall illuminate the path of progress." Supporting Booker T. Washington's view, Gilman warned about unrealistic expectations and said that blacks should limit their sights to becoming "well trained teachers, artisans, and tillers of the soil. . . . Work, work, work has distinguished every progressive and prosperous race while sloth, sloth, sloth has been characteristic of decadence and imbecility."

Gilman reflected the thinking of the time and of his peers. Nearly all of the Municipal Art Society's twelve board members were WASPs—except for the B&O engineer Mendes Cohen and William M. Ellicott, a Philadelphia old-stock Catholic. Gilman was pretty much a figurehead who brought prestige, while Theodore R. Marburg ran the show.[6] The architect Josias Pennington was secretary. S. Davies Warfield was treasurer; he would soon extend his Seaboard Air Line Railroad to Florida, bringing its winter sunshine closer to northeastern markets. "If Baltimore had an upper class dominant in the city, it included these men," historian James B. Crooks writes.

The organization was the brainchild of Marburg whose German father, an heir to an iron fortune in Wiesbaden, built a tobacco empire in Baltimore. It was sold to the American Tobacco Company, allowing the son to enjoy a Renaissance man's life. He was a jurist who attended Princeton and Hopkins (lecturing at the latter), studied at Oxford and École Libre des Sciences Politiques in Paris. He wrote knowingly about economics, translated notable textbooks, and published poetry. He was a strong advocate of world peace, promoting Woodrow Wilson's League of Nations, and judicial settlements in international disputes. President William Howard Taft made him the U.S. minister to Belgium.

Marburg believed in eugenics in immigration. "We have the right to exercise a choice not only in the character and health of the individuals we admit but in the races we admit. It might be well to try, for a generation at least, the experiment of limiting the numbers of immigrants, declaring definitely how many we will receive from each of the European peoples, and giving a decided preference to the hardy northern blood. . . .If shutting out immigrants seems unfair, it is unfair in a bigger way to permit the overcrowding which will place a strain upon our institutions."[7]

Marburg briefly toyed with a mayoral run in 1895 as a Republican good-government candidate, but instead chose to concentrate his efforts on building the Municipal Art Society into the influential civic lobby that it became. The society had no headquarters other than Marburg's home at 14 West Mount Vernon Place. Lectures were held at the upstairs halls of Hollins, Cross Street, and Broadway markets. Marburg could count on the support of Progressive mayors, on the backing of *The Sun*, and on the endorsements of the Merchants and Manufacturers Association, another power base. His links to the Johns Hopkins University were strong. He was a university trustee (as was his brother) and bankrolled the opening of the faculty club—in the Homewood mansion. When he died in 1946, Hopkins president Isaac Bowman and trustees president Carlyle Barton were among the pallbearers.

The Progressives' big tent accommodated reformers of various ilk. One Democratic leader was President Woodrow Wilson, who received his PhD from Hopkins. During that time, in the 1880s, Gilman sent him to Princeton—which had a law school at the time—to see whether Hopkins should have one. (No law school was added. Wilson in due course became president of Princeton.) Progressives included suffragettes, workers' rights activists, child labor critics, eugenic birth control advocates, and academics of all stripes. Conservationists made a strong contribution under the leadership of the Republican Theodore Roosevelt. In Wisconsin, Robert M. La Follette launched the Progressive Party. He had been a GOP congressman, governor, and senator. Although white males (who often were upper-class Protestants) dominated the movement, considerable numbers of activists exhibited concerns about America's big cities and the ills affecting immigrants. On race matters, Progressives tended to be white supremacists and ardent segregationists, and in Baltimore blacks were the only population group that the movement did not embrace. Many Progressives believed that blacks were intellectually inferior and not ready for equal citizenship. Wilson was among those. As president of the United States from 1913 to 1919, he oversaw the racial segregation of the federal civil service. Jim Crow, he asserted, "was not a humiliation but a benefit" for blacks.[8]

Gilman, by that time, was dead. In life he approvingly quoted President Grover Cleveland: "When the attempt is made to delude the people into the belief that their suffrage can change the operation of natural laws, I would have our universities and colleges proclaim that those laws are inexorable and far removed from political control." Gilman then gave his own opinion: "Let me express a belief that the distinction between the two races is as permanent as the distinction between the colors white and black; that this distinction is natural and cannot be set aside by human action; that the lessons of history make it clear that differences of race are ineffaceable, by legislation or volition."[9] His assessments carried weight: He pulled purse strings at such leading charitable trusts as the John F. Slater Fund for the Education of Freedmen, the Carnegie Institution, John D. Rockefeller's General Education Board, the Peabody Southern Education Fund, and the Russell Sage Foundation.

RACIAL ROTATIONS AROUND CITY HALL

One of the Municipal Art Society's principal aims was to redevelop the city hall area, which contained blocks of antiquated houses on narrow and steep streets and alleys. The society commissioned plans by the Beaux-Arts consultants Carrère and Brunner to instead create a "civic center" of governmental offices and showpiece edifices, all clustered around a ceremonial plaza in front of city hall. That's how today's War Memorial Plaza came about.

Germans first dominated the city hall area. They formed the bulk of some eight hundred thousand European immigrants who landed in Baltimore in the nineteenth century. Significantly, most immigrants rushed onward as fast as they could. In Europe they had bought combination tickets that included the voyage as well as a B&O train trip to their final destination. But hostility also may have been a factor. Baltimore was a national stronghold of the American Party, which controlled city hall during the terms of Thomas Swann, the erstwhile B&O president. The anti-Catholic, anti-Irish nativist party was commonly called the Know Nothing party, not because members were necessarily ignorant but because the answer had to be, "I know nothing," if anyone asked about party activities.[10] At peak immigration in 1890 "less than 16 percent [of Baltimoreans] had been born abroad—a percentage smaller than that of any of the other cities among the ten largest in the country," writes Crooks.

Although the country of Germany did not yet exist, 60 percent of the foreign-descended were classified as "Germans," culturally and linguistically connected ethnicities. They established themselves as historically the largest immigrant group in Baltimore and included several thousand Jews. The most consequential were Forty-Eighters who came after revolutions in 1848 failed to produce unification at home, or a more democratic government. With steamships running on regular schedules across the Atlantic, America became the beneficiary of an unequaled brain drain of intellect and talent. The freedom seekers were respected, educated, well-to-do, and politically aware. "Baltimore has five German banks, three German fire insurance companies, eight German newspapers, and five German bookstores," the president of the Maryland Historical Society, the Rev. Dr. John G. Morris, reported in 1895.

He was of German extraction. Of more than 160 ethnic savings-and-loan associations—the backbones of wealth accumulation and homeownership that enabled the massive building of row-house neighborhoods—more than 130 were German; the rest were Bohemian, Polish, Lithuanian, and Italian.[11] Nearly fifty-seven hundred pupils attended classes at five city-operated public schools that taught in German and English. (By comparison, the total enrollment of twenty-one "colored" public schools was 7,858.) According to Morris, who counted churches as well as synagogues, "there are thirty-two places of worship in Baltimore in which all the pulpit instruction is imparted in the German language." The city bestowed the name German Street on a financial district thoroughfare of shipping offices that was originally called Lovely Lane. During World War I, the recognition was taken away after a 1915 plot to blow up industries in Manhattan and Jersey City was tracked down to saboteurs operating out of German Street's Hansa Haus, still extant.[12] In September 1918, the city council renamed the street to honor Lieutenant George Buchanan Redwood, Harvard Class of 1910. He was a *News* reporter and a fluent German speaker, the first local officer to lose his life in the fight against the Kaiser. *The Sun* praised "the ordinance wiping out the Hunnish appellation."[13]

The German Lutheran Zion Church stood across from city hall, and still does; its oldest surviving part was erected in 1807. Founded in 1755, the congregation had a turbulent history of schisms over creed and language. Then, during the pastorate of Henry Scheib from 1840 to 1870, the church relaxed its Lutheran tenets, "coming close to the position of the Unitarian Church in America," according to church historian Klaus G. Wust.[14] This rationalist thrust won favor among independent-minded Forty-Eighters. Scheib himself was a vintner's son from Rhineland who came to America in search of freedom from religious dogma. Educated in Bonn and the Netherlands, he built Zion into a cradle of cultural activity. He formed Liederkranz, America's second-oldest singing society; the pioneering Frauenverein women's guild; and Bildungsverein for overall uplift. He mastered Latin, Greek, and Hebrew. His crowning achievement was the independent Zion School that opened next to the church. It may have been the first Baltimore school in the modern sense of the word, and it became a model for such nearby academies as Professor Knapp's, which the writer H. L. Mencken attended and wrote about later. Zion classes were held in both German and English; religion was taught strictly as an extracurricular subject. "Soon the number of Anglo-American, Catholic and Jewish children, together with the children of Protestant German families who were not members of Zion Church, exceeded by far the number of Zion's own boys and girls enrolled in the school," Wust writes.[15]

During all this time, a slow but steady ethnic and economic churn took place—the number of blacks increased. They first established an institutional presence in the city hall area in 1797 by renting Zion's old sanctuary, a steepled white clapboard church on a hill on Fish Street (today's Saratoga). The African Bethel Church was a breakaway congregation, formed twelve years earlier by protesters who walked out after the birthplace of American Methodism—the Lovely Lane church—bowed to white worshippers' wishes and banished blacks to "nigger pews" and "African corner."[16] Many blacks nevertheless chose to stay with the familiar congregation, and Bethel's early days were rough. Yet it grew from a puny gathering, thanks to Daniel Coker, a twenty-one-year-old slave escaped from Frederick County, Maryland.[17]

An offspring of a white indentured servant from England and a black slave—and fair-skinned enough to pass as white—Coker got access to education when his master's son refused to go to school without him. In his early teens he escaped to New York, where Methodists welcomed, nurtured, and trained him. Bishop Francis Asbury, one of the denomination's founders, ordained him as a deacon. In 1801 Coker returned to Maryland, still a fugitive until a white benefactor bought his freedom. He became the first black teacher at the African Academy, a school founded by the Abolition Society.

Coker made a name for himself, cooperating with like-minded Philadelphia preachers in the creation of the African Methodist Episcopal movement. He was even elected AME's first bishop, but promptly resigned in favor of the more African-looking Richard Allen, of Philadelphia. Color was a fact of life, symbolism mattered. A man of rebellious principles, Coker eventually burned bridges to his denomination, instead allying himself with the American Colonization Society. He led some ninety settlers to Liberia. "O God! thy name be praised that it is not a lion, a tyger, or company of slave traders," he wrote on arrival. Named Justice of Peace, he got a taste of difficulties ahead when one settler refused to be judged by a mulatto, a remark that necessitated a lecture about how Coker was as African as the rest of them. Meanwhile in Baltimore, Bethel thrived. Prominent members included the educator Fannie Coppin, for whom Coppin State University is named, and John Murphy, founder of the *Afro-American* newspaper. Today Bethel remains a mainstay of the AME movement, and well over a dozen of its pastors have risen to bishop.[18]

Three other celebrated congregations worshipped in city hall's shadow. St. James Episcopal was on Saratoga Street. Founded in 1824, it was the nation's third oldest "colored" parish of the Anglican faith. At Calvert and Pleasant streets was St. Francis Xavier (1863), the nation's first Catholic church established for blacks. Then there was Saratoga Street African Baptist Chapel (1855), one of the predecessors of today's Union Baptist Church. Four whites organized it as an outreach mission for the Domestic Board of Southern Baptist Convention and the Maryland Baptist Union Association. The congregation first worshipped in a rented walk-up on Courtland Street, then erected a custom-built brick edifice at Saratoga and Calvert. The $18,000 structure was easily the most imposing building in "colored" use. "It is the height of four stories, and has a commanding appearance, adding greatly to the neighborhood," *The Sun* reported.[19]

The venture was the creation of a wealthy white merchant from Richmond, William Crane, who conducted business in Baltimore and superintended the congregation's Sunday school. It was he who acquired the site, and arranged for the design and construction of the building, where his businesses owned and occupied the ground floor. The congregation's trustees—all white—owned the rest of the building, including a high-ceilinged church hall, with galleries and eight tall windows fronting on Saratoga. Two more floors contained classrooms. His brother, James C. Crane, donated $1,000 to the building fund. He was finance chairman of the Southern Baptist Convention, the largest of that faith's central bodies. Blacks were the brothers' passion, historical sources assure us. James headed the Virginia Colonization Society and saw to the assignment of the first two black Baptist missionaries to Liberia. The Baltimore congregation never exceeded thirty members, and collapsed in the havoc of the Civil War when Southern contributions ceased. The tiny congregation merged with others to form Union Baptist.[20]

That's how the story ended. This is how it began: The Southern Baptist Convention bought a slave to serve as pastor. He was Noah Davis, of Virginia. His father was the chief miller to a rich Fredericksburg merchant and was privileged enough to be "allowed to keep a cow and horse, for his own use; and to raise and feed his hogs and poultry from the mill." When the mill was sold, his parents were set free and given a plot to till, but the rest of the family remained in bondage, including Davis. Trained as a carpenter and cobbler, he had no formal schooling, yet he was ordained a Baptist deacon. So trusted was he that his master allowed him to tour northern cities in efforts to raise the $600 price for freedom. He fell short. Then a letter arrived. It was an offer to set him free "if I would come to Baltimore, and accept an appointment as missionary to the colored people of that city," he writes in his 1859 autobiography *A Narrative of the Life of Rev. Noah Davis, a Colored Man.*

A frontispiece woodcut shows a serious, erect man of darkish color, with a haircut suggesting an Afro.

When Davis, now free, moved to Baltimore, his wife and children stayed behind in bondage.[21] Because of his status as a missionary, he was able to visit them three times a year, a frequency unheard of among ordinary free blacks. Freeing his family became his obsession. To raise money, he toured on speaking engagements, selling copies of his autobiography and building a committed network of well-wishers with resources. With help from white "brothers" he first bought the freedom of his wife and two youngest children, then interceded to prevent two daughters from being sold down South. He was creative. When he lacked the balance to free one daughter, he hired out another. "I studied out a plan; which was to get some gentleman who might want a little servant girl, to take my child, and advance me three hundred dollars for the purpose of paying my note, which was now due in Virginia." As a security he took a $500 life insurance policy "and made it over to this gentleman." Gradually he was able to free five of the children at a total cost of more than $4,000. Two still remained in bondage. The ethical dimensions of the situation were fascinating. One supporter said that as much as he wanted, he could not bring himself into giving money because doing so would involve him in human trafficking!

Today Davis is forgotten. Yet this self-taught missionary tended to the first sprouts of black public education in Baltimore. His autobiography notes: "It may be remarked, that the large colored population of Baltimore, now from thirty to forty thousand souls, have no sort of Public School provision made for them, by the city or state governments. They are left entirely to themselves for any education that they may obtain." That he set to change. His church's building became an incubator for privately sponsored black schools. The most significant was the predecessor of today's Douglass. The Colored High School was born above Davis's church hall, sponsored by the Baltimore Association for the Moral and Educational Improvement of Colored People. That Quaker-led organization existed for only six years after the Civil War, yet it set up and ran the first statewide education system for blacks. Municipal subsidies covered more than half of the $42,000 annual budget. Substantial contributions came from Quakers in Britain, as well as from freedmen's aid groups in New England and Pennsylvania. Two local rabbis contributed: Henry Hochheimer, spiritual leader of Nidche Yisrael ("The Scattered of Israel"), today's Baltimore Hebrew Congregation, which built the historic Lloyd Street synagogue, and Benjamin Szold, of Oheb Shalom ("Lovers of Peace"), Henrietta's father.

It is almost certain that Johns Hopkins donated to the school cause, anonymously, the way he did his charitable work. Many of his Quaker relatives—including Uncle Gerard—and friends educated blacks at a "Sabbath School at Sharp Street Church" for black adults who could not attend during the week. Sessions were held from 8 to 10 a.m., and again from 1 to 3 p.m. Relatives Elisha Tyson and Evan Thomas headed a group of Quakers who maintained a night school at the Bethel AME church. One report said there "could not have been less than six hundred" men, women, and children taking lessons.[22] Among other leaders of the Baltimore Association for the Moral and Educational Improvement of Colored People were Francis T. King, a wealthy dry-goods merchant, whom Hopkins appointed as executor of his will, and Galloway Cheston who would succeed King as president of the Hopkins trustees. Jesse Tyson was the treasurer. Theirs was a transformative venture. In its third year, the group operated "seventy-three schools, including twenty-two in Baltimore city, numbering in all seventy-two teachers and 7,000 scholars. Most of the teachers are colored."[23]

Despite support by the city and its "largest taxpayers," as the society put it, the school network was always in dire financial straits.[24] Black education was an explosive issue. No real trouble was recorded in the city, but Maryland's Eastern Shore across the Chesapeake Bay was a different matter. Irate whites pummeled and tarred a teacher in Cambridge; resolutions in Dorchester County called for the expulsion of teachers. In Millington, Kent County, a church school was torched, and black churches were burned in Cecil, Queen Anne's, and Somerset Counties. In 1867, when the city created public schools for blacks—nearly four decades after the white system was launched—it simply took over the association's classrooms and teachers.

The colored public education system came under the authority of the white school board, an unwieldy construct where each political ward was represented by a commissioner appointed by the city council. The result was a twenty-four-member board that critics accused of shady insider dealings involving textbooks, hiring, and supply contracts. In 1897 Mayor Alcaeus Hooper had enough. He dismissed the commissioners, and appointed a new board with Gilman as president. Council politicians went crazy at their loss of power. They legally challenged Hooper's action. For three months, two separate bodies claimed to be the school board, each making decisions and denying the other's authority. The case went to the Maryland Court of Appeals, which declared the Gilman board illegal.[25]

A WHITE MAN'S CITY

The U.S. Supreme Court's 1896 "separate but equal" ruling established segregation as the law of the land. Three years later, Baltimore's revengeful

Democrats roared back to power under the banner of "This is a White Man's City." Thomas G. Hayes became the new mayor. He was a machine politician who reinvented himself as a Progressive reformer, bringing in good and efficient governance—and the first moves toward formal segregation. Mencken described him as "a very shrewd lawyer, an unreconstructed Confederate veteran, a pious Methodist, and a somewhat bawdy bachelor."[26] Voters also approved a charter reform that Gilman had crafted to overhaul the public school system. Instead of twenty-four members chosen by the city council, the mayor alone appointed the new board, subject to confirmation by the council. Gilman was on the board, along with seven other men; he presided over the first meeting.[27] Also on the board was Lillian Welsh, MD, the first woman member. Tellingly, no black replaced C. F. Eggleston, the minister of Grace Presbyterian Church, whom the Republicans had appointed in 1896 as the first African American. He was seen as a troublemaker. "I'm opposed to separate schools for white and colored pupils," he declared in a newspaper for all to see. "I am also opposed to separate churches for the white and colored races."[28]

For over a decade a building specifically designed for the Colored High School had occupied a prime parcel on the north side of Saratoga, between St. Paul and Charles Streets. When it was inaugurated in 1889, Mayor Latrobe hailed its twenty-seven classrooms as an example of an equitable arrangement, a demonstration of separate but equal in action. "This is an event of importance to the city and to the colored citizens," he declared. "The city council proposes to furnish all classes with suitably-equipped school buildings, and to make no distinction in their character. . . . Its excellent location is also to be noted, standing as it does but three doors from Charles Street, one of the fashionable thoroughfares. The situation is more conspicuous than that of any other school in the city." He reflected: "Thirty-four years ago there was a law in Maryland which prohibited the colored citizens from receiving the benefits of public education. Now in this city you have just the same schools and the same instruction as the white scholars. You have your primary schools, you have your grammar schools, you have this splendid high school, and you have a manual training school. In all of them the teaching is of exactly the same character as in the white schools."[29]

That was then. Thirteen years later, the school board evicted the Colored High School from Saratoga Street, which was in the midst of gentrification. Racial attitudes had sharpened, color lines hardened. A brand-new showpiece court house (today's Mitchell Courthouse) opened in 1898, just a block from the colored school. The Maryland Historical Society was nearby, and so were the upper-class homes, O'Neill's department store, and fine caterers to the needs of the carriage trade.[30] If blacks were allowed to expand, what would be the fate of such investments?

The idea to move the school had a surprising sponsor, Hiram Watty. He was one of the first blacks elected to the city council. A Republican, he was worthy enough to be rewarded with jobs at the Customs House and U.S. Treasury. He championed the relocation because he wanted the Colored High School and its six hundred students—an enrollment that was projected to double—in his power base, the Seventeenth Ward along Pennsylvania Avenue; at the same time he did not want the old Saratoga Street building given to a white school.[31]

The message to blacks to vacate was delivered in various ways. In November 1903 a mob of more than two hundred white men and boys attacked the black Masonic Temple on Courtland Street. One attack was preceded by a bonfire to mark the mob's staging area. Masons arriving for a meeting at the temple were harassed. After nine o'clock that night, the mob began pelting the temple with stones, breaking windows. The central police station was just a couple of blocks away but when it finally responded, after several complaints, it was with one patrolman. A week later, the scene was repeated, sending a message to such other fraternal organizations as the Grand United Order of Odd Fellows and Knights of Pythias which had meeting halls in the vicinity.[32]

Such antics kicked off systematic municipal efforts to separate the races and segregate residential areas. Then came the Great Fire of 1904. The city hall area escaped the inferno that incinerated 1,526 buildings on 140 downtown acres. Afterward it was deluged by burned-out companies needing relocation sites.[33] Black residents and organizations were made offers they could not refuse.[34] Bethel AME vacated its twelve hundred-seat sanctuary near the old high school, and so did Union Baptist, by then a mega-church of twenty-five hundred members. Both headed for the ward where the Colored High School had been moved. *Afro-American* relocated from St. Paul to Eutaw and Druid Hill, two blocks from the Johns Hopkins University's original campus. Leading black lawyers packed up, including W. Ashbie Hawkins, George McMechen, Harry S. Cummings, and Warner T. McGinn, each a notable civic leader. Doctors and dentists pulled up stakes and followed their clients. Also relocated from Saratoga Street was the Colored Normal School, created to train teachers by the Baltimore Association for the Moral and Educational Improvement of Colored People and then continued by the state. It was transferred to Prince George's County, near Washington, where it evolved into today's Bowie State University.

In the 1850s, when New York assembled more than seven hundred acres to implement Frederick Law Olmsted's plan for Central Park, that city resorted to condemnation. In the process, the black hamlet of Seneca Village was wiped out. After the 1904 fire, Baltimore similarly used condemnation to refashion the city hall area into an extension of the rebuilt business district and a "civic

Much of the city hall area survived the 1904 fire but the central business district along the shoreline did not.
Courtesy of the Maryland Historical Society, Image #MC4709

center" of municipal headquarters. In 1908 Progressive Mayor Barry F. Mahool began planning the widening of St. Paul Street, a narrow, winding thoroughfare that cut through the black area. When James H. Preston took the oath in 1911, the year after the residential segregation law was enacted, he expanded the authority of the Burnt District Commission. With access to bond money, the five-man commission he headed furthered the Municipal Art Society's vision by acquiring a great number of properties around city hall and the courthouse. Edward D. Preston, no relation to the mayor, acted as the enforcer. A member of the Burnt District Commission, he was the city's chief building inspector, the sole judge and jury who ordered structures torn down. In one case, the owner of a small hotel still occupied the premises, praying for a last-minute reprieve, while wreckers kept tearing up the roof. A ten-story office building was erected at the site.[35] Across from today's Mercy Hospital,[36] demolition sites were refashioned into Preston Gardens. The City Beautiful-inspired park became ringed with tall buildings, including the monopoly Chesapeake and Potomac Telephone Company which hired no African Americans until 1974.

The dispersal of the city hall area's black concentration created the racial dynamics that have shaped Baltimore ever since. The largest number of those evicted—including the socially most prominent and economically most successful—relocated to the west side, edging steadily farther and farther up along the twin spines of Pennsylvania and Druid Hill Avenues. A French-speaking refugee community of all races had existed around Franklin and Pennsylvania since the Haitian revolution in 1791. That Seton Hill nucleus now grew and spilled over, the numbers swelled not only by evictees from the city hall district but also by hundreds of blacks dispersed from Sharp-Leadenhall, near Federal Hill, where the B&O needed more land for its train yards. So frenzied was the pace of racial turnover that between 1900 and 1910 the Seventeenth Ward's black population increased from 1,499 to 12,738 and then to 16,736 in the next decade. The white population fell from 18,926 to 3,900.[37] The expansion put blacks in close proximity of Eutaw Place and Druid Hill Park, upscale areas that ethnic rotation had made noticeably Jewish as WASPs moved on to new exclusive suburbs. Thus the fates of blacks and Jews were twinned in adjoining neighborhoods. On the east side, another transition took place. As dispersed blacks sought new living quarters, the dominant white population groups, the Irish and the Jews, withdrew. They had done well in America and could afford nicer neighborhoods.[38]

The city's racial geography was formalized after the African American lawyer W. Ashbie Hawkins in 1910 disregarded an internalized demarcation line on the west side and leapfrogged to 1834 McCulloh Street, buying a thirteen-foot-wide, three-story row house on a white block. He did not move there, instead renting the property to his black law partner, George McMechen, a Yale graduate. The presence of blacks triggered white anxiety. *The Sun* warned about dire consequences unless this "Negro invasion" was stopped.[39] With municipal elections approaching, the city council imposed residential segregation throughout the city. No whites or blacks anywhere could move to blocks where their race was not the majority. A key motivation for the legislation was the whites' fear of disease.[40] One of the Hopkins Hospital's Big Four—Welch—advocated the segregation of blacks on health grounds. He made this public declaration: "Tuberculosis, infant mortality and pneumonia have wrought the greatest havoc, and we cannot be indifferent to this condition, because the death rate among the colored people has a great influence upon the whites because of contact through the kitchen, nursing and other forms. It is clearly a problem of self-interest, if not one of humanity."[41] Similar fears prevailed elsewhere. Copying Baltimore's law—the nation's first residential segregation law—dozens of cities crafted segregation tools of their own, among them Richmond, Birmingham, Atlanta, and Louisville.

Decades before Photoshop, A. Aubrey Bodine used darkroom magic to highlight the monumentalism of city hall and the War Memorial Plaza in keeping with City Beautiful thinking.
Courtesy of the Maryland Historical Society, Image #B64-9

Northern cities joined the residential segregation effort. They were trying to cope with racial change on a giant scale: the Great Migration. Black sharecroppers streamed from the Mississippi Delta to fill industrial jobs vacated because World War I cut off immigration from Europe. Then, after peace returned, Congress ended the traditional open-door immigration policy. Instead of the "huddled masses," the federal government's eugenic immigration quotas in force from 1924 until 1966 favored northern European professionals, entrepreneurs, farmers, and craftsmen. Asian immigration was restricted; no quota existed for black Africans.

THE REDLINING OF AMERICA

Distinct class, ethnic, racial, and religious concentrations were as old as America itself. In the mid-1930s, such segregation received the U.S. government's stamp of approval, when officials redlined 239 big cities, creating the racial expansion patterns that remade the country's big cities after World War II.

Redlining grew out of a New Deal attempt to stabilize a Depression-era housing market. Influenced by eugenics, it rated neighborhoods' credit risk on the basis of the age and condition of housing but also according to residents' race, religion, ethnicity, income, and class. Maps were color coded from the lowest to the highest risk: green, blue, yellow, and red. Red was "hazardous," denoting houses that lacked modern conveniences and had undesirable neighbors. President Franklin D. Roosevelt's bailout agency, the Home Owners' Loan Corporation, supervised the actual mapping. Its guidelines reflected the thinking of Homer Hoyt, the Federal Housing Administration's chief economist. Relying on the judgments of a Chicago real estate man, he listed ethnicities in the order of their desirability as homeowners, neighbors, and lending risks in his 1933 PhD dissertation at the University of Chicago:

1. English, Germans, Scots, Irish, Scandinavians;
2. North Italians;
3. Bohemians or Czechoslovakians;
4. Poles;
5. Lithuanians;
6. Greeks;
7. Russian Jews of the lower class;
8. South Italians;
9. Negroes;
10. Mexicans

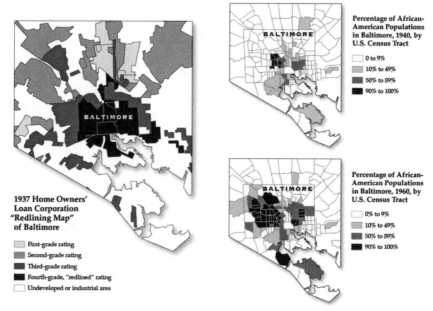

The 1937 redlining map divided the city into four categories of real estate risk, based on the quality of housing as well as the race, ethnicity, religion, and social class of residents.
Robert Cronan. Lucidity Information Design, LLC

Hoyt's list became the nation's real estate gospel and banking mantra; it kept reappearing in appraisal manuals until the 1960s. Being a White Anglo-Saxon Protestant, or at least sharing WASP aspirations and values, was hoisted up as the American ideal. In city after city, homeowners of English, German, Nordic, and Irish ancestry occupied the neighborhoods deemed to be the most desirable, a map category colored green. Those residents tended to be old stock, or at least native born, well-off, and educated, and mostly Protestant. Their houses were modern showpieces—the cliché "upscale" had not yet been invented—and their neighborhoods barred blacks and Jews through legally enforceable homeowners' joint agreements called restrictive covenants, a strategy the government recommended nationwide for combating "inharmonious elements." The next category, blue, was broader. It included some desirable Jewish suburbs that maintained their homogeneity by banning blacks *and* Jews of different origin and lower social standing. The federal government told bankers to go ahead and lend prudently in those two top color categories. Such guidelines were uniform and used nationwide.[42]

In Baltimore distinguished WASP families tended to live far from madding crowds in new garden districts built on one-time estate lands north of

Johns Hopkins University's Homewood. That's where the grandest exclusive neighborhood, Guilford, was located. Once the estate of Arunah S. Abell, founder of *The Sun*, owners of its stone and brick mansions banned both Jews and blacks, except for servants. The Home Owners' Loan Corporation maps gave Guilford the top ranking, green. Nearby was Roland Park. It only merited the second rank, blue, or "still desirable," even though it shared identical restrictions. The reason was the age of housing. The garden district had been inaugurated in 1891; thus the oldest Victorian homes, constructed of wood, had been built more than forty-five years earlier. By the government's 1937 reckoning, those homes were time worn, and held little long-term appeal for status-conscious homebuyers who sought to project success. The homes were "like a 1935 automobile—still good, but not what the people are buying today who can afford a new one," a document explained. Nevertheless, the government encouraged lending in both blue and green areas.

From downtown to North Avenue and as far up as Waverly along Greenmount Avenue, all residential neighborhoods were colored red between Fulton Avenue in the west and Patterson Park Avenue in the east and again in Highlandtown and Canton. They were *dangerous*, the government said. Lenders were cautioned against doing business in such neighborhoods that have since come back—Mount Vernon, Eutaw Place, Bolton Hill, Reservoir Hill, Station North, Charles Village, Remington, Butchers Hill, and in Federal Hill and the rest of South Baltimore. Any loans made in those sections should be done at stricter terms and higher rates, the government advised. Those were white neighborhoods, but that did not matter. Applicants there were subjected to the same clampdown on lending that was imposed on black areas, where no conventional financing took place. Residents were left at the mercy of loan sharks and assorted improvement scammers. "In most 'hazardous' or 'red' areas it is difficult to see how any improvement can take place" was the HOLC's verdict. That became a self-fulfilling prophesy. As loan money at any terms dried up, deterioration set in.[43]

Beyond the redlined areas lay transitional zones, colored yellow on the maps. They consisted of older housing and were predominated by working-class families. The government classified them as "risky" for lending because, it said, their eventual fate was to be redlined. In this thinking, transitional neighborhoods went in only one direction, downward. There was no consideration of an alternative course—encouraging lending and improvement in declining neighborhoods—that would support income and social diversity. To bankers, planners, and bureaucrats of the day the very idea of investing in down-at-heels or racially changing neighborhoods would have sounded wacky. Their thinking was grounded in the rotation theories of the trailblazing Chicago School sociologist Robert E. Park. Cities, he argued, expanded in concentric circles outward, with the most desirable and ambitious groups steadily moving farther out.[44] Once a neighborhood lost its luster, less desirable elements succeeded one another. At the end of the cycle, there would no longer be an economic reason for the neighborhood to exist, and it would be razed and redeveloped for a more desirable use.[45]

The Johns Hopkins Hospital area became a prime example of such transitions at work.

Chapter Seven

Governments Create Slums

World War II turned Baltimore into a smoky and overcrowded industrial camp, a smokestack boomtown. Some 250,000 streamed in from outside Maryland in search of well-paying defense jobs.[1] Many had been unemployed during the Depression and thought they struck gold. At Bethlehem Steel's mills and shipyards alone, some forty-eight thousand men and women toiled around the clock, seven days a week—including legendary Rosie the Riveters and eight thousand African Americans of both genders. One shipyard was located right on Key Highway at the foot of Federal Hill, where the Ritz-Carlton and Harborview waterfront condominiums now stand near the American Visionary Art Museum.

Key Highway was operated by Bethlehem Steel, whose giant Sparrows Point steel mill on the other side of the Patapsco included wharves. When more capacity was needed, yet another shipyard opened. Once Fairfield, too, proved too small, Bethlehem took over a Curtis Bay factory two miles away that manufactured sleeping cars for the Pullman company. It was converted into a plant prefabricating ship sections which then were transported by rail or truck to a forty-acre open-air staging area outside Fairfield's gates. In 1941, when the government ordered the first Liberty ship, that boxy, utilitarian freighter was delivered in forty-three days after the contract was signed. A new ship was then launched every thirty-five hours, according to the official history, which lists the production of 383 additional Liberty ships (out of an overall fleet of 2,710 vessels of that type), thirty landing craft, and ninety-four Victory ships.[2] Glenn L. Martin's bomber factories in Middle River employed another fifty-three thousand workers. Thousands more toiled at Bendix, Western Electric, Westinghouse, and General Motors, helping the war effort.

Housing shortage was desperate. There were no vacancies for whites or blacks, and many renters took subtenants. In 1942, 590 whites—nearly half

115

of them out-of-town war workers—shared 121 rooms on a block near the Key Highway shipyard. Health inspectors counted fifty-three bathtubs among the units.[3] When one shift worker woke up, another grabbed the "hot bed" and dozed off. So it went. War workers slumbered in chicken coops and coal cellars, or stole shut-eye in newsreel theaters operating around the clock. The money was good. The outsiders left their mark on the city. The largest group consisted of tens of thousands of white Appalachian men, women, and children. Many "hillbillies" eventually returned home. By contrast, African Americans, mostly from the Carolinas, came to stay. As a rule, blacks paid higher average rents than whites, according to several government surveys.[4]

At the end of World War II, vast expanses of row houses lay southeast of Hopkins Hospital. Those belonged to white ethnics, who worked union jobs, bowled, whooped it up at bull roasts, and cracked steamed crabs with wooden mallets on long tables covered with newspapers, and then went to mass to count their blessings. In the founder's time, farms occupied the rolling hills. Since then, endless blocks of redbrick row houses had been erected to enable immigrant families to fulfill American dreams. The rows stretched all the way to Highlandtown, which used to be called Snake Hill until it became part of the city in 1918, the same year as the neighboring Canton. Closer to the Hopkins medical institutions, Butchers Hill's imposing houses overlooked Patterson Park, a 137-acre oasis of walks, a boat lake with swans and the Pagoda observation tower. Home air-conditioning had not yet become common. On hot summer evenings whole families fled stifling houses and headed to the park, where they camped overnight under the stars on a hillside where a hundred cannons defended Baltimore in the War of 1812.

The Home Owners' Loan Corporation redlining maps marked all this territory red, dangerous for lending; a narrow belt near Bayview was given the yellow transitional marking. The problem was not housing because that was mostly solid. Instead, HOLC was worried about a eugenic downward shift in the ethnic and socioeconomic makeup of residents, who were mostly of immigrant stock in various stages of assimilation and who still often socially identified with their country of origin. HOLC went by the book. One government appraiser praised a Polish neighborhood for its appealing appearance and fastidious upkeep, then declared it transitional because of "Negro and Italian infiltration."[5]

Yet, despite redlining, these white ethnic enclaves between Hopkins Hospital and Highlandtown emerged stable from the sixteen-year calamity of the Great Depression and World War II. They were close-knit and self-reliant communities with thrifty values and Old World skills, kept tidy by Bohemian, Hungarian, Polish, and Ukrainian womenfolk who carried buckets of hot water, rough brushes, and Bon Ami scouring powder (available since the

An idealized stoop-sitting scene by A. Aubrey Bodie, circa 1930.
Courtesy of the Maryland Historical Society, Image #B360-2

1880s) to Saturday competitions in scrubbing white front steps, their pride of homeownership. Numerous ethnic building-and-loan institutions mitigated the impact of redlining. Some were so small that weekly business meetings were held in the treasurer's kitchen. Four Polish Catholic parishes operated banks for regular depositors. Parochial schools provided further glue. Then there was politics. At election times heavily voting precincts had an understanding with the ethnic Democratic clubs: We vote, you give us service and patronage jobs in government. For white ethnics, East Baltimore beyond the hospital was a good place at the end of World War II.

The situation was quite different on the opposite side of Broadway. Downhill from Hopkins Hospital was Old Town, separated from the city hall district by the Jones Falls stream. The philanthropist Johns Hopkins had known the area well because he took the main drag, Gay Street, whenever he rode from his counting rooms to his Clifton estate. Old Town was the commercial center of the whole east side in his time. Few bridges crossed the Jones Falls and repeatedly were wiped out in floods. So instead of crossing the stream, farmers from highlands simply rolled downhill on York, Harford, and Belair Roads until they reached Belair Market stalls along Gay Street. That part boasted imposing commercial buildings, and a fire station with a fanciful tower worthy of an Italian villa (still standing). Factories, warehouses, and businesses clustered near the North Central Railways' Calvert Street Station which the *Sunpapers* demolished in 1949 for its printing plant, newsrooms, and offices.

The Old Town district had always served as a way station for a rotation of ethnicities, classes, and nationalities. In the early years, the wealthy lived next door to newcomers. Charles Carroll of Carrollton, the signer of the Declaration of Independence, occupied a mansion at 800 East Lombard Street, near the 234-foot-high Phoenix Shot Tower, which at one point was the tallest structure in the United States. (Molten lead was poured through a sieve at the top; lead droplets, like raindrops, formed into perfect pellet spheres and solidified as they hit a vat of cooling water below.) Carroll was a Catholic of Irish descent. At the time, the neighborhood was heavily German, and many prominent families lived on Front Street.[6] But a few years after his 1832 death, the Catholic parish of Heilige Jakobus, at Eager and Aisquith Streets, spun off St. Vincent de Paul's, at Front Street, to serve the English speakers. That came just in time for an influx of tens of thousands of poverty-stricken refugees from Ireland's potato famine. The first arrived in 1847 on three vessels so ghastly they were called coffin ships.[7] Those who survived the Atlantic crossing were sick, hungry, uneducated, and Papists—underclass. Nevertheless, they had the rudiments of the language. They soon spread to many parts of the city. Irish churches were established in the Locust Point, Canton, and Fells Point industrial waterfronts where jobs were plentiful, and near B&O's Mount Clare depot in the Hollins Market area, west of today's University of Maryland downtown campus.

Old Town, however, remained the heart of the Irish, who took over homes vacated by the Germans. Heilige Jakobus became St. John the Evangelist Roman Catholic Church, the soul of the Baltimore Irish, whose passion was Tenth Ward politics. The storied Democratic machine dispensed favors at city hall and patronage in the port, enabling upward mobility. The ward ran "roughly, from Maryland Penitentiary to Green Mount Cemetery, from Jones Falls to Greenmount Avenue," remembered James H. Bready, an *Evening Sun* journalist, who first got to know it during war years. "It was fairly homogenous, in the late 1940s—working class whites in rental rowhousing: Irish, Italians, wartime leftover hillfolk." On feast days native sons returned for processions, politicians like Governor Herbert R. O'Conor and Representative Ambrose J. Kennedy. They were products of much history. "In the mid-1800s, the mobs that terrorized the polling places were largely ethnic groups—Irish, Greeks, Italians, Poles, Germans, each seeking political superiority over others," observed political journalist Frank A. DeFilippo. "The Irish won the skirmishes and dominated Baltimore (and Maryland) politics well into the 1930s. At that juncture the Jews, later joined by the Italians, snatched politics from the Irish."[8]

Rich or poor, Baltimore's earliest Jewish families also settled in Old Town. They came from Bavaria and Hesse, or the Netherlands and the Austro-Hungarian Empire. Collectively referred to as German Jews, they sought to blend in and Americanize quickly. Thus the Har Sinai congregation, instead of Fridays, held Sabbath services on Sundays in a synagogue opened in 1849 on High Street, near Fayette.[9] Then in 1881 Czar Alexander II was assassinated, and Russia's Jews were scapegoated. Amid slaughter by Cossack horsemen, millions fled pogroms to America.

As thousands of "Russian" refugees flooded Old Town, well-to-do German-Jewish families departed, moving crosstown and concentrating on streets along Eutaw Place and around Druid Hill Park. They felt crowded out among newcomers from the Pale of Settlement, the vast territory stretching from Poland to Ukraine to Belarus where the czarist authorities required Jews to live. Those refugees were *shtetl* folk. Even after settling in Baltimore, they insisted on speaking guttural Yiddish, adhering to religious laws and wearing stern Orthodox garb, provocations that upset many old-timers who feared they would be excluded from membership in German societies. Despite apprehensions, local and international donors, including the French financier and philanthropist Baron Maurice de Hirsch, aided the newcomers. Agents were present in the port to advocate for people who had been denied admission. If security was needed, they posted bonds. They secured twenty houses on Gay Street to get newcomers started. "We say to these oppressed people, 'Come, we'll assimilate you,'" vowed Simon Wolf, an aid advocate.[10]

In eighteen years Baltimore's Jewish population soared from ten thousand to sixty thousand. The main "Russian" colony stretched from Front Street to Broadway and from Gay to Pratt. This district was the local equivalent of New York's Lower East Side. It included a slum on Exeter, High, Low, and Harrison Streets, which later rotated to the next wave of newcomers, becoming Little Italy. Carroll Mansion bore the marks of the area's shifting fortunes. An 1895 visitor found a junk shop on the ground floor (which had previously been a tavern). A Hasidic congregation, Anshe Niesen, worshipped in the faded parlor. It was a gathering of *landsleit*, a tightly knit group of families who had fled pogroms in Nizhyn, a Ukrainian town of a Christian majority but also of traditions of mysticism. Theirs was Baltimore's original Lubavitcher shul. Fifteen "Russian" families with their broods filled the rest of the building. Yiddish was a dominant tongue. "The speech of the loungers in the streets and shops is polyglot. The signs over the stores are in foreign characters. Russian, Polish, Lithuanian and Bohemian mingle with Italian, Greek and German," *The Sun* wrote. "The old, substantial houses of the early settled locality still remain. Formerly the residencies of the wealthy, they were later on invaded by the foreign element of German and Irish nationality, but are now for the most part tenanted by a race from the far East, the exiles and refugees from Russia."[11]

That was the past. By the end of World War II, the bulk of East Baltimore's Jewish families had hopscotched to the west side, where restrictive covenants against them were weak. The Jewish community's center of gravity thus shifted across the city, first to the Monroe Street corridor, then Garrison Boulevard and Liberty Heights Avenue, then to Park Heights Avenue and Reisterstown Road, and ultimately all the way to Pikesville, Reisterstown, and Owings Mills. Relics remained. The Jewish Educational Alliance, a precursor of today's Jewish Community Center, was at 1216 East Baltimore Street, next to Hendler's ice cream factory, the fortress-like redbrick home of "The Velvet Kind." Nearby were the historic Lloyd Street synagogue and B'nai Israel ("Russische shul").[12] On Lombard Street, kosher butchers expertly wrung the necks of caged turkeys and clucking chickens whenever there was demand for fresh birds. Pushcarts did a brisk trade.

By that time, the Old Town Irish were largely gone. Quick to assimilate, many had been migrating north and northeast since the 1910s. Neighborhoods along York, Harford, and Belair Roads became Shamrock land where taverns had Irish names, and the Hibernians ruled. The Irish experienced much job and social discrimination and were excluded from some tony neighborhoods, so they, in turn, built row-house enclaves that discriminated by barring non-Catholics. An example was Anthonyville, near Gardenville's

St. Anthony of Padua parish, as surviving real estate ads confirm. Other migrations took place elsewhere. The Irish and Lithuanians living in the vicinity of Hollins Market and the Mount Clare depot moved west along Frederick Road to Irvington and ultimately to Arbutus. The Poles and Ukrainians proceeded along Eastern Avenue to Dundalk, Rosedale, and Essex. "Each generation moved twenty minutes farther out," reflected Richard T. Lawrence, the pastor of St. Vincent's.

Some of the ethnic migration patterns out of Old Town over the years.
Robert Cronan. Lucidity Information Design, LLC

During these transitions the city acquired Carroll Mansion, turning it into a vocational school and then a recreation center for whites. Special intervention programs were held there for youngsters from Little Italy who had been caught in all kinds of mischief, including "molesting" couples returning from dances in Patterson Park.[13] In the 1960s a proposal was floated to tear down the mansion and build a gas station at the site. Mayor Theodore McKeldin put a stop to that idea and had the landmark restored. It still stands, now part of a hotel operation.

In relocating, all those white ethnicities left behind not only the old neighborhoods but also the stigma of redlining. By simply moving a few miles out, whites could get loans, and build a nest egg through homeownership. Blacks did not have that option.

ALL THAT JAZZ

In the 1930s three jazz greats lived within a few blocks from one another downhill from Johns Hopkins. The singer Billie Holiday dwelled at 219 South Durham, a two-story redbrick row house still in existence in a narrow alley (with a plaque commemorating her tenancy); the ragtime pianist Eubie Blake at 414 North Eden; and the drummer Chick Webb at 1313 Ashland. They all soon moved to the Big Apple in search of stardom, but in 1939 Webb returned to his native city for a week of sold-out engagements at the Hippodrome, an all-white downtown theater. "Chick Webb represented the triumph of the human spirit in jazz and life," writes the musicologist Richard S. Ginell. "Hunchbacked, small in stature, almost a dwarf with a large face and broad shoulders, Webb fought off congenital tuberculosis of the spine in order to become one of the most competitive drummers and bandleaders of the big band era. Perched high upon a platform, he used custom-made pedals, goose-neck cymbal holders, a 28-inch bass drum and a wide variety of other percussion instruments to create thundering solos of complexity and energy."[14]

Webb was at the peak of his powers. Coast-to-coast radio broadcasts made him a crossover star, the black mascot of the white college set. Yale hired him for a dance; Boston University fans gave him an MS (Master of Swing) degree, and a senior class prom at New York University bestowed on him an MD (Master of Drums).[15] His big draw was a teenage songstress he discovered—Ella Fitzgerald. Harlem's Savoy was their home base, a nightclub known all over the world thanks to "Stomping at the Savoy," a hit penned by one of his sidemen. The band was often on the road. During the Hippodrome gig Webb wasn't feeling well. He consulted Dr. Ralph Young, Baltimore's

leading black physician who had treated him since boyhood. Young recommended a checkup at Hopkins. Except that he had no privileges there, nor
did any other black; a white doctor had to make the referral. That's how it
worked. (In 1946 Hopkins would appoint Young to the hospital staff and in
1952 to the university faculty.)[16]

Webb had been deformed at birth, then broke his back in a fall when he
was five years old. It was Young who taught him to walk again, encouraged
him to take a newspaper delivery route, and recommended drums as the best
upper-body exercise to "loosen up" bones. After Webb died at Hopkins,
aged thirty-four, of tuberculosis of the spine and liver on June 16, 1939,
Young issued a citywide challenge. He announced that Webb's deathbed
wish was to construct a community center for the slums of East Baltimore,
which had none. For years there had been a plan for a colored YMCA, but
it got nowhere. The idea was to donate the center to the city, which would
run it. With the initial $5,000 contribution coming from Young himself, the
cause electrified the black community; some seventy-five hundred people
from all walks of life packed the Fifth Regiment Armory for the first fund-
raiser. The master of ceremonies was boxing champion Joe Louis, the
Brown Bomber, a close friend of both Webb and the Pennsylvania Avenue
entrepreneur William L. Adams.

Even representatives of the segregated city's white power structure took
notice. Governor O'Conor, Senator George Radcliffe, Representative Kennedy, and former Mayor William F. Broening all attended the fund-raiser.
Duke Ellington came, and his son, Mercer, played. The singing Ink Spots
came, and so did the Nicholas Brothers, the astonishing acrobatic dancing
duo soon to be featured in *Stormy Weather* and two Glenn Miller films,
Orchestra Wives and *Sun Valley Serenade*. Mostly, though, the evening
belonged to star-struck young musicians and singers who had found their
inspiration in Webb. In the wee hours Ella belted out the finale, "St. Louis
Blues," and the thousands spilled onto sidewalks in the armory area, which
at the time was a black slum south of the white bastion of Bolton Hill. (The
slum was demolished in urban renewal in the 1950s; the State Office Building
complex now occupies the area.)[17]

It took seven years for the Chick Webb Recreation Center to open on
Eden Street. The hitch was finding a suitable site. There were no appropriate vacant lots in the overcrowded black sections, and whites east of
Broadway, struggling to maintain segregation, did not want a black magnet.
The *New York Times*'s Turner Catledge reported in 1943 that Baltimore's
estimated two hundred thousand blacks, or about 20 percent of the total
population, were compressed to neighborhoods comprising *less than four
square miles of the city's total 78.6*. "Additional Negroes are still coming

to Baltimore at an estimated rate of 2,000 a month to work in defense factories. Where are they going to live?"[18]

As early as 1933, the state's Joint Committee on Housing identified a seventeen-block slice of Old Town's Tenth and Fifth Wards as Slum No. 1, the city's worst. Remarkably, the chronic housing shortage compelled various socioeconomic classes and races to mix. There were roughly thirty-four hundred residents, 67.9 percent of whom were black. According to an *Afro* writer, they could be grouped: "There are the old-timers who have lived there many winters, and would not now choose any other section; there is the group who is trying every possible means to 'move out': a large number are neither interested in leaving nor staying, they are just there eking out a living. Numbers of them are there for the time being—till they can do better. Included among them are new comers from the farther South, professional men and not few of the old residents who will die nursing the desire."[19]

Bordered by Forrest, Eager, Aisquith, and Monument, Slum No. 1 was a hodgepodge of residential, business, industrial, and entertainment uses. Eubie Blake got his start there—in a lawless pocket called Hell's Kitchen—playing ragtime piano in a "hookshop," as he called brothels. Some distance away, Billie Holiday premiered as a preteen "pretty baby" at an Upper Fells Point whorehouse. The slum was wracked with diseases. Its mortality rate was 75 percent higher than the average; the incidences of tuberculosis and fatal syphilis were ten times higher. With the lowest real estate assessments in the city, "It is not teeming with life," an observer wrote. "A walk through Slum No. 1 gives one the impression, rather, of a city in ruins, half deserted. Hundreds of houses lie vacant, and many of them are wrecked and ready to cave in."[20]

LITTLE BOHEMIA

A nearby concentration of white immigrants kept blacks in check—Little Bohemia. Straddling Broadway were some ten thousand Czechs, whose well-kept row houses (with obligatory white marble steps) surrounded Hopkins. With roots in the Austro-Hungarian Empire, the Bohemians provided another illustration of how neighborhoods rotated. When St. Wenceslaus Catholic Church first came into being in 1872, congregants worshiped in a former Lutheran sanctuary at Central Avenue in Old Town, above Baltimore street. By 1901 the immigrant community had prospered enough to move outward and St. Wenceslaus built a veritable cathedral on Ashland Avenue, near Hopkins hospital. Known for its stained glass, grand organ, and choirs, St. Wenceslaus became the community's anchor. A thriving parish school and a convent for nuns soon followed.[21] The parish had six thousand members, and more than fifteen hundred pupils attended the St. Elizabeth's of Hungary school overlooking Patterson Park. Bohemians were everywhere. "Several thousand of them are garment workers, a thousand or so are cigar-makers, while others have control of important bakeries, furniture-houses and machine shops. There are also Bohemian butchers, Bohemian organ-builders, a Bohemian lawyer and a Bohemian physician," *The Sun* reported in 1896.[22] Seven "flourishing building associations" bound the settlement together, financing row-house purchases and creating such landmarks as Bohemia Hall, at Broadway and Eager.

Many Bohemians worked at breweries near Gay Street and North Avenue. Nothing could compare with the J. H. Von Der Horst & Brewing Company. It is long gone, and even its lasting claim to fame is forgotten: In early 1880s, the brewer constructed an adjoining ballpark and beer garden and purchased an American Association franchise, which it named the Orioles. A Baltimore baseball tradition was born.[23]

A few hundred yards west, at North Avenue and Harford Road, was the Samuel Ready School for orphan girls. When Ready moved to the suburbs in 1938, Sears, Roebuck and Company bought the fifteen-acre site for its first Maryland store. Sears was a change agent. Chicago's Julius Rosenwald was no longer alive, but as a part owner of Sears he had donated a fortune to support the education of African American children in the rural South. His philosophy lingered on. Sears served blacks, in contrast to Howard Street department stores, which did not.[24] Yet it was unthinkable that any quick racial transformation could occur around the store. For one thing, the vicinity's many big employers—including Coca Cola and rival Suburban Cola bottlers, envelope and office supply manufacturers, metal fabricators, and dairies—depended on a white workforce that lived in Little Bohemia. Goetze's, a family meatpacking operation, alone employed a thousand people near the site of the erstwhile ballpark where the first Orioles had played.[25]

However, as soon as peacetime conditions allowed, whites decamped. In search of more space, lawns, and modern conveniences, they trekked further out, taking advantage of feverish building in the suburbs that was financed by government-subsidized FHA loans. Their departure freed more houses for blacks. Like an inkblot, the slum kept creeping outward. In 1945 the area's first white landmark institution announced its departure. It was Sinai, the Jewish community hospital. Having been located on Monument Street since before its neighbor Hopkins was built, it unveiled plans to move to near Pimlico race track to better serve its ethnic base which was concentrating in the northwest.[26] More relocations soon came. St. Joseph, a Catholic hospital, abandoned its century-old building on Caroline Street that had 250 beds but had been allowed to deteriorate so badly that the fire marshal repeatedly threatened to close it down. In 1958 the hospital relocated to Towson, the seat of Baltimore County, which was growing by leaps and bounds, thanks to whites fleeing the city.

The next to go was Faith Presbyterian Church, a congregation of some note. Its buildings are still at the confluence of Gay and Biddle Streets, and so are the church's famed stained glass windows, protected by bulletproof glass. It was another link to the philanthropist Johns Hopkins. George Stewart Brown donated the Gothic sanctuary and bell tower—to which a stone-built school soon was added. A family friend of Hopkins, he headed the Alex. Brown financial empire (founded by his grandfather) and made the gift as a tribute to his family's roots.

Designed to resemble Scots-Irish country churches, the sanctuary was built of bluestone from local Falls Road quarries on the grounds of a cemetery. A faded old photo shows how the foundations were simply dug amid existing headstones which were removed only as needed. (A few still remain.) When Broadway was extended north, it cut through the graveyard. Soldiers from the War of Independence and the War of 1812 were dug up, along with the city's fourth mayor, merchants, shippers, bankers, and other notables and reinterred at Green Mount Cemetery.[27] Substantial three-story Victorian row houses rose all around. But that was in the 1880s and 1890s; now it was 1947. Faith Presbyterian was the first white church to surrender. It announced that it had bought four suburban acres along Loch Raven Boulevard, near Woodbourne Avenue. Three years later it moved, selling its old compound to Knox Presbyterian, a prestigious black church. About the same time, the nearby Bohemian and Moravian Presbyterian Church, a missionary offshoot of Faith, sold its sanctuary at Ashland and Washington, also to a black congregation. Whites were on the run.[28]

DESTABILIZING THE INNER CITY

Federal agencies and city hall conspired to destabilize the vicinity of Hopkins Hospital and the rest of Baltimore. That's not my opinion but a finding by federal judge Marvin J. Garbis in a 2005 landmark discrimination suit, *Thompson v. HUD*.[29] Government intentions may have been benign but the accumulated results were disastrous.

The most destructive tear in Baltimore's overall urban fabric was a 1944 proposal to dig an expressway through Howard Street, Baltimore's Fifth Avenue, just north of the leading department stores. The bulldozing plan came from Robert Moses, the legendary Manhattan powerbroker, who reshaped New York City by building expressways at the expense of public transit.

Baltimore hired him to unclog the east-west traffic congestion, one of the worst in the nation during the war.[30] Moses proposed a sunken expressway that would have barely skirted the Roman Catholic Basilica, the Walters Art Museum, and the Enoch Pratt Free Library (but destroyed the architectural harmony of Mount Vernon square) before continuing on an elevated path to Orleans Street, just blocks south of the Hopkins Hospital.

To clear the expressway's path on the west side, Moses proposed to raze some two hundred blocks and relocate some nineteen thousand residents, mostly black and poor. "Nothing which we propose to remove will constitute any loss to Baltimore," he assured. His sunken freeway never materialized. But over the next three decades, his Franklin and Mulberry Street alignment resurfaced in no fewer than nine plans. In 1960 the corridor was designated as the route of an eight-lane east-west expressway. Only 1.5-mile of intended highway—nicknamed the "road to nowhere"—was constructed after the city acquired and demolished swaths of row houses.

This destruction necessitated the resettlement of thousands of poor residents, who unsettled other fragile neighborhoods in the midst of racial change. Those included two northwest corridors, lower Reisterstown Road and Park Heights Avenue below Northern Parkway, which Jews, white Catholics, and recent black pioneer first-time homeowners abandoned after the 1968 riots when a lower socioeconomic class of African Americans began moving in. Most relocated to the county.[31] In East Baltimore, city hall began large-scale demolitions near Johns Hopkins Hospital about 1940. Not for roads. Instead, acres and acres of slums were cleared to make land available for the city's largest concentration of public housing.

Congress created public housing in 1937 as one of Franklin Roosevelt's New Deal initiatives. The program originally intended to serve the needs of the "submerged middle class," who were temporarily outside of the labor market during the Depression. Being selected to move to public housing was regarded as a badge of honor. The units were new and came with modern bathrooms and kitchens, even refrigerators. Rents were reasonable. Competition for units was keen. Preference was given to veterans' families. Tenant screening was tight, and only stable traditional families with jobs were considered. Spot checks kept the tenants on their toes.

In conformity with local traditions that meshed with federal policy, separate public housing was built for the races. That made no difference. Newspaper ads accused all "projects" of spreading "vile social diseases, tuberculosis, juvenile delinquency and mental ailments." One exhorted that "our school children and people should not and must not be subject to the dangers of a slum housing project in our community. The slum families will of necessity use the same public transportation facilities—street cars and buses—and the

same public schools."[32] Housing authorities in various cities ran the program
quite independently and according to local racial preferences. "There is little
doubt that local authorities in Baltimore seized the new federal tools and
resources to fulfill longstanding desires to effect a greater separation of the
races than previous history allowed," writes Arnold R. Hirsch, the University
of New Orleans urban historian.[33]

Baltimore's first public housing project opened in August, 1941. It was
the 688-unit Latrobe, located in the heart of the fading Irish stronghold of
Tenth Ward in the shadow of the Maryland Penitentiary and the separate City
Jail. Latrobe was built for whites. Two weeks later, public housing came to
the hospital's doorsteps, when the 393-unit Douglass Homes, named for the
Maryland-born slave and abolitionist, opened on Orleans Street. Two other
projects for blacks were constructed near the hospital. They were Somerset
and Lafayette Courts, the city's first high-rise project, totaling 1,225 units.
Saturation continued. Two additional projects--688-unit Perkins and 490-unit
Flag House Courts--were built for whites. Consisting of three eleven-story
towers, Flag was located on twenty-one acres next to Little Italy in the middle
of Lombard Street's nostalgic Jewish "Corned Beef Row," between Old
Town and Hopkins. These projects were filled with low-income occupants
and formed the highest concentration of public housing anywhere in the city.
No public hearings were held during their planning; all decisions were settled
in administrative negotiations between municipal authorities and the federal
government. There were hitches. In one case, the city acquired 275 houses
near Hopkins. More than a year later, at the peak of housing shortage, they
remained vacant while government bodies pondered what to do with them,
including how they should be segregated.[34]

The spanking new Lafayette Courts development, in 1955, made history as the first desegregated public housing project. Whites had no faith
in integrated living in its six eleven-story towers and seventeen low-rise
buildings—just four of Lafayette's 807 tenant families were white.[35] Other
whites, qualifying for low-interest mortgages through VA and FHA, deserted
public housing. "The distribution of federal benefits made it possible for
mostly white working-class people to move out of public housing, and contributed to a downward income shift in the public housing population after
the 1940's," writes historian Jennifer Amy Stoloff.[36] In many cities, public
housing became a minority program. At least it still strived for standards.
The rental market did not. A worsening slum kept creeping toward Hopkins.
Of 785 properties surveyed in 1954 in a twenty-four-block area around Gay
and Biddle—the intersection north of the hospital which Faith Presbyterian
abandoned—556 were "actively infested with rats"; others with bedbugs
and roaches. One hundred and seven houses had no inside toilet, only an

Baltimore Public Housing in the 1960s

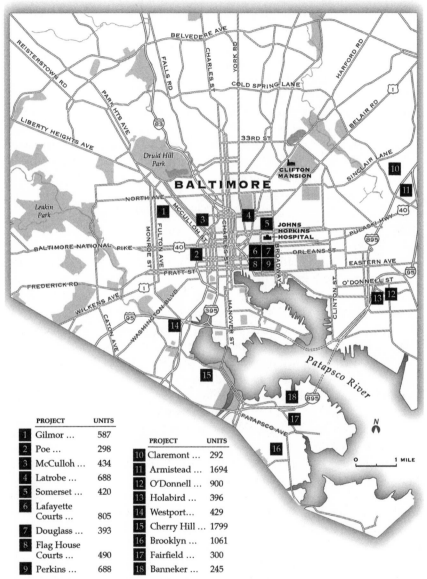

PROJECT	UNITS
1 Gilmor ...	587
2 Poe ...	298
3 McCulloh ...	434
4 Latrobe ...	688
5 Somerset ...	420
6 Lafayette Courts ...	805
7 Douglass ...	393
8 Flag House Courts ...	490
9 Perkins ...	688

PROJECT	UNITS
10 Claremont ...	292
11 Armistead ...	1694
12 O'Donnell ...	900
13 Holabird ...	396
14 Westport...	429
15 Cherry Hill ...	1799
16 Brooklyn ...	1061
17 Fairfield ...	300
18 Banneker ...	245

The Johns Hopkins Hospital vicinity contained the city's highest concentration of public housing projects.

Robert Cronan. Lucidity Information Design, LLC

outhouse; ninety-two had more than ten persons use a single toilet, and forty-five apartments had no sink or water supply. Inspectors counted 272 broken plumbing systems, 146 leaking roofs, 513 sagging floors, 835 worn, broken, or otherwise dangerous stairways.[37]

THE BALTIMORE PLAN

Frances Morton knew those numbers by heart. To her that slum represented an opportunity. She began an unusual urban experiment, a privately financed rehabilitation program that became known around the country as the Baltimore Plan. She was a Smith alumna who did graduate work at the New York School of Social Work and then spent two more years as a medical social worker at Hopkins. She studied twenty-one hundred "bad blocks" around the city and counted twenty-six thousand unsanitary outhouses in backyards. She founded the Citizens Planning and Housing Association to demand action. The political establishment responded to her cajoling. In 1941 the city council passed the Hygiene of Housing ordinance, one of the strictest such measures in the nation. The law empowered Dr. Huntington Williams, the city health commissioner, to take appropriate action if he found conditions "unfit for human habitation." The Hopkins man could even demolish houses, and did. When peace returned and material shortages eased, the city introduced new codes. Bathrooms and inside toilets became code requirements. A housing court was created to whip recalcitrant property owners into compliance. Meanwhile, the *Afro-American* newspaper continued organizing annual summertime "Clean Block" campaigns. Since 1935 thousands of children and adults were involved in prettifying and repairing hundreds of blocks. The winners received prizes and accolades were written up about them.

Back in 1933 the Joint Committee on Housing had recommended that Slum No. 1 be cleared of blacks, leveled, and then rebuilt for whites because its location was desirable and public transit good. Two decades later that was not what the Baltimore Plan hoped to do. Instead of moving settled residents out, it pledged to help families stay put and abate the slum conditions. This proved to be quite a task. Landlords owned 42 percent of housing; the rest belonged to individual families, whose median income was 20 percent below the citywide average. "Few were actually in dire poverty; the men were steady providers with year-round jobs in the steel mills or shipyards. Some were prosperous Negro families, to whom the outlying suburbs were still closed," Martin Millspaugh writes in *The Human Side of Urban Renewal*. Those homeowners felt targeted when the Baltimore Plan's crackdown ordered them to make and pay for costly repairs.[38] This is where the Fight-

Blight Fund stepped in. Since no conventional financial institutions lent to blacks, it arranged rescue plans in complicated situations.

James W. Rouse, a mortgage broker, headed the Fight-Blight Fund, which helped homeowners with repair costs and procedures. No taxpayers' grants were involved. Instead, the fund was supported by real estate interests, including the Mortgage Bankers Association and the National Association of Home Builders. Rouse was a tireless salesman who marketed the concept as a workable way to turn around declining neighborhoods without bulldozing them. The Baltimore Plan strategy caught the attention of the Twentieth Century Fund, which gave *Encyclopedia Britannica* money to do a twenty-minute film about the plan. NBC television showed it coast to coast (and you may watch it at https://www.youtube.com/watch?v=-52MmEdIqOU). Rouse is remembered as a visionary builder of suburban malls and such "festival market places" as Faneuil Hall in Boston and Harborplace in Baltimore. He created the new city of Columbia halfway between Baltimore and Washington. The Enterprise Foundation posthumously continues his commitment to neighborhood revitalization. In this book, Rouse will resurface several times.

Tellingly, Rouse's Fight-Blight Fund never exhausted its treasury. Money, it turned out, was less needed than good counsel. One couple was raising five children on a total income of sixty-five dollars a week from the husband's job at the Army's Edgewood Arsenal and the wife's janitorial chores. They were paying $43.72 a month on a G.I. mortgage. When the Baltimore Plan came to their neighborhood in 1951, they still owed $3,000 on the mortgage. "Then things started to go wrong," Millspaugh reported in 1954 in the *Evening Sun*. "There was illness in the family, and one child died." The couple could not keep up on installment payments for furniture, groceries, and oil. Their creditors obtained five judgments against them, totaling $485. The city's code enforcers told them to make repairs estimated to cost $230. That did it; the couple had enough. They threw up their hands and put the house on the market, figuring they could pay the judgments and overdue bills, and still have money for a down payment on another house. They found a buyer. But because they had not made the required repairs, the sale fell through. The real estate broker sued for his $200 commission; the couple was told their mortgage was going into foreclosure. It was a holy mess. Rouse's Fight-Blight fund straightened it out.

The Baltimore Plan began with high hopes in 1951; four years later it was in shambles. One cause was infighting. When Morton initiated the program, she wanted the health department to be in charge. And why not? Until 1963, when a separate housing department was finally created, all enforcement was done by the health department's housing bureau. Rouse quickly realized that did not work. Unlike Morton, he wanted a dedicated housing office and pressed the issue. When "Old Tommy" D'Alesandro sided with Morton, Rouse quit in frustration and moved on to other pursuits. His successor was Hans Froelicher, headmaster of the nonsectarian Park School, who would wed Morton several years later. But Rouse's was not the only departure. Yates Cook also quit. He was the plan's dynamic coordinator. After they left, bureaucratic and political interference increased. The city's own building inspectors, saying they were busy elsewhere, refused to work in the pilot area. This meant delayed inspections for electrical and plumbing work, much of which was belatedly deemed to be unsatisfactory. Big slumlords reckoned that it was cheaper to pay fines (and bribes) than make the ordered repairs on hundreds of units. They found allies among political appointees on the zoning board who showed little sympathy toward a community trying to turn itself around. The same with the liquor board. No fewer than fourteen liquor outlets existed in the pilot area; nevertheless, the liquor board granted new licenses.[39] "If a political machine could obtain the appointments of friends, it could hamstring the Baltimore Plan without resorting to open interference," Millspaugh writes. Thus the Baltimore Plan, the first private/public renewal effort, failed because of bickering and city bureaucratic sabotage.

A societal earthquake put the Baltimore Plan out of misery altogether.

When the plan was introduced, the unwritten assumption was that blacks did not have housing choices outside their segregated territories. That had been essentially true ever since 1910, when residential segregation was formalized. But soon after World War II, the U.S. Supreme Court reshuffled the deck. In the 1948 landmark case *Shelley v. Kraemer*, the justices declared that courts could no longer enforce racially restrictive covenants, which were used to exclude blacks and Jews from certain neighborhoods. Six years later, the justices ordered the nation's public schools to desegregate "with all deliberate speed." So controversial was this decision that most school systems delayed implementation. Baltimore was an exception, the only big city to desegregate in the fall of 1954, system-wide and without delay. The city that had pioneered legislated residential separation now became among the first to comply with school desegregation. It was an odd twist of history, with many contradictions and conflicts. Walter Sondheim, a forty-four-year-old vice president of the Hochschild Kohn department store, headed the school board. On the board he advocated school desegregation, but his department store would continue to discriminate for six more years. D'Alesandro accepted the board's vote. "This is a time for cool heads and calm considerations," he told the public as thousands of protesters demanded that blacks be barred from white schools. "Kick Them Out," one sign exhorted.[40]

Because of the long tradition of segregated neighborhoods, little changed at most schools that autumn. Near the yet-to-be-built Mondawmin Mall,

Gwynns Falls Parkway Elementary School was an exception. Its student population went from all white to 44.5 percent black. A stampede ensued. A sixth of the school's white pupils withdrew, and their families moved, resulting the next year in a student body that was 77.4 percent black. The school was in the Lake Ashburton vicinity, an area that had once been blanketed with covenants barring Jews. Following the typical West Baltimore pattern, white Christians ran when Jews moved in; now Jews fled when blacks appeared nary three decades later. Black strivers grabbed the houses whites vacated, calling one upscale stretch the "Gold Coast."

Access to desegregating neighborhoods killed the Baltimore Plan. By 1955, one year after school desegregation was implemented, many of the plan's "proven neighborhood leaders—who had fought the battles of zoning and liquor licenses in the city hall, and carried on the work of the Neighborhood Committee"—had given up and moved away from the pilot area. Now that they had alternatives, they relocated crosstown to the vicinity of Gwynns Falls Elementary. The departure of those strivers robbed the slum of its socioeconomic diversity and role models. Among those headed to the west side was a probation officer named Vernon Dobson, who became pastor of the historic Union Baptist congregation on Druid Hill Avenue and a significant figure in civil rights struggles.

In those days, Gwynns Falls Elementary adjoined Western High School. The nation's oldest all-girls public school had been located in a turreted brick fortress on McCulloh Street, but moved after blacks appeared. Now the school again was relocated for racial reasons. It ended up at Falls Road and Cold Spring Lane, where a black portion of the village of Cross Keys was demolished to create space for two schools—Western and Polytechnic—and an expressway interchange. Douglass, the one-time Colored High School, took over the Mondawmin campus.

U.S. Supreme Court rulings implicitly gave a green light to the dismantling of segregation in neighborhoods. Wherever black students appeared in numbers, near hysteria broke among residents who were not accustomed to blacks walking through their segregated neighborhood. The professional code of conduct of the National Board of Realtors, of which Baltimore was a founding member, forbade sales and rentals to blacks in white areas. Instead, speculators who were not realtors started systematically acquiring houses on the cheap from fleeing whites and selling them to blacks at double or triple. Once these "blockbusters" targeted a white neighborhood, they intentionally fanned panic in order to create listings and bring acquisition prices down. They knocked on doors, leafleted, and called at all hours to warn that blacks were coming and whites would be smart to sell while prices were still decent. "Did you hear about the rape?" a caller would ask,

whether one had occurred or not, just to drum up sales. Blockbusters operated on the margins of real estate. Some had a license, many did not because
the law was full of loopholes.

As I detailed in *Not in My Neighborhood*, speculators used every trick to
create listings. Manning-Shaw, the city's leading blockbuster of upscale individual homes, planted a dysfunctional black family on an all-Jewish block
in Ashburton. Joseph and Audrey Carter had eight children, ranging in age
from four months to twelve years. There was no heat or food in the house.
The children had no shoes, which prevented them from walking six miles to
school. Manning-Shaw was a pioneering firm, a partnership between Manuel
Bernstein (white) and Warren Shaw (black). Agents told anxious neighbors
that the Carters constituted a "pilot project." Meanwhile, an orange-colored
Day-Glo SOLD sign was erected on the Carters' lawn. That sign—and dozens of similar ones elsewhere in targeted neighborhoods—stayed there for
months after the sale, signaling that Manning-Shaw was in action and the
neighborhood's racial change was a done deal. Shaw saw blockbusting as his
civil rights mission to increase housing choices for his race. It was not his
problem if whites could not take it.

The more panicky whites became, the less speculators offered. They then
flipped the properties to house-hungry blacks. Such flipping occurred in the
Baltimore Plan area too. In 1955 one speculator acquired a row house for
$3,700, repaired it for an additional $1,900, and then sold it for $8,900, a re-
markably high price considering the neighborhood. Many speculators owned
building-and-loan associations or attracted investors who wanted to profit
from racial change.

Although blockbusters represented themselves as sellers, no actual sale
took place. Instead, they retained the deed, took a mortgage on the house
being bought on a rent-to-buy basis, and then relied on a peculiar, shady,
and exploitative instrument called the land installment contract, or renewable
ninety-nine-year lease, as Britain knows it. The essence of the arrangement
was that the speculator would continue owning the ground for which the
buyer would pay rent. During the war landlords used rent-to-buy arrangements as a tax dodge. They converted renters into contract buyers so that federal rent controls could be circumvented. Some speculators used strong-arm
tactics—including evictions—to persuade renters to sign on the dotted line.
Little changed for the buyers, except that the payments went up. However, as
titular owners, contract buyers became responsible for all repairs, including
retrofits that may have been previously ordered by city code inspectors but
not yet done. Few knew what they were doing. A 1963 contract stated: "It is
understood and agreed that the seller shall have the right at any time during
the life of the contract to do any repairs or improvements now or hereafter

required by law and add the cost of such repairs and improvements to the purchase stated in this contract."[41] The rules were onerous. Even one missed payment could make the buyer lose everything, including a new roof, or heating plant that he had paid for. There was no foreclosure, or a process for contingencies, just summary eviction. Despite these known pitfalls, families signed sweeping agreements.

In this lottery of life, blockbusters sold chances to eventual homeownership. Conventional financing was so difficult to obtain that before the 1968 riots two-thirds of all black real estate sales consisted of rent-to-buy schemes. Thousands of contract buyers made it, with sacrifices. Many others didn't. But for a long time, many African American neighborhoods on the west side exhibited an amazing stability. Its cause were families who had risked all and acquired their homes through rent-to-buy arrangements. Making the payments had involved so many balancing acts and sacrifices that they never wanted to relive that stressful experience. So they stayed in the "home houses," aging and retiring with their neighbors who also skimped on maintenance and repairs. Those who had the means broke out, hastening the spiral of slummification.

Chapter Eight

Mobtown in the 1950s

In June of 1952 a night watchman traced a foul stench around the Fish Market to a corpse, with four bullet holes in the head, rotting away in the locked trunk of a green sedan. The car had been ditched just a block away from the police headquarters and across the street from Little Italy, a working-class row-house neighborhood anchored by St. Leo's Catholic Church and spaghetti houses. Few mourned the fifty-four-year-old victim, Anthony Messina, a hoodlum who had sought refuge in Baltimore decades earlier after a notably gruesome upstate contract killing made New York too hot for him.[1] He was last seen taking a train north. Investigators deduced that he had been shot in Delaware inside a Cadillac originally stolen from a New York doctor, and then transferred to the sedan that transported the bloody mess to Baltimore.

The gruesome execution sent a warning—this is what happens to a hot-headed fool who disrespects Frankie Carbo, "America's unofficial boxing commissioner." The boxing journalist Budd Schulberg, who authored *On the Waterfront*, coined this title for Carbo, a Gambino gangster who lorded over professional boxing. Through the International Boxing Club, he controlled New York's Madison Square Garden, where his wife, under her maiden name, drew an astoundingly high salary for a woman, $40,000 a year. Through the club's top executive, Jim Nolan, Carbo fixed championship matches at the highest levels, and owned several top boxers outright, including Sonny Liston, the world heavyweight champ.[2] "Not every fight was fixed, of course, but from time to time Carbo and his lieutenants, like [Frank] Blinky Palermo in Philadelphia, would put the fix in," said Schulberg. "It was an open secret. All the press knew that fights were fixed."[3]

Carbo was born on New York's Lower East Side—in and out of juvenile institutions since age eleven. He was suspected of engineering the killing of Benjamin "Bugsy" Siegel, the celebrity gangster as good-looking as he was

lethal, and was charged with the slaying of big-time bootleggers Max Green-
berg and Max Haskell. This was just a partial list. With witnesses refusing to
testify, he routinely beat the rap. In Baltimore, where Sicilian relatives lived
in Little Italy, Carbo owned the premiere sporting venue, the Coliseum, a
dank and dreary forty-five hundred-seat shrine of pugilism in the then-white
Monroe Street area. (The New Shiloh Baptist megachurch now stands there.)
The Gambino family also had influence over the port and its unions.[4]

The Messina murder remained unsolved when James M. Hepbron became police commissioner three years later. He was Mr. Clean, a sixty-
four-year-old native of Chestertown on the Eastern Shore, who moved to
Baltimore as a kid, graduating from the City College High School and the
University of Maryland law school. He and his wife, a dance instructor,
lived in an ivy-covered cottage in the tree-shaded Cedarcroft section, near
the northern city-county line.[5] Erect, immaculately tailored, gray-haired,
and with an aquiline nose, he cut a distinguished figure. For more than three
decades he headed the Community Chest, a predecessor of United Way,
while at the same time serving as managing director of the Criminal Justice
Commission, a private law-and-order group with considerable political
clout.[6] Highly regarded nationally, he taught criminology at the Johns Hopkins Institute for the Study of Law. He established a reputation as an expert
on organized crime. In 1951 Maryland's Senator O'Conor, chairing a U.S.
Senate probe into organized crime that later became known as the Kefauver
committee, designated the criminologist as his right-hand man.[7] Among the
first things Hepbron learned as police commissioner was that Carbo was the
main suspect in Messina's murder.

Baltimore's ancient nickname, Mobtown, had been due to brawling political and firehouse gangs that caused havoc and mayhem but disappeared
around the Civil War. Organized crime activity now gave a new meaning to
the tag. "It was always my understanding that the Mafia crime lords decreed
Baltimore to be an 'open city,' where, roughly speaking, Jews did gambling,
blacks did drugs and Italians did a little bit of everything," explained Stephen
H. Sachs, a federal prosecutor in the 1960s.[8] In Carbo's case, by tapping telephones, detectives accumulated hours and hours of intercepts that implicated
the gangster and his goons. The case was just about sealed. Just about, except
that Carbo had not yet been taken in for questioning and, possibly, arrest. As
Chief Inspector Fred L. Ford detailed the case, the commissioner listened in
silence, letting it all sink in. It was an awkward moment, the moment of truth.
"I guess you have my voice on those tapes, too," he said tentatively.[9]

Ford nodded. Over the years recording devices had indeed captured Mr.
Clean repeatedly talking familiarly with Carbo. He was also recorded with
Benjamin Magliano, Carbo's enforcer in Baltimore. Better known as "Fat

Benny" Trotta, the convicted draft dodger was a made man, a member of the Gambino family's "Baltimore Crew," which had been in the killing business since the 1920s.[10] He was another suspect in the Messina murder. A partner of his in a boxing club, "Big Sam" Zannino, took Messina on his fateful last ride to a New York–bound train at Pennsylvania Station. After that, Zannino was never seen again; police assumed both were liquidated on orders from Carbo.

As a lawyer, Hepbron had been carrying water for organized crime at least for the previous decade. He defended Fat Benny in the draft-dodging case and, after the hood returned from prison, got him a job at Bethlehem Steel—but Fat Benny found working for the city highway department more rewarding. They stayed in touch, with Hepbron repeatedly visiting Fat Benny's home and his friends' hangouts. Hepbron's usefulness greatly increased in 1953, when he was made a commissioner on a three-man board that advised Governor Theodore R. McKeldin on all paroles in Maryland. He was so corrupt that he saw nothing wrong with arguing his private clients' cases on the board. He interceded on behalf of Carroll "Cappy" Goldstein, an all-around hoodlum and accused white slaver. Next Hepbron took care of a problem for Louis Comi, a Little Italy numbers and vending-machine racketeer. He visited local and federal judges, hoping to sway them. On behalf of Fat Benny, he and Dr. Frank L. Marino appeared before the Federal Parole Board in Washington. It was quite a spectacle: Mr. Clean and Marino, the mobster's physician and treasurer of the winning Baltimore mayoral campaign of then-judge J. Harold Grady, a former FBI agent and top prosecutor, asking lenience so that the gangster—described in raw FBI files as a "companion" of Mayor Thomas D'Alesandro Jr., a former congressman—could get a liquor license on The Block.[11] Fat Benny got his pardon. Soon thereafter Hepbron went to a Turkish bath downtown. That was his lunchtime routine. "After the bath I lie down for a while in a little cubicle. Then I sleep for twenty minutes or half an hour. It's very invigorating, gives you new energy to go through the day."[12] On that particular day a stranger approached him and said, "It's nice of you to be willing to help a friend of mine, Benny Trotta." The stranger turned out to be Frankie Carbo. That was the beginning of a beautiful friendship.

We know all this because the Baltimore delegation in the Maryland Senate eventually launched a probe into Hepbron, exercising an oversight role it had because of the police department's previous scandals. Hepbron was politically connected, always had been. Then-Governor McKeldin, a Republican, appointed him to the parole board, where he advanced from an ordinary member to chairman. In becoming the chief of Baltimore's twenty-two-hundred-member police force, Hepbron took a $2,500 pay cut, quite a bit of bread in those days. So from the beginning there were whispers. After a few years, when allegations multiplied, a city grand jury was convened to investigate. It said it ran out of time. Then its jurisdiction was challenged. Legislators eventually managed to hold hearings, mostly without his cooperation. Although sworn testimony was taken, it was not a trial, leaving successor Governor Tawes, a Democrat, to decide the case as the sole judge and jury. Tawes ruled that Hepbron was guilty of "poor judgment" but that allegations of misconduct were not proven. The governor left the compromised commissioner to serve for two more years, until 1961.[13] (The legacy of Tawes's own corruption was to bring down Vice President Spiro T. Agnew and Governor Marvin Mandel.)

We also know how the Messina murder investigation ended. Inspector Ford gave the newly minted commissioner summaries of the Carbo eavesdropping transcripts: "It was quite a big report. It gave the background of all racketeering in Baltimore—gambling, procuring of women, dice—all that." After reading, Hepbron pleaded naiveté. He promised to disassociate himself "from these people," saying that it was "very peculiar that people can throw sand in your eyes." At that point, homicide detectives were planning to pick up Carbo for questioning. But according to Ford, just when the mobster was to be taken in, the commissioner remarked that he had spent the previous evening with Carbo and Fat Benny. Ford and Clarence W. Forrester, another deputy chief, did not know what to do. They mulled over the conundrum for a few days. In the end, the two top commanders took the evidence to the city incinerator and tossed more than a hundred thousand wiretap tapes, along with most transcript summaries, into the blazing inferno. This made the bothersome case vanish, and Carbo, Fat Benny, and Hepbron could worry about other things. There was no public outcry when all this was revealed. Ford later had regrets. "We made a real mistake in 1955 in burning those wiretap tapes," he testified at the hearings that proved nothing, according to Governor Tawes.

All this happened before Facebook and tweets existed, or even live television news. The media still lived in the age of ink-stained newspapers; Baltimore had one morning paper and two evening dailies. Today, Hepbron never could survive relentless tweets and other coverage. Charles Whiteford's outstanding reporting in *The Sun*—including transcript excerpts—makes it difficult to see how he survived all the damaging evidence in 1959 either. Except that powerful interests wanted him to survive. "Hepbron Friendly with Figures in Underworld and Influenced by Them, Probe Hearing Is Told" screamed one two-deck banner headline on the front page of the staid *Sun*, the city's newspaper of record. Two detectives swore that in late 1956 they saw the commissioner and Carbo exit an elevator together at the Emerson Hotel in the company of two good-time girls from Fat Benny's Club Troc on The

Block. Hepbron strongly denied that particular allegation, but acknowledged extensive dealings with gangsters.[14,15]

Law enforcement agencies had extended professional courtesies to mobsters in the past. When Al Capone came to Baltimore's Union Memorial Hospital for syphilis treatment in 1939—after Johns Hopkins rejected him—a state police sergeant, with superiors' approval, hid the mobster on the second floor of his home near Druid Hill Park.[16] But never before had the Mob had a commissioner in its pocket. When promoters worked out a much-ballyhooed scheme to move televised boxing matches from New York's crime-ridden rings to Baltimore's Coliseum, the plan died a sudden death after a Manhattan official identified Fat Benny as Carbo's front as president of the Coliseum. A farce then ensued. Governor McKeldin sent Hepbron to New York to investigate, and ordered the boxing regulators to revoke Fat Benny's license.[17] After some interval Hepbron made an official recommendation that Fat Benny's boxing license be restored, as it was.[18]

Wiretaps of Fat Benny's telephones contained voices of policemen "asking help in getting promoted."[19] Many a cop accepted gratuities. That was how it had always been. Bakers gave free donuts, bar owners, drinks or a little something, and so on. All just to spread good cheer and to prevent misunderstandings.[20]

THE BLOCK

Organized crime activity centered on The Block on Baltimore Street. It was America's oldest continuing hotbed of harlotry, far older than Bourbon Street in New Orleans.[21] The Block illustrated how cities recycle. During the philanthropist Johns Hopkins's lifetime it was the heart of the financial district, and the starting-off point of stage coaches to Philadelphia and to Ohio. The chief cross street, Gay, contained several edifices built by Hopkins, including his ornate headquarters. All that legacy was destroyed in the fire of 1904; nothing survived. Among the rubble were all seventy revenue-producing commercial buildings that Hopkins Hospital inherited from the founder. The destruction nearly brought the hospital to its knees. The oil giant John D. Rockefeller emerged as saving angel. He covered the hospital's uninsured losses.

When the devastated area was rebuilt, the business core shifted some five hundred yards west to Hopkins Place, so named because Uncle Gerard once had a shop there. Later, streetcar lines intersected there at the doorsteps of main Howard Street department stores—Hutzler's, Hecht's, Hochschild Kohn's, and Stewart's—as well as such discount houses as Brager-Gutman's and Epstein's.[22] Nearby also was O'Neill's department store, favored by

Catholic families for confirmation dresses and good linens. The famous Miller Brothers restaurant served turtle soup, rockfish (a favorite of the FBI director J. Edgar Hoover) and elk that was slaughtered right on the premises, with select patrons invited to witness the ritual. Outside *The Sun*'s headquarters, a stone colossus with an impressive colonnade and baroque roofline, an illuminated news ticker drew hundreds of the curious, sometimes thousands. Then, beginning in the late 1950s, the whole area was demolished for Charles Center, a heroic effort by the Greater Baltimore Committee to reconstruct and revitalize downtown.

Hookers had plied their trade near the waterfront since early days. After the 1904 fire, a red-light district formed along a rebuilt stretch of Baltimore Street, near Gay. As strange as it may sound, the garish sin district's neighbors were the police headquarters and city hall. Italian mafiosi, Jewish gamblers, and thugs of assorted other ethnicities (except for blacks) shared the turf, plotting scams, bank heists, loan-sharking, striptease, prostitution, and an occasional contract murder. Those itching for high-stakes gambling could always find dice and card games. "Dates" were readily available. Overpriced ladies' drinks allowed groping in a dark corner, and a certain number of "champagne" bottles (and a hefty tip) bought a rushed romp in some seedy backroom. Pretty much any perversion was catered to, and ignored by the authorities, as long as "exotic" dancers on stage respected public morality by covering their nipples and pubic hair with "pasties," as required by law.

The Block was Baltimore. Whenever a ball team won a pennant, the whole town descended on The Block to celebrate. Even Roland Park made accommodations. The hoity-toity garden district excluded Jews (and blacks) of any standing in 1943, when a bar owner of Lithuanian descent, a Lutheran Pigtown native named Bettye Karl Mills, was able to buy a three-story light-yellow stucco mansion with two ionic columns supporting an elegant semicircle-shaped portico at 501 Somerset Road. She was a madam on The Block, who first married at twelve and later collected four more husbands. (It is said that some Roland Park fathers favored Bettye's girls for their sons' initiation.) In 1945, when *The Sun* hired a feisty "news hen," as women journalists were nicknamed in those day, the future U.S. maritime commissioner and Republican congresswoman, Helen Delich Bentley, moonlighted as Mills's night manager to supplement her paltry reporter's pay, which was lower than that of male colleagues.[23]

The Block was quite a place. At its peak, some seventy establishments held liquor licenses on six city blocks and spilled over to Old Town, on the other side of the Jones Falls, where cheap grog houses served the thirsty, a variety of sin bins—including Bettye Mills's—took care of the lusty, and where after-hours clubs gave losers one last chance to get lucky.[24] Another collection of sleazy venues clustered a few blocks away around Belair Market, the murdered Messina's stomping grounds on Gay Street. Among those was Cicero's, an early lesbian dive. With a live band, it was crowded with patrons of all persuasions and genders.[25] In the 1980s that area was bulldozed in the name of urban renewal. By contrast, The Block lingered on.[26] It shrunk and deteriorated, and real estate values plummeted. The Anglican Sisters of the Poor, it was discovered, was landlord to the biggest pornographic bookshop and a Catholic group rented to a girlie bar. Lawyers explained that the inherited properties did not produce any income and that the religious organizations were hanging on to them in hopes that the city would buy them for urban renewal. That did not happen.[27]

Aside from the Johns Hopkins institutions and The Block, Baltimore was nationally known for the Pimlico racetrack. It was America's second-oldest track, after New York State's Saratoga, and home to the Preakness Stakes, second jewel in the racing crown of events each spring. Horse racing was a big gaming sport in those days; *Life* magazine declared it to be "the most gigantic racket since Prohibition." While nineteen million Americans headed for baseball games, an estimated twenty-six million went to the tracks. Among other gambling gambits, racetracks fueled the illegal lottery industry, which was popularly known as numbers or policy. Results from Pimlico and other racetracks determined the winning combination. Newsstands, bootblack stands, barbershops, dry cleaners, beauty parlors, pool halls, and corner grocery stores took bets, and a "numbers man" could be found in practically every tavern. Some preachers' popularity was based on the belief that they gave "good numbers."[28]

It was well documented that organized crime controlled the racing industry and the attendant numbers rackets, in which local operators "laid off" bets with out-of-town syndicates in order to diminish their exposure to losses. Yet J. Edgar Hoover on many Saturdays left the "SOG"—or "the Seat of Government," as he modestly called his FBI headquarters in Washington—to take a one-hour ride to Pimlico in a bulletproof limousine with his partner, Clyde Tolson, an assistant FBI director. To satisfy news photographers, he made an obligatory appearance at two-dollar windows, while agents placed bigger bets for him out of sight. He received tips about "a sure thing" from the Mob-friendly gossip columnist Walter Winchell and from Frank Costello, a big-time New York gangster, who once sighed: "Hoover will never know how many races I had to fix for those lousy ten-dollar bets."[29]

Numbers fed corruption. As early as 1893, the *Baltimore News* reported that the racket existed as a privilege of the reigning Democratic political machine, which also ran the police department. Bookmakers employed two thousand runners and netted a couple of hundred thousand dollars every day in today's money. Of the turnover, 25 percent was used for expenses (including paying off corrupt cops), and 10 percent for payouts, leaving a staggering 65 percent as profits for the backers. How reliable those figures are is anyone's guess. But in later years, particularly during the vicissitudes of Prohibition and the Great Depression, numbers were in great demand as antidotes to hopelessness, requiring generous protection payoffs to the lawmen. Just like bootleg liquor. Still, in the 1950s, numbers was a big racket that united hoodlums of various ethnicities in alliances with policemen, political clubs, and neighborhood taverns, where the Mob had jukeboxes, cigarette vending machines, pinball games, coin-operated pool tables and shuffle boards, and where stolen goods were sometimes fenced.[30] Many a tavern, in fact, was acquired with loans from the Mob. "The experience of the City of Baltimore in alliance of officers with the gamblers was not different from that of Chicago, New York, New Orleans and the other great cities of the Republic," the jurist John D. Lawson wrote.[31]

IT'S ALL POLITICS

Among big, white numbers kingpins was Isaac "Ike" Sapperstein, who first made headlines as a thirteen-year-old urchin when he stole twelve penknives from a department store with an associate, ten-year-old Billy Landsman, who snatched five. Sentenced to the Maryland School for Boys, the two grew up in crime and mayhem.[32] At twenty-two, Sapperstein killed a fellow gang member's girl by throwing her out of a speeding car for resisting his advances; he served five years. That was only one of several killings tied to this onetime boxer known as "Kid Wendell."[33] Cappy Goldstein was another scoundrel of note. He was a member of the liquor board commissioner Irvin Kovens's Democratic organization, which placed him as a state racetrack inspector and made his wife a stenographer at the liquor board.[34] Hepbron had defended Goldstein on the parole board. The commissioner testified that he repeatedly received information from the thug about "good" cops and those who "are stepping on our toes," as a wiretap put it. He confirmed that at Goldstein's say-so he transferred officers, including a lieutenant, from The Block to the Siberia of the Southwestern District. His private secretary testified that Goldstein called the commissioner several times a week on an unlisted private line.

Kovens was a rising political godfather. He ran an installment-plan furniture store on West Baltimore Street, near Hollins Market, where he could be seen with his trademark cigars, mostly unlit. From there salesmen fanned to black neighborhoods to sell furniture on payment plans and then knocked on doors every week to collect. Behind that mundane facade stood a connected man. His wife's kin were Hoffbergers, Jewish princelings who owned the National Brewing Company and the Orioles. Another relative manufactured vending machines. Through Jimmy Hoffa, the president of the International Brotherhood of Teamsters, the Furniture Man had contacts with the Mob. He owned West Virginia's Charles Town racetrack with the jailed Teamster boss's daughter, a federal judge. Together with the Teamsters' pension fund, he controlled much of the Caesar's Palace gambling casino in Las Vegas.[35] His brother, Cal Kovens, was a big Miami builder with even stronger ties to Jimmy Hoffa and the Mob, which paid a ransom for his early release from a federal prison where he was in for fraud. The price tag? A $50,000 contribution to President Richard M. Nixon's reelection campaign. That's how things worked in simpler days.[36]

As a Maryland political kingmaker, the Furniture Man was famous for his loose-leaf binder of 125 names. It was a money tree he could shake to raise quick cash for political purposes because each person on the roster was good for perhaps ten more contributors. He assured officials he elected that he wanted nothing in return, except kindness to his friends and understanding to strangers he was trying to help. He would lift Vice President Spiro T. Agnew, mayor and governor William Donald Schaefer, and the house speaker and governor Marvin Mandel to the pinnacle of their varied careers. Like Mandel, he would end up in prison.[37]

In his quest for dominance, the Furniture Man elbowed out an older political rival, Jack Pollack. Pollack was a bootlegging enforcer who got his break from hoodlum life in 1933 when Governor Albert C. Ritchie appointed him to regulate boxing on the State Athletic Commission.[38] With the two other members living in faraway counties and seldom attending meetings, he effectively ran the commission with Jack Cohen, the executive secretary, who was a stalwart of his Trenton Democratic Club and a former first baseman on its celebrated softball team. The Easterwood Boys team was Pollack's pride. Players came from row-house streets of Jewish needle-trade workers, carpenters, and roofers and sported such nicknames as Coddie, Dodgie, Binch, Moocher, Boogie, Schnickles, and Yoodle. They toured regionally and were written up in out-of-town newspapers. Their coach added to Pollack's luster as a magician who could fix anything. He was David "Dutch" Baer, chief of delinquent collections at the Internal Revenue Service.

For more than two decades, Pollack controlled votes in the then-majority Jewish Fourth District, where he lived at 2306 Anoka Avenue in an ordinary-looking porch-front row house that had marble floors inside. When racial change came, he tried to stem the tide. He subsidized the rents of Jews who agreed to move to the district. Still, the exodus swelled. A 1962 canvass of his home district revealed that one-third of voters on the rolls no longer lived there, and seventeen were dead. They were his voters.[39]

As his day job, Pollack sold insurance. Many politicians—including Old Tommy D'Alesandro—favored that line of business because those wanting consideration didn't have to be sold on protection. Pollack had a price list.[40] The understanding was that if he got someone a city job, the first year's pay went to him. A document in the Baltimore Jewish Council's files says he gave all the Jews a bad name. Still, he was an important change agent because he opened doors to the Jews in the municipal government and, as a consequence, in banking, the legal profession and private-sector professional offices as well, all of which were devoid of Jews. "His entry into public life gave Baltimore's unorganized Jewish population a sense of political identity and a powerful vehicle for winning recognition in government," Laurence Stern wrote in the *Washington Post*. Keeping blacks at bay was the glue.[41]

Pollack derived much of his clout from his friendship with Old Tommy. They were practical men. Once, Pollack wanted to land someone in a city job.

"What can he do?" the mayor asked.

"Well, he really can't do anything," said Pollack.

"Good, then we don't need to break him in."[42]

Pollack spent much time in Florida. One day a relative was killed in a shoot-out. To make things right for surviving children, a go-between approached Ettore "Eddie" Coco, the Lucchese family boss, demanding restitution. The mafioso declared that if Pollack ever as much as showed his mug again in Miami, "I'll send him back in a cigar box."[43] Pollack skirted trouble in Baltimore as well. In 1963 police questioned him about an attempt to kill a political rival, Verda F. Welcome, America's first black woman state senator. She was struck by two bullets and wounded in a drive-by shooting outside her office. He went unscathed but his black state delegate, Ernest Young, was among those charged with the failed assassination. He was acquitted; two allies went to prison.[44]

Underworld life had risks. Before World War II, one black numbers kingpin counting profits was gunned down inside his Druid Hill Avenue Democratic club. He was Wallace Smith, who briefly inherited the franchise when his more famous brother died of old age. Thomas R. Smith was a real-life Uncle Tom, Baltimore's "black King," according to the *New York Times*. For five decades, from the 1890s onward, he rigged elections for the white-supremacist Democrats. He did whatever was needed to minimize the impact of blacks who still overwhelmingly voted for the party of Lincoln. He paid them not to vote. He took them out of town on boat excursions on election day. Once he was caught stuffing a ballot box. His "record shows that he has given a valiant service for the 'white man's party,'" *The Sun* wrote. He was richly rewarded. "Not only does he run one saloon himself, but he is interested more or less directly in nearly a dozen of others, in some cases owning the places outright and in others merely selling the supplies to the keepers."[45]

In the lobby of Smith's twenty-six-room hotel was his shrine. Clustered around a life-sized photo of Joe Gans, the great lightweight boxer and Baltimore native, were his protectors—the white Democratic bosses John S. "Frank" Kelly, John J. "Sonny" Mahon, and Senator Millard Tydings. Completing the collection was a bust of boss Kelly, nicknamed "Slot Machine" and "the King of the Underworld."[46] Twenty-four-year-old Little Willie Adams succeeded the Smith brothers in 1938. A country boy from North Carolina, he was fifteen when he moved to the big city. The very next year saw him selling numbers and making deliveries on his bicycle for Kovens's parents, Russian immigrants who owned a neighborhood store, initially on the east side.[47] In just a few years, the high school dropout became so successful that Philadelphia mobsters attempted to take over his Lucky Number syndicate. They firebombed his base, Little Willie's Tavern at Druid Hill and Whitelock. He fought back, living up to his nickname that was derived from the Edward G. Robinson gangster movie *Little Caesar*.

Adams wanted his Lucky Number syndicate's men and women to be as inconspicuous as possible. He drove a modest Buick himself, instead of a flashier car, and expected everyone else to do the same. He was another Tom Smith, except that when civil rights battles came, he financed lawsuits against segregation and bailed out protesters. He owned taverns and clubs through front licensees, with protection bought from politicians and police. Without ever spending a night in jail, he remained the undisputed black numbers king until about 1950. He then parceled out the operation to friends, went legitimate, and became the first truly important African American businessman in the city.[48]

Adams addressed his friend as Mr. Kovens, whereas the latter called him Willie. Their families invested together, owned real estate and a suburban liquor store together, backed the same candidates and collected rewards of patronage. Kovens even invited Willie to join his Teamster buddies in the Caesar's Palace gambling venture, but the latter, much to his later regret, declined. Adams's wife, Victorine, a former school teacher, was the first elected woman of any color on the city council; her Woman Power, Inc., was still training future leaders sixty years later. She gave lessons in social graces at Charm Centre, her dress shop on Pennsylvania Avenue and one of the few places that allowed black women to try on the latest fashions; previously they had to travel to Philadelphia or New York to do that.[49] Adams once invited me to their home near Lake Ashburton. The "maison," as the *Afro* called it, was a big but unremarkable brick house on a small lot a block from the Ashburton reservoir; the living room was decorated with Japanese touches. They and a daughter were the first blacks to move to the Jewish neighborhood; Kovens arranged the deal.[50]

The police department introduced two significant innovations during Hepbron's six-year tenure. A tactical squad was formed to respond to emergencies. After reading a newspaper story, Hepbron also borrowed the K-9 dog unit idea from London and hired a former Scotland Yard sergeant to train the department's German shepherds. From Birmingham to Selma, many southern cities came to visit and copied the idea, later to sic dogs on civil rights demonstrators.[51] In general, Hepbron's force was full of rogues who did whatever they pleased. His men routinely disregarded wiretapping laws, systematically monitored phones illegally, and in some cases did so after a judge had denied an application for a tap.[52] Another hallmark of the Hepbron command were raids in which police planted incriminating evidence and booked suspects on trumped-up charges simply because someone wanted them out of circulation. In 1957 a squad raided an Auchentoroly Terrace basement apartment across from Druid Hill Park where a handful of young black businessmen and some ladies were watching a boxing match on television and gambling. Among those arrested was Charles Thurgood Burns, a numbers backer, and the sausage manufacturer Henry G. Parks, both close associates of Little Willie Adams. A passing motorist, Philip Taylor (who just happened to be in numbers) was dragged from a car to the raided premises and booked on made-up charges to bolster the case.

Burns, a first cousin of the future Supreme Court justice Thurgood Marshall, pursued the case doggedly even after he was convicted. A Douglass High School and Morgan football player, he told me that his parents wanted him, too, to go to law school but he chose the fast life instead. He took over much of Adams's numbers business and bought three hundred-acre farm in White Hall, Baltimore County, with a hundred head of pure Holstein cattle, three tractors, and two trucks. He later operated the now-defunct Super Pride supermarkets, which at one point was the largest black-owned grocery chain in the nation.

Burns had served two years in prison when lawyers established that cops had falsified evidence to "get" him. When that was confirmed, there was hell to pay. One sergeant committed suicide.[53]

That same year mobsters complained about "pansies" invading The Block, and police raided a gay bar, Pepper Hill, on Gay Street. Officers seized 162 male and female patrons, each of whom was handcuffed and taken to the nearby police headquarters to be shamed with an overnight stay. Among the arrested—just for being in the bar—were numerous Washingtonians; most charges were dropped. Amid a political storm, Hepbron blamed the mess on underlings, saying he was not in day-to-day command. By then his No. 1 deputy was Inspector Forrester. The former FBI instructor became a fall guy and went to prison, as did Captain Hyman Goldstein, of the rackets division. Among other crimes, Forrester was convicted of operating a whorehouse near the Pimlico track with Albert Weinstein, who owned the Diamond Cab Associates taxi company, the city's largest, and also ran a gambling den. The latter got probation.[54]

SEGREGATED SIN

Before television, suburbanization, desegregation, and urban renewal killed them, several sin districts existed around the city. Pennsylvania Avenue was the unrivaled center of black carousing, part of the "Chitlin' Circuit" touring itinerary that stretched from Harlem's legendary Apollo all the way to roadhouses in Dixie. Pretty much everything was available: jazz, vaudeville, comedy, gambling, foxy ladies, and, still on a tiny scale, reefer and heroin.[55] "Sporting tonight, sir?" was the come-on. This is how a regular described the scene: "Every night on the Avenue is Halloween, and Saturday is Mardi Gras." Little Willie owned several clubs through front licensees and booked national talent. Visiting big names in jazz and rhythm and blues often also gigged at Carr's Beach, his African American amusement park in Annapolis which catered to the whole region between Delaware and Washington and had legal one-arm bandits. Radio station WANN broadcast live from Carr's Beach.[56]

In the segregated city, the Avenue vicinity was the black hub, location of professional offices, trailblazing entrepreneurs, and "colored" hotels where black ballplayers stayed because downtown hotels refused them. The bulk of businesses, however, was in white hands. Scattered white families also remained on side streets, but social interactions between the races were kept to a minimum because police raided private homes in search of "interracial whoopee houses." Hundreds were rounded up in such raids. In 1930 two white couples were arrested in the Dolphin Street apartment of Mrs. Eva Moody, "a well known church worker" who was black, after complaints of interracial dancing.[57]

Overall, Jim Crow was much in evidence. Pennsylvania Avenue retailers served blacks, unlike the big downtown department stores, but many restaurants catered only to white shoppers and storeowners, dispensing takeout orders to blacks at the back door. Tellingly, the No. 1 black restaurant was not on the Avenue but on Division Street, near Provident Hospital and the elite Druid Hill Avenue residential areas of Marble Hill and Sugar Hill. It was

Sess's, famous for its fried chicken. "All of the stars from the Royal Theater used to go there for dinner—Pearl Bailey, Billie Holiday, Sarah Vaughan, Dinah Washington. To say nothing of a heavy contingent of black doctors, lawyer and business types," recalled one competitor.[58]

Pennsylvania Avenue[59] attracted crowds of white shoppers because neighborhoods above North Avenue had not changed racially yet and contained the city's largest concentration of aged Jews, working-class renters who had gravitated there from Old Town. Among white-owned businesses was a slaughterhouse founded in 1868 by a German immigrant, a great-great grandfather of longtime Maryland politician Charles "Dutch" Ruppersberger. The city-operated Lafayette Market was an Avenue chief attraction. It was a horn of plenty, surrounded by specialty vendors, such as Covington's, which took telephone orders for chicken, ready for pickup. Nearby were discount department stores and a plethora of other businesses. Then in 1953, a monster blaze destroyed Lafayette Market in the wee hours. All of its 219 stalls were destroyed; some seventy-five nearby businesses were wiped out and dozens of residents displaced. Then the next year, nine replacement stalls were swept by fire.

"It was a neighborhood killer," remembered real estate man James Crockett, a firefighter who eventually became a member of the city's historic preservation panel. The fires were part of a rash of suspicious blazes at municipal markets and coincided with the spread of commercial supermarkets. The famous Lexington Market was destroyed in March 1949; Old Town's Belair Market was partially obliterated in May 1951, and Federal Hill's Cross Street Market was incinerated two weeks later. None was solved.[60]

In the midst of this calamity, the municipal liquor board, on which Irv Kovens sat, delivered the final blow to Pennsylvania Avenue as a destination where the races mixed. The action was another illustration of how governmental decisions earmarked areas for racial turnover. For a long time, the liquor board had licensed all outlets to serve only a specified race. Places with a "white" license could only serve whites and "black" licensees—who often were white—could only serve African Americans. Or were supposed to. At the peak of the Avenue's popularity in the early 1950s, many black bars and clubs bent the rules, serving drinks to all comers.[61] Now the three-member liquor board read the riot act. It threatened to take away the license of any black bar that served whites. This happened just months after school desegregation was implemented. A seventeen-block stretch of Pennsylvania Avenue boasted no fewer than fifty-four liquor licenses issued for "black" drinking. As soon as the crackdown began, more than a dozen remaining whites-only liquor outlets applied to be relicensed to serve blacks only, including bars that quickly became fronts for package goods stores. They knew the area was going all black. Such classification changes could tear apart social fabric because bars, with their television sets and air-conditioning, served as communal club basements and often sponsored Little League or bowling teams. Without drinking holes for their race, remaining longtime white residents abandoned the old neighborhood. They moved on to better and more modern housing in a socioeconomic recycling. White patronage at Avenue retail stores plummeted, and white nightlife slummers headed elsewhere.

MOUNT VERNON AND STATION NORTH

Among white nightlife areas, Mount Vernon also was changing. The high and mighty—the B&O Garretts and other friends of Johns Hopkins—had lived in mansions on the prestigious Mount Vernon Place, where a colossal Doric column soars as a tribute to George Washington. At the time, the lands northward still belonged to the vast Belvedere estate of John Eager Howard, a Revolutionary War hero and statesman, and were so wooded that the main drag, today's Charles Street, was called Forest Street. Eventually trees were cut down, and fields subdivided into fashionable addresses. The development of those lands kicked off a class and economic rotation that is a hallmark of all American cities. As suburbanization gained strength in the 1910s, the mansions and huge stone row houses went out of vogue. One-family edifices were cut up into offices, shops, and apartments. Mount Vernon was losing its cachet.[62]

Mount Vernon circa 1950 straddled a territory that housed big insurance companies, advertising agencies, several hotels, including the posh Belvedere, the Medical Arts Building of doctors' and dentists' offices, and the Lyric opera house. Its Charles Street spine was a popular nightlife district that stretched from the Washington Monument beyond Pennsylvania Station to North Avenue, the one-time city border, which boasted movie palaces, a busy privately owned market hall, luxury-car showrooms, trendy restaurants, quality retailers, and WFBR, the city's oldest radio station. Alan Shecter witnessed that rotation. In the 1930s, when his family bought an old trolley car barn at 1717 North Charles, the cavernous edifice was a newsreel theater known as *The Times*. During World War II, the theater stayed open until 4 a.m. to accommodate Bethlehem Steel workers. It became a hundred-lane bowling alley, then the Famous Ballroom, a big-band venue, where Benny Goodman, Artie Shaw, Glenn Miller, and the Dorsey brothers, Tommy and Jimmy, played. After the area declined, the building went vacant for several years in the 1990s, then reemerged as the Charles, a premier multiscreen theater that contributed to Station North revitalization.[63]

Charles Street thrived in the 1950s as a shop and nightlife stretch because Pennsylvania Station was the gateway to North, South, and Midwest. Trains were still the chief mode of travel for business and pleasure.[64] Hotels and rooming houses dotted the station vicinity, giving it a transient character.[65] Dry cleaners were part of the service industry and so were girls. A striptease bar, *Les Gals*, was located where the University of Baltimore business school stands today on Mount Royal Avenue; it provided takeouts. In a nearby Charles Street stone row house with an inconspicuous entry through a busy Chinese restaurant, Pearl Williams kept a stable of wholesome fillies hot to trot; her husband, Frank, was a Pimlico habitué, a pimp corralling high rollers.[66,67]

Mount Vernon was a free-spirited place. Beaux-Arts and Queen Anne–style buildings on tree-lined, stone-paved streets accommodated a variety of shops, restaurants, supper clubs, cocktail lounges, and piano bars. They all did a brisk business in the age of Frank Sinatra. There was something for everybody, even homosexual hunting grounds on side streets.[68] Then there was the Peabody Book Shop, where shelves of serious tomes (which seldom sold) and bins of eclectic phonograph records concealed a beer stube that looked like the smoky, backroom speakeasy it was reputed to have been. Mencken had imbibed there, or so said Peabody and Maryland Institute students, who came by to see Dantini the Magnificent, a violinist and magician who was so prematurely hip that he wore a tux and sneakers, in the 1950s.

A few blocks north was the Club Charles, a trendy supper club that brought patrons from New York. Dean Martin, Tony Bennett, and Jackie Gleason entertained there. So did Lenny Bruce, the edgy social critic. His obscenities-laden stand-up routines attracted so much unwanted attention that his contract was bought out. Things had to stay orderly, under control—the Club Charles and many other night spots hid gambling dens with ownership ties to the Mob. Some openly laundered money. Chanticleer, a nightclub at Charles and Eager, sanitized cash by selling $3,500 money orders that were paid to nationally known bookmakers, according to the Kefauver commission.[69]

FUCKOLOGY

As sexual mores relaxed, The Block became smuttier and raunchier. Old characters disappeared, including Julius Salsbury, a racketeer known as "The Lord." Headed for prison on gambling conviction, the operator of the Oasis nightclub jumped bail, never to return. (Barry Levinson ended his *Liberty Heights* movie with that scene.) Some traditions persisted. Blaze Starr reigned as the striptease queen at her Two O'Clock Club. At fifteen she was Fannie Belle Fleming, a West Virginia hill girl working at a D.C. donut shop when her fiery red hair and well-developed personality—she measured 38-24-37—recommended her for a different line of work. As Blaze Starr, she would become Louisiana governor Earl K. Long's mistress, but before that she did a thing or two with John F. Kennedy when he was a congressman. "Very quick and very wild" was her take.[70]

Blaze Starr was still on The Block in 1969 when I came to Baltimore as a reporter for *The Sun*. There I was, a citizen of Finland, in an alien city working in a language not my own. I saw myself as a foreign correspondent, except that I reported on Baltimore to readers who were Americans. My first assignment was to cover cops. District stations, courts, firehouses, hospitals, and funeral parlors were my lodestars. When I first visited The Block, I saw a hot new attraction, "Million Dollar Baby." The stripper was Johns Hopkins's contribution, a medical curiosity who earned that name because that's how much it supposedly cost to fix a man to a woman.

Hopkins was among global pioneers in surgical gender reassignment. In 1965 the hospital became the first in the United States to perform genital reconstructions. Those surgeries grew out of a body of theoretical work that psychologist John Money and the husband-and-wife psychiatric team of Joan and John Hampson did on gender roles. They all were doctors, but not of medicine. In groundbreaking articles on intersex in the *Bulletin of the Johns Hopkins Hospital*, they argued that children's gender was determined not by biological factors alone but by how they were raised. What followed was one of the most controversial chapters in the annals of Johns Hopkins medicine.

Money was a New Zealander, a Harvard PhD. Pretty much everything he did was controversial, including a recommendation that physicians read pornography. He authored more than five hundred articles and some forty books on sexuality. A shameless self-promoter, he was the Aquarian Age's academic sex guru, a man who conducted university-sponsored public forums on sex in a conservative city. He coined pop terms like "fuckology" for his field of research and "lovemap" to describe a person's adoption of sexual identity which he likened to the early embrace of a native language.[71] "He was an expert in the problems of children born with genitals that weren't clearly male or female," wrote the journalist Jonathan Bor. "He believed that children could be assigned to either gender before the age of 3 and adapt happily, despite the influences of biology." So after a Canadian hospital horribly botched the medical circumcision of eight-month-old Bruce Reimer, the boy's parents took the baby to Hopkins. Money recommended—and the parents acceded—to have the boy castrated at the age of two. A vagina-like artificial cavity was then constructed, Bruce was dressed in girls clothes, renamed Brenda, and administered hormones. But instead of adjusting to the change, the subject rebelled. Bruce/Brenda felt like a freak. At fourteen she told her parents she wanted to be a boy again. She went through another excruciating series of operations and hormone treatments and was equipped with an artificial penis. She reemerged as David, got married, adopted two children, and earned his living scrubbing meat grinders at a Winnipeg slaughterhouse.

It wasn't a happy existence. David blamed Money for his misery. He claimed that instead of helping him, the researcher subjected him and his identical twin brother, who also had an abnormal penis, to harrowing psycho-anatomical experiments. More accusers came forward, bringing up Money's bisexuality and allegations about pedophilia. Even though Money no longer had any contact with David, he continued to describe the Bruce/Brenda treatment as a success. By the time David committed suicide, at thirty-eight, in 2004—two years after his identical sibling, Brian, killed himself—Money had gone senile. His reputation was in tatters. According to Dr. Harry Benjamin who was part of the research team, Money "was probably more responsible than any other individual for the decision that such an august institution as Johns Hopkins Hospital would . . . endorse sex-altering surgery in suitable subjects."[72]

The pendulum then swung back. The more controversial sex research grew, the less adventurous Hopkins became. In 1979 it stopped gender-change operations altogether. Dr. Paul R. McHugh, the psychiatrist, was in charge at the time. His much-debated view was that transgenderism was a mental disorder, sex change was biologically impossible, and that people who promoted sexual-reassignment surgery were promoting a mental disorder that often led to suicide.

Hopkins resumed gender-change surgeries in 2017.

Chapter Nine

Activism Builds Up

For a long time, Johns Hopkins was an ingrown place. Key posts were filled with lifers, who knew no other university and tolerated the shabby gentility of low pay and frugal classrooms as fair trade-offs for the prestige and freedom they enjoyed. G. Wilson Shaffer was an example. During his career he advised seven Hopkins presidents.[1] A Patterson Park boy and 1920 graduate of the City College high school, he turned down a pitching offer from the New York Giants. Instead, he studied economics and psychology at Hopkins, receiving his bachelor's in 1924 and doctorate in 1928, the year he was named chief psychologist at the Sheppard and Enoch Pratt psychiatric hospital. He joined his alma mater's faculty six years later as a lecturer in psychology and director of sports, who built up Hopkins as a lacrosse powerhouse. Two years later he created the Hopkins Mental Health Clinic and was its director until 1973, the year he retired after being dean of the Homewood schools for a quarter century. Two other deans received their degrees from Hopkins and never left.

Another constant was Ross Jones. The New Jersey native first visited the Homewood campus on a lark, liked it—including the quaintness of a corner of the Hopkins Club called Woman's Dining Room—got an undergraduate degree and stayed for forty-two years. When he retired in 1998 as a vice president, he had advised six presidents. He was the keeper of secrets, counseling five presidents of the trustees, the body that kept Hopkins afloat.

Then there was Chester Wickwire, a puckish man with a crew cut and a wry sense of humor. For half a century he was the university chaplain, although his initial employer was the Levering Hall Young Men's Christian Association, which also owned the Levering Hall building in the middle of the Homewood campus. This separation gave Wickwire rare independence and sometimes put him in conflict with the administration. He witnessed how activism by the 1960s engulfed the country's campuses in turmoil. Radicals occupied administration buildings, protesting the U.S. quagmire in Vietnam and wanting universities to get rid of their ROTC programs. Hopkins was a conservative school but it had an energetic chapter of Students for a Democratic Society (SDS), part of an informal coalition that became known as the movement and overlapped with other causes, including equal and civil rights, feminism, nascent environmentalism, and gay liberation. This was the groovy age of "roaches" being passed among friends, of LSD, magic mushrooms, psychedelic rock, and hedonistic sex without fear of pregnancy, thanks to the Pill.

During all that turbulence Wickwire served as a symbolic link to the founder, who had been a YMCA man himself.[2] Indeed, without YMCA there might not be the university, hospital, or medical school.

YMCA in Johns Hopkins's days was a mighty international movement of social and spiritual uplift to counter urban secularism and ill consequences of the Industrial Revolution. In 1870 Hopkins promised to make a $10,000 lead gift for the construction of a High Victorian Gothic YMCA edifice (which still stands) at Saratoga and Charles Streets, steps away from his city mansion, so that "the merchant, the mechanic, the professional man, Christian could unite" to "promote material interests, purity of life, integrity of character and the salvation of souls," as expressed by his friend John W. Garrett, a member of the YMCA board.[3] But the very day when he was to present that check, the Baltimore Copper Company in Canton announced staggering losses. Finding himself $300,000 poorer, Hopkins tried to weasel out of the commitment. Garrett, his partner in the venture, lost a similar amount. The latter was privy to the full extent of Hopkins's wealth. He pointed out to his friend that in the larger scheme of things their losses were minor, and talked the entrepreneur into honoring the pledge. Once they got started, they also discussed financial arrangements if Hopkins died. The very next day, Garrett hosted a four-hour dinner meeting between Hopkins and George Peabody, the London moneyman and onetime Baltimorean. Inspired by that session, Hopkins began working on his bequest.[4] He sought additional guidance from Enoch Pratt, another Unitarian originally from Massachusetts, an ironmonger who sold horseshoes and nails on a big scale and operated highly profitable bay boats for passengers and freight on the Chesapeake and its tributaries. Pratt was experienced in philanthropy and was working on creating the Baltimore city public library system that carries his name.

Johns Hopkins was a practicing Quaker, but his will contained no instructions about religion's place on the campus. In 1876 some rich and pious attendees got quite upset when the first buildings on Howard Street were dedicated without a benediction. "The university must be unsectarian," declared the main speaker, Harvard president Eliot, but not "irreligious." Three years later, Eugene Levering donated a YMCA building.[5] A Baptist, he was a banker, who formed the Baltimore Trust Company and United States Fidelity and Guaranty Company (USF&G), was among founders of the American Red Cross, and served as a trustee at Hopkins and Georgetown, the Jesuit school in Washington. Thanks to its degree of separation from Hopkins, Levering Hall "became a conduit through which much of the work of the university's Department of History, political economy and political science passed," the historian Jessica Elfenbein writes. "The partnership that resulted between Levering Hall, the Charity Organization Society [coordinating body led by Gilman] and the Johns Hopkins Hospital allowed YMCA to play a critical role in the making of modern philanthropy from 1880 to 1900, the impact of which was felt across the country for years to come."[6]

About faith at the hospital Hopkins's will was specific: "It is my special request that the influences of religion should be felt in and impressed upon the whole management of the hospital; but I desire, nevertheless, that the administration of the charity shall be undisturbed by sectarian influence, discipline or control." In 1896 Gilman—who would end his career as president of the American Bible Society—placed a donated statue, *Christus Consolator*, in the hospital's ornate Broadway rotunda. Carved from a single block of Carrara marble, the statue arrived by ship from Italy, then was placed on rollers and hauled up a steep hill from Fells Point to the hospital, where doors were taken off the hinges to fit it through. Three brick columns were built under the rotunda's marble floor to support the statue's weight. "The Great Healer," said Gilman, wrought "more wonderful cures than any physician or surgeon that had ever lived."

The glistening ten-and-a-half-foot statue was eugenically correct. It depicted Jesus as a Nordic man, being a replica of an 1820 sculpture by Bertel Thorvaldsen, which stands in Copenhagen's Lutheran cathedral.

CHET THE JET

Chet Wickwire came to the university the year after Herbert C. Kelman in 1952 declared war on status quo. Kelman, while working at Hopkins Hospital's Phipps psychiatric clinic, formed a chapter of the Congress of Racial Equality (CORE), which advocated nonviolent civil disobedience, the tactic that Gandhi had used to win India's independence. The timing was impeccable. Four years earlier the Supreme Court had outlawed the judicial enforcement of racially restrictive covenants. The court would soon bolster that antisegregation ruling by its school edict. Segregation began unraveling. "When I arrived in Baltimore, it was a completely segregated city but one that was ready for change," reflected Kelman, who was to become a legendary professor of social ethics at Harvard. He exuded the urgency of someone who had cheated death. As a youngster he escaped Vienna just before Hitler rolled in.[7]

CORE stands out in the annals of local civil rights activity. It burst into the activist scene through small but sustained sit-ins that redefined direct action and changed the downtown retail scene. It targeted symbols of white entitlement: Miller Brothers restaurant, Ford's Theater, the Lyric, and the whites-only lunch counters in the five-and-dime store district near Lexington Market that excluded blacks. "Before that period, the only eating places open to African-Americans in downtown Baltimore were the Greyhound bus station, railroad stations and the YMCA," veteran activist Charles Logan remembered. "The first initiative was to change the racial policies of Kresge's, Woolworth's, Schulte's, McCrory's and Grant's." [8]

Leafletting was enough to convince Kresge's and Woolworth's to lift the race bar. Schulte's followed, then McCrory's. Grant's held out. So in the hectic spring and summer of 1953, activists targeted the store for sit-ins. The tactic did not work, and it took until the following May for Grant's to desegregate. The chain surrendered nine days after an activist stockholder raised the Baltimore situation on the floor of the annual stockholder's meeting in New York, which itself was picketed. The labor leader Bayard Rustin and nonviolent activist James Peck participated in negotiations to settle the dispute.

The CORE emblem depicted a black hand clasping a white one. Indeed, nonracialism was a founding principle of the organization which, like NAACP, was midwifed by whites. CORE's roots were in the Fellowship of Reconciliation, a Quaker-influenced pacifist direct-action group formed during the European bloodbath of World War I. The small Baltimore chapter's "success lay in its ability to recruit from a broad spectrum of people," writes CORE historian August Meier, who was a Morgan professor. "The membership of about twenty-five or thirty was unique, for in addition to the usual types of middle-class whites and Negroes, its members included a black minister and his wife, and a significant contingent of upwardly mobile black trade unionists who were active in the International Garment Workers Union."

In its glory days in the sixties, the Baltimore CORE organized sit-ins and demonstrations to desegregate some fifty restaurants along U.S. Route 40, the main highway link toward New York. Those actions garnered headlines around the world because among those refused service due to their skin color were many Third World diplomats and dignitaries motoring between the United Nations and Washington; the State Department was constantly apologizing for discrimination in the Land of the Free. Now students not only from Baltimore but also from Ivy League schools bused in to join the action. CORE also was a main sponsor of a campaign to desegregate Gwynn Oak Amusement Park, owned by the Price brothers, one of whom was the president of the city council. The decade-long campaign began as a protest to Gwynn Oak inviting foreign embassies to its International Day, while barring blacks. Demonstrators came from all over the country. They represented various races, ethnicities, and religions. Catholic priests marched with rabbis, Protestants, and Baha'i activists. Hundreds were arrested, including Wickwire. On August 28, 1963, the same day Martin Luther King Jr. delivered his "I have a dream" speech, Social Security Administration supply clerk Charles C. Langley Jr. was able to perch his eleven-month-old daughter, Sharon, on a wooden carousel horse at Gwynn Oak. A victory was won. Ten years later the park was gone, wiped out by a tropical storm, changing entertainment preferences and prejudices.[9]

Wickwire was an unusual man. Raised as a Seventh-day Adventist in Colorado, he was born on the Nebraska prairie, where his ancestors had trekked in Conestoga wagons from New England. He earned his bachelor's and PhD at Yale, financing his studies by selling spring-mounted rocking horses known

The singer, actor, and activist Paul Robeson (left) lends support to efforts to desegregate Ford's Theater; Paul Henderson photo.
Courtesy of the Maryland Historical Society, Image #HEN.00.A2-178

as Wonder Horse (which became the title of his 2000 poetry collection). Polio interrupted his studies at Yale, and he was hospitalized for thirteen months. An acquaintance was connected to Eleanor Roosevelt; the First Lady got him a place for rehabilitation at Warm Springs, Georgia. For the rest of his life he could be recognized from his cane or crutches, which he employed so adeptly that he became nicknamed Chet the Jet. He was a humanist, a religious universalist, ordained by the United Church of Christ. He was also a political progressive, who used his bully pulpit to preach friendship with the Soviet Union (even after he was arrested in the Crimea for distributing leaflets against nuclear weapons deemed to be anti-Soviet), and support for Central America's anti-imperialist movements. He brought newsworthy speakers to the campus, including Daniel Ellsberg, the civilian military analyst who leaked to the press a top-secret Pentagon study about the Vietnam War that President Nixon tried to suppress.

During many of those years, President Dwight D. Eisenhower's kid brother headed Hopkins. Milton S. Eisenhower only had a BA from the state university of his native Kansas. But by the time he came to lead Hopkins in 1956, he had left a strong imprint as president of two major state universities, his alma mater and Pennsylvania. He was an educational statesman, whose good counsel several occupants of the White House sought. He arrived in Baltimore only to find out that Hopkins was about bankrupt. "It was pitiful," he remembered; it "had had a deficit in thirty-two of the preceding forty-two years." Eisenhower avoided public statements on controversial issues. He saw the fallacy of Vietnam early on, and understood why protesters were agitated. But he feared that if he spoke out on such issues, his words would be taken not as "Milton Eisenhower's views but President Eisenhower's brother's views."

Also his imperative was to bring the university back to fiscal health, and controversy was bad for aggressive fundraising. He was an independent-minded progressive Republican, a breed that would disappear a few decades later. On race, he moved stealthily. He increased black admissions without taking up the matter with the trustees. Despite initial qualms, he also supported a student initiative to require the university housing office to offer nondiscriminatory rentals. Remembered one student, "I immediately found out that he was really a liberal on human rights and civil liberties issues, while a conservative on fiscal affairs."[10]

When Eisenhower retired in 1967, an architect of America's Cold War foreign policy succeeded him. Of Jewish origin, Abraham Lincoln Gordon was an eastern establishment figure who hated his first name and never used it. Raised in Manhattan's Ethical Culture environment, he rose to become W. Averell Harriman's right-hand man in the Marshall Plan to rebuild war-torn Europe. Then, from a Harvard professor of international economic relations he became John F. Kennedy's and Lyndon B. Johnson's lead advisor on Latin America. He authored the blueprint of the Alliance for Progress, a failed U.S.–financed hemispheric politico-economic program aimed at countering Fidel Castro's lure. As ambassador to Brazil, he orchestrated an army putsch that removed a popularly elected leftist government from power. In a top-secret cable he called for clandestine U.S. shipment of untraceable arms to be "pre-positioned prior to any outbreak of violence" and to be "used by paramilitary units working with Democratic Military groups."[11]

Two proven university administrators were also finalists for the president's job. They all had PhD degrees because there had been grumbling about Eisenhower not having one. Gordon's credentials looked good on paper and his international experience dazzled the trustees. He quickly proved to be a bad fit. He was a nice enough fellow, but had no academic administration experience. He also was such an incurable talker that it was said he spoke not in sentences but in chapters and books. Interminable meetings achieved little. Gordon was lost when Dean Shaffer retired with Eisenhower, and then the longtime provost P. Stewart Macauley died. Another loss was the retirement of Charles Garland, the president of the trustees, who made possible a building expansion that reshaped the campus.

There also was the trust issue. About the time that Gordon was installed, *Ramparts* magazine revealed that the Central Intelligence Agency—through private foundations—bankrolled the activist National Student Association as a way to penetrate campuses and influence student movements around the world.[12] There was no mention of Hopkins in the exposé, but the student association was active at Homewood. Gordon denied he was with the CIA. Nevertheless he was viewed with suspicion by the university community, which was not radical by any means but was getting riled up as the war dragged on in Vietnam.

Gordon lasted four years before he was forced to quit in 1971 after students occupied the administration building and the faculty revolted, telling him point-blank that they had no confidence in him. A delegation then marched to see the president of the trustees with the same message; Gordon was out within four hours. Hopkins was relieved to get rid of him. He had inherited the university from Eisenhower with a $2.5 million dowry, but then messed it up, acquiring $4.5 million in new debt. Eisenhower agreed to hastily come back. "I realized that there was no one else that I knew of who could do the job, because it had to be done quickly and therefore you had to know the place intimately, both personnel and finance and organization." He slashed budgets, rearranged priorities, and raised millions for the Homewood campus and the medical school. Eisenhower also hastened the arrival of a provost Gordon had hired, Steven Muller, whom he trained as the next president.

Muller was a child refugee from Nazi Germany who went on to earn a doctorate in political science at Cornell University. Over an eighteen-year tenure
at Hopkins, he oversaw an unprecedented expansion. "Steve was a doer, a
mover, and had tremendous amount of creativity," Ross Jones remembered.
"An extraordinary guy."

Under Wickwire, Levering Hall served as a safety valve. He sponsored
a summer Freedom School to educate whites about black life. He founded
the local Free University; Hopkins was not happy about the noncredit program.[13] There were causes galore. Environmentalism was budding. So was
feminism after president Lincoln Gordon made the undergraduate programs
coeducational in 1970. Few gays were out of the closet yet, but Levering Hall
welcomed them too. Then there was race. In Wickwire's early days, the city's
segregated YMCA operated two "colored" branches—on Druid Hill Avenue
and in Baltimore County's Turner Station, near Bethlehem Steel's Sparrows
Point. Because of its special status, Levering Hall became a unique sanctuary
where integrated organizations could have annual dinners. He sponsored the
city's first interracial jazz concerts. During the 1960 Johns Hopkins "Brotherhood Week," students ushered the featured Duke Ellington to a nearby
restaurant named the Blue Jay, after the Hopkins mascot, where the seminal
jazz figure was refused service. "This place is white and will stay that way,"
owner Fred Paxenos vowed. That night, a slow-burning fire began in the
basement of the Blue Jay. "Restaurant Fire Baffles Inquiry," stated a small
headline in *The Sun*, the last anyone heard about it.[14]

Wickwire transcended race as much as anyone could. The overwhelmingly
black Interdenominational Ministerial Alliance elected him president, the
first and only white in that position. The Black Panthers insisted on having
him as an intermediary when police demanded the surrender of suspects. (He,
along with Hopkins students, spent a couple of nights protecting the Panthers
headquarters when police assault was feared.) He supported the People's Free
Medical Clinic on Greenmount Avenue, which relied on Hopkins volunteer
doctors (and was operated with the Black Panthers in its beginning).[15] He
recruited hundreds of volunteers—faculty, students, and outsiders—to tutor
inner-city kids, a program that continues. "No one who knew Chester Wickwire thought of him as white or black," said black activist clergyman Marion
C. Bascom. "They thought of him as a totally human person."[16]

LUMPENPROLETARIAT

Of the five main civil rights organizations, only Martin Luther King's Southern Christian Leadership Conference did not have a Baltimore office. This

may have been a calculated political move on his part because his relations with NAACP were complicated and Baltimore was known as an NAACP town, a stronghold of two family dynasties.[17] One consisted of the Murphys. They owned the *Afro-American*, which came out twice a week in Baltimore and also had editions in Washington, Philadelphia, Richmond, and Newark, New Jersey. The company was headed by Carl J. Murphy, who had a PhD from Harvard and was happily teaching German at Howard University, when he was called back home to take charge of the paper founded by his grandfather, a former slave. "Mr. Carl," as even his daughters called him, offered readers a diet of serious news and commentary, laced with the passion and blood of salacious love triangles, preferably involving doctors and ministers. The paper employed much of the Murphy clan, made money and spent it. During World War II, the *Afro* sent six staffers, including Mr. Carl's daughter, to cover U.S. troops as war correspondents.[18]

The matriarch of the other dynastic family was Lillie May Carroll Jackson. She was Mr. Carl's grade-school classmate, and claimed descent from Charles Carroll of Carrollton's dalliance with a slave woman. A daughter of a minister, she was a sought-after speaker, married to a traveling projectionist of religious and educational films. Their daughter, Juanita, ran the City-Wide Young People's Forum with Clarence M. Mitchell Jr., an *Afro* reporter. Thousands came to Forum meetings to hear such speakers as the educator Du Bois and the folklorist Zora Neale Hurston. When the Mitchells married, fifteen hundred guests attended.[19]

Back in 1933 Clarence Mitchell was in Princess Anne to report on the aftermath of the last recorded lynching in Maryland. More than a thousand boisterous whites witnessed the hanging and burning of a feeble-minded twenty-two-year-old laborer in that sleepy hamlet of white supremacy (and also home of a black state college). George Armwood died that way because the authorities delivered him to the mob. Charged with assaulting a seventy-one-year-old white woman, he was initially taken to Baltimore for safekeeping. But when a local judge and prosecutor guaranteed his safety, politicians demanded that he be brought back to await justice. As soon as he was returned to Princess Anne, a mob overpowered and disarmed twenty-five state troopers guarding the jail, ripped off his clothing, and dragged his naked body behind a car around town, including past the house where the judge was eating dinner, and hanged him from a nearby tree. "The rope was cut into small pieces and distributed as a souvenir," the *Washington Post* reported.[20] Later the body was cut down and taken to the public square where it was burned. So many cars with people descended on Princess Anne, said a spectator, that "the roads looked like a long funeral procession." No one was convicted of the lynching.[21] The white townspeople's attitude was that

Photographer Paul Henderson took this early portrait of Juanita Jackson Mitchell and Clarence Mitchell Jr. with Clarence Mitchell III (standing) and Keiffer Mitchell.
Courtesy of the Maryland Historical Society, Image #HEN.00.B1-041

"there was a nasty job to be done, there was no other way around it—and why so much fuss?"

The murder galvanized Baltimore's activists. With the City-Wide Young People's Forum as his base, Clarence Mitchell tried his wings in politics. It was true that Baltimore was run by Democrats, but other parties also fielded candidates, including the Communists. Clarence Mitchell was not that extreme; he ran as a socialist in 1934, seeking a General Assembly seat from the Fifth District. Broadus Mitchell, the longtime Johns Hopkins economics professor and biographer of Alexander Hamilton, was the party's gubernatorial hopeful. They did poorly and regarded the endeavor as educational propaganda. "Privately, [Clarence Mitchell] thinks that the Democratic party, many years in power, has been robbing the colored citizens of jobs, education and privileges of social justice," *Afro* columnist Ralph Matthews wrote. "He believes that they do it deliberately with malice aforethought with the air of a highwayman who sticks a gun under the nose of a defenseless pedestrian."[22]

That was Clarence Mitchell's last try at elective office. Instead, he would become the NAACP's lobbyist in Washington, known as the "101st senator" in the halls of Congress. A bevy of relatives ran on his coattails and got elected to city, state, and federal offices.

Much of the black community's agenda was shaped in the *Afro* office at Druid Hill and Eutaw. There, Mr. Carl, a short man peering through Coke-bottle eyeglasses, presided from his elevated desk. Among causes that won his backing was a boycott of Pennsylvania Avenue merchants who refused to hire blacks in their stores. The "Buy Where You Can Work" drive was started by an outsider, a charismatic turban-headed faith healer named Kiowa Costonie, who modeled it after similar efforts in Chicago and New York. When the prophet mysteriously left town, Mr. Carl in 1936 assigned Lillie Jackson to take over. Next he tasked her and her daughter to revive the moribund local NAACP chapter. They built it into a powerhouse, one of the nation's largest, and jealously guarded their territory.

However, from the mid-1960s onward, direct-action organizations no longer felt cowed or constrained by the *Afro* or NAACP. The insurgents now had access to a panoply of rival black publications and the megaphone of black-formatted radio stations. Black Power was on the rise. Stokely Carmichael coined the term. The rallying cry swept through activist organizations. At its national convention in Baltimore in July 1966, CORE cast aside its nonracialist past and emerged as a Black Power organization. The overall tenor was militant.[23] The new emphasis scared some away. "Among those missing from the convention were Martin Luther King, who got his schedule mixed up, Julian Bond, the Georgia Negro fighting for a seat in his state's Legislature, who got his plane ticket mixed up; the ghetto Negroes in any significant numbers and all of Baltimore's civil rights leadership, including the ministers and the governmental appointees who concern themselves with problems facing Negroes," *The Sun*'s Richard H. Levine reported.

Assertiveness sprang from many factors related to desegregation. The Civil Rights Act of 1964 outlawed discrimination based on race, color, religion, sex, or national origin. President Lyndon B. Johnson's War on Poverty empowered the disfranchised further. It created Medicare and Medicaid and expanded Social Security benefits for retirees, widows, and the disabled; made food stamps permanent; established the Job Corps vocational training program, the Volunteers in Service to America (VISTA), and Head Start, and launched the Title I program to give impoverished students a free lunch. Then, in response to civil rights agitation, Johnson ushered through the Voting Rights Act of 1965. On demand, he was giving a voice to the previously voiceless.

Community outreach was written into many federal guidelines. In that environment the National Welfare Rights Organization (NWRO) established a branch in Baltimore. That group was another offshoot of CORE, inspired by a seminal 1966 *Nation* article, "The Weight of the Poor: A Strategy to End Poverty." The authors, Richard Cloward and Frances Fox Piven, argued that if everyone demanded what they were entitled to, welfare rolls would explode, paralyze the bureaucracy, and trigger a fiscal crisis. That, in turn, could lead to the authors' preferred outcome—guaranteed annual income to all people, instead of a bevy of separate programs. This was a novel idea then. NWRO organizers found fertile ground in many public housing projects near Hopkins Hospital. Women were the foot soldiers, men the generals.

Such was the promise of radicalization that in the five years before Martin Luther King's murder, Gay Street evolved into a veritable testing ground for groups challenging Karl Marx's axiom that the raggedy underclass ("Lumpenproletariat") was too consumed by mundane daily worries to be capable of revolutionary action. And who were members of Lumpenproletariat in a ghetto context? According to Eldridge Cleaver, "To be a woman, one had to have a man with a job. To be a man without a job or a woman with a man without a job was to be Lumpen."

Cortez W. Peters showing his skills by typing blindfolded. His business school trained many clerical workers hired by the federal government.
Courtesy of the Maryland Historical Society, Image #HEN.00.A1-063

After CORE fell into disarray and closed its Baltimore office in 1967, the Union for Jobs and Income Now (U-JOIN) continued the effort. That organization was created by the Hopkins campus Students for a Democratic Society, with input from the Civic Interest Group of Morgan students and participation from Goucher coeds. It said quite a bit about Baltimore's racial realities that U-JOIN, while preaching equality, conducted parallel organizing along color lines. Its headquarters at 1042 North Gay Street, near the hospital, had black organizers, whereas an office about a mile away at 326 South Broadway had white organizers catering to Fells Point residents—Poles, Italians, Ukrainians, Czechs, Appalachians, and a settlement of Lumbees from North Carolina. "There is, of course, a lot of racism in the area," wrote Kim Moody, the white Hopkins graduate student in charge on Broadway. "Most of the people with whom we have had direct contact seem to respond to economic arguments for black-white unity in economic organizations, but it remains to be seen how the race question will affect us."[24]

The national SDS's roots went back to 1905, when the activist Upton Sinclair founded the Intercollegiate Socialist Society (ISS), with the help of writer Jack London and the advocate Clarence Darrow. Newspaper editorialist Walter Lippmann joined the anti-Communist organization, and so did future Supreme Court justice Felix Frankfurter, and Roger Baldwin, who was among founders of the American Civil Liberties Union. In the 1930s the society was rebranded as the League for Industrial Democracy (LID). That was the Old Left. In 1959 the youth wing split off and reconstituted itself as Students for a Democratic Society, the nation's most influential New Left organization. Overwhelmingly white, it was inspired by the civil rights movement and initially concerned with equality, economic justice, peace, and participatory democracy. With the escalation of the Vietnam War, SDS extended rapidly to hundreds of campuses, radicalized, and occupied university and college administration buildings across the country. A splinter group, the Weatherman faction, gravitated to bombings. In ten years, SDS would dissolve.[25]

Theoretical reasons invited U-JOIN to concentrate on the Hopkins Hospital area. "The socialist view of the working class as a potentially revolutionary class is based upon the most obvious fact about the working class, that it is socially situated at the heart of modern capitalism's basic, and in fact defining institution, industry," Moody, Fred Eppsteiner, and Mike Flug wrote in a national SDS convention position paper. They all lived in Baltimore and could see how two industries increasingly dominated the east side as packinghouses moved to the south, canning industries closed, and smokestacks no longer billowed. Those two expanding industries were Hopkins and the prison complex, two bookends of an area trying to figure out its future. Both now became organizers' holy grail. Inmates working in state-run workshops inside the overcrowded Maryland Penitentiary, including several Black Panthers and Muslims, formed a union. Authorities did not let it exist long, but it was an audacious try.[26]

Walter Lively became U-JOIN's face. In the end, he was a tragic figure, an ascending civil rights star who just burned out. In the few published accounts of this period, he is often omitted. Yet "from 1964 to 1974, Walter was probably the most well-known and recognizable Negro in Baltimore," Rudolph Lewis wrote in his *ChickenBones* journal. "He was known by the highest political figures in the state as well as the most lowly on Gay Street or Pennsylvania Avenue, the petty hustler as well as the storefront church madam. He was one of them. He could stir them up and he could quiet them down. He rubbed elbows with gangsters as well as the polished businessmen of the Chamber of Commerce and the Greater Baltimore Committee. He was many things to many people."[27]

Lively was born in South Philly, the eldest of eight children. Raised in a public housing project by his mother after his father left when he was thirteen, he grew into a civil rights movement comet. He was a Freedom Rider, arrested twenty-two times. He organized the University of Pennsylvania's NAACP chapter, started a CORE chapter there, and at the age of twenty-one, was chosen to be the Philadelphia director of the 1963 March on Washington. He came to Baltimore to work for U-JOIN. It was his view that "fighting for bread and butter and a good roof is a fight for freedom." U-JOIN registered voters, endorsed political candidates, tried to outlaw potbelly stoves and unvented gas heaters, sponsored cleanups of parks and playgrounds, advised the unemployed of their rights and helped them to collect money due them. A subgroup, Mother Rescuers from Poverty, organized welfare recipients and tried to find jobs. Tenants for Justice in Housing organized a rent strike, persuading judges to hold rent money in escrow while settlement was sought.

Having established hood credentials, in 1967 Lively ran for the city council from the Second District (Gay Street, Hopkins, Bolton Hill, Guilford). A member of Norman Thomas's Socialist Party but registered as an Independent, he was added at the last minute to the Republican ticket, thanks to mayoral candidate Arthur Sherwood insisting that GOP carry a black. "Never in memory has a major party put forward as a standard bearer a civil rights activist of the Lively type," *Sun* political reporter Charles Whiteford wrote.[28]

Lively shaved his beard and shaggy hair and changed to old suits a preacher donated. He had tea in the homes of Bolton Hill and Guilford whites. He got the backing of liberal Republican mayor Theodore R. McKeldin. Republican governor Spiro T. Agnew also supported him. In the previous year's election, Agnew had carried the city's black districts (in contrast to his white county base, which he lost); he was regarded as a moderate on race, running against a segregationist Democrat, George P. Mahoney. In just thirty days of shoe-leather campaigning, in less than a month, Lively garnered a remarkable vote total against Democratic incumbents. Even though he lost (as did Sherwood), he emerged as a young man to watch. Some whispered that one day he might be the city's first black mayor.

At the end of his second city hall stint, Mayor McKeldin launched a public-private pacification program that hoped to counter growing restiveness in black neighborhoods. Called the Urban Coalition, it was financed by the city as well as corporate and do-gooder money. He named Lively executive director. This was Lively's big moment. But the window of opportunity shattered and slammed tightly shut when the riots came in 1968. He became a marked man. He was seen around so many trouble spots—trying to bring peace, he said—that the police arrested him and charged him as a suspect. Several white councilmen attacked him as a "subversive" troublemaker, cut the coalition's funding and made life otherwise miserable for him and other young leaders, including Walter P. Carter. Meanwhile, Agnew, his onetime supporter, became a curse word by accusing "Negro leaders"—from militants to Uncle Toms—of collusion with rioters. (That particular dressing-down brought him to the attention of Richard M. Nixon, who was looking for a running mate.)

Another complication was Lively's skin color. As black consciousness gained traction, darker brothers claimed he was too "white" to be a credible leader. "What can I say?" I heard him once answer to one such complainant. "The whitey did a worse job on me than on you." Eventually, he grew back his shaggy hair, and returned to his scruffy attire. "He built no lasting institutions," Lewis wrote in his journal. "All those fell by the wayside for whatever reason." That's how I remember him as well. Lots of initiatives somehow failed to pan out: Liberation House Press publishing house, an Afrocentric bookstore; a history museum in a former Broadway library branch near Hopkins. About the last time he appeared in newspapers was for boosting two steaks from a supermarket. Then, at thirty-four, he died at the Hopkins Hospital, from an aneurysm.

WOMEN TAKE CHARGE

In 1966, two years before the riots, starvation-wage black women changed Baltimore's labor dynamics. Shifts of mothers, sisters, daughters, and aunts struck at Franklin Square's Lincoln nursing home, protesting thirty-five-cent hourly wages, dismal conditions, and sixty to seventy-two-hour work weeks.

They were fired. Women at other nursing homes then also walked out, chanting Black Power slogans. Coordinating the drive was the newly created Maryland Freedom Union. That, too, was a CORE offshoot, even though the chief organizer came from SDS, as did many supporters. "Our position would be that any unorganized workers, no matter what their industry, could get help from us," explained Mike Flug, the organizer.

AFL-CIO unions did not interfere; they were predominantly Jim Crow and had shown little interest in organizing low-wage blacks. But when Maryland Freedom Union began unionizing employees in such popular Pennsylvania Avenue stores as the Tommy Tucker five-and-dime, the Retail Clerks Union got mad and notified the United Auto Workers president who headed the nationwide AFL-CIO trade union federation. "It's no secret that one of the big contributors to CORE then was Walter Reuther (through several of his fronts)," Flug writes. "Reuther got the word all the way from the Retail Clerks that CORE was doing something in 'his field' in Baltimore." He called CORE director Floyd McKissick and "told him to stop or no more money."[29]

Divided and strained by quarrels between the New York headquarters and the local operation, the Baltimore CORE collapsed.[30] But the struggle went on, watched by the Big Brother.

Chapter Ten

A Cat of a Different Color

Dozens of American cities blew up in fiery rage after a sniper's bullets killed Martin Luther King Jr. in Memphis on April 4, 1968. Baltimore hesitated for two days. Trouble then began on Palm Sunday eve just downhill from Hopkins Hospital. There, pamphlets distributed around Gay Street's Belair Market demanded that businesses close immediately to honor the civil rights leader. But stores, full of kids looking for new sneakers and other Easter regalia, were slow to clear. Suddenly an orgy of shattered glass, flames, rampage, and looting erupted. Even closer to Hopkins, pilferers threw kerosene bombs into long-established furniture, home furnishing, appliance, and clothing stores on Monument Street, the onetime retail heart of Little Bohemia. Disorders spread. Flames soon burst over Greenmount Avenue, Cherry Hill, Lombard Street, Baltimore Street, Pratt Street, North Avenue, Harford Road, Edmondson Avenue, Pennsylvania Avenue, Liberty Heights Avenue, Park Heights Avenue, Reisterstown Road. Six people were killed, and more than five thousand arrested. It took four days and nearly eleven thousand Maryland National Guard and regular army troops to quell the unrest. A thousand businesses were pillaged, including 288 liquor outlets. Some fifteen neighborhood retail districts were torched and looted. None of those commercial strips would fully recover. After three decades of white residential flight, businesses joined the exodus.[1]

Pimlico races aside, J. Edgar Hoover was no stranger to Baltimore. The bulldog-faced FBI director once personally conducted a highly publicized morals raid, and in 1936 he and Clyde Tolson were among more than six thousand spectators who witnessed how the FBI baseball team, Sleuths, crushed the Baltimore police,12–5. Then there was the U.S. Army intelligence. In 1955 it relocated its headquarters, training facilities, and administrative offices from Kansas to Fort Holabird. That waterfront base between Canton and Dundalk is now an industrial park, but in the fifties a sphinx statue at the headquarters entrance reminded everyone that mum was the word.

Hoover had worked with the military since 1919, when as a young Department of Justice lawyer he took over the newly created General Intelligence Division. The army's wiretappers and decoders helped him establish linkages among subversives—to determine the scope of their activities and decide what prosecutorial actions should be taken. He worked to impress. In the first year on the job, his G-men created card files on more than 450,000 subjects, including some 60,000 individuals ranging from anarchists to sexual nonconformists. His operation grew steadily during World War II. A decade later, at the height of the Cold War in 1956, Hoover formed a coordinated covert intelligence command, COINTELPRO, to undermine the Moscow-allied Communist Party of the United States of America (CPUSA). Aside from the FBI, this secret all-out effort involved the various intelligence agencies, postal inspectors, Treasury agents, the Internal Revenue Service, various military intelligence agencies, as well as local police, including Baltimore's. All available means were used. The CPUSA became such a honeycomb of FBI stool pigeons that sometimes it seemed as if Hoover singlehandedly kept the party alive.

In the mid-1960s, with red menace receding, he refocused. Nearly a year before King's assassination he targeted black activism as priority No. 1. He was an old hand at that. After World War I, when Marcus Garvey created the Universal Negro Improvement Association, Hoover so thoroughly infiltrated that one-million-member organization—the first African-American mass movement—that he knew everything worth knowing, including Garvey's suicidal thoughts at moments of despondency. That enabled his agents to harass Garvey, the Moses of the Back to Africa movement. After years of hounding, he had Garvey convicted in 1923 on a flimsy mail fraud charge, jailed, and deported back home to Jamaica.[2]

By the mid-1960s, Garvey and his assemblies were long gone. Instead, a bevy of civil rights organizations vied for prominence. The National Association for the Advancement of Colored People (NAACP) was the oldest, established in 1909 with Du Bois at its helm. Others included the Congress of Racial Equality (CORE) and the Southern Christian Leadership Conference (SCLC). But it was the Black Panther Party for Self-Defense that captured the imagination of urban discontents. While the preacher King had a dream, the Panthers had a plan—they wanted to rid America's black communities of white control. Whereas Garvey's African Legion, wearing military dress uniforms and carrying unloaded rifles, had engaged in theatrics, strutting in formation up and down Harlem avenues, the *Black Panther* newspaper's powerful graphic artist Emory Douglas depicted Panthers in fatigues ready to fire loaded AK-47s, the legendary Soviet assault rifles favored by Third World guerrillas. "Off the pigs," the paper exhorted, urging readers to kill police officers. Individual Panthers were involved in fatal shoot-outs with cops and were also linked to several murders of informants. "Ratlords," as the paper called slum landlords, were also to be exterminated. "All Power to the people! Right on!"

The party's membership was not great but its militant combativeness pushed other groups toward extremism. Just look at Martin Luther King! The 1964 Nobel Peace Prize laureate became a campaigner for the dispossessed of the land, but also a prominent critic of the government's war in Vietnam. He even questioned the very tenets of capitalism, the system that made America great. While he was courting Coretta Scott, he wrote her: "I imagine you already know that I am much more socialistic in my economic theory than capitalistic."[3] He went further. Seven months before he was shot, he declared to a Southern Christian Leadership Conference meeting in Atlanta: "And one day we must ask the question, 'Why are there forty million poor people in America? And when you begin to ask that question, you are raising questions about the economic system, about a broader distribution of wealth.' When you ask that question, you begin to question the capitalistic economy. And I'm simply saying that more and more, we've got to begin to ask questions about the whole society."

Then came the call to arms: "These are revolutionary times. All over the globe, men are revolting against old systems of exploitation and oppression, and out of the wombs of a frail world new systems of justice and equality are being born. The shirtless and barefoot people of the land are rising up as never before. 'The people who sat in darkness have seen a great light.' We in the West must support these revolutions. It is a sad fact that, because of comfort, complacency, a morbid fear of Communism, and our proneness to adjust to injustice, the Western nations that initiated so much of the revolutionary spirit of the modern world have become the arch anti-revolutionaries."[4]

On August 25, 1967, nine days after that King speech, Hoover directed COINTELPRO to cut out the heart of black consciousness, remove the brain, and paralyze the muscles. He ordered the FBI to "expose, disrupt, misdirect, discredit, or otherwise neutralize the activities of black nationalist, hate-type organizations and groupings, their leadership, spokesmen, membership and supporters." He further ordered COINTELPRO to "prevent the rise of a 'messiah' who could unify and electrify the militant black nationalist movement." Was King a messiah? Hoover thought so. Among hate-type organizations he listed King's nonviolent Southern Christian Leadership Conference. Also on the list was another proven mobilizer, the Nation of Islam. Hoover saw it as ripe for sabotage because the militant sect was being torn apart in a rivalry between the founder, Elijah Muhammed, and Malcolm X, whose parents had been Garvey firebrands. The Student Nonviolent Coordinating Committee (SNCC) and the Maoist Revolutionary Action Movement (RAM) also topped Hoover's list. But the Panthers were the main enemy. "The Black Panther Party, without question, represents the greatest threat to the internal security of the country," J. Edgar Hoover wrote.

This is what brought Warren Hart to Baltimore's Gay Street a few months after the riots. At five-foot-eight and 190 pounds, the forty-year-old army veteran was a bulldozer of a man. He rented a storefront in Old Town, near the Maryland Penitentiary. There he set up a makeshift Panther outpost and started recruiting disciples, who resold copies of the *Black Panther* newspaper which he bought from a bookstore. He brought his proselytizing to the Oakland, California, headquarters' attention and pestered it until his pop-up was legitimized as an official chapter. Appointed the Baltimore defense captain, he added other houses on Gay and Eden Streets, near Hopkins hospital. He started a free breakfast program at St. Martin de Porres Church, near the penitentiary. He was soon in charge of a five-state Mid-Atlantic area, gaining access to the party central committee. He traveled repeatedly to Oakland and met with the inner circle: minister of defense Huey P. Newton, chairman Bobby Seale, minister of information Eldridge Cleaver, chief of staff David Hilliard, minister of justice H. Rap Brown, and prime minister Stokely Carmichael. "The Baltimore chapter is important because it played an instrumental role in the success enjoyed by the organization on the East Coast," writes the Black Power historian Judson L. Jeffries.[5]

The Panthers were an odd mélange of Marxist phraseology, calls for armed struggle at home and anti-imperialism abroad, in-your-face attitudes, and serious efforts to promote self-reliance. The boxer Muhammed Ali never became a member but he was the party's inspiration and symbol. The party's historical origins were in Alabama, where it was born in 1965 as an affiliate of SNCC under its chairman, Carmichael. He had gone to organize in Lowndes County, which was 80 percent black but had not allowed a single black to register to vote. The party then split from SNCC, and Newton moved it to Oakland, the city across the bay from San Francisco. In some forty cities, the Panthers' free breakfast programs fed undernourished children, free clinics provided medical care, liberation schools indoctrinated. Many white celebrity liberals raised money for the Panthers, regarding them as the ultimate in radical chic.[6] Abroad, anti-U.S. governments, guerrilla groups, and revolutionary fronts recognized the Black Panther Party.

Back in Baltimore, Hart distributed Chairman Mao Zedong's *Red Book*, taught about Kim Il-sung, Ho Chi Minh, Malcolm X, Kwame Nkrumah, and Frantz Fanon. "I was learning an entirely new history of world dynamics and the conditions of black and poor people," Steve D. McCutchen wrote in his published diary.[7] Overall, though, Hart's Panther branch often functioned like a social club. Members drifted in and out. A couple were Vietnam veterans. Some held regular full-time jobs: One was with the post office, another a data clerk at a bank. This puzzled those who thought that being a Panther was a full-time commitment. "Some Panthers still live at home," McCutchen marveled. "They're part-time Panthers, at least that's what I understand. Hart explained that was understood at National Hq. that we did that here. Part-time Panthers." The Panthers excluded whites, but their support was welcome. Among Hart's visitors was an auxiliary from Detroit named the White Panthers.

The Panthers glorified guns. Throughout the nation they were frequently involved in confrontations with the police or in the executions of suspected informants. Baltimore was no exception, although no proven evidence links Hart to such cases. He did have licenses for four guns: a Derringer .38 special, two .38 Smith & Wessons, and a .32 H & R revolver.[8] Then on July 4, 1969, fireworks exploded and flak rained on him. McCutchen noted: "Field Marshal D.[onald] C.[ox] from National arrived with [Henry] Mitch[ell] and a lawyer named [Arthur] Turco. A white lawyer with Panthers. Strange. I tried to search them at the front door. Fucked up. Turco was packing, and I missed his piece. All Panthers had to depart for a general meeting. Hart was criticized for fucking up. D.C. said that the branch might be closed down. Some Panthers were told to get out if they didn't understand what had to be done. Lt. [Charles] Butler and Lt. [Zeke] Boyd was expelled. Hart was busted down to Panther." He resigned the same day that Governor Mandel appointed him to the seventeen-member state Commission on Childhood Nutrition as a recognition of the importance of the Panther breakfast program, which was partially funded with grants from the Catholic archdiocese's controversial Urban Commission. That support created such a backlash among the archdiocese's white parishioners that the commission was quietly phased out.

Hart departed the way he arrived, never exposed. For the man who started the Baltimore Black Panther Party was in fact a COINTELPRO agent provocateur from the National Security Agency, which had opened a new headquarters at nearby Fort Meade. His mission was to infiltrate the Panther leadership, penetrate Baltimore's radical scene, and cause havoc.[9] As the Baltimore defense captain, Hart took it upon himself to spread dissension among the various factions of the New Left. He quarreled with Soul School. That black cultural gathering on Fremont Avenue was formed by Benjamin "Olugbala" McMillan, who became disenchanted with CORE. Hart squabbled with SDS. That overwhelmingly white organization supported the Panthers, but was splintered. The Progressive Labor Party wing advocated stern Marxism-Leninism, the Weatherman wing planned bombings. True, there were suspicions about Hart, and one close call: Larry S. Gibson, who later became a University of Maryland law professor, remembered seeing Hart's NSA identification card. A volunteer lawyer, Gibson spotted the card while sifting through the belongings of Hart, who had been arrested and was held at the city's Western police district, along with nationalists from Soul School.[10] No one connected the dots.

Hart moved on. In the spring of 1970 he resurfaced in Canada, which at the time was in the midst of bombings in separatist Quebec, student takeovers on campuses, pro-Castro agitation among Caribbean immigrants, and unrest among Indians on reservations. Yet the Royal Canadian Mounted Police had not a single homegrown black operative, nor enough agents who could claim kinship with restive Indians. So they borrowed from the U.S. Justice Department. As a black American, Hart was hard to miss. Many radicals wondered about him, about his fancy car and the arsenal of arms he displayed so freely in his apartment. To some he hinted that he was in the Mob. (Indeed, his superiors expressed worries about his chumminess with mobsters.) He burrowed into the anthill of radicalism, trying to fan dissension and provoke confrontations by helping student militants plan takeovers of public buildings. When the Black Panther icon Angela Davis visited Toronto, he peremptorily took over as the old comrade's road manager, bodyguard, and driver. He reported everything. True to his provocateur calling, he suggested (but was overruled) that sharpshooters flank Davis during a speech in a university auditorium. He traveled widely in the Caribbean on assignments. When Canada soured after three years, he went freelance. He plotted assassinations in Antigua from a rented house with a "concealed rifle, four hand grenades and a phial of poison" and worked for an embargo-busting arms trader that supplied South Africa's white-supremacist apartheid government with "approximately fifty thousand 155 mm artillery shells, two artillery control radar vans, eight 155 'Long Tom' artillery barrels," according to a CIA document.[11]

All this may be found in dated newspaper reports and magazine articles in Canada and the Caribbean.[12] The most authoritative source is the 1981 Royal Commission of Inquiry into Certain Activities of the Royal Canadian Mounted Police, a sweeping probe into illegal wiretapping, unauthorized break-ins, and other unsanctioned spying on a wide spectrum of social movements and public organizations in the early 1970s. The inquiry was the equivalent of the probe Frank Church's U.S. Senate commission conducted into similar rogue FBI activities. In the Royal Commission investigation, Hart was a somewhat incidental figure. Sworn testimony, including his own, depicted him as a black James Bond wannabe touting Soviet-made weapons to anyone prone to violence. The overall plan was none of his concerns.

Canada twice expelled him as an undesirable alien. The first time was just for show, a ploy necessitated by his supervisors' change of heart, according to the voluminous Royal Commission report. At the last minute, they decided to abort a bombing, ostensibly by radicals, for which Hart was to deliver the explosives. Kicking him out was the easiest way to abandon the plot without harming his credibility and usefulness as an agent.[13] Among Mounties, Hart's swagger triggered envy. Colleagues described him as an egomaniac, a "sandlot thug." So when he was expelled for a second time, many were glad to see him go. The commission rendered a different verdict: Warren Hart "performed laudable service for the people of Canada and should not be prevented from returning."

By contrast, hardly any documentation existed about Hart's Baltimore days. In 2013, long after he died, I went to an address in the northwest part of the city, a tidy individual home on a quiet tree-shaded street. All I knew was that he had once bought it and it was still deeded to his widow. I stopped in my tracks. In front of me, parking an SUV, appeared a startlingly young version of Warren Hart. That was his son, Christopher. We traded nods; he knew instinctively why I was there. As a proof of his identity he flashed his smartphone screen. It showed his father in Panther regalia, giving a clenched-fist salute. Christopher half-promised to talk but then failed to respond to my calls and emails.

FBI was no help either. It said it destroyed Warren Hart's file on January 1, 2001.[14] The timing was curious. Nary three weeks before, on December 12, Officer Cherylann Young steered a marked Miami-Dade County police cruiser toward the perimeter of MIA, the international airport. She was forty-five, armed and in uniform, a twenty-year veteran of the force. Sitting next to her on the front seat was an old dude known as The General, who was on yet another mission. One time he moved five kilos of cocaine from the airport, with Miami Beach Officer Kevin Coleman, thirty-seven, driving the patrol car and receiving $5,000 in cash for his troubles. Likewise, Officer Young herself, while off-duty, had transported two kilos of blow in a police cruiser, with The General riding shotgun. She received $2,000. As to the task at hand, nothing to it; a piece of cake. Except that on that day they all got busted: The General, identified as Warren Hart, seventy-two, Young, Coleman.[15] Geezers must have been transporting an awful lot of cocaine in patrol cars in Florida those days because no newspaper followed up the arrest story or reported that he was sentenced to prison for seven years; he served less than three.[16]

THE MAN WHO KNEW ALL

Baltimore's city police department had long operated a "red squad" to track subversives. Donald D. Pomerleau brought that surveillance capability to new heights, when he was sworn in as police commissioner in 1966, five years after Hepbron's retirement and two years before the riots. He first came to Baltimore as a consultant. The International Association of Chiefs of Police dispatched him in 1964 to sort out the mess left behind by Hepbron, whose successor also failed miserably. That man was Bernard J. Schmidt. *The Sun*'s Richard H. Levine got him fired after digging seven months into various layers of the disorder. The force was "manned, equipped and financed heavily enough for modern warfare on crime, yet it is waging a primitive kind of guerrilla action marked by inefficient administrative procedures, haphazard planning and lax discipline," Levine concluded.[17] Meanwhile, consultant Pomerleau studied the problems, biding his time.

On his first day as commissioner, Pomerleau created the Inspectional Services Division (ISD) to spy on citizens, organizations, and institutions not necessarily suspected of wrongdoing. To him, ISD was what COINTELPRO was to Hoover, a surveillance machinery to keep tabs on known and potential troublemakers, and make sure that friends did not stray. The unit was also tasked to surveil organized crime, but that was a secondary mission, according to a Maryland Senate's investigation. Instead, answerable only to him, ISD focused on challenges to the existing order, particularly from blacks and leftists. To head this political policing, Pomerleau brought in Maurice duBois from FBI—to be later succeeded by another FBI agent, Bernard F. Norton Sr. Pertinent reports were routinely routed to FBI and Fort Holabird. Historian Frank Donner writes that no major police department did as much to neutralize dissident groups as did Baltimore's Inspectional Services Division.[18]

Being the collector, guardian, and disseminator of Baltimore's secrets enhanced Pomerleau's power. He often slipped something into conversations to signal that he knew everything and that he had a file on everyone, whether civic leaders, businessmen, do-gooders or militants. Like, "I know where you meet, when you are going to meet before you meet, what you do."[19] He testified how he summoned the mother of one black state delegate to see him. In her presence, the adult son fell on his knees, begging Pomerleau not to show compromising evidence to her.[20] "It is not intimidation, it is cooperation," the commissioner insisted. "She didn't know it and I thought she ought to know it. I would do the same for you if you have a son and he gets out of hand."[21]

For a boy who grew up on a ranch in Medicine Lake, Montana, Pomerleau had traveled far and wide. As a strapping marine he served in China for three years in the 1930s, and in World War II chased the Japanese from Guadalcanal to Tarawa. After additional duty in Korea, he rose to lieutenant colonel and was eventually promoted to provost marshal at the Marine Corps School and University at Quantico, Virginia. On retiring, he simply moved across the huge base to the FBI National Academy. After graduation, he became director of public safety in Kingsport, Tennessee. Miami-Dade County then hired him to modernize its force. His ways so antagonized local politicians that, after a few confrontations, he decided not to waste any more of his time in Florida. He was a macho man, a cowboy who donned a Stetson on his horseback patrols during a record snowstorm in Baltimore. He didn't take crap from anyone and was quite open about his prejudices. He knew he had to be political about blacks, but women didn't count. "All women are little balls of fluff in the eyes of the Creator," he told a judge in a federal courtroom.[22]

Pomerleau was a defining commissioner. In his fifteen years he organized the force along military lines, insisting on a strict chain of command. He was able to beef up salaries, reduce chronic vacancies, buy new vehicles. He improved training and equipped the force with the latest in eavesdropping technology and such potent weapons of crowd control as teargas and Mace. He experimented with lie detectors, including voice stress analysis. In the sky, the "Foxtrot" helicopter hovered over the city. Many white Baltimoreans saw Pomerleau as a rock of stability in a city undergoing a racial shift from majority white to majority black. Blacks vocally criticized him for perceived bias when it became known that he had designated vast spreads of the inner city as "gray areas," where police were to ignore routine calls due to racial tensions. The mere presence of police could cause a mini-riot, or so it was argued. Pomerleau's kennel of fifty-four K-9 dogs contributed to that friction. After one dog bit a woman, their use was halted, with white politicians from the First and Sixth Districts protesting the decision.[23] In the spring of 1970, a police radio dispatcher sent a patrolman to a Gay Street address two blocks from the Black Panther headquarters, only to be advised that "we don't respond to that area." Such was the uproar over the arbitrary policy that Young Tommy D'Alesandro, Governor Mandel, and the commissioner saw it necessary in a joint appearance to assure the city that all neighborhoods got equal police coverage.

Many in the department's overwhelmingly white rank-and-file did not like the commissioner. The feeling was mutual. Disregarding his vocal warnings, a police union formed and defied him by going on strike, while garbage kept piling up on sidewalks because the municipal collectors walked out, then some three hundred prison guards. Teachers also struck. The whole city seemed to be unraveling in a veritable general strike. There was some looting. Pomerleau fired most striking officers, and took away the police union's bargaining rights.[24] Amid subsequent recriminations, someone spilled the beans on ISD surveillance to *News American* reporters Joe Nawrozki and Michael Olesker. The latter remembered that criminal case folders sometimes contained a handwritten notation barring the information's use in courts so as not to reveal unauthorized wiretapping. A city grand jury was assembled to conduct a probe but its jurisdiction was challenged because the police department was technically a state agency. The Maryland Senate then exercised its oversight prerogative and conducted hearings on ISD spying activities.

It was a minor miracle that any hearings were held at all. When the Senate took up the mission, Pomerleau sued to stop the process. Then he sued again. No dice. Forty-five witnesses gave forty-three hours of testimony in Annapolis; the official transcript ran 1,754 pages. Olesker remembered Pomerleau packing the hearing room with his brass so that all seats were taken and no protesters could get in. "A significant inhibiting factor experienced by the Committee was the lack of cooperation and, in fact, active resistance of Commissioner Pomerleau and his counsel, George L. Russell, Jr.," the Senate's sixty-page report stated. Russell was a prominent black lawyer. He agreed to represent Pomerleau, who insisted that he also represent all the testifying police officers, active as well as retired. The commissioner got what he wanted. No civilian review board was established. He also got the mayor put in charge of the police department, instead of the governor. He retired in 1987, having notably contributed to the sense of omnipotence and arrogance that helped explain the police department's frequent subsequent troubles.

Some early police departments were created by slave owners, and while Baltimore's was not among them, cops long acted as if they were plantation overseers. For the first eighty-five years the department had no black officers at all. True, a number of African Americans took the test but they were always failed. In 1920 General Charles D. Gaither put an end to the charade. He declared once and for all that white privilege was not going to accept blacks, regardless of how well they did in the examinations. "The psychological time had not come in Baltimore for the appointment of negroes on the force," he stated.[25] His belief in white privilege was such that he reprimanded Sergeant William A. Howard for "having handed over to a negro man to deliver a warrant which had been issued for the arrest of a negress." That was a white privilege. This is what happened, according to Howard: "I went to the woman's house and found her at a washtub. I try to police according to the teachings of Christianity, and I saw that the woman was trying to make an honest living. The charge against her was trivial, and the collateral was set at $11.70. I told her to get the collateral and meet me at Calvert and 21st Street at 10 p.m. She met me there with a colored man and I gave the warrant to him, as he told me that he would go to the police station with the woman. . . . The Lord guided them to the police station."[26]

The black hiring issue did not go away. In 1922 an all-white grand jury recommended that black policemen and policewomen be employed in "colored sections of the city."[27] Nothing came out of that proposal. It took fifteen more years before Policewoman Violet Hill Whyte was sworn in as the first African American officer in 1937. She was soon joined by three men: Harry S. Scott,

Milton Gardner, and J. Hiram Butler Jr. But such was white sensitivity that they had to serve unarmed, wear civilian clothes, and were not empowered to arrest whites. Blacks were put in uniform during World War II, but were limited to foot patrol until 1966, when they were permitted to ride in radio cars.

Pomerleau arrived in Baltimore at a time when the city's racial balance of power was shifting as a result of continuing postwar migration from the Carolinas. The interim commissioner, Maryland National Guard Adjutant General George Gelston, recognized the realities. He was a change agent. He forbade racism on the police force and ordered a stop to the use of epithets. He brought William "Box" Harris from the desegregated Maryland National Guard as the highest ranking black officer, first major, then colonel. Black hiring was stepped up. Gelston had distinguished himself through his skillful handling of a 1963 race conflict in the Eastern Shore river town of Cambridge. Whites there did not want to end segregation, even refusing federal funds meant for poverty-stricken black areas. They did not want low-paid poultry workers and seafood processors radicalized, to unionize and become cheeky and more demanding.

After peaceful protests against segregation failed, pent-up black anger burst into rioting. Governor Tawes declared martial law, and the National Guard was called in, commanded by Gelston. When whites learned that he was a Confederate soldier's grandson, they celebrated. But instead of siding with them, he took the blacks' concerns seriously and found common ground with a protest leader, Gloria Richardson, president of the local SNCC branch. The two saw themselves as the only sane people in the madhouse of Cambridge. Ending the confrontation was so important that U.S. Attorney General Robert F. Kennedy got involved in negotiating a way back to normalcy. Tensions persisted however. In 1967 H. Rap Brown, the former SNCC and Black Panther chieftain, incited another riot in Cambridge. He renounced peaceful means and declared, "I say violence is necessary. Violence is a part of America's culture. It is as American as cherry pie. Americans taught the black people to be violent. We will use that violence to rid ourselves of oppression if necessary. We will be free, by any means necessary."

In Baltimore, Gelston demonstrated levelheadedness. When a sit-in blocked the busy Calvert Street in front of Horizon House, a brand-new, whites-only high-rise in center-city Mount Vernon, Gelston simply redirected the rush-hour traffic, took a smoke, and chatted with other officers on the scene. As the clock ticked, UPI reporter Dan Riker heard a protest leader complain: "What the fuck is he up to? He is supposed to arrest us. That's the whole idea." Gelston knew that. Soon the early television news would be over and the whole sit-in would become irrelevant. Film at eleven—since it had to be processed in a darkroom.[28]

Where Gelston endeavored to open lines of communication to maintain a dialogue, Pomerleau regarded all black doers as potential suspects. It was only natural that his agents occupied a house across from the Black Panther headquarters on Gay Street, filming comings and goings and eavesdropping on conversations. But his ISD spied also on emerging black leaders. It snooped on Joseph C. Howard Sr., who in 1968 challenged the establishment's all-white ticket and became the first African American judge in the felony court. It spied on Milton B. Allen, who in 1970 made history as the first African American elected to a citywide office, and the first black person to hold a chief prosecutor's position in a major U.S. city.[29] Surveillance on Parren J. Mitchell was keen before and after the member of an influential civil rights family, a bachelor, was elected Maryland's first black congressman in 1970. Next year, when a white bachelor, city council president William Donald Schaefer, was elected mayor, he told his aides never to antagonize Pomerleau.[30] He knew only too well what the commissioner was capable of doing. During the mayoral election race, ISD infiltrated the campaigns of Schaefer's black opponents, George Russell and Clarence M. Mitchell III. Pomerleau then fed reports to Francis B. Burch, the state attorney general who was a member of Schaefer's (and Governor Mandel's) campaign team, with the Furniture Man Irvin Kovens greasing the wheels. All police commissioners were subject to the prevailing political winds. Where Hepbron was influenced by the elder Mayor D'Alesandro and his cronies, including Pollack, Pomerleau promoted Kovens allies during Schaefer's mayoral years. The upper ranks of black officers were dominated by Little Willie Adams's protégés.[31]

ISD, according to the Maryland Senate investigation, "amassed a data bank containing the names of, and information pertaining to, hundreds, perhaps thousands, of citizens of this state, many of whom did nothing more than testify with respect to a particular piece of legislation before the Baltimore City Council, or peaceably walk a picket line." Illegal tapping of telephones was common, including at least three at *The Sun*. Pomerleau informants penetrated campus groups at Johns Hopkins, Goucher, the University of Maryland law school, Morgan, and the Community College of Baltimore. He spied on organized labor. He collected information on environmentalists and citizens who opposed the gas and electricity monopoly's rate hike. Agent Terry Josephson became a vice president of the United Credit Bureau of America in order to gain easy access to credit information; he later returned to ISD and infiltrated the Jewish Defense League. The most notorious ISD agent was Leonard Jenoff, who infiltrated the office of a big heroin dealer's lawyer and tipped Pomerleau to defense strategies. Remembered Michael Olesker: "Jenoff later fled to Philadelphia, where he got involved with a rabbi who was having an extramarital affair with a woman radio personality and thus wanted his wife out of the way. The rabbi hired Jenoff to kill his wife, which Jenoff did. He bludgeoned her to death. Jenoff and the rabbi both went to prison."[32]

ISD's numerical strength was never disclosed (although I put it at "about 20" in a 1971 news story), nor was how many volunteers or paid informants it recruited. A hundred, perhaps.[33] When the *News-American* unmasked the surveillance operation and the Maryland Senate launched its investigation, Pomerleau destroyed all ISD files and records. This much is known: At least five ISD operatives were trained at the army's intelligence headquarters at Fort Holabird in eavesdropping and surreptitious entry; many others had links to the base through joint operations when trainees were sent to the city on undercover assignments.

On really sensitive tasks, Pomerleau did not trust his own personnel. Instead, he used Marshall "Mike" Meyer, a private investigator who had done contractual work for the police for years. (Governor Mandel also used him occasionally.) Six feet tall, Meyer had once been a bodyguard to the Hollywood child stars Judy Garland and Shirley Temple. His intelligence work began in World War II France, then continued in Japan and Korea. After he left the army he went into the gumshoe business, running the Inter-State Bureau of Investigation, located in the city's Roland Park neighborhood. Even then he continued to advise a special intelligence unit he created at Fort Holabird. A useful man. So strong were his links to the monopoly Chesapeake & Potomac Telephone Company that he routinely tapped lines without court authorization. In fact, it was often difficult to know who was up a pole because Meyer's wiretappers drove decommissioned C&P trucks that still bore the company's colors. Whenever a call came from a certain number to a tapped phone, a small box on the pole linked it with the police monitoring room.[34]

In addition to three mainstream dailies, several "underground" newspapers existed. One was *Harry*, a biweekly tabloid. Among its principals were such Hopkins students as Michael Carliner, P. J. O'Rourke, and Art Levine. Another in the mix was Tom V. D'Antoni, a white Morganite. The unpaid staff photographer was Glenn Ehasz. I remember him as a personable twenty-eight-year-old with a mop of reddish hair, sideburns, and a handlebar mustache, always toting 35mm cameras. As a member of the Baltimore Defense Committee, he attended a Chicago meeting of the Weathermen, the splinter group from SDS. He also accompanied D'Antoni to Milwaukee for a strategic planning conference. Instead of his own name, he used playful photo bylines that paid tribute to popular camera brands. On one page he was "Kosmic Konica," on another "Leiky Leica." The most appropriate was "Papa Topcon," because con was his game: He was a 1969 honors graduate of the police academy. His first mission was to infiltrate the Peace Action

Center, a clearinghouse of dissident activities. Photography for *Harry* provided a perfect cover.

Surveillance of dissidents was nothing new. Hopkins had a reputation as a conservative school, but informants had watched it ever since Albert Blumberg. Born in Vienna and educated at Yale and Sorbonne, he was a Hopkins professor of philosophy in 1937, when he became the district administrative secretary of the Communist Party (CPUSA). The Kremlin-controlled Stalinist party was at the peak of its influence. In his party role, he kept hanging around the campus. Then there was Owen Lattimore. He was a Hopkins Far East scholar whom Senator Joseph McCarthy, in a four-hour speech, accused of being a top Soviet spy.[35] The baseless claim prompted a tortuous investigation of intellectuals. A trustee, Jacob France, was so upset over Hopkins's failure to fire Lattimore that he canceled his bequest to the university and instead used it to create the France-Merrick Foundation.[36]

About the same time, Alger Hiss was convicted of perjury. He was a local boy wonder, a City College and Hopkins graduate who received his law degree from Harvard Law School, became a diplomat, accompanied Roosevelt to the fateful Yalta conference where postwar Europe was split, and oversaw the creation of the United Nations. For such contributions Hopkins awarded him an honorary doctorate. Then a former friend, Whitaker Chambers, claimed that Hiss was a secret Communist. Hiss sued, and lost. He was sent to federal prison where, he told me, he practiced his Italian with his cell mate, a Mob boss. Taking place at the height of McCarthyism, the Hiss case divided liberals who argued about his guilt or innocence for decades. Most scholars now accept his guilt.

In the middle of all this, Carl P. Swanson, an associate professor of botany, reported a visit by a tall, well-dressed man who announced: "I'm from the FBI. You have been recommended to me as a conservative citizen and I'd like to ask you some questions." The agent wanted information about a particular graduate student pursuing a doctorate in embryology, a former army captain, member of the Genetic Society of America, Phi Beta Kappa, and the Progressive Citizens of America, whose father-in-law, a professor emeritus of music, left Russia before the Bolshevik takeover. Said Swanson: "What worries me is that a member of the FBI can come to me, say, 'You have been recommended to me as a conservative citizen,' and then accept whatever I have to say."[37]

Then there was Gunther Wertheimer. The World War II U.S. Navy ensign was a tall man with a Prussian officer's bearing, a scholarly man happiest wading into streams to fish and listening to Wagner and Mahler. It had been his family's good fortune to leave Germany in 1936, just when all Jews were deprived citizenship. In America Wertheimer wanted to become a professor.

He was a member of the Progressive Party and at Hopkins headed a peace group that attracted the attention of the House Un-American Activities Committee. After Wertheimer was summoned to testify in 1951, Hopkins expelled him. With a career in academia blocked, he worked in industrial jobs and as a union organizer, then founded a construction company with Milton Bates, a University of Maryland law graduate who passed the bar examination but was disqualified because of his political beliefs.[38]

Pomerleau claimed not to spy on church groups, but few believed him. There was turbulence everywhere, particularly in the Catholic Church. Baltimore was the "premier see," America's earliest diocese, where Archbishop Lawrence J. Shehan was trying to shepherd a resistant flock toward desegregation while implementing the controversial reforms of the Vatican II conclave. A racial progressive, he was a native of Old Town's Irish Tenth Ward. Just before Pomerleau took over, an angry white crowd booed Cardinal Shehan at a jam-packed city council hearing when he advocated desegregated housing. Irate opponents spat on him, including fellow Catholics. "It was a bad thing to bring the cardinal down here. This is not the kind of an issue a clergyman should get involved in," a Catholic councilman admonished.[39]

Informants kept Pomerleau abreast of the activities of a Catholic antiwar faction led by Minnesota-born brothers Daniel and Philip Berrigan. They were sons of an Irish Catholic trade union member, socialist, and railway engineer. Daniel was a Jesuit priest. Phil did combat duty in Europe during World War II, then joined the Josephites, a priestly order ministering to African Americans. They were inspired by the Catholic Worker Movement. Founded by Dorothy Day and Peter Maurin in 1933, it had since grown to include some two hundred autonomous communities of believers who pledged to "live in accordance with the justice and charity of Jesus Christ." The community run by Phil, by now defrocked, and his wife, Elizabeth McAllister, a former nun, was called Jonah House and located on Park Avenue in Baltimore's Reservoir Hill. Another place where activism flowered was Viva House, a spiritual outpost and soup kitchen near Union Square, the neighborhood where Mencken once lived. This is how it came about: Brendan Walsh, a seminarian, came to Baltimore to work with the Berrigan brothers, and met Willa Bickham, a nun. They married and raised a family dedicated to fighting for peace and dignity, serving a declining neighborhood of drug addicts and prostitutes but also of struggling families wondering where their next meal might come from.

The activists felt they had the moral right and obligation to break laws because they regarded all wars as inhuman and the U.S. involvement in Indochina as criminal. They thrived on publicity. The Berrigans led a contingent—the Catonsville Nine—to raid the Selective Service's suburban

Catonsville office, where they carried out hundreds of draft files and poured blood on them. They then doused them with napalm concocted by Johns Hopkins physics student Dean Pappas, and set them on fire. Napalm was the flammable liquid that U.S. forces used to incinerate jungle supply trails and villages in Indochina. Countless similar "actions" followed, each with a new dramatic twist that earned headlines. More than once Phil chain-locked himself to military base fences, throwing the key away.

Catholic antiwar activists were of particular interest to law enforcement agencies because they connected with the rest of the movement. In 1970 Mary Moylan, a nurse who was a member of the Catonsville Nine, came up with the idea of opening the People's Free Clinic on Greenmount Avenue. "Look, the Black Panther Party has established free clinics in a number of cities. Why don't we establish a free clinic, together, with them, as partners?" she said, according to Jim Keck, another prime mover. The group voted and said, 'Yes, this would be a good thing, let's do that.'[40]

Meanwhile, a Catholic underground group in Philadelphia performed the most audacious caper. On a March night in 1971, as America watched the first Joe Frazier–Muhammad Ali heavyweight championship fight, eight members of the Citizens' Commission to Investigate the FBI burglarized the agency's Philadelphia office in Media. Unbelievably, there was no security— no surveillance cameras, no alarms, not even locks on many file cabinets. The FBI office shared the building with apartments. All went without a hitch; residents were glued to their television sets, too excited to pay attention to any strange noises.

In Catonsville, the Berrigans burned and soiled records. What the Catholic underground group did in Pennsylvania was far more devastating. It stole the FBI office files, and carted the contents out to their vehicles. Members then pored over each document. At first the abbreviation COINTELPRO rang no bells, but then they realized that the acronym hid J. Edgar Hoover's top-secret domestic spying program. They began releasing occasional documents from their explosive haul. Now that COINTELPRO had been exposed, Hoover ended it. He launched a big manhunt to catch the perpetrators. He came back empty-handed. No suspects, no fingerprints, nothing. His vaunted bureau proved incapable of solving the case. When the identities of the burglars and their painstaking planning were finally revealed forty-two years later, it was the work of a gutsy veteran journalist, Betsy Medsger, who documented everything in *The Burglary: The Discovery of J. Edgar Hoover's Secret FBI.*

Baltimore's right-wing groups also were monitored. The local Ku Klux Klan's heyday was in the 1920s, when its two top leaders were the city's chief highway inspector, and a dental surgeon and a clubhouse, Klan Home, existed in a former Presbyterian church at Madison Avenue and Biddle Street.[41] The

Klan's influence then steadily decreased, but still, four decades later, Klansmen tried to force confrontations at Horizon House demonstrations. In the early 1970s, I covered two rural KKK cross burnings, and saw men surreptitiously writing down car tag numbers. I also reported on Charles Luthardt's Fighting American Nationalists. That Klan auxiliary gathered around a sound truck in Riverside Park to listen to harangues and racist songs. Luthardt also proselytized in Patterson Park, where around the corner on Eastern Avenue the National Socialist White People's Party operated a bookstore in a three-story redbrick row house. With a swastika flag flying outside day and night, it was the outpost of a would-be fuehrer, Wolfgang Schrodt, a German-born unemployed truck driver, who filled it with Nazi regalia and white-supremacist propaganda. Neighbors tried to have him evicted but ACLU took his case as an important First Amendment issue and won. When Schrodt departed, he told me, "I'm just trying to make ends meet, just like everybody else."[42]

Such was Baltimore.

Part III

PUSHING OUT THE LUMPENPROLETARIAT

Chapter Eleven

A Citadel of Hope

Ever since its founding, the *Afro-American* had been trying to figure out what to call people of color. "I think the term 'Negro' [black] is disgusting. If not African, why not call us colored?" a letter writer opined in 1895. The editor agreed. Black was evil—angel's food cake was white, devil's food cake black. Little girls burst into tears if called black, tar-baby. "The term 'Negro' has always been offensive . . . and should never be used," he wrote in a front-page editorial.[1]

That became the editorial policy. Nearly seventy-five years later, after the 1968 riots, the *Afro* published a commemorative text of Martin Luther King's "I Have a Dream" speech. In the paper's version King's references to "Negroes" and "Negro children" were edited out and changed to "colored." Except that the *Afro* was badly out of touch. By that time the once-hurtful term black was increasingly in vogue as a self-characterization.[2] The soul singer James Brown almost single-handedly changed the usage shortly before King's killing, when he busted the charts with an anthem that replayed endlessly on WEBB, a radio station he owned in Baltimore:

> *I've worked on jobs with my feet and my hands*
> *But all the work I did was for the other man*
> *And now we demand a chance to do things for ourselves*
> *We tired of beatin' our head against the wall*
> *An' workin' for someone else*

> *Say it loud! I'm black and I'm proud*
> *Say it loud! I'm black and I'm proud*
> *Say it loud! I'm black and I'm proud*
> *Say it loud! I'm black and I'm proud, oh!*

Ooh-wee, you're killin' me
Alright, uh, you're out of sight!
Alright, so tough you're tough enough!
Ooh-wee uh! you're killin' me! oow!

Black consciousness was in the air. Activists at inner-city parishes would soon darken statues of white Jesus with mahogany stain. This was the atmosphere in 1969, when the Hospital and Nursing Home Employees' Union set up noisy picket lines in front of Hopkins Hospital, hoping to win recognition as the bargaining agent for menial workers. Hopkins was a tough nut to crack. In the 1940s the mighty Congress of Industrial Organizations (CIO, before its merger with AFL) had tried to unionize eight hundred orderlies, laundry workers, cooks and kitchen help, laboratory technicians, and maintenance personnel. It got nowhere. The hospital simply refused to recognize the union. Administrators and trustees argued, with the support of leading newspapers, that because Hopkins provided essential public services regardless of the patient's ability to pay, unions and strikes did not belong there.[3] "The hospital's sole purpose is the care of the sick and injured," said Dr. Russell Nelson, the hospital president. "We cannot do this work under conditions where a group could interfere with or even interrupt services." The law was on the hospital's side. The Taft-Hartley Act specifically forbade union activity at private nonprofit hospitals like Hopkins.[4] The hospital defeated another unionization attempt in 1959 by raising wages.[5]

The Hospital and Nursing Home Employees' Union that now tried its luck was originally formed by Jewish drugstore clerks in Manhattan in 1932. It had recently won a bitter 114-day strike at two hospitals in Charleston, South Carolina, partnering with Martin Luther King's old organization, the Southern Christian Leadership Conference. Now SCLC targeted Hopkins.[6] "With soul power and union power we are going to tear down the walls of injustice in Baltimore," SCLC president Ralph David Abernathy vowed. "We are going to sock it to Baltimore."[7]

That kind of talk scared many whites in a city traumatized by the previous year's riots. It was no empty talk either. From a rented storefront on Broadway, across from Hopkins, a thirty-three-year-old army veteran of stints in Korea and Japan spearheaded the Local 1199E effort.[8] "The trouble with too many unions today is that you can't tell the difference between the union and management," he told me. In Fred Punch's case there was no mistaking. Blessed with that kick-ass name, he looked like a union firebrand from central casting. The eldest of ten children, the native of New York's Bedford Stuyvesant had been a hospital worker himself. He thrived on keeping his adversaries off balance. "By skillfully alternating the rhetoric of brotherly love and non-violence with the rhetoric of militancy and Black Power, he made it difficult for administrators to know his true intentions; they never knew what to expect from him," Gregg L. Michel wrote in his examination of the effort, "Union Power, Soul Power: Unionizing Johns Hopkins University Hospital, 1959–1974."[9] A leading labor lawyer described Punch as "the most aggressive and worst" union leader he had ever encountered.[10] Recalled a Hopkins official: "The first time I met Fred Punch was one of those High Noons at Hopkins—I stood under the statue of Jesus. He marched out there and called us every name in the book."[11]

Punch succeeded because years of past Gay Street organizing by CORE, the Black Panthers, and U-JOIN had prepared the soil. Rallying around race, the union demonstrated how Stokely Carmichael's original black power cry had been mainstreamed. Punch didn't waste any time in slamming the race card on the table. You only had to watch the evening television news to see pickets with raised fists, shouting, hoisting placards, and carrying on: "Johns Hopkins Hospital is Racist," "End Poverty at Johns Hopkins." He promised more punch to come: "We have a lot of angry blacks at Hopkins, and only when we put 10,000 workers on the street will they [management] begin to understand." In one year, his small cadre of zealots brought some six thousand workers into the union at eight hospitals. It also represented twenty-five nursing homes, including locals originally created by CORE's Maryland Freedom Union.[12]

The unionization campaign was long and arduous. It made national headlines when Coretta Scott King, continuing her slain husband's focus on poverty and income equality, joined Local 1199E picket lines, gave speeches, and raised funds.[13] Of Hopkins workers she said: "They are sick and tired of working full-time jobs at part-time pay."[14] The hospital workers' demands became a broader civil rights issue. Baltimore's postal workers, municipal garbage men, teachers, and policemen also were in the process of unionization, pressing for respect, better wages, and an end to racial discrimination. Wickwire, the Hopkins chaplain, supported 1199E and so did the Interdenominational Ministerial Alliance.[15] The union also won the backing of some two hundred members of a liberal group of doctors, nurses, and medical students. "We support the right of the union to organize hospital employees," said Dr. Thomas C. Washburn, cochairman of the group. "We feel this is a basic civil liberty regardless of the fact that the hospital is a non-profit institution."[16]

An assistant professor of pediatrics at the medical school, Washburn illustrated the caste system that prevails to this day. As university employees with an academic rank, he and other doctors enjoyed the perks and benefits of a faculty appointment, including retirement, and members of their professional and clerical staffs were in the same system. The worked together at the hospital with black women and men occupying menial jobs (along with whites) who were not employees of the university but of the hospital. Their hours were long and their pay and perks were inferior. That's why they demanded higher wages and benefits.[17] "When the workers won, it was the first time Hopkins was beat—and by its own work force," Robert Moore, an SNCC activist and 1199E organizer told me.

"A HOSTILE BLACK COMMUNITY"

Labor tensions continued, however, adding to the hospital's crisis. Back in 1889, when it opened, the hospital was a charity taking care of the poor. For a long time, hospitals, such as they were, did not appeal to anyone who could avoid them. They presented no advantage over home care because conditions were primitive, and no breakthrough medical technology or cures existed. Instead, horse-and-buggy-riding doctors, medicine men and women on foot, including midwives, made house calls, with family or friends caring for the sick. When Johns Hopkins himself fell ill with cholera, leading physicians brought him back to health in his city mansion, with his own servants feeding him and giving him around-the-clock attention. Breakthrough hospitals changed all that, Hopkins included. The advent of asepsis, anesthesia, modern technology and medicines brought about a revolution. As technical diagnostic tools, electronic monitors, scanners, specific medications, and teams of technicians became commonplace, the hospital was "no longer looked upon as the haven for the incurable; its reputation for miracles has made it a citadel of hope," a 1970 Hopkins report stated.[18] Aided by new health insurance schemes, paying patients seeking specialized treatment turned Hopkins into a growth engine. "The medical care now provided is fantastically complex and effective in comparison to that available one or two decades ago."[19]

With medical miracles came market demand for creature comforts. As a result of the introduction of jet airliners, wealthy and famous people could shop for treatment near and far. Hospitals became niches of the *hospitality* industry. A well-heeled patient wanted a room resembling a luxury hotel, complete with an à la carte menu of fine steaks and lobster, served by a tuxedoed butler. And what about family members? They also had to have nice places to stay, with attractions and conveniences that helped them cope with a stressful situation. If Hopkins—and Baltimore—did not provide the desired services and amenities, rival hospitals in other cities were eager to step in. In any case, why would any important person want to come to Hopkins? True, the citadel of hope was a bastion of breakthroughs and excellence. But nothing could erase the stigma of its location smack in the midst of squalor and abandoned buildings, surrounded by poor blacks of all ages whose mere presence and demeanor some visitors viewed as threatening.

This was the backdrop when Hopkins began weighing its options in the midst of the Local 1199E tumult. What was the hospital's future? Did it even belong on Broadway, the site the founder himself had handpicked?

Those questions had been on the table since shortly before the riots, when a committee began evaluating the long-term viability of the hospital's Broadway operation. It became the task of Dr. David E. Price to sort things out. He was fifty-two at the time, retired from the U.S. Public Health Service, and on a consultancy assignment in India for the Ford Foundation when he was appointed the hospital's director of planning. He held bachelor's, master's, and medical degrees from the University of California and a master's and a doctorate in public health from Hopkins. Close to the riots' first anniversary, chiefs of clinical departments and their deputies weighed options at a two-day off-site meeting. In an April 1970 paper, *Hospital Services in the 1970's*, Price presented three scenarios to move forward:

> The first is to strive for institutional self-sufficiency that would put under one roof, as it were, a desirable mix of health services—ranging from primary care through intermediate level inpatient service, and diagnostic outpatient service, to highly specialized inpatient and intensive care, rehabilitation and extended care.
>
> The second alternative would be to retain under the Hopkins roof only selected aspects of a comprehensive model of health service and to depend on affiliation with other institutions to provide an educational linkage through which our students and house staff would be exposed to a complementary way to those aspects Hopkins chose to retain.
>
> The third alternative would be to become the nucleus of or to participate in the formation of a consortium of health care facilities each of which specializes in the provision of some level of health service and which taken together would represent a model of comprehensive health services with all members of the consortium participating in the educational activities.

Price confronted the Broadway problem head-on. "A hostile black community, constantly reminded of past expansion, limits future enlargement of the site. The characteristics of the neighborhood make the area uncongenial for employees, staff and students," he wrote. "The choices made by other patients from outlying areas of the city to enter outlying hospitals for their care reflect a general repulsion from the inner city."[20] Worse still, the poor black residents' routine medical needs clashed with the ambitions of the hospital and medical school—"the first American medical institutions dedicated to scientific clinical investigation and instruction," as historian Karen Kruse Thomas put it.

Wrote Price: "A large proportion of the care Hopkins is now called upon to give does not require the complex, expensive resources needed to perform a highly special mission. Because the staff is overworked and the hospital overwhelmed, neither the very sophisticated specialized care which is considered its distinctive role, nor the simpler primary care so much in demand, is being performed to the satisfaction of the faculty and staff, or the consumers, their patients." To overcome this, Price wrote, Hopkins should discontinue "primary care of a kind generally rendered out-of-hospital," "intermediate level care of a kind adequately performed in a community hospital," as well as "long-term care of chronic illnesses." Instead, Hopkins should specialize in referral and diagnostic medicine and "highly specialized and intensive care of complex illness."

Price discussed the idea of abandoning Broadway altogether and building a new hospital and medical school near the Homewood campus. The University of Chicago had done something like that in the 1920s when it moved the medical school to Hyde Park. A more recent example was Stanford, in California, which in 1959 relocated the medical school from San Francisco to the main campus in Palo Alto. But the Homewood option was closed to Hopkins: The campus did not have enough space and was ringed by built-up residential neighborhoods with considerable clout. Instead, Hopkins officials discussed a move to suburban Howard County, young and growing town of Columbia, midway between Baltimore and the nation's capital. Columbia "offers one possible relocation point," Price wrote.

Columbia was the invention of James W. Rouse, the real estate developer who had spearheaded the failed 1954 Baltimore Plan to revitalize a slum near Hopkins. Since then he had built trendsetting shopping malls, and brought life to abandoned city sites. Among his earliest projects was Underground Atlanta, which turned post–Civil War brick catacombs into a shopping and entertainment draw. He soon moved on to refashion postindustrial waterfronts into tourist destinations. But before that he stealthily patched together fourteen thousand acres of farmland for his new town. When the first of Columbia's ten villages was inaugurated in 1967, the metropolitan real estate market was still segregated racially. Columbia was different, Rouse pledged. It welcomed all races, religions, and classes. Television commercials touted it as "The Next America." In time, escalating home prices constrained the founder's egalitarian ideas, and some congregations rejected his wish that various religions worship at communal Interfaith Centers, instead of building sanctuaries of their own. Even so, Columbia was a success. Over the next half century, it ranked among the most desirable communities anywhere. (I once asked Rouse what he would have done differently in hindsight. "Density," he answered, "higher density, so that public transit would work.")

In future years, Hopkins Medicine would embark on a steady suburban expansion strategy through partnerships and acquisitions—even operating a children's hospital in St. Petersburg, Florida—but the move to Columbia never happened. Any relocation would have been wrought with perils and may have seemed irresponsibly risky because Columbia was still a promise, not the state's second-largest town, as it is today. On the other hand, Hopkins was already involved in Columbia. It ran Maryland's first HMO there, a health insurance and managed-care plan with its own doctors and facilities.[21] In the end, what guided decision making in choosing the location was access to human clinical material. Wrote Price: "When the question of a complete relocation of the Medical Institutions is considered, a number of factors other than the substantial investment in current facilities come to bear. The educational program needs the contact with the inner-city poor and their special burdens of physical and social pathology. At the same time it needs the different pathology of the more affluent, who can communicate deeper insights on the history of their ailments to illumine the learning and research processes of students."

The hospital was swamped with run-of-the-mill patients because East Baltimore was so grossly underserved. The ten census tracks surrounding one of the world's premiere hospitals had one doctor serving six thousand people—or fifteen serving a population of a hundred thousand—whereas national average was one doctor for 750 patients. The level of health was markedly lower than elsewhere in the city, and residents sought medical help only in dire emergencies. Concluded a Hopkins study: "The infant mortality rate in census tracts 10-1 and 10-2 (the old Tenth ward, centering on Latrobe Homes west of the hospital), in 1967, was as high as 37 deaths for every 1,000 live births, as compared to a rate of 21.6 for Baltimore's white population . . . tuberculosis, with 887 newly reported cases in 1967, places the inner city of Baltimore as the third highest in the country." Thirty percent of TB cases involved children.[22]

Once the decision was made to keep Hopkins's medical base on Broadway, steps were taken to divert routine patients elsewhere. Hopkins created the East Baltimore Medical Plan, Maryland's second HMO, with its own doctors and treatment facilities. The prepaid plan initially covered about five thousand people in the Somerset, Latrobe, Douglass, and Lafayette public housing projects and then expanded fivefold. Other patients were diverted to Good Samaritan Hospital, a Hopkins-run Catholic facility built in 1968, and to collaborating clinics.[23] To further ease the burden on Hopkins, Price proposed the establishment of a separate, two hundred-bed community hospital, "staffed, like the Columbia program, with physicians recruited to provide intermediate level services, backed up by the specialist services of the Johns

Hopkins Hospital and its staff." It was to provide emergency services and have "such outpatient services as may be necessary to supplement ambulatory care provided by community clinics."

It took more than a decade for the community hospital to materialize. And when it did, William Donald Schaefer played a key role. On becoming mayor in 1971 he inherited the troubles of City Hospitals at Bayview, a 134-acre compound on the grounds of a one-time almshouse for paupers that had been a favorite of grave robbers. The capacity of City Hospitals peaked at some seventeen hundred beds before veterans' hospitals were built. For periods, its medical operations were overseen by Hopkins, whose experimenters accessed human clinical material there. A 1907 article in the Hopkins *Bulletin* received wide coverage in the British press and aroused controversy on both sides of the Atlantic. It described a Hopkins doctor at City Hospitals testing the effects of overdosing with thyroid extract on eight lunatics, one of whom was "murdered scientifically," the Anti-Vivisection Society of Maryland charged. "It was determined in this scandalous torture den to induce grave symptoms of poisoning in certain incurable patients whose minds were so enfeebled that no complaints they could make would be likely to be listened to." Hopkins defended the experiment.[24]

By the time Schaefer appeared on the scene, half a century had gone by and City Hospitals was full of excess beds in ramshackle buildings. The city did not have money to fix the antiquated sick-house four miles east of the Broadway campus. The oversized relic was a drain on the municipal budget, a never-ending mess, whose record-keeping auditors repeatedly found spotty and billing haphazard. Outside operators had been tried but Schaefer was not satisfied. After periodic earlier contacts, he spent two years negotiating a deal with Hopkins.[25] It was a sweetheart deal. The city gave the buildings, equipment, and much land to Hopkins, which also received a $5.4 million onetime subsidy. Hopkins offered the best way to put valuable assets to their full use, Schaefer believed.

I remember from conversations with him how consumed he was about unloading the burdensome Bayview. Over years, he developed a rapport with Ronald Peterson, a Hopkins negotiator in the1984 transfer deal. In a mere decade after arriving at the hospital as a graduate student ("administrative resident") in an eleven-month management training program, Peterson had impressed everyone. He soon administered the Henry Phipps Psychiatric Clinic, headed the hospital's cost-improvement program, and ran the Johns Hopkins Children's Center. He now was put in charge of transforming the City Hospitals complex first into the Francis Scott Key Medical Center and then rebranding it as the Johns Hopkins Bayview Medical Center. Peterson directed an initial $100 million physical redevelopment program at the seven hundred-bed hospital, turning a $7 million-a-year loss under city ownership into a "positive bottom-line performance." He eventually became a rare non-physician to head the whole Hopkins Medicine colossus.

Schaefer was a true Smalltimorean, as quirky as his provincial hometown. I knew him as a hardworking, shrewd politician. He graduated from the storied City College high school, whose alumni network veritably ran the town. In World War II, he reached the officer ranks and administered field hospitals in England and on the continent. Back home, he obtained a law degree from the University of Baltimore, a poor man's night school that produced title lawyers and politicians; he became both. In a city of traditionally segregated neighborhoods, he was an oddity. He lived with his mother, Tululu Irene, in Edmondson Village where they were among the last white holdouts after blockbusters engineered a rapid wholesale racial change. He was a frugal and dutiful son who fussed over his African violets and regularly took his widowed mother to dinner at Connolly's, a modest seafood shack built of corrugated metal along one of the piers downtown. His vacation spot in Maryland's Ocean City was a trailer park.

Little in Schaefer's early years suggested that he would be a "Messiah Mayor," so called because he took on to resurrect a city left for dead after the riots. He lost his first two tries at elective office, and was so awkward that Irv Kovens nicknamed him "Shaky." Then, with Kovens's blessings, he got voted onto the city council from the mostly Jewish Fifth District, the only goy on the ticket. He rose to city council president, the No. 2 elected position at city hall. When Young Tommy D'Alesandro, emotionally exhausted from the destructive riots, decided not to seek reelection, Schaefer succeeded him in 1971. Up to that time many had speculated about the possibility of Baltimore electing a black mayor like some other big cities had done. But when Democratic primary votes were counted (by hand) in a city where Republicans did not count, Schaefer garnered 94,809 votes and carried all white precincts. Of the blacks, George Russell's interracial ticket received 58,223. Clarence Mitchell III got 6,582 votes.[26]

Schaefer was fifty years old. He played for keeps by preempting predictable future challengers from the field. He co-opted his main black opponent, Russell. The forty-two-year-old former judge agreed to continue as city solicitor, running a governmental law office bigger than the downtown law firms. With Kovens's backing, Russell then tried, unsuccessfully, to unseat Parren J. Mitchell, Maryland's first black congressman.[27] Majority black Baltimore might seethe at its political impotence, but not until Schaefer resigned to become governor did an African American rise to mayor. Among white politicians, Schaefer's chief rival, Councilman Robert C. Embry Jr., dropped out. At thirty-three, the Harvard-educated Embry, a fellow City College alumnus, was a good-government advocate, who ended up serving as Schaefer's housing commissioner, worked as a high federal housing administrator in Jimmy Carter's administration, tried his hand as a developer (with his City College classmate David Cordish), and sat on the school board. As the head of the Abell Foundation, he became the gray eminence of the nonprofit sector who pulled strings behind the scenes. He awarded grants, commissioned policy studies and op-ed pieces, and supported the *Baltimore Brew* Internet newspaper, known for gutsy reporting and penetrating analyses of municipal practices. But he never returned to elective politics.[28]

As mayor, Schaefer inherited a gritty, declining industrial town with low self-esteem and with physical and emotional scars from the riots three years before. Baltimore had once been America's third largest city—after Philadelphia—but then became an also-ran after the state politicians took away annexation powers and the city could no longer grow its territory and population. Bethlehem Steel's Sparrows Point illustrated Baltimore's slide. It was the world's largest steel mill when in the early 1960s "Beth Steel completely reversed course, deciding to build a new steel mill at Burns Harbor near Gary, Indiana," said Mark Reutter, a railroad historian and author of *Making Steel: Sparrows Point and the Rise and Ruin of American Industrial Might.* "At the same time, Baltimore's onetime pride and joy and source of riches, B&O, was a total mess. It had lumbered through the mid-40s from its sheer bulk and geographic scope, then came undone by its sheer bulk and costly antiquated facilities." The Chesapeake & Ohio, a much smaller railroad, then got its hands on B&O and downgraded Johns Hopkins's and John Garrett's erstwhile line. Its top officers were furloughed or moved first to Cleveland, and then to Jacksonville. Overall, Baltimore was on its way to becoming a branch office town.[29]

Despite a steady exodus to nearby counties, many Baltimoreans found the city as comfortable as a pair of worn-out slippers. It was a nickel city, big enough, cheap, and unpretentious; Washington down the road was a dime city. Each year, Straw Hat Day on May 15 marked the return of straw boaters and seersucker attires to be worn until Labor Day. Summertime fun included snoballs, cheap bleacher seats at Memorial Stadium where the Orioles played, and visits to neighborhood crab houses where waitresses called everyone "hon" and where whole families hammered steaming crustaceans at long newspaper-covered tables groaning under pitchers of beer. A municipal park band, formed in 1914, concertized in neighborhoods.[30] Each performance began with the singing of the city's official anthem, with the audience standing and following the lyrics through a bouncing ball on a screen:[31]

Baltimore Our Baltimore,
where Carroll flourished, and the fame of Calvert grew!
Here the old defenders conquered as their valiant swords they drew.
Here the starry banner glistened in the sunshine of the sea.
In that dawn of golden vision that awoke the song of Key.
Here are hearts that beat forever for the city we adore.
Here the love of men and brothers—Baltimore, our Baltimore!

This was the wholesome image Schaefer wanted to promote. An advertising agency came up with "Charm City" as a gimmick in which visitors would purchase charms at tourist stops and attach them to a bracelet. The charm part did not take hold, but the nickname stuck. The more people laughed about the hokey slogan, the more they wanted to believe it. Schaefer had downtown sidewalks painted pink as part of a "pink positive" campaign. In another stunt, he stepped into the National Aquarium's seal pool, wearing a straw boater and a striped, one-piece Victorian swimsuit. He clutched a rubber duck. Those pictures made newspapers around the world.

In his free time, Schaefer drove around, inspecting neighborhoods, counting potholes. One summer day, with windows down, he was at a traffic light on Baltimore Street when someone snatched his wristwatch. That made him mad. Incidents like these produced feared "action memos" that became legendary. Once, instead of giving the address for a derelict car he wanted removed, Schaefer challenged the bureaucracy to find the vehicle. "City crews ran around like hungry gerbils for a week. Must have towed five hundred cars," reported *Esquire*'s Richard Ben Cramer, a former *Sun* reporter, in an article about Schaefer. A series of memos involved the city's four unsuccessful attempts to sell a Fells Point house that deteriorated before Schaefer's very eyes. He grew increasingly annoyed as his memos produced no action. One afternoon, about 4:30, housing administrator J. Randall Evans received a call from the mayor, who barked a deadline: "Young man, I'm sick and tired of hearing your excuses. I want that house fixed up by morning." There was no way to do that. Instead, Evans and an aide scrambled to Sears to buy curtains, rods, and other props. "The house didn't have any floors. I stood on [an assistant's] shoulders to put the curtains up." Then they put out a sign that read: "Brought To You By Mayor William Donald Schaefer And The Citizens of Baltimore." Schaefer called Evans by nine o'clock the next morning. "You could hear him smiling over the telephone."[32]

Schaefer's direct involvement in the Bayview deal illustrated his hands-on management style. He was a do-it-now mayor, frustrated by the slowness of the municipal government. The tortoise pace was due to all kinds of rules and regulations enacted to protect taxpayers. For example, borrowing development money through the municipal bond process took a couple of years because voters had to approve each request. Such time-consuming red tape harmed deal making, or so Schaefer believed. He cut the Gordian knot by ostensibly privatizing a bevy of city agencies—such as the economic development arm—and creating a private development bank, the Loan and Guarantee Fund. "The Shadow Government," as his biographer C. Fraser Smith dubbed it, was an ingenious piece of hocus pocus. One trustee was Charles L. Benton Jr., the powerful city finance director; another was Larry Dale, the city treasurer. By simply switching back and forth between their city and private-trustee roles, they could strike and finance deals without public scrutiny and bypass ordinary procurement processes. The trustees gave Schaefer things he coveted for breathing life into the city—"new money, speed and flexibility, advantages that would not be available to them if they confined themselves to activities that were strictly in conformity with the city's charter," writes Smith. "The trustees and their agencies began to make marginal or high-risk projects, projects the banks would not touch." Many succeeded, many failed.

Schaefer could be rude and abusive. He did not take criticism well and once publicly called the whole Eastern Shore "the shithouse of Maryland." When he was striking a deal to construct a new stadium to keep the Orioles in Baltimore, he met with the team owner, New York financier Eli Jacobs, at Dalesio's restaurant in Little Italy to hash out details. This is how part of the conversation went, according to Schaefer's friend, the elections administrator Gene Raynor, who owned the restaurant and witnessed the exchange:

"Look now, Elijah."

"My name is not Elijah, it's Eli."

"And my name is Schaefer."

Pause.

"Look, Mr. Jacobson."

"My name is not Jacobson, it's Jacobs."

"And my name is Schaefer."

That was the mayor's clumsy way of trying to convey that he wanted the stadium named after himself. "Eli got up and took the check," remembered Raynor. "Schaefer said: I tried, that's all I can do."

THE INNER HARBOR

Schaefer was a bullheaded man of German ancestry, prone to temper tantrums, usually in private but occasionally also in public. Remarkably, he was aware of his limitations, and surrounded himself with doers, dedicated and bright men and women of all ages, ethnicities, and religions, who saw the diversity of neighborhoods as worth celebrating. Their imagination promoted city living, reenergized the Citizens Planning and Housing Association and inspired an annual city fair that attracted hundreds of thousands of visitors to celebrate the promise of tomorrow. *Esquire* dubbed Schaefer America's best mayor, and that may have been so for a while. But Cramer wondered: "How will they ever make a statue of him. They'll have to, you know. He saved the town. But how could they bronze that stubby little body, the melon head, the double chin?" A likeness was eventually erected; the sculptor got the gait right.

Today that bronze Schaefer waves from a harbor promenade at all he created.

He turned that stinky old basin into the glistening Inner Harbor, right? Not quite. In fact, the harbor's urban renewal was put in motion by Theodore R. McKeldin, a two-time mayor and two-term governor. He is an unsung hero of Maryland politics, a progressive Republican and a civil rights reformer, who rejected his party's 1964 presidential candidate, Barry Goldwater, and instead endorsed the Democrat Lyndon B. Johnson. He was responsible for many infrastructure projects. The rebirth of the Inner Harbor, tunnels underneath, a new airport, and the construction of the Baltimore Beltway were conceived on his watch.

Thus it was McKeldin, who in 1946 submitted a bond issue to voters' approval so that new bulkheads could be constructed in the basin.[33] That's how today's Inner Harbor began. A few years later, the real estate developer James Rouse sent McKeldin a letter outlining ideas for the waterfront. By the time Schaefer became mayor, so much infrastructural work had been done that it was left for him to mostly come up with the bells and whistles that would bring tourists to the Inner Harbor. Tourists? You gotta be kidding, no tourists came to Baltimore. In the old days, The Basin had been so odorous that H. L. Mencken wrote that by each August it reeked like "a billion polecats."[34] Schaefer's predecessors changed that, and he kindled the public's imagination during the 1976 bicentennial celebrations by a display of tall ships visiting from around the world. Nothing had been built along the harbor embankment yet. Huge crowds of visitors came at all hours of the day and night to admire the majesty of the ships. They saw the potential.[35]

Heated debates raged over what the Inner Harbor should be. Some citizens demanded that it remain undisturbed open space, dedicated to Sam Smith, a mayor who was a hero of the 1812 war. But Schaefer wanted a strong life pulse. To provide that, he engaged Rouse, who came up with Harborplace, a two-pavilion arcade of shops and restaurants. That hugely popular centerpiece attraction today is a victim of its own success—a collection of chain operations that could be anywhere. The original Harborplace was different. It served a real slice of Bawlamer, the native pronunciation of the city's name. It was a tourist version of Lexington Market. The vendors were local entrepreneurs, handpicked by Paula Rome, a CPHA activist, who toured the region in search of interesting concepts and products. A delightful stall sold flavorful spices; its knowledgeable owners were visibly gay and proud of it. Among other vendors, Michael Butler quit his job as the telephone company's personnel manager to open a burger joint; Jay Harrison gave up his job in the mayor's office to sell galoshes. One store sold plush, cushy, toy versions of animals. Operated by a former director of the Baltimore Zoo, it was called "Arthur Watson's Embraceable Zoo."[36]

As visitors came by the millions, the range of merchandise changed to cater to mass tastes. Other tourist attractions were added: National Aquarium, Maryland Science Center, a collection of old ships, the PowerPlant entertainment venue. Foreign experts streamed in to see how Baltimore had rejuvenated the waterfront. The gospel spread, imitators cropped up. Sydney, Australia, was so inspired it did its much-acclaimed version of the Inner Harbor, the Darling Harbour, with the sail-like Opera House as the crowning feature.[37] Yet it was a miracle that the Inner Harbor even existed.

In Johns Hopkins's days The Basin was a smelly nuisance. In floods, its muck frequently merged with Jones Falls debris, inundating much of downtown. In July 1868 two storms collided in the wee hours. By midday, the Jones Falls had risen twenty inches over its walled banks, with waves eroding the foundations of the current city hall, then under construction, contributing to its persistent rat problems. Seven bridges were swept away. "Its yellow flood came down with a turbulent roar like some mountain torrent, bringing in its headlong rush fragments of bridges and buildings, uprooted trees, drift wood, fences, outhouses, sheds, oil tanks, barrels, merchandise &c."[38]

Such periodic floods were preventable, Dr. Thomas H. Buckler believed. He was a prominent physician, whose patients included General Robert E. Lee and Chief Justice Taney. For the previous decade the pathologist had been urging the city to demolish Federal Hill and use the clay and dirt to fill up The Basin so that the Jones Falls could be redirected to empty farther down in Anne Arundel County waters. Buckler hated The Basin, which he saw as a diseased and hazardous cesspool. But he hated Federal Hill even more. The name celebrated the nation's "federal" constitution, but during the Civil War the Union occupation forces were headquartered there. He wrote: "How long is that uncouth, ill-shaped, ill-looking, unmetropolitan monstrosity and idiosity [*sic*]—Federal Hill—to be allowed to stand and prevent ventilation by shutting off all sea and land breeze from the lower part of the town? For what object is this Federal Hill allowed still to rear its head in the very front of a democratic city unless to commemorate the occupation for a night by General Ben Butler."[39] (After the Civil War Buckler found conditions in Baltimore so intolerable that he took his practice to Paris for three decades, preaching his harbor ideas on visits and in newspaper articles. He invited Lee to join him there, but the general declined.)

Buckler's reading of the law convinced him that while the city owned the water in The Basin, the ground below the surface was anyone's to claim. He filed a warrant "for the purchase of 80 acres of vacant land"—the bottom of The Basin. He said he did so protectively in order to prevent any speculators from making a killing because it was obvious that The Basin would soon be filled. Once that happened, he would gladly give the bottom to the city for the price of incidental expenses. The only action he got was a city council move to "prevent any party or parties from acquiring a legal title to the open space now occupied by the Basin within this city, or to any ground that may be made in that locality hereafter should the same ever be filled up."[40]

Johns Hopkins had his headquarters on the banks of the basin, where he owned some seventy substantial commercial buildings. Three decades after his death, the Great Fire of 1904 incinerated the whole district. Until then, its north-south thoroughfare, Light Street, "was hardly more than an alley, thronged with horses and wagons and scurrying pedestrians, pervaded with the odor of spices and overlaid with the music of a dozen honky-tonks," remembered *The Sun* chief editor Hamilton Owens, writing under the pen name John O'ren. "But the little steamboats still left its many wharves every day and the stevedores still sang their songs as they wheeled their trucks up and down the gangplanks."[41] By the time post–World War II urban renewal came, the oldest buildings were less than a half-century old, yet they chronicled a lifestyle that had vanished. The Light Street terminals and warehouses were the last relics from the once-thriving traffic on paddle wheelers to the Eastern Shore and overnight steamers to Virginia, traditions that began as transport necessities and ended in the early 1960s.[42]

Since Buckler's days, several plans have been put forward to partially fill the Inner Harbor. The most serious was the Greater Baltimore Committee's 1957 proposal to use federal urban renewal funds to fill ten acres and build a civic center on reclaimed land. The committee hired Pietro Belluschi to do the plan. He was a modernist guru, the Italian-born architecture dean of the Massachusetts Institute of Technology. His plan won the support of mayor Old Tommy D'Alesandro, the city council, the Citizens Planning and Housing Association, the American Institute of Architects, and a long list of dazzled do-gooders. They were jerked back to reality, when the McCormick spice company, whose nearby plant emitted wondrous fragrances from exotic lands, declared the project insane because high tides in storms would inevitably flood sports and convention facilities (including parking lots for twenty-five hundred cars). A scramble then began for alternative sites. Among those were three in and around Druid Hill Park, where surrounding blocks were turning from Jewish to black. Blacks saw the proposals as destabilization efforts. State senator Verda Welcome reminded me how Schaefer was the only white on the council to hear them out and vote against the proposal. She said such good deeds explained the goodwill he enjoyed among many blacks.[43]

Schaefer's contributions to the Inner Harbor are justly celebrated. However, his role is complicated. At one point in his council career he supported a proposal that would have demolished Federal Hill properties for an interstate, complete with a huge bridge to carry the roaring traffic to today's Harbor East, Fells Point, and Canton. The route was part of the Robert Moses vision. Several neighborhoods were condemned before the proposed alignment was scrapped. As a councilman Schaefer also supported road alternatives that required the condemnation of hundreds of row houses and would have bulldozed through Leakin Park, the city's 1,216-acre urban forest. However, once public opposition to such destructive roads mounted, he shifted his position and did his best to repair the damage. He took Bob Embry's "dollar house" concept and ran with it. A qualifying citizen, committing to a timetable, could plunk down one dollar, buy the shell of a house condemned for the road, rebuild it, and return it to the tax rolls. So many applied that the properties had to be allocated by lottery. Changing economics, a dearth of affordable restorers and trouble with contractors later took the air out of the program, which ended after federal funds were cut.

CANTON

Schaefer stood in awe of "smart fellows," who could be relied on to produce results. Among such was Willard Hackerman, whose Whiting-Turner construction company delivered—for a price. Hackerman was a public-spirited man who shared his blessings. In 1984 he and his wife donated to the city a Mount Vernon Place mansion that became the Walters Art Museum's Asian gallery. About the same time, the Hopkins civil engineering graduate claimed to have found a solution to the city's worsening vacant house problem. With great fanfare, a crane lowered a prefabricated two-story insert into the twelve-foot-wide shell of a row house. This was supposed to begin a drive to cheaply modernize hundreds of derelict vacants. But Hackerman's engineers had overlooked a crucial detail. Nearly all old row houses, despite their cookie-cutter appearance and claimed measurements, were nonstandard and incapable of swallowing prefabricated units. Another defeat in the city's efforts to combat vacants, a struggle that continues to this day![44]

Every year on Schaefer's birthday, Raynor hosted a small dinner party at his Waterfront Hotel in Fells Point (and later at Dalesio's). The Bread Man was there to congratulate, of course. He was John Paterakis, who inherited his Greek immigrant family's' small H & S bakery and expanded it to America's largest privately owned bread business, an empire so big that in addition to stocking supermarkets it baked all McDonald's buns east of the Mississippi. When a savings-and-loan scandal derailed a plan to redevelop a stretch of abandoned industrial shoreline south of Little Italy, Schaefer persuaded the Bread Man to buy the land and do something with it. The result, eventually, was Harbor East, a concentration of towering waterview hotels, condominiums, and prestige offices that in time moved Baltimore's corporate downtown east of the Jones Falls for the first time in history.

Like the Furniture Man before him, the Bread Man invested in politicians. Incumbents counted on his largesse; would-be candidates gauged their chances by seeing how he reacted to their begging. He called in his chips to kill an award-winning shoreline plan so that he could greatly exceed densities and height limits so that he could build his Harbor East towers. He could be generous. But then one day the tables were turned. He did not quite know what to make of the scene that unfolded before his drowsy eyes when he woke up at Hopkins after having collapsed during his regular Saturday breakfast with cronies. There, talking to him, were two dark suits who said they were from Hopkins. They wanted to thank him for his past generosity, they said, for all those millions he had given. But, they coughed, did Mr. Paterakis understand that for a reasonable lump sum a building could be named after him?

"Get out," he ordered.

"But Mr. Paterakis, sir, you don't understand."

"I understand alright. Every year I give you money to keep me alive. If I give you all that money now, you have no reason to keep me alive. Get out."[45]

Louis Grasmick came to the Schaefer birthday dinners with his spouse. Nancy Grasmick was Schaefer's state school superintendent, with a PhD degree from Hopkins (where she later became a codirector of the Kennedy Krieger Institute.) Lou, by contrast, dropped out of school at thirteen when his father died and the surviving family needed to be fed. He played baseball, advancing from sandlot teams to the Phillies, then got a job with a lumber company. He did well and bought into it, growing it into one of the largest on the East Coast.[46]

Grasmick had been among Kovens's coinvestors in the Caesar's Palace venture in Las Vegas, but in the 1971 mayoral race he raised money not for

Schaefer but for the rival Russell ticket that included a city council president running mate, James J. Lacy, the white fire board president with strong Irish connections and a family foundry at the harbor. After the election, Schaefer let it be known that he wanted Grasmick's harbor lumberyard for the Pier Six music pavilion. Fine, but the yard had to be relocated. During negotiations, the two were kicking rubble and looking at sites in Canton, when at one of them Schaefer told him to build housing there. "Housing!" Grasmick shouted. "That's a rat-infested dump that I'm going to convert into a lumber company. But he told me it could become our gold coast," said Grasmick, who had never before built anything.[47]

Grasmick's homes, the first new houses built in Canton, began the postindustrial gentrification of the shoreline. Once the city's center of heavy polluting industry—including a copper company that the philanthropist Johns Hopkins controlled—Canton was reinvented. Long before federal laws required costly decontamination of brownfields, erstwhile canning factories were turned into waterfront condominiums. Plenty of land was available for gentrification because vast areas had been condemned for the interstate road that never came. Grasmick's townhouses, as "row houses" now came to be called, overlooked the water and came with adjoining boat slips. Residents soon got addicted to watching harbor traffic day and night. Once gentrification took hold, he also constructed a condominium tower at the Anchorage. He still couldn't figure it out. It's "absolutely mind-boggling to me," Grasmick said, that well-to-do families spent good money to buy in Canton.

Nearby, another erstwhile Russell supporter, Little Willie Adams, heeded Schaefer's call and added momentum by building the Canton Square townhouses.[48] He had hired a Harvard MBA, Theo C. Rodgers, to run their A & R Development Company. Taking a risk in Canton—and a risk it was—was a small price to pay for city contracts to build federally financed senior housing, which was the company's niche. The townhouses were the first new homes constructed inland in Canton, away from the water. They were well built and much in demand because they were originally designed as roommate condominiums. This is how gentrification gained strength.

Chapter Twelve

Rough Road to Renewal

Following a time-honored Baltimore saying that urged citizens to "vote early and often," an aspiring Dixieland jazz saxophonist living near Hopkins Hospital registered to vote as soon as he turned nineteen in 1937. Never mind that Clarence H. Burns was two years shy of the then-required voting age. He had a job to do. The white Young Men's Bohemian Club hired him as a ward heeler to get out the black vote along Gay Street, a task his laborer father had performed in earlier days. Every vote counted.

Burns was a born hustler, known as "Du" for all that he was doing. "Billie Holiday was a good friend of mine," he said, recalling that the singer lived about four blocks from his house. "I would go up on a train to New York and she'd be singing all night long in some club and she'd let me stay in her apartment up there."[1]

Du got his break in 1946—and it was not in music. Instead, he got a patronage job as a locker room attendant at Dunbar High School. It came courtesy of Young Men's Bohemian Club leader Richard A. Lidinsky, who had accompanied Old Tommy D'Alesandro to city hall as the mayor's right-hand man. A St. Wenceslaus faithful, Lidinsky was a City College alumnus and University of Baltimore law graduate, a mannerly man always wearing black undertaker-style suits; he remained in municipal gatekeeper positions from 1946 until 1991. Remembered Schaefer: "When Old Tommy got sick, Richard was the mayor. He never made a big deal about it and did what he was supposed to do. And he had everyone's confidence."[2]

For two decades, Du paid dues, picking up wet towels at Dunbar and washing uniforms. He allied himself first with Old Tommy and then with Irv Kovens and Little Willie Adams. In 1971, the year William Donald Schaefer began his mayoral rule, he was elected to the city council. He rose to president of that legislative body when the previous occupant was imprisoned for corruption. In 1987 Du was automatically elevated to become Baltimore's first African American mayor when Schaefer went to Annapolis. Said the governor: "Du was a man who got his degree on the street. He's the kind of a guy who is rare in politics now."[3]

Next year Kurt L. Schmoke ousted the sixty-nine-year-old "roads scholar" mayor. Schmoke was a *Rhodes* scholar, having attended Oxford with one of the academe's most coveted honors. The thirty-three-year-old lawyer was every black mother's broadly smiling dream son. By his senior year in high school, he was a minor celebrity, leading an undefeated City College football squad to the state championship while serving as student body president. "When Schmoke showed up in the stands at Johns Hopkins lacrosse games, heads of (mostly white) local high school and prep school spectators would turn. 'Kurt's here,' they would say. 'There's Kurt Schmoke.'"[4]

A graduate of Yale College and Harvard Law School, Schmoke was a textbook liberal. He did not rely on old-style political organizations. Instead, in a city where the typical voter was likely to be a black woman in her fifties and sixties, he networked through sorority sisters in the Alphas, Deltas, and Zetas, and through upwardly mobile professional parents in the Jack and Jill uplift organization. He won support among churchgoers; his stepbrother, Frank M. Reid III, was pastor of the storied Bethel AME church and much later became a bishop. Schmoke also did well among liberal whites.

In the early months of his three terms as mayor, from 1987 to 1999, Schmoke tried politically daring things. He proposed decriminalization of narcotics as a way to reduce turf-battle killings in a city highly addicted to drugs.[5] He launched a campaign against illiteracy, ordering "The City That Reads" slogan painted on benches in parks and at bus stops. Despite the howls of pastors, the health department let high schools decide whether to offer the contraceptive Norplant to sexually active students. The city's teenage pregnancy rate was among the nation's highest, leading to snarky comments about "The City That Breeds" and, as murder rates kept climbing, "The City That Bleeds." Eventually, he convinced HUD to dynamite the public housing high-rise complexes and replace them with mixed-income duplexes, which included not only subsidized rentals but also units for sale.

Still, Du Burns remains germane to the story. Had he been reelected mayor, the Hopkins Hospital area's current reconstitution approach might have taken a different turn. Instead of the landgrab and wholesale razing of eight hundred properties in the eighty-eight-acre extension to the medical campus, it is possible that residential rehabilitation might have become a more widely used strategy. That is because James W. Rouse's Enterprise Foundation had partnered with Hopkins and four housing nonprofits to rehabilitate distressed housing in a hospital neighborhood called Middle East. The developer, who had tried to do the same thing under the Baltimore Plan three decades earlier, now had seed money from the Rockefeller Foundation, plus grants and participation from the city, Hopkins, and various Enterprise subsidiaries. Despite a modest scope, the ambitious goal was to produce a comprehensive neighborhood redevelopment strategy of "housing rehabilitation, employment and training programs, day care, early childhood development, elementary and secondary education and health care."[6]

Once Schmoke took office in 1987 everything ground to a halt. East side voters had overwhelmingly gone for Du, a native son. Why should they get anything? After all, Schmoke had his west side base to consider, including a coalition of activist church groups called Baltimoreans United in Leadership Development (BUILD). Driven by this political imperative, the city axed the embryonic Hopkins redevelopment initiative, instead focusing on Sandtown. That section ran from Fulton and Pennsylvania Avenues below North, adjoining Harlem Park.[7] It once was an area known for its a-rabber horse-cart vendors and other hardworking families whose sons left the hood behind and became leading lawyers, photographers, teachers. Over several decades it became a vast wasteland of distressed row houses.

Rouse initially fought the shift to Sandtown but then became a booster. He had been there before. In the 1960s he had won federal support for an urban renewal plan to construct a thousand new apartment units in the Pennsylvania Avenue corridor—but when Richard M. Nixon came to the White House that funding went away. Now, twenty-five years later, he returned to the west side. But whereas Hopkins would have served as a job-generating anchor in East Baltimore, now there was no institutional anchor. "I thought that was fatal," David Cramer, a planner who worked with Rouse, told me.

BUILD, Habitat for Humanity, and New Song Community Church were among those joining Enterprise in the Sandtown effort. From 1989 to 1999 at least $130 million in public and private money was spent to build or renovate about a thousand homes. Millions more went to develop specialized curriculum for Sandtown schools to ensure that babies were born healthy and to provide job training for residents. Yet revitalization never took hold. The whole Sandtown approach was flawed. Without jobs there was no income to maintain homes or to sustain a community. Some housing was built, for sure. But the neighborhood lacked the economic underpinnings for a turnaround. Without big employers few jobs were accessible to poorly educated residents, many with criminal records and at the mercy of the city's notoriously unreliable public transit system that makes crosstown commuting problematic even today.

Despite all the money spent on revitalization schemes, Sandtown kept losing population. A big national bank was supposed to inject new development capital, but bowed out after running into financial trouble. Sandtown grew increasingly poor and dysfunctional. In April 2015 it gained international notoriety as the wretched home turf of Freddie Gray, twenty-five, whom police arrested for alleged possession of an illegal switchblade. Gray was apparently given a "rough ride" in a police van—a common extralegal retaliation treatment for perceived troublemakers—during which he suffered a broken spine and fell into a coma.

THE PLANTATION

Miles away on the other side of town, Gay Street residents called Hopkins "The Plantation." For decades, they had accused the whites controlling the university and hospital of racial hostility, superciliousness, and remoteness from the community. They remembered how the homes of twelve hundred blacks were demolished in order to build dormitory housing for two hundred white Hopkins nurses and doctors. "The Compound," as the resulting complex was called, was separated by a tall fence erected to protect the whites from "vandals."[8] Black neighbors witnessed land banking by Hopkins, its nonprofit Kennedy Krieger Institute affiliate, and such for-profit divisions as Dome Corporation and Broadway Corporation (real estate development), and Broadway Services (security, linens, cleaning, transportation, maintenance) which did nothing with the properties they acquired. Whether that was by design or incompetence was unclear. "When the Johns Hopkins Institutions plunged in to the world of profitmaking in 1984, grand visions abounded. Their new Dome Corp., Hopkins officials said, would direct the development of a $500 million East Baltimore research park, create a string of moneymaking subsidiaries and help commercialize university research," *The Sun*'s Liz Bowie wrote. A decade later, little had been achieved, except that most Dome subsidiaries were sold off or dissolved.[9]

The incompetence evidenced itself much earlier—as soon as Hopkins built a 150-room Sheraton Inn across from the hospital on Broadway in 1960. Entirely financed from the hospital's endowment fund, it was part of a forty-acre redevelopment effort that Henry J. Knott, in cooperation with the city, launched to reconstitute a belt of land between Broadway and Old Town. Derelict old row houses were demolished and in their stead new garden apartments arose, as did a shopping center. Knott was an American success story. Turning his father's masonry business into magic, he was the first local developer to manufacture prefabricated wall panels in a factory, and then send them out to construction sites. He became a contractor of choice for Hopkins—to whose hospital he gave millions—as well as for the city. As the

Catholic archdiocese's moneyman, with close ties to politicians, he donated generously to causes of faith. [10]

Sheraton quickly lost its luster. Operated by Hopkins, it gained a reputation as the city's worst hotel. When *Sun* restaurant critic John Dorsey visited the dining room, he was unable to order one of its three steak items, the principal chicken dish, or the special of the day, or a baked potato because the "restaurant is out of those things," according to a server. "And this isn't, remember, some diner on the side of the road in the sticks with a sign outside that says 'Cabins $3.' This is a Sheraton Inn," Dorsey wrote. (The hotel was demolished in 2010 for the construction of a unit of the Wilmer Eye Institute.)[11]

Blacks were not only suspicious of Hopkins but of municipal authorities as well. Repeated "slum clearance" announcements from city hall had followed the construction of public housing projects after World War II. But promises made had often fallen short or been broken. In the late 1960s, a group of east siders met in the kitchen of Du Burns's modest fourteen-foot-wide row house on Mura Street, vowing to give black residents a voice. "Basically, what we decided to do was to use political power to deliver services to the East Baltimore community," Robert L. Douglass told me. He was a South Carolina native, who had grown up in the shadow of Bethlehem Steel in Turner Station, the same black township where Henrietta Lacks later moved. A 1946 graduate of Dunbar High School, he served in the army, earned a Bachelor of Science from Morgan and a second bachelor's degree, in electrical engineering, from Hopkins. He was elected to the city council in 1967.

A political rift gave Douglass and Burns the opening they needed. In 1968 a group of liberals bolted out of Bolton Hill's Mount Royal Democratic Club, which two years earlier had made headlines by unveiling a biracial ticket. Since then, Martin Luther King Jr. and Senator Robert F. Kennedy had been assassinated and the United States was bogged down in Southeast Asia's rice paddies and jungles. Now, led by an assistant professor of chemical engineering at Hopkins, delegate Maclyn McCarty, fourteen liberals marched out after club leaders, state delegate Julian L. Lapides, and his law partner, Thomas Ward, rejected demands that Mount Royal support gun control and condemn the Vietnam War. Ward was a gun enthusiast, former city councilman, and future judge, who had worked for Hubert H. Humphrey's losing presidential campaign against Nixon that year; McCarty had backed Eugene McCarthy. Yet another delegate, Walter S. Orlinsky, a former Mount Royal president, had been with Kennedy.[12]

The insurgents formed two new organizations in the Second District. Predominantly white Bolton Hill, Charles Village, and Guilford liberals coalesced around the New Democratic Club, whose president was a Hopkins Hospital biomedical scientist, Dr. Keith D. Garlid. Existing Douglass and

Burns Clubs, in turn, merged into the Eastside Democratic Organization. In the next election, NDC and EDO united behind a joint ticket of candidates that they split fifty-fifty in order to produce a racial balance. The timing was perfect. Two longtime Bohemian incumbents, Joseph V. Mach and Clement J. Prucha, saw the demographic writing on the wall and bowed out. "Why butt your head against a brick wall?" said Mach, president of the First Bohemian Club. He was a tavern owner, a line of business favored by many because one could provide constituent services while selling drinks. Prucha, too, was in the liquor business. President of the Young Men's Bohemian Club (which had admitted Du as the first African American member), he headed the city council's panel that passed on mayoral patronage.[13] The interracial NDC/EDO alliance triumphed. Among the winners was Du, who was elected to fill one of the seats vacated by the Bohemians. "Everyone said it couldn't be done, because it hadn't been tried before. To everyone's surprise, we won 17 out of 18 local positions," Garlid remembered.[14]

The council had been an exclusively Democratic province since before World War II; the partnership now put it in control of a "Negro-white liberal coalition," according to *The Sun*. Burns became chair of the council's powerful urban affairs committee. Schaefer then tapped him as the floor leader. These gatekeeper positions were useful for EDO which unabashedly tied legislative votes to black economic advancement. Robert Douglass by that time had risen to the state Senate, where he preached taxpayer-supported black capitalism and urged that minorities get 10 percent of state contracts in the Metro subway and other critical infrastructure projects under planning or construction. (That minimum was never adopted.) He owned Baltimore Electronics Associates, which made AC/DC power supply equipment and whose business model relied on federal and state contracts. He served as vice chair of the National Association of Black Manufacturers. In Annapolis he chaired the Maryland Legislative Black Caucus.[15]

Douglass had media interests as well. He owned *Metropolitan*, a glossy monthly magazine that for a time was the best resource for understanding what was going on in the black community. He participated in the cable television gold rush in the 1980s. Comparable to the scandal-ridden awarding of streetcar franchises a hundred years earlier, the wheeling and dealing was all about using political clout to win licenses that could then be flipped at great profit. The dominant local entrant was Caltec Cablevision, headed by Dr. Leonard P. Berger, a physician who was chummy with Democratic totems and involved in all kinds of investment schemes. Caltec won the franchise in Baltimore County and made a killing by selling it to Comcast.

In the city, too, a blue-ribbon commission recommended Caltec. The fix seemed in. White majority investors included Jerome S. Cardin, who would go to prison in a savings and loan scandal, and his wife, Shoshana; Louis Grasmick; Homer Gudelsky, a leading Washington real estate developer; Henry J. Knott Jr., and family members, all big players in construction and donors to Catholic causes. The Bread Man, John Paterakis, was an investor, and so was Calman J. Zamoiski, a wholesale distributor who was a power in the Jewish community and sat on the boards of Hopkins University, Hospital, and health system.[16] Among blacks, Douglass and family members held a 10 percent share; another 10 percent stake was shared by investors who included George Russell; a councilman, Dr. Emerson Julian; and Bishop Monroe Saunders, whose church missions included the First United Apostolic Federal Credit Union as well as prison, bookstore, and library ministries. Several city council members had conflicts of interest, including Victorine Adams, Little Willie's wife. Her cousin, parking lot operator Allen Quille, was an investor.[17]

Reading the tea leaves, one applicant, Cox, offered to buy out Caltec. The privately owned Atlanta firm assembled a star-studded cast of Baltimoreans to lend credibility to its bid. Put together by attorney Ron Shapiro and Ted Venetoulis, a former Baltimore County executive, they included Jack Moseley, chairman of USFG; Henry A. Rosenberg, chairman of Crown Central Petroleum; Matt DeVito, chief executive of the Rouse Company; Edward Bennett Williams, the legendary Washington lawyer, Democratic bigwig, and Orioles owner; black broadcast pioneer Dorothy Brunson; and commercial real estate developer Bernard Manekin, immediate past president of the Greater Baltimore Committee. Among "rent-a-citizens" furnishing their names to the effort were Tom Bradley, president of the Maryland–D.C. AFL-CIO, and Ray Clarke, president of Local 44 of the American Federation of State, County and Municipal Employees.

Everyone stood to make money. "Say someone legally contracted to buy $100,000 worth of stock," Berger explained. "They only had to put up a $500 deposit, with the rest to come after we got the franchise. For that $500 investment they will get $10,500 if the franchise is granted to Cox."[18] Little Willie Adams was in for a windfall. Cox promised to sell a one-third interest in its franchise to a group that included his daughter, Gertrude Venable; his partner in A&R Development, Theo Rodgers; and two Parks Sausage owners, Henry Parks and Raymond Haysbert. For its studio, Cox pledged to buy land from Adams for five times the market value.

Schaefer voted for the Caltec bid (to support his blue-ribbon panel, he said) but then got cold feet. "I'm concerned. I am worried, I have uneasy feelings," he told television cameras. The city council took care of his worries. Instead of awarding the franchise to Caltec's or Cox's well-connected local Democrats, it gave the license to an affiliate of United Artists, whose investors were less political and whose minority partners were not players in Baltimore's black community.[19] That franchise, too, soon ended up in Comcast's hands, giving the conglomerate a cable monopoly that continues.

MANY HATS

The Eastside Democratic Organization was an anomaly in an age when such old-line white Democratic clubs as the Bohemians and South Baltimore's Stonewall (named after the Confederate general) were disappearing.[20] Douglass and Burns did not hand out Thanksgiving turkeys, or bags of coal, as bosses of old had done. EDO had no Internet access, nor a clubhouse, and it rarely held membership meetings. Instead, a politburo of directors, hand-picked by Douglass and Burns, dispensed patronage through a network of affiliated—but outwardly nonpolitical—community organizations. On Election Day, those fronts generated volunteer workers who were paid "walk-around-money," another Baltimore tradition, and whose job it was to usher citizens to the polls and make sure they voted right. Taverns, by city law, were closed on election days but some were known to surreptitiously dispense free drinks to EDO loyalists. Power had its privileges.

Political organizations could not legally receive direct taxpayer support. EDO solved that inconvenience by creating an intermediary, the East Baltimore Community Corporation, headed by Douglass and Burns. Federal, city, and state funds to the district were channeled through that economic development arm. With a $5 million annual budget, EBCC operated the HMO that served twenty-five thousand residents and was nearly entirely funded by Medicaid and the U.S. Public Health Service. Board members basked in the glory. But quiet as it was kept, little could happen without input from The Plantation. EBCC's medical plan underscored that fact. Its chief architect was a state delegate, Dr. Torrey C. Brown, associate director of health-care programs at Hopkins (and future state secretary of natural resources). An NDC leader, he was an ally of EDO. Overlaps like these caused some awkwardness. On one hand, explained Burns, "we didn't have any confidence in Hopkins. People looked at it as some sort of monster in the neighborhood, not doin' anything for anybody."[21] On the other hand, they depended on Hopkins, which eventually bailed out the medical plan and took it over after EBCC ran into financial difficulties.

With elections approaching in 1975, Burns and his city council colleague Nathan C. Irby were able to provide 1,532 federally funded Youth Corps summer jobs to loyalist families, or one half of such slots available citywide. Jean E. Spence, EDO's corresponding secretary, controlled twenty jobs through the Preston-Bradford Community Organization and an equal number through the Superior Neighborhood Community Association. And so on. She said she sent some enrollees to work directly at city hall, ten at Faith Lutheran Church, three at the Loving Care Day Care Center, and thirty more at EBCC. EDO had been central in the planning and construction of a reconstituted Dunbar High School's new building. Delegate Hattie N. Harrison an EDO cofounder and board member, received four hundred summer jobs for Dunbar. Waverly Blockbuilders took another twenty jobs and the Neighborhood Development Corporation 150. Other affiliates receiving summer jobs included the East Baltimore Medical Plan.[22]

The city steered to EBCC millions of federal and state dollars to construct new housing. After delays and mismanagement, an affiliate, Central Ashland Housing Associates, erected some two hundred new "townhouses" and rehabilitated a hundred old ones intended for low- and middle-income families. U.S. Department of Housing and Urban Development auditors said funds were improperly used to cover cost overruns or to finance buyers who did not meet the income qualifications.[23] Connections between EBCC, EDO, and the Douglass firm were murky, some dealings questionable. Federal prosecutors, in trying to figure out what was going on, subpoenaed EBCC files.[24] There was "a thin line that separates the corporate effort from the political effort," Du Burns acknowledged to me. "I don't want to separate politics from economic power."[25]

The American Brewery Building highlighted the labyrinth of tie-ins. That Gay Street landmark still miraculously stands near North Avenue, surrounded by abandonment and destruction. The Victorian storybook castle, built in 1887 by John Frederick Wiessner, a Bavarian, is the most fanciful temple of suds left from the glory days of Baltimore brewing. The huge copper vats that used to dominate the cavernous edifice are long gone—along with the sweet smell of malts and hops—but at least a statue of King Gambrinus, the patron saint of brewers, was rescued and can still be seen in the Maryland Historical Society.[26]

The old brewery was vacant and harboring vagrants in 1977, when the city awarded it to EBCC to redevelop. The first phase called for rehabilitation of the warehouse section which was then to be leased to Douglass's electronics firm. The rest of the complex was to be renovated in stages. That's as far as it got. Douglass's company ran out of money. Schaefer tried to prop it up, and extraordinarily raided funds restricted for upgrading businesses in the neighboring predominantly white First District. Councilman Dominic Mimi DiPietro was furious. "The mayor didn't tell me nothing about it," he complained to me. "When we have money in the district, I want to keep it in the district."[27]

In 1988 it was disclosed that Douglass's firm had no valid lease and had not paid a penny in rent to the city for five years. The EDO and EBCC president refused to vacate the premises, and no one had the will to evict him. "The city doesn't go and throw [businesses] out who can't pay rent," said Burns, the city council president and EBCC chairman, who had managed Douglass's unsuccessful reelection campaign for a state Senate seat. By that time the electronics firm was bankrupt. Work on the old American Brewery stopped altogether. The building went vacant again, and squatters took over. Another decade would pass and millions of additional taxpayers' dollars would be required to bring it back to life. Particularly at night it is a wondrous sight. "It is simply breathtaking," said C. William Struever, a Baltimore developer who bought the colossus for $5,000 and completed a $21.2 million restoration in 2008. "It's full of irreplaceable, idiosyncratic wonders."[28]

THE NEW FACE OF HOPKINS

In 1990 Mayor Schmoke woke up to new political imperatives. Needing east side votes for reelection and hoping to split Du Burns's EDO base, he announced his commitment to a vast undertaking around Hopkins Hospital that would include new housing, education, medical programs, new streets, business incentives and job training for more than forty-seven thousand people. "Tens of millions" in development money would be spent, he pledged. Dr. James A. Block, who headed Johns Hopkins Hospital and Health Systems, said the institution provided seed money because "we are an integral part of this community. We're interested in seeing further development around the hospital."

This was the new face of Hopkins. Throughout its existence, the hospital had uneasily coexisted with neighbors, white and black. After clumsy sporadic earlier efforts, Hopkins now wanted to stabilize its surroundings and accumulate enough real estate to satisfy its future expansion needs. The target area was huge—180 square blocks. Stretching from the Somerset and Douglass public housing projects to Dunbar High School to Hopkins, it covered more than twice the territory of Sandtown and also had more than twice the population. In a competition that would give empowerment-zone grants to six cities, an initially reluctant Schmoke applied to the Clinton White House for $100 million. The windfall was announced the week before Christmas. "I'm really excited. This is really a big victory for our community," the mayor said.

To get the Hopkins area empowerment zone off the ground, the city created an implementation agency, the Historic East Baltimore Community Action Coalition (HEBCAC), which soon became perceived as a stalking horse for

EDO. When its chair, "Mama" Harrison, an EDO cofounder, showed independence, the political organization dumped the veteran state delegate from its ticket. A bevy of other fronts appeared. Marie Washington, an EDO vice president and Douglass's right-hand at EBCC, won state funding for her jobs program that required expensive taxpayer-paid alterations in a Gay Street building she acquired.[29]

The $100 million grant was not for the Hopkins project alone, however. The money was to be shared with Schmoke's pet project, Sandtown, which was on the ropes, and five other communities. Among those was Pigtown, the old slaughterhouse district near the University of Maryland downtown campus, which also bordered Poppleton. Also in the mix was Fairfield, home to petrochemical and heavy industry and the abandoned World War II shipyard which had built Liberty ships. The goals were lofty, and remain relevant as yardsticks of failure. A promised ecological-industrial park in Fairfield to squeeze oil and energy out of solid waste never materialized and the idea was abandoned as unworkable.[30] Other goals included a one-stop capital shop to provide $20 million in revolving credit for businesses, and a $15 million community development bank to pay for housing rehabs, commercial revitalization, and entrepreneurial growth in East Baltimore. A $20 million mortgage pool helped zone residents buy or fix up homes, with the goal of raising from 30 percent to 50 percent the percentage of homeownership.

A designated school was promised for each zone to offer affordable after-school and weekend activities, including educational, recreational, and artistic programs. A training fund was to be set up to provide workers with stipends of up to $400 a week for six weeks, allowing them to get on-the-job experience. Nonprofit van pools were promised to transport workers to jobs not accessible by public transportation. Neighborhood Child Development Resource Centers were to provide quality low-cost day care and preschool programs. Family Resource Centers were to be set up to help elementary- and middle-school children improve their performance. Two goals involved law enforcement. "Mobile police stations," similar to those used as command posts at special events, were to be employed in high-crime and open-air drug market areas. In order to incentivize police officers to live in the zone, low-cost mortgages were to be provided. Those taking part in the program were also eligible to take home their squad cars, according to promises made.

In the middle of this, another partner was added to the Hopkins renewal's roster of stakeholders—the Annie E. Casey Foundation. Named after the widowed mother of the UPS founder, Jim Casey, the foundation spent its riches on child welfare initiatives nationwide and compiled the widely used reference tool *Kids Count Data Book*. Relocating its headquarters from Connecticut, the foundation selected the Hopkins Hospital area as its testing

ground. I followed all this as an editorial writer for *The Sun*, with Michael
Seipp as my guide until politicking led to his ouster from HEBCAC executive
director's job. He was a pro, a capable taskmaster who ruffled feathers; I had
known him for years.

Despite the Schmoke administration's promise of ribbon-cuttings galore
to heap praise on President Clinton, nothing much happened. "Five years
after the Historic East Baltimore Community Action Coalition drew up its
renewal plan—and four years after $34.1 million in federal money was se-
cured to fund it—only 47 row houses have been rehabilitated or are in the
process of being rehabilitated," *The Sun*'s Eric Siegel reported in 2000.[31] The
worst bureaucratic bungle involved $21 million in federal funds that were
lost because the empowerment zone failed to spend the money within the
required five-year time limit.[32] To make up for lost time, renovation of old
buildings was scrapped altogether in favor of demolition. There had been a
long-standing bias against old houses anyway. Years earlier during his time
in the city council, Douglass called houses along Stirling Street, a charming
cobblestone stretch off Gay Street, "slave houses" and therefore not worth
saving. He didn't know what he was talking about. Those houses had never
been slave houses, but residences of white artisans and small merchants.
Thanks to the advocacy of Mount Royal Democratic Club's Lapides, by then
a state senator, Stirling Street became Schaefer's first dollar-house renovation
project and survives as a Dickensian time capsule.

HEBCAC was seen as so lucrative that Bernard "Jack" Young thought
about resigning from the city council when the top manager's job opened up
in 2000.[33] (He was a radiology manager at the hospital.) Despite the failure
of the organization's overarching renewal missions, federal money made a
difference. Several east siders were able to escape the hood and buy homes
in the county, while pretending to live in the city, and coming there every
Election Day to cast their votes. They had their feet planted in two jurisdic-
tions, which challenged their civic focus. There was historic precedent for
that. Decades earlier Jack Pollack's Jewish voters had done the same. Living
outside one's district—or even outside the city—became so widespread that
Jack Young, by then the city's No. 2 elected official as city council president,
had to defend himself against accusations that a vacation home he owned in
Harford County was his primary residence.[34]

The tortuous pace of the HEBCAC-led makeover convinced Hopkins
to revamp the whole renewal effort. Lawyer Richard Berndt, the Catholic
archdiocese's consigliere, played a pivotal role. He was a Hopkins Hospital
trustee and a behind-the-scenes manipulator so skillful Schaefer nicknamed
him the "German general." He was close to U.S. senators Paul Sarbanes and
Barbara Mikulski and also managed Martin O'Malley's 1999 campaign for

mayor. The thirty-nine-year-old O'Malley was a suburbanite from Montgomery County, a University of Maryland law graduate whose wife, Katie, was a daughter of the state attorney general, J. Joseph Curran Jr., and would become a judge. Despite having married into the Democratic establishment, O'Malley claimed a rebellious streak. Wearing black muscle shirts, he fronted an Irish folk rock band and on occasion burst into anti-British diatribes. All this time he dreamed about the White House, and in 2016 he ran for president.

With O'Malley in power in 2002, Hopkins announced another redevelopment plan. It went big. It wanted to bulldoze, with certain exceptions, eighty-eight acres of row houses and abandoned industrial blocks north of the hospital. O'Malley authorized the city to seize up to three thousand properties. As a first step, the city condemned about seventy derelict houses *outside* the boundaries of the proposed "bio-technical park," signaling an even more ambitious push to reconstitute East Baltimore. Perhaps the plan truly intended to create the bio-technical park of incubators and research offshoots, as official announcements promised, but economic headwinds morphed it chiefly into a mixed-income housing plan for Hopkins students and employees. The plan's governance minimized EDO interference. A new HEBCAC chief, Lawrence Cager Jr., was pointedly excluded from East Baltimore Development, Inc., a partnership the city created to wrest implementation from political hacks.[35] Repeated failures and false starts had raised the stakes.

Condemnation for the vast footprint proved controversial. Some owners were only too happy to get rid of worthless vacants. For "zero consideration," an ophthalmologist, Dr. Barbara S. Hawkins, turned over to the city a Broadway row house she owned near the hospital. The Columbia resident had bought the house two decades earlier in the hope of fixing it up and living near her work at Hopkins. That never happened and the structure eventually collapsed in a snow storm. At Collington Square, Virginia computer consultant Robert A. Benjamin took the city's offer of $2,500 for a row house that he said had been vacant for at least ten years. "It was a pretty worthless property," he said.

Far more challenging were disputes over what constituted fair compensation to live-in owners. The market dismissed their houses as worthless but those "home houses" were full of memories celebrated on holidays when generations gathered to enjoy grandma's cooking. Quick-take was supposed to be a streamlined process guided by federal and state compensation tables and regulations. But in this case the number of condemnations was big enough to create a legal class. Owners contested quick-take, only to be rebuffed in the U.S. Supreme Court in a relevant case.[36] Theirs was a peculiar predicament. Many owners simply could not afford to move elsewhere. That was a particular dilemma for those who had used their marginal real estate as collateral to accumulate debts. In the end federal funds and Hopkins typically paid owners $70,000 for their property, plus moving costs—much above the true market value and often ten times or more the tax assessment. Renters forced to relocate received up to three years' rent compensation.

Again, progress was maddeningly slow. "The nation's largest urban redevelopment, a projected $1.8 billion effort to transform 88 acres of East Baltimore into a world-class biotech park and idyllic urban community, lies derailed amid vacant lots, boarded houses and unfilled dreams a decade after it began," Melody Simmons and Joan Jacobson reported in a 2011 *Daily Record* investigation.[37] Dr. Marisela B. Gomez wrote a whole book about the reconstitution controversy and how it rekindled resentment toward Hopkins. In *Race, Class, Power and Organizing in East Baltimore: Rebuilding Abandoned Communities in America*, she outspokenly took the side of the displaced residents, whom she portrayed as victims, Davids in a battle against the mighty institutional Goliath.

She depicted the renewal area as a "historically African American community." I had a problem with that characterization. If taken literally, it ignored previous ethnic and class rotations, particularly the Bohemian phase, and held that history began only after blacks became the majority in the 1950s and 1960s. The view also seemed to argue that socioeconomic, class, and racial successions could somehow be tempered in the future. That wasn't going to happen—and you could see it. Black strivers moved out of the hood whenever their economic situation allowed. Despite promises of renewal, they did not want to live amid ambulances wailing 24/7 or the roar of emergency helicopters. Their decision to decamp was not surprising. The same had happened with the Baltimore Plan in the 1950s, when go-getters departed as soon as better alternatives came along (see chapter 7).

Over its existence, EDO managed to maintain its predominance amid frequent infighting. However, the organization had never before faced a challenge that posed a threat to its very rationale. The farther along the Hopkins project progressed, the more the district's characteristics were certain to change. Most newcomers would likely be white and not wedded to status quo, or the politics of the past. With the hood gone, they would put their imprint on new surroundings, and decide priorities. All those fears crystallized in suspicions about a partnership with Morgan State University that created a new K–8 education center in the shadow of St. Wenceslaus. Critics saw the Henderson-Hopkins School as an arbitrary agent of regentrification because it handpicked students to create a certain mix. The controversy, said a *Sun* editorial, "is not Hopkins' fault, nor that of the parents from surrounding neighborhoods who clamored to get their kids into the school. It's the fault of decades of racial segregation that robbed generations of poor, black Baltimore residents of the opportunities others take for granted. Even an effort as well resourced as this one was swamped by the magnitude of Baltimore's concentrated poverty."[38]

Importantly, the Hopkins area reconstitution no longer was happening in isolation. A miracle had occurred. A gamut of small and large renewal efforts started under several mayors had surprisingly begun to jell. Despite those measures' patchy record and disparate locations on the east side, a constellation of tentative revival formed. This archipelago of renewal kept spreading outward, converging with other islets of hope. This was a remarkable turn of events in a city where neighborhood turnarounds, if they occurred at all, took an inordinately long time, compared to Washington, D.C., and other hot cities. Now the once-unfathomable promised to become a reality. All because of economics. The Fells Point and Harbor East shoreline had been so saturated with luxury apartments that developers began looking for opportunities in unconquered territories farther inland, but not too far away from the waterfront. They began inching toward Hopkins.

A PATTERN OF SUCCESSIONS

It had been a long slog to reach this point, as Fells Point illustrated. Less than a mile downhill from Hopkins Hospital, the ancient seafaring community was founded in the 1730s by William Fell, a Quaker merchant. His grave monument on Shakespeare Street is an obligatory stop on nighttime ghost tours, which also dispense all kinds of other lore. According to one story, the tip of Fells Point was once known as the "hook," whose womenfolk so eagerly welcomed sailors that they became known as hookers. Alternatively, they got the name in the embrace of the Civil War general Joseph Hooker's troops. Many other cities offered competing legends.

Grounded in verifiable facts was other trivia. When Fells Point wharves still made wooden clippers (chapter 1), African Americans dominated the ship caulking trade. A number of them banded together, unionized and pooled their resources to form the Chesapeake Marine Railway and Dry Dock Company. The cooperative soon employed over three hundred black and white workers. Its organizer was Isaac Myers, a free black who had been schooled by the Quakers at the Sharp Street church. One caulker, the abolitionist Frederick Douglass, later returned to Fells Point in his seventies to build a row of five handsome redbrick houses in Strawberry Alley, later renamed Dallas Street, where they still stand.

Fells Point had once been an overwhelmingly Irish community but then underwent repeated ethnic, racial, and economic rotations. In the 1960s,

Interstate highway builders targeted it for demolition. As the city condemned a pathway of properties, hundreds of families were evicted, just as were residents of Federal Hill on the opposite shore. Citizen activists applying civil rights tactics to development issues stopped the road before all condemned houses were torn down. This was a turning point in Baltimore's recent history. If the road, initially supported by Schaefer and the rest of the city council, had been rammed through, the Inner Harbor would be little more than a bridge and Interstate exchange. There would be no gentrification of neighborhoods from Fort McHenry to Canton and beyond. Instead of condos, ribbons of asphalt and concrete tunnels of traffic would mar the shoreline.

The reprieve started gentrification—and Schaefer bought into it. Federal Hill properties overlooking the harbor attracted moneyed renovators; Fells Point drew a peculiar mix of habitués—old Polish ladies, dock workers and sailors, greasy spoons, artists, shift workers, weirdos and whores, and missions offering soup, bed, and salvation. The sketchy waterfront became a nighttime magnet for young suburbanites, a bar district with eclectic shops, striptease joints, and characters like Turkey Joe Trabert, a barkeeper who was an elementary school teacher. Rock and hillbilly songs mixed with bouzouki, and the Acropolis restaurant, at the time located at the foot of Broadway, featured belly dancers.

Popularity then unleashed yet another socioeconomic rotation—Fells Point went upscale and homogenized. Conventional retailers replaced edgy shops. Bars changed hands; old warehouses were turned into luxury apartments, new condos constructed. This recycling crawled up Broadway from the waterfront toward Hopkins. Rising rents pushed a changing array of residents to move. Hispanics succeeded Lumbee Indians who had settled from North Carolina in the 1950s. "Black spots" were removed. A 173-unit Section 8 rental complex in an otherwise white area along Baltimore Street was razed and became part of three blocks of apartments marketed to Hopkins doctors and students. With space for future additions, that colossus bordered an earlier successful reconstitution that dated back to the 1970s, the Washington Hill cooperative apartments. It consisted of 218 cooperative units in a bevy of restored buildings occupied by various races and persuasions.

The name Washington Hill went back to Jameson's erstwhile medical school, Washington College (chapter 3), whose main building, the onetime Church Home and Hospital, had ended up in Hopkins ownership. Its hilltop location offered a splendid panorama of Baltimore's repurposed waterfront, increasingly defined by the towers that the Bread Man built in Harbor East on grounds where foundries and metal refineries once belched smoke. Paterakis had bought the land as a favor for Schaefer, when previous investors' redevelopment plans fell through. The master baker knew how to make dough rise and became a billionaire. In Harbor East, he constructed a city within a city. Everything was brand-new, except for one Civil War relic—President Street Station, the focal point of the mob attack on federal troops (chapter 2). Under Paterakis, Harbor East evolved into the new heart of the central business district. Lines separating it from Fells Point and Little Italy vanished.

Central Avenue, which parallels Broadway, led from Harbor East to the vicinity of Hopkins through desolate blocks ripe for reconstitution. It was clear that redevelopment would eventually link the medical institutions to the repurposed waterfront. Close to Harbor East, old Central Avenue factories were already converted into condominiums, and warehouses refashioned into trendy eateries. Paterakis's H&S bakeries continued to occupy a cluster of buildings, but for how much longer? He was dead and the ground was far too valuable for low-return industrial use. Holding back reconstitution were two World War II–era public housing low-rises, Perkins and Somerset Courts. But their days seemed numbered. Several proposals called for their razing, a prospect that might involve land swaps and the resettlement of a thousand dislocated residents within the eighty-eight-acre Hopkins reconstitution footprint. Other candidates for razing included such landmarks as the Chick Webb Recreation Center (chapter 7), the art-deco building of the Eastern Health District, and a vacant behemoth that belonged to the failed Soujourner-Douglass College. Those parcels were situated between city hall and Hopkins; whatever happened there could either make the rest of the eastside renewal efforts advance or doom them to failure.

Central Avenue intersected with Old Town's Gay Street. In the philanthropist Johns Hopkins's day, that latter artery was the beginning of a wagon route to Philadelphia and beyond. Urban renewal in the 1960s cut it up in places, ending its thoroughfare role as a feeder to U.S. Route 1. That was not all: Urban renewal destabilized the business area. In an effort to reverse the declining fortunes, the city reformatted Gay Street's old retail core in 1976 into Oldtown Mall, whose seventy stores occupied rehabbed Victorian row houses on a stretch that was closed to vehicle traffic. With an old-fashioned town clock, the mall might have been a quaint hit in a suburban setting, but in the hood it never took off. It went into a death spiral after the city closed Belair Market and demolished nearby public housing high-rises.

With Daniel P. Henson as housing commissioner, Mayor Schmoke replaced many of the high-rise towers with subsidized mixed-income communities that had suburban-sounding names like Pleasant View Gardens. Their residents had no reason to venture to Old Town, where various plans to bring life and jobs failed. The city had cleared much acreage which lay fallow, earmarked for future development. In the meantime, Gay Street

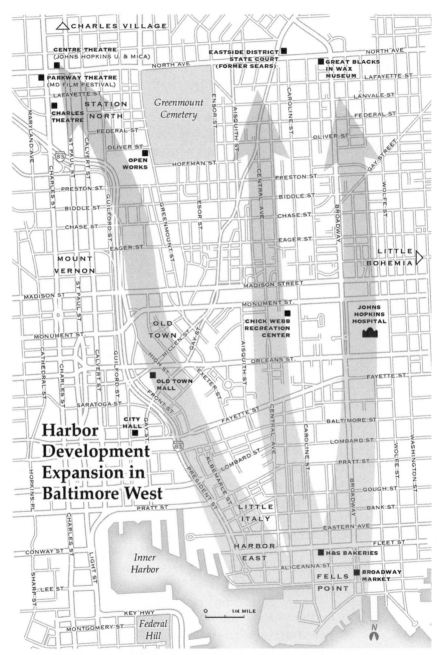

This map speculates on future redevelopment thrusts originating from the shoreline. It is based on trends in evidence in 2018.

Robert Cronan. Lucidity Information Design, LLC

became the location of a new juvenile jail, an addition to a growth industry that included the state penitentiary and city jail.[39]

Bridges across the Jones Falls connected Old Town with Mount Vernon (chapter 8), which was regentrifying. Revitalization from there then continued to Station North, sandwiched between Mount Vernon and Charles Village. The Station North name paid tribute to Pennsylvania Station, a 1911 Beaux-Arts edifice that once had been surrounded by well-to-do residences off North Avenue, fashionable churches, and the original home of Goucher College, which later moved to Towson. The arts district's main attribute was its location, steps away from the main Amtrak and commuter station. Among Station North renewal sponsors were the MICA arts institute and Hopkins, which cooperated on turning the old WFBR radio headquarters into a multipurpose cultural activity center. A few hundred yards away, Stavros Niarchos shipping riches helped renovate a faded movie palace, the Parkway, as the new permanent home of the Maryland Film Festival.

All this activity inspired revitalization talk further east on North Avenue, past Green Mount Cemetery, where Johns Hopkins was buried, and past the erstwhile Sears department store to a corner, where the Great Blacks in Wax Museum opened in the 1980s at the fringes of the one-time Little Bohemia (chapter 7). The museum was a tribute to the perseverance of educators Elmer and Joanna Martin, who started by taking a few wax figures to show at various schools, community centers, and malls. The couple acquired an old firehouse near Broadway to tell the story of the Atlantic slave trade. Thousands came every year to see lifelike figures of slaves bound in shackles and chains inside a realistic replica of a slave ship. Wax likenesses of important African American historical figures were added, and U.S. Congress designated the repository as the National Blacks in Wax Museum. In 2018 it was building a brand-new headquarters and exhibit complex. The stretch in front of it was repaved, with new sidewalks constructed and old-fashioned streetlights installed to evoke the past. Joanna Martin talked about creating "our Station North."

The museum corner was more than a dozen blocks north of the Hopkins medical institutions on Broadway. It was another kernel of renewal promising to germinate new life and vitality in a tough corner of the city.

Chapter Thirteen

The Knockers

It was like *The Wire* going on the air live, a decade after David Simon's HBO series ended.

On a dimming November afternoon in 2017, Sean Suiter, a forty-three-year-old plainclothes homicide detective and father of five, was shot once in the head with his own gun on a narrow vacant lot between row houses near Sandtown. Precious minutes were lost when the police cruiser rushing him to hospital crashed on the way; he could not be saved. At the scene, three spent casings were found, all from his service revolver. Signs of struggle were discovered. For six days, police cordoned off the crime area. All outsiders were barred, and residents had to show ID and get permission to enter or leave the neighborhood. Despite a record $215,000 reward, weeks went by without any suspects, then months. That was unheard of in a Baltimore cop killing. Rumors swirled, one suggesting that Suiter committed suicide.[1]

The medical examiner ruled that his death was homicide.[2]

Suiter died on the eve of his scheduled testimony before a federal grand jury probing bounty hunters on the police department's elite Gun Trace Task Force. For years, a dozen times on "slow nights," and more than fifty "easy" on busier nights, its undercover "knockers" rolled in, slammed the brakes, and pulled over "dope boy cars"—Honda Accords, Acura TLs, and Honda Odysseys. Wearing dark face masks and black clothing, cops claimed that the occupants had no seatbelts on, or that the windows were too heavily tinted. They ransacked vehicles and grabbed those who ran. Money and drugs that they discovered they often split, or gave to the evidence control room, if formal charges were pressed. Most illegal guns they turned in because the police department rewarded such confiscations.

The knockers' trunks contained their tools—crowbars, lock cutters, machete, and grappling hook—all ordered from Amazon, which kept records.

"If you could put together a crew of guys and rob the biggest drug dealer in town, who would it be?" the GTTF supervisor, Sergeant Wayne Jenkins, asked those he searched. His men hid BB guns in their vehicles "so that we could plant them" on suspects. The assumption was that everyone was guilty of something and would not complain about missing ill-gotten cash or illegal drugs.

The knockers showed the futility of the "war on drugs" by fencing heroin, cocaine, marijuana, and guns that they stole. Six knockers pleaded guilty to a variety of federal conspiracy, gun, and narcotics charges. Two others opted for jury trial but did not testify in their own defense; they were found guilty. It was one of the biggest scandals in the department's history, unearthed when Drug Enforcement Administration agents heard the voices of cops in wiretaps of a heroin ring supplying The Alameda section in the city, and the suburban communities of Perry Hall, Towson, and Bel Air.[3] As the racket unraveled, prosecutors had to toss out some three thousand criminal cases because so many were tainted or bogus.

Trial testimony detailed wider police corruption. Systematic overtime falsifications throughout the force enabled cops to buy homes, SUVs, Jeeps, and fishing boats, or try their luck at casinos. Raifu Makanjuola was the department's "million dollar man." He was an ordinary Eastern District officer, who earned $437,034 in base pay between 2012 and 2017 and a whopping $620,060 in overtime, enabling him to pay off a $464,000 mort-gage on his Baltimore County home. The fifty-two-year-old took in more than anyone else in the police department or in city hall—more than the mayor, more than the commissioner! He averaged seventy-five-hour work weeks—"far beyond the hour limits of truck drivers or railroad engineers," Mark Reutter wrote in *Baltimore Brew*.[4]

The overtime racket had been common knowledge for decades. It drained the municipal budget, but no one stopped it. Witnesses now implicated a deputy commissioner, the head of internal affairs, and an assistant state's attorney. In the middle of this, Mayor Catherine Pugh fired Commissioner Kevin Davis and replaced him with a deputy, Darryl D. De Souza. The thirty-year veteran of the force was Baltimore's third police commissioner in six years. "It's very few bad apples that spoil the entire barrel," he declared.[5]

As testimony exposed the vast criminal enterprise, Pugh said she did not read the coverage in newspapers, or watch it on television. "I have to run the city, I don't have time to sit in a trial," she said.[6] Such world-weariness had been a defining characteristic of the city for a long time. Thomas Buckler, the cranky doctor who wanted to demolish Federal Hill in the 1870s, wrote that "past experience has taught me that, in their collective or municipal capacity,

[Baltimoreans] are the most silly, unreflective, procrastinating, impracticable and perverse congregation of bipeds to be found anywhere under the sun."[7]

The police department's troubles mirrored Baltimore's overall condition. Much of the municipal government was dysfunctional. Republicans had not elected anyone for more than half a century, so they could not be blamed. The Democrats' grip on the city had produced a one-party town where few politicians bothered to challenge a tradition of indifference. Reutter blamed the apathy on "the 'original sin' of Johns Hopkins's generation (if not Hopkins personally)—failure to give up refighting the Civil War (hence Democratic Party hegemony) and slavery."

Despite frequent revelations about waste, misuse of public funds, graft, and incompetence, the one-party town kept reelecting incumbents. Audits had traditionally been few and far between, and even after the public clamored for such accounting, Mayors O'Malley, Sheila Dixon, Stephanie Rawlings-Blake, and Pugh let the issue go.[8] The school system's messy finances were not audited, and neither were the rampant overtime padding in the police department and public works, where employees often made more in claimed overtime than their base pay. Elsewhere, corruption became commonplace. Female public housing tenants won an $8 million settlement after they proved that city maintenance men demanded sex in return for repairs.[9]

Baltimore's shoddiness was known far beyond U.S. borders. In April 2015, when Freddie Gray sustained fatal spinal cord injuries while in police custody, Vladimir Putin's cyber attackers unleashed a storm of Facebook and Twitter messages on Baltimore, inviting those upset about the death to converge at Mondawmin Mall for a "purge" that was about to begin. The provocation was a Kremlin trial run, the first known tactical use of social media to successfully create a riot in America. It came as similar controversies in other parts of the country had created the Black Lives Matters movement. Moscow, the purge's sole initial organizer, orchestrated expertly. Tweeting began just as Douglass High and other area schools were letting out. Simultaneously, someone—who was never identified—halted all MTA transit service at the Mondawmin hub, stranding thousands of kids at Metro and bus stops without a way to get home. Aimlessly wandering around, some joined the purge of looting and arson that ended up doing $20 million worth of damage.[10]

Police response was disorganized and timid. Less than a half century after the 1968 riots, Commissioner Anthony W. Batts had no contingency plan for civil unrest. Rawlings-Blake's tin-eared comments branded as "thugs" all protesters upset about Gray's death in questionable circumstances.

All this time the knockers kept doing their thing. Oreese Stevenson was among targets. At eighteen, he killed his older half brother, who objected to his loud music. He was twice that age when the knockers interrupted a drug deal, took his cash and his house keys, invited themselves in without a warrant, broke into his safe and found two kilograms of heroin, along with an additional $200,000. They grabbed $100,000 worth of cash to share among themselves, closed the safe back up, then video-recorded themselves pretending to open it for the first time. "Nobody touches it, understand me right now," Jenkins said on the video as money was counted. "We're not even gonna fucking touch it. Keep your camera on it." Later, he listened to jail calls in which Stevenson wanted to hire a good lawyer to go after the cops who stole his money. Since Stevenson's wife was arranging his legal matters, Jenkins wanted her out. He left a note on the couple's doorsteps, purporting to be from another woman. It said the husband had gotten her pregnant. Then he knocked on the door.[11]

Before Suiter died, he was involved in several arrests with the knockers. Jenkins called him to a crash scene after an Acura his men were chasing slammed into a Monte Carlo, killing its driver, Elbert Davis. The eighty-seven-year-old father of a Baltimore officer remained trapped inside the wreck. "Dude's unconscious, he ain't saying shit," one of the chasers reported in a car FBI bugged. Instead of helping him, the knockers tried to figure out what to do about the heroin they had planted in the Acura. Because Suiter was "clueless" about "the shit," Jenkins summoned him to search the car and find the dope. The twenty-eight grams of heroin sent Umar Burley and Brent Matthews to fifteen-year terms in federal prison. (They were freed after the knockers' racket was uncovered.)[12]

Jenkins sometimes portrayed himself as a federal agent, telling drug dealers that he was taking their money and drugs but would let them go because they were not his ultimate targets. He planted illegal GPS homing devices. During the disorders following Freddie Gray's death, he took two big trash bags of looted pharmaceutical drugs to a confederate who testified to making more than $1 million from reselling them. That buddy was bail bondsman Donald Stepp, who did some robberies and whom Jenkins occasionally dressed as a cop. Two members of the team, Momodu Gondo and Jemell Rayam, worked directly for a drug crew, providing protection.[13]

THE BLACK GUERRILLA FAMILY

Suiter was gunned down on a trash-strewn lot in the nine hundred-block Bennett Place. That desolate stretch of derelict row houses in Harlem Park, a neighborhood adjoining Sandtown, was one of the city's poorest. In 2010 almost 56 percent of the households subsisted on incomes less than $25,000, compared with 33 percent citywide, according to the health department. The substantially vacant block was stained with blood. To restrict access, police in 2013 installed four metal gates across the alley's mouth, and a uniformed cop was posted nearby around the clock. Nevertheless, three years later three young African American men were gunned down in a Black Guerrilla Family hangout on the block. Neighborhood folk suspected it was a robbery gone bad—and some wondered whether the knockers had anything to do with it. On that fateful afternoon in 2017 when he died, Suiter was scouring Bennett Place to find a witness to the unsolved triple homicide.

If the Gun Trace Task Force's bounty hunters exemplified law enforcers gone astray, the Black Guerrilla Family illustrated how anger and hopelessness steered Muslims and erstwhile Black Panthers to violent criminal enterprise. Inmates who once spent their time studying black nationalism and poring over religious texts instead ran drugs and engaged in bloody turf wars on streets.

BGF's roots went back to 1960s agitation in California prisons by George Jackson, a Black Panther. "I met Marx, Lenin, Stalin, Engels, and Mao when I entered prison and they redeemed me," he wrote in his best-selling prison memoir, *Soledad Brother*, published after he was charged with murdering a guard. In 1971 he took several guards and two inmates hostage. Felled in a hail of bullets, he rose to the pantheon of black liberation, and was even memorialized by Bob Dylan, the troubadour of troubled times:

> *Sometimes I think this whole world*
> *Is one big prison yard*
> *Some of us are prisoners*
> *The rest of us are guards*
> *Lord, Lord, they cut George Jackson down*
> *Lord, Lord, they laid him in the ground*

Baltimore's BGF organization was born out of a massive 2007 fight among City Detention Center inmates, who deposed the Crips gang and put Sunni Muslims and Black Panther–influenced inmates in control of cell blocks. Emphasizing cultural awareness, BGF leader Eric Brown authored *The Black Book*, a 124-page study guide, which was distributed throughout Maryland prisons. What do we believe in, he asked?

We believe in Black Power

We believe in Black Liberation

We believe in Black Nationalism

Drugs financed BGF's elusive revolution. Brown could be a Robin Hood, occasionally paying electric bills or providing groceries to the needy. BGF "regimes" controlled Sandtown, Greenmount Avenue, and the Perkins Homes public housing complex, where Brown was born, half a mile from Hopkins Hospital. A federal indictment said the regimes' 2009 open-air meeting drew a hundred top operatives to Druid Hill Park.

After Brown was transferred to a federal prison, a new leader took over the 750-inmate detention center. "This is my jail," Tavon "Bulldog" White announced. "I'm dead serious. I make every final call in this jail . . . and nothing go past me, everything come to me."[14] For several years everything did. White controlled the supply, prices, and availability of smuggled cell phones, tobacco, and drugs, and all other contraband circulating inside the prison. From a smart phone in his cell, he made deals, punished turncoats, and transferred money between bank accounts. He regarded jail guards as "homies" from the hood. He had them couriering Grey Goose vodka to him and platters of crab imperial, for which they were richly rewarded. Women opened their legs. In trysts behind bars, he fathered five children with four guards. He showered his women with expensive gifts, one with two Mercedes Benz vehicles. One guard mother had the name Tavon tattooed on her neck, another woman had his name tattooed on her wrist. He was the king of the jail. "What if I name the baby King?" one expectant guard mother asked in a wiretapped call to her sister. "I like the name King. King Tavon White."

In 2013 Governor Lawrence Hogan closed the lawless jail because gang penetration had so compromised its operation. He made that decision after U.S. attorney Rod J. Rosenstein, the same man who would become President Donald Trump's embattled deputy attorney general, declared war on BGF. Rosenstein left quite a mark. Dozens of guards and inmates were indicted and convicted.

Rosenstein succeeded in defanging the Black Guerrilla Family. But the emasculation of the disciplined gang network had adverse consequences. True, aspirants to the gang had to prove their mettle by killing someone. But once BGF's dominance was ended, violence by outsiders rekindled. Score settling among rival gangs surged. Then controversies surrounding police involvement in Freddie Gray's death curtailed patrolling. State's attorney Marilyn J. Mosby charged six officers with complicity; none was convicted. Violence soared. In 2017 Baltimore went on the record books as the nation's deadliest city, per capita. Despite having fourteen times fewer people, it had more homicides than New York City. Less than 50 percent were cleared, in contrast to New York's claimed 88 percent clearance rate. Baltimore's death toll would have been far higher still, except for emergency medicine interventions, particularly at the University of Maryland Shock Trauma Center.

Nearly all Baltimore victims were African Americans, shot by other blacks. Rosenstein blamed the record killings on decisions authorities made in 2015 to cut back policing and prosecution. Wrote Patrick Burke in *War Is*

Boring, a web magazine: "Unfortunately, without any hierarchy to control the reciprocal killings, and with proactive police work remaining at an all-time low, it's difficult to see how violence ends."

It was significant that the Black Guerrilla Family and Gun Trace Task Force prosecutions came about as results of federal investigations. City police and prosecutors lacked sophisticated resources like accountants, whereas the U.S. attorney, appointed by the White House, could rely on FBI, DEA, and IRS assistance. It had been that way for a long time. An example was a 1972 federal probe involving the treasurer of Robert Douglass's and Du Burns's Eastside Democratic Organization, James A. "Turk" Scott. He was a man of many faces—an insurance agent who had served in the army in Europe during World War II, owned a pool hall with a liquor license in his native D.C., and had done graduate work at Howard University and Hopkins.[15] Intrigued by his assertion that the bulk of his most recent earnings came from "gambling income," IRS hauled in his tax returns for six years.[16]

Scott owned Alpine Village at Harford and North, across from the Sears department store that is now a courthouse. In the 1930s it had been a Bohemian cocktail lounge. It retained the old name even after the neighborhood became black. I went to Alpine Village about 1971 to use a pay phone. There I bumped into off-duty police personnel having drinks, including a female clerk I knew from the Western District station.

Eastside Democratic Organization unsuccessfully lobbied Governor Mandel to appoint Scott to the city liquor board. Just before Christmas in 1972, the interracial political alliance between the New Democratic Club and EDO designated him to succeed a deceased House of Delegates member. Four months later, the newly minted forty-nine-year-old legislator was arrested outside the State House in Annapolis. A federal grand jury indicted him on nine counts of drug dealing, including making several trips to New York in the previous two years to secure and transport forty pounds of heroin. In Baltimore he wholesaled it to some of the city's biggest dealers, such as John Edward "Liddie" Jones and his brothers.

By Bastille Day in July, Scott was dead, a month before his trial. He was gunned down in the basement parking garage of Sutton Place, a Bolton Hill high-rise, where he lived in an eleventh-floor apartment. Someone wanted him deader than dead. On the torso, the chief medical examiner counted eight pellet blasts from a 12-gauge shotgun and shots from a .22-caliber handgun. "He was shot when he was alive, he was shot after he died," homicide lieutenant Stephen Tabeling said. Blue and yellow sheets of paper next to the body contained this mimeographed message: "These people are known drug dealers. Selling drugs is an act of treason. The penalty for treason is DEATH!!" The pages were signed: "Black October." No one had ever heard of such

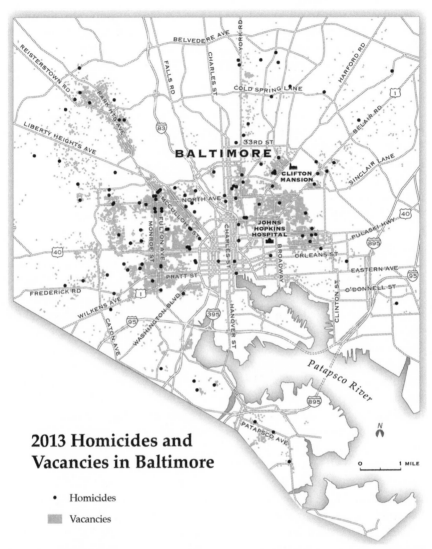

2013 Homicides and Vacancies in Baltimore

- • Homicides

  Vacancies

This map pinpoints the locations of homicides in 2013, correlating them with the shaded areas of vacant houses.

Robert Cronan. Lucidity Information Design, LLC

a Baltimore organization. Sherman Dobson, a troubled son of a family of prominent Baptist ministers, was eventually charged with killing Scott. He pleaded guilty to lesser offenses and went to prison.

No snitching. Hear nothing, see nothing was a Baltimore tradition. For many years in the 1900s, persistent testimony linked high-ranking police officials to protecting a white chemist nicknamed the "Cocaine King." Operating from 400 Gay Street, Dr. William H. Dull controlled illegal sales to blacks in Old Town's Belair Market area and paid $10,000 for protection. Two sergeants and three patrolmen were charged. Testimony before a police trial board revealed payoffs and how one cocaine dealer was recruited for the job by an officer as a reward for keeping fifteen blacks away from the polls on Election Day. Large-scale violations of Sunday liquor laws also were detailed. Black gofers in the case were convicted, the white accused—from Dull to the officers—were acquitted because the evidence was regarded as unreliable. So it went.[17]

The U.S. Senate's Kefauver Committee report in 1951 caused some ripples. Talking about vice in Baltimore, Judge Joseph Sherbow, of the Supreme Bench, said: "If any gambling or other illegal venture is in existence for any length of time and is not discovered by the police, then one of the following of several things is true: (1) the policeman on the beat is blind, (2) or he is incompetent, (3) or he is corrupt."[18]

In 1977 a city grand jury heard evidence of possible police involvement in the narcotics trade. The next year, deputy commissioner James H. Watkins was indicted on sixteen drug-related charges stemming from ten separate incidents. He was originally from Sandtown, a big man whose nickname was "The Bear." He got his GED diploma in the army where he rose to master sergeant. He joined the police force in 1951, becoming a protégé of Little Willie Adams and a protector of Charles T. Burns. He moved through districts, Criminal Investigation Division, Inspectional Services, and Tactical Squad until he became a lieutenant colonel, the second-highest black commander on the force. He was accused of taking a $15,000 bribe to alert a big drug dealer, Charles R. Burman Sr., a friend and neighbor who also had grown up in Sandtown. Watkins was found guilty by a jury but a judge overturned the conviction; a second jury found him not guilty.

He had been under a cloud several times before but Commissioner Pomerleau protected him. After acquittal, he retired from the force. He founded a group of five businesses that included a security agency employing a thousand men and women. It operated in Baltimore, Washington, and Cape Town in South Africa, where he bought a second home after Nelson Mandela came to power.

Suspicions of police involvement in drugs refused to go away. It was estimated that as many as a tenth of Baltimore's 611,600 residents were addicted to opioids. Heroin fueled holdups and burglaries; it turned decent women into bargain-basement hookers. In 1981 a city grand jury alleged "gross misconduct" in the police department and in the city state attorney's office. The twenty-three-member panel wrote that its six-month investigation "clearly demonstrates a hands-off approach when the targets were certain well-connected members of the community. The report specified that "there is an organized structured effort of some present and former members of each agency to perpetuate the protection of a select few to further obvious illicit gains."

This grand jury report so upset Stuart O. Simms and Patricia C. Jessamy that the two state's attorneys had a judge quash it. Circuit court judge Edward Angeletti ruled that the grand jury "exceeded its powers" by criticizing the local criminal-justice establishment without handing down indictments. He ordered the report expunged.[19] Enough copies floated around to enable *City Paper* reporter Van Smith to summarize: "It claimed that the police department's rotation policy, in which officers are reassigned to other police units, was used to thwart criminal investigations; it noted a pattern of investigations halted by the upper echelons of the police department and the state's attorney's office; it alleged there was abuse of the police overtime-pay system and that there were racially discriminatory employment practices; and it claimed the police department mismanaged its criminal investigation division's drug-enforcement section (CID-DES), which was said to operate 'on its own terms with little control or direction.'"

Those long-standing problems remained mostly unresolved nearly four decades later.

The grand jury, whose work now was erased was empaneled by circuit court judge Kenneth Lavon Johnson. To hear him tell it he was "just a simple country boy from Mississippi," who liked nothing better than hunting alligators on a spread of more than two hundred acres that his African American family had hung onto since Reconstruction. In fact, the Howard law graduate was a wily troublemaker who was expelled from Southern University and A & M College in Baton Rouge, Louisiana, for participating in a desegregation sit-in. In Vietnam, he helicoptered around to investigate allegations as a judge advocate corps captain. After he moved to Baltimore, he challenged the business-as-usual slate of "sitting judges" and won a seat on the circuit court.

We were friends. We usually met on his porch at 6 a.m., summer or winter. After retiring, he told me what happened. The grand jury was probing allegations of drug-related money laundering among the storied "Diner Guys," Jewish fellows who hung around Pimlico's Hilltop Diner before the neighborhood rotated to black. They were part of the 1950s and 1960s social tapestry in Barry Levinson's movies *Diner*, *Avalon*, and *Liberty Heights*. Among them were two go-getters, Leonard "Boogie" Weinglass and Harold Goldsmith. They created Merry-Go-Round Enterprises, a Baltimore-based nationwide peddler of the latest fad clothing at fifteen hundred mall stores operating under a dozen different concept names. Merry-Go-Round was at its peak when the grand jury began investigating allegations that the chain was used in money laundering. That was the testimony that Angeletti wiped out.[20]

Baltimore lost its will. It refused to investigate obvious policing and prosecutorial problems. Along with the state, the city also rebuffed efforts to overhaul a clogged justice system that made lawyers rich by postponing their clients' cases into eternity. Witnesses were intimidated and flaked away. All this was documented by *Sun* and *News American* reporters. In 1999 I wrote a yearlong editorial series, "Getting Away with Murder," which demanded reforms. Two decades later, little had changed. The top prosecutor and police still did not trust each other or work well together, and the various cogs in the creaky and jurisdictionally splintered "criminal justice" system moved out of sync. Baltimore accepted killings so long as violence was limited to drug neighborhoods, and victims were black.

It was like Rio de Janeiro, where skin color and neighborhood determined one's predictable exposure to violence. Planning a trip, I remember asking *The Sun*'s foreign editor, Richard O'Mara, about safety in Rio, where he had lived. He was aghast: "You live in West Baltimore and you worry about Rio."

Chapter Fourteen

The Price of Poison

The Hopkins medical institutions embodied the great technological strides that had taken place since the founder's days. But technology had its limits. Nothing more exemplified how unresolved social and political issues affected health than the city's lead paint crisis. For over a century, Hopkins had been the ringer of alarm bells, a worldwide pioneer in research about the dangers of lead. Nevertheless, decades after the paint was outlawed nationwide in 1978, the toxin kept poisoning families, highlighting the city's dysfunction, poverty, and ignorance.

Lead caused all kinds of ailments—neurological disorders, aggressive behavior, dimwittedness, even death. Many speculated that Baltimore's high homicide and overall violence rates were somehow linked to lead. To homeowners this seldom presented litigation problems but potential lead liabilities ruined Baltimore's resale market for rundown row houses. This produced more vacant houses. That, in turn, caused havoc in rentals as tenants sued for health damages. High jury awards drove landlords to bankruptcy. A landlord friend of mine in his nineties, Stanley Sugarman, wondered whether he would end up in the poor house. He reported that his insurance company offered him $700,000 to cancel a long-standing policy that protected him from lead liability.

Such an offer was an act of desperation. No new lead insurance policies could be bought for love or money because in 1975 the federal government lowered the level of lead concern in blood from sixty micrograms per deciliter to thirty micrograms, then to ten micrograms in 1991. Some advocates demanded that the latter risk percentage be further halved to five micrograms.[1] A Catch-22 came in 2011, when the Maryland Court of Appeals, in *Jackson v. Dackman Co.*, ruled that expensive lead abatement completed under old standards offered no immunity from future suits. Not even demolition got rid of lead. Whenever an old house was torn down, lead particles blew around, spreading contamination. Lead truly was a gift that kept on giving.

"Lead poisoning is a classic example of what happens when we take a material that was once buried deep underground and with which humans rarely had contact and introduce it widely into humans' ecology," Gerald Markowitz and David Rosner write in *Lead Wars: The Politics of Science and the Fate of America's Children*. "In the 1920s, the additive for gasoline, tetra-ethyl lead, was called a 'gift of God' by an industry intent on profiting from it. Despite warnings at the time that this industrial toxin might pollute the planet, more than a half century passed before it was finally removed from gasoline."

Lead was part of our common heritage. Ancient Romans mined lead and applied it—the English word for plumbing was derived from the Latin word for lead, *plumbum*. The Romans' cooking utensils and pots contained lead. Poisoning was widespread, particularly among the wealthy, who spiked their wine with sweet-tasting lead.[2] In modern times, doctors sometimes prescribed lead as medicine. Lead drove the Industrial Revolution. In Baltimore, the philanthropist Johns Hopkins and many of his Quaker kin owned shot towers that cast leaden bullets, or ran refineries that smelted lead. The Canton waterfront also accommodated a big canning industry, which used lead to seal metal containers. Tin Decorating Company on Boston Street alone employed more than a thousand men, who produced four million tins a day, including one million ten-cent tobacco tins. The plant's floor area covered seven acres. Of that complex, one building remains—Tindeco Wharf, an old canning factory converted into luxury apartments.

"Lead is a normal constituent of the earth's crust, with trace amounts found naturally in soil, plants, and water," writes Dr. Herbert L. Needleman, a pediatrician and psychiatrist. "If left undisturbed, lead is practically immobile. However, once mined and transformed into man-made products, which are dispersed throughout the environment, lead becomes highly toxic. Solely as a result of man's actions, lead has become the most widely scattered toxic metal in the world." Needleman demonstrated that children exposed to even small amounts of lead could suffer intellectual and behavioral deficits. That research convinced the federal government to outlaw lead paint and phase out lead from gasoline. Those measures, however, could not rid America of accumulated contamination. Inner-city neighborhoods along expressways had been particularly polluted with decades of emissions; previously industrial building sites were rezoned for residential but not de-leaded. In one big downtown apartment conversion I saw how flaking lead paint was simply covered with a false ceiling.

Lead's ill effects were assumed long before a groundbreaking 1904 interior paint study in Australia for the first time documented the harm the metal caused children. Elite physicians scoffed at the findings. However, consistent results convinced Australians otherwise, and in 1914 lead was banned from house paint—sixty-four years before the United States did the same. Also in 1914 Hopkins published the first North American lead paint study. Dr. Henry Thomas and Dr. Kenneth Blackfan wrote about a five-year-old white boy at Hopkins's Harriet Lane Home for Invalid Children who died after digesting white paint he gnawed from the metal railing of his crib. That's how many children got sick, by chewing and eating sweet-tasting lead paint from windowsills or plaster.

Hopkins was surrounded by lead. Nearby were forges and manufacturing industries that used lead, and thousands of row houses with tainted wood and plaster. Lead was used in water pipes. The poorer you were, the more you were likely affected. Doctors reported that during the Great Depression poor families commonly burned lead-contaminated wood casings from discarded car batteries, breathing toxic fumes from the oven.[3]

A hero in the battle against lead was Dr. Huntington Williams, who combined research with public health applications and actions. He was a Hopkins man through and through, a Gilman and Harvard graduate, who got his doctorate in the first class of the Hopkins School of Hygiene and Public Health (today named after Michael Bloomberg, an engineering graduate, who made his fame as a billionaire entrepreneur, philanthropist, and New York mayor). Williams first became interested in public health when typhoid fever killed his father, the university's first geology professor. Two Hopkins luminaries mentored him—Welch and Dr. Henry Hurd, the hospital's director until 1911. Another influence was Dr. Hermann Biggs. A powerful and progressive reformer, he was New York State health commissioner when Williams worked as a district health officer in Albany.[4]

In 1931 Welch summoned Williams back to Baltimore, where the latter headed the health department and established the Eastern Health District around the medical campus. The fifty-thousand-resident belt became a training field for public health students and personnel, and a testing ground for such city initiatives as prenatal care and well-baby clinics, medical care for recipients of public assistance, rat control, and rehabilitation of old and dilapidated housing. Williams was an educator during his tenure as health commissioner that lasted until his retirement in 1962. He had a weekly program on local radio, and on slow news days newspapers called him because he was so quotable. His department published a popular monthly magazine, the *Baltimore Health News*.

Lead was Williams's chief focus. Thanks to him, Baltimore became the nation's most aggressive city in curbing poisonous paint. Beginning in 1935—much earlier than anywhere else—free blood tests were offered to diagnose lead poisoning. Each year thereafter he updated the tallies in reports to mayors. In 1951 fifty-seven poisoned children were reported. Seventeen of them lived in the old Slum No. 1, a fifteen-square-block area of Old Town within the Eastern Health District; three of those died. That same year, Williams prohibited lead-based paint from interior use in all new private dwellings as well as public housing throughout the city.[5] Writes historian Elizabeth Fee: "Whereas some commissioners of health owed their loyalty to a political leader, a party machine, or the economically powerful, Williams owed his loyalty to Welch, who had groomed him; the Hopkins professors who had taught and inspired him; and the example of Biggs, who had shown him what an effective public health organization should be."[6]

After Williams retired, Baltimore grew lax. The lowering of the poisoning threshold gave rise to aggressive lead paint litigators, who carved a profitable niche by matching potential plaintiffs with property owners with collectable wealth. The ambulance chasers targeted investment groups, widows, and retirees as people who could be sued before the complainant's twenty-first birthday. Many cases were settled out of court and involved genuine victims of lead poisoning. But many others sued as just part of a racket. Lawyers knew that as long as their case ended up before a jury, a jackpot was within reach. It was a poverty game; nearly all lead plaintiffs were black, landlords and lawyers, white. "And now, ladies and gentlemen of the jury, look at this landlord in his fine suit. And now look at the young life he destroyed. How do you rule?" The juries' sympathies were obvious. One jury awarded $7.5 million in compensation, even though a state law set the ceiling at a fraction of that.[7]

Among lead plaintiffs was Freddie Gray, the hustler who got arrested because an officer didn't like the way he looked at him. Cops regarded Gray as a troublemaker, who had a rap sheet of eighteen arrests for drug dealing and stickups. During a rough ride in a police van he was left handcuffed and put in leg irons, but without a seat belt. He likely fell in the van, became paralyzed, and died. Thus ended a troubled twenty-five-year life span. It began in Sandtown, where he lived his formative years in houses so poisoned with lead that he tested as having between 11 mg/dL and 19 mg/dL in six blood samples taken between 1992 and 1996.

Freddie Gray's mother was a heroin addict who had not gone to high school and could not read or write. He didn't do very well with the alphabet, either, but was good with numbers. His life was a case study in the effect of lead paint on poor blacks. "A child who was poisoned with lead is seven times more likely to drop out of school and six times more likely to end up in the juvenile justice system," said Ruth Ann Norton, executive director of the Coalition to End Childhood Lead Poisoning. Kids who were poisoned decades ago grew into adults showing disruptive behavior.

Freddie Gray and his siblings went to Kennedy Krieger for treatment because the institute provided inpatient and outpatient medical care for children and adolescents with learning disabilities, disorders of the brain, spinal cord, and musculoskeletal system. Dr. Winthrop Phelps opened it in 1937 as the Children's Rehabilitation Institute, the first treatment facility in the country dedicated solely to children with cerebral palsy. The institute was renamed in 1968 to honor President John F. Kennedy's initiatives on behalf of people with disabilities. It was acquired by Hopkins and, in 1992, Zanvyl Krieger, an original board member of the old Children's Rehabilitation Institute, got an equal billing on the marquee.

Born to a beer and liquor fortune, Krieger was another City College boy. He graduated from Hopkins with a degree in political science in 1928, and earned his law degree at Harvard. He became immensely rich by controlling a start-up company called U.S. Surgical, which owned the rights to closing surgical incisions without cloth fiber stitches; the product was a game changer and soon gained 75 percent of the market. His greatest single gift was a $50 million challenge grant to the Hopkins division that deals with the humanities, social sciences, and natural sciences. The Zanvyl Krieger School of Arts and Sciences is named after him, an owner of the baseball Orioles and football Colts, who gave generously to the Baltimore Symphony Orchestra.

After treatment at Hopkins's Kennedy Krieger Institute, Freddie Gray and his two sisters sued Stanley Rochkind, a big inner-city landlord who owned seven hundred pre-1950s rental properties, accusing him of poisoning them. They won out-of-court settlements but then agreed to be cheated out of most of their windfall. Gray himself sold $146,000 worth of his structured settlement, valued at $94,000, to Access Funding for around $18,300. His sisters relinquished $435,000—valued at around $280,000—for about $54,000, or less than twenty cents on the dollar. After Gray's death, the city paid a $6.4 million wrongful death settlement to the family. (In all, Baltimore paid out $12 million in settlements and court judgments in police-misconduct cases from 2010 through 2015.)[8]

The Kennedy Krieger Institute's research became increasingly controversial after lower thresholds were adopted to measure lead harm and the number of lead-poisoned multiplied. If not cured, how could their health be stabilized? Kennedy Krieger experts set to work. Throughout the 1970s, they divided 107 housing properties into five categories on the basis of the abatements made and their cost. Researchers found single mothers with a total of 140 children, aged six months to six years, to live on the test premises.

The aim was not to cure them but to establish economically feasible and "practical" means to ameliorate lead poisoning. In each case, the researchers measured lead content of homes and took periodic blood tests over a two-year period. Follow-up measurements were to be made every couple of years after to track how the lead concentration changed in children, many of whom ended up with neurological complications.

Critics accused Hopkins researchers of endangering the victims' health. In 2001 Maryland Court of Appeals judge Dale R. Cathell slammed the university. In a scathing ninety-eight-page opinion, he declared that Kennedy Krieger researchers used children as "canaries in the coal mines, but never told the parents." He likened the research project to the notorious Tuskegee experiments that withheld treatment to black men infected with syphilis. A robust academic debate raged over whether the institute acted ethically in putting research of amelioration techniques over treatment. A class action suit against Kennedy Krieger limped along. The way the litigation would be settled had wide implications. "As new synthetic toxins—such as bisphenol A, polychlorinated biphenyls, other chlorinated hydrocarbons, tobacco, vinyl, and asbestos—are discovered to be biologically disruptive and disease producing at low levels, lead provides a window into the troubling dilemmas public health will have to confront in the future," Rosner and Markowitz wrote.[9]

POVERTY OF MEANS AND MINDS

I worked in Africa for more than two years as *The Sun*'s correspondent, followed by five in the Soviet Union. Coming back in 1989, I was startled to see how rapidly Baltimore had acquired some lifestyle features of underdeveloped Third World countries. Like unlicensed "jitney" cabs, hack predecessors of Uber and Lyft; like illegal sales of loose cigarettes because people were too poor to buy a whole pack; like prostitutes bringing tricks to city senior complexes where retirees needing money for a fix rented tryst space. "Like sidewalk grills," I wrote, "operated without permits or health inspections, that sell snacks in the wee hours of the night along Pennsylvania Avenue and other thoroughfares. Like other types of unregulated street vendors, with their makeshift tables. Like a population that increasingly tends to live without bothering to obtain building permits—or even zoning approvals—because it doesn't seem to make any difference. Add to this such truly meaningful social indicators as high rates of infant mortality and childhood illness, unplanned births and sexually transmitted diseases, poverty, drug addiction and chronic unemployment, and it becomes evident Baltimore is a Third World city in the First World."[10]

The federal government made that designation official. In 1994 the U.S. Agency for International Development began sending to Baltimore its experts returning from Kenya and Jamaica. Their task was to see whether micro-lending—granting small loans to entrepreneurs who were starting a business—could be replicated in the row-house city. Hopkins hosted an international conference on the matter. "I lived in India," said city hall official Lee Tawney. "When I travel around Baltimore, I see the same issues I saw in India."

There was a big difference, however. Unlike exploding Third World cities, Baltimore kept shrinking. Since the 1950s, its population plummeted from 949,700 to about 611,600—with more and more black strivers joining the exodus. Most headed for Baltimore County, a separate jurisdiction that rings the city like a neck collar. In the 1970s the county's population had been 95 percent white. In 2018 whites still formed the majority, but enrollment in the public school system revealed the future. So many students were African American, Hispanic, or Asian that it was "majority minority." Prominent churches followed the outflow. Many families simply wanted out. They had experienced urban living—loud music at all hours, quarrels and dysfunctional behavior, wailing ambulances and fire engines, and horns honking in front of row houses at 3 a.m. The city's property tax was the highest in the state, double Baltimore County's rate. Car insurance was far more expensive than in the suburbs, yet life without a vehicle was unthinkable.

Old-timers rhapsodized about the days before desegregation. The city was orderly, whites said, everything worked. Blacks remembered how their community was cohesive, with beauty parlors and barbershops next to churches and movie theaters, all within walking distance. Schools were better, kids acted respectfully, not wearing pants prison-style halfway down the buttocks. Local radio talk-show host Marc Steiner put it all in perspective: "Nostalgia is remembering the past, with the pain removed." There was pain in Baltimore's present. Things had so deteriorated that in 2016 a vacant row house collapsed and killed a sixty-nine-year-old retired truck driver, Thomas Lennon, who was sitting in his pride, an inherited cream-colored Cadillac, with red interior, listening to Otis Redding on the stereo. "Every day, he would come out and sit in that car," said a cousin.

Those in the work life found the Maryland Transit Administration service unreliable. Big employers operated their own transportation systems. Amazon vans ferried workers to its huge fulfillment center in an old General Motors auto plant near Canton; Hopkins ran a fleet of buses between its widely scattered installations. Patricia Williams, a billing coordinator living in Dundalk, could take an MTA bus to Bayview and then hop on a Hopkins shuttle to the hospital on Broadway. Similarly, a visitor coming by train could take a

Hopkins shuttle to the medical campus. That was the quickest way because the nearest Metro stop was half a mile away from Amtrak's Pennsylvania Station. That was the mad genius of Baltimore's transit system—the Metro, buses, and light-rail did not interconnect anywhere. Then in February 2018 the Metro line serving the hospital was suddenly shut down for a month without any advance warning. It was in such bad shape that it needed an emergency overhaul. Some forty thousand daily commuters were left in the lurch.[11]

MISEDUCATION

Nineteen-year-old Markel Scott did not make it. Someone shot him six times in 2017 as he walked home near Hopkins Hospital, carrying his schoolbag. He was two months from graduating from Excel Academy, an alternative high school for dropouts and others trying to get their lives together. "I am appreciative of being alive, healthy and sane," he wrote in his journal a month before he died. Excel students' odds were not great: Six of Scott's Excel schoolmates were murdered within fifteen months of his death.

Most of Excel's six hundred students were so poor that they qualified for taxpayer-paid free lunches, 22 percent were proficient in reading and math, and 27 percent graduated.[12] Those numbers actually were quite good: Of thirty-nine other high schools, thirteen had zero students proficient in math. Social interruptions rendered schools unable to teach. Up to 75 percent of elementary pupils in some hoods transferred during a given academic year because families led a nomadic life of drama ahead of bill collectors.[13] The state mandated preschool—so that children would enter elementary grades able to read and write—but many single mothers skipped it because they could not arrange for a pickup in early afternoon. Overall, few parents were involved in education. When one superintendent attended a PTA meeting, two parents showed up—along with a rat that scurried across the room.[14]

All kinds of experiments were tried to bring about hope. The most curious was an effort to extract seventeen at-risk seventh and eighth graders from Baltimore hoods and fly them to Africa for alternative schooling by American teachers. The scheme was dreamed up and financed by the Abell Foundation, and the way it came about was fascinating. An aging Gilman and Princeton graduate, George L. Small, who was white, inherited from his brother fifty thousand acres of Kenyan bush. Leaving the land unfenced, he turned it into a wildlife preserve with Africa's largest herd of elephants and helped find a site for the $800,000 school called Baraka, or blessing in Swahili. Small had made a fortune in his native York, Pennsylvania, running a food wholesale business that had been in the family since the philanthropist Johns Hopkins's days. He had grown up in Baltimore, and helped set up Charles T. Burns's pioneering African American Super Pride grocery chain. The city school board bought the Baraka idea and subsidized the school for six years. It closed in 2006 due to a worsening security situation in Kenya but also because the experiment had not stamped out alienation or behavior problems.[15]

At home, school disappointments continued. Until 1954 the city operated two public education systems—one for whites, the other for blacks. After desegregation, the systems merged and then, under Mayor Schaefer in the 1970s, became a racial battleground. At stake were well-paying jobs. Schaefer inherited two outspoken black school board members from Young Tommy—Larry S. Gibson, a lawyer, and James Griffin, a one-time CORE chair. These two activists championed assertive Roland N. Patterson, the first black superintendent. I remember attending acrimonious school board meetings that went past midnight; one lasted until 2:20 a.m. After Schaefer had Patterson fired, subsequent superintendents kept reorganizing. Various philosophies were tried out, with the pendulum swinging between centralization and decentralization. One constant stayed on—the school bureaucracy. It became a black reserve, and demonstrated a peculiar form of tribalism based on fraternity and sorority ties and church memberships. Miseducation was tolerated, and so was fiscal mismanagement.

This became the school system's permanent condition. It was dramatically revealed in the winter of 2018. Old heating systems failed in a third of 170 schools, turning classrooms into freezers and busting pipes. The whole system had to be closed. It should have been a big scandal, but it wasn't. The state had awarded tens of millions of dollars to update heating plants but school system bureaucrats did not follow procurement requirements and forfeited the money. Business as usual.

THE HOPKINS BRAND

In a branch-office city of limited ambitions, Johns Hopkins was the exception—a global premium brand, a diversified $6.3 billion corporation. Its medical operations networked with hospitals throughout the United States.[16] Hopkins also cooperated with institutions from Lebanon to India, and from Canada to Brazil to Chile. In Saudi Arabia alone, Hopkins managed health care for some 360,000 employees and dependents of the government's Aramco oil company. It did not hurt that Prince Bandar bin Sultan, the fixer and former Saudi ambassador to the United States, received a master's degree in international public policy at the Johns Hopkins's School of Advanced International Studies in Washington.

Then there was the United Arab Emirates.

That Persian Gulf state's modernization began with oil discoveries in Abu Dhabi deserts in 1958. Since then, some of the world's tallest and most ambitious skyscrapers had risen from sand dunes where camel caravans once traipsed and bedouins pitched their tents near harbors full of dhows that carried spices, gold, and silks from Asia and Africa to Europe. In the oil-fueled jet age, Abu Dhabi rebuilt its ancient trading prominence and then some. Along with neighboring Dubai, it was a feat of outsourcing, a strange place that I found soulless. Arabs owned it, but they accounted for only 10 percent of its 9.2 million people. The rest were foreigners, with no path to citizenship. These "expats" came from all corners of the world to work on temporary employment contracts in white-collar, blue-collar, and service industry jobs. They kept everything humming. They ran the IT infrastructure, managed and staffed offices and hotels, and oversaw skyscraper construction—by other foreigners. Indians counted for 27 percent of the population, followed by Pakistanis (12.53), Bangladeshis (7.31), and Filipinos (5.49). "For Sale" signs in Abu Dhabi were in English, Chinese, and Korean.

The moneyed elites wanted the best, regardless of cost. Huge shopping malls were their modern oases, open until midnight. In addition to exclusive brand merchandise, fashion shops, and restaurants, those malls offered a mind-boggling array of leisure options—including indoor ski slopes for downhill racing and snowboarding. Each year, Formula One Grand Prix auto races were a big event. As to culture, the Louvre and Guggenheim art museums opened branches. Even Rolls-Royce was part of the culture kick, exclusively introducing to Abu Dhabi customers a collection of Phantom, Ghost, and Wraith models inspired by composers from Bach to Beethoven. "The musical notes from the actual compositions were meticulously included in the veneer marquetry and inlays of these incredible motor cars. The notes have also been embroidered into the headrests, the rear centre armrest and across the headliner," a publicity release enthused.

The Abu Dhabi elites' brand consciousness allowed Johns Hopkins (and the rival Cleveland Clinic) to become big players in the health-care market. Hopkins managed the government's Tawam and Al Rahba teaching hospitals that specialize in oncology, neurosurgery, and pediatric surgery, and also ran the Corniche maternity hospital. Hopkins was a presence at the College of Medicine of the UAE University, just as Abu Dhabi was a presence in East Baltimore, where the Heart & Vascular Institute's $1.1 billion Sheikh Zayed critical care tower on Orleans Street had 560 beds and thirty-three operating rooms. It honored the first UAE president, a big donor, who was celebrated at home with a breathtaking storybook mosque straight out of the *One Thousand and One Nights* tales—and Disneyland.

Hopkins's interest in the Middle East was longstanding. Before Iran's Islamic revolution of 1979, the university was building a relationship with the shah. It granted an honorary doctor's degree to his twin sister, Princess Ashraf Pahlavi, who dished out government contracts. "Johns Hopkins University smelled money in Iran," wrote Dr. William Rawlings, a Sandersville, Georgia, physician and historian. He was a senior resident at Hopkins in 1975, when he took an offer to go to Teheran as a teaching resident at the shah's Reza Pahlavi University Hospital. "Everything was to be paid for, including my airfare, lodging, meals, etc.," he wrote. "And the best part was that I was given a grant of $3,000 per month on top of that for 'expenses,' with no real need to account for how I spent it." That came in addition to Rawlings's $9,000-a-year Hopkins salary, which he kept receiving.

"It was a strange world, to say the least," wrote Rawlings. "I was assigned living quarters which I shared with a professor from Hopkins who was there with his wife. It was, by Iranian standards, a luxurious apartment. The floors were covered with hand-woven silk carpets that would have cost several years of my salary at home. There was maid service. Our food was—for the most part—provided, or we could eat for free at the hospital. I discovered that my assigned duties were relatively minimal."

He garnered medical rewards. He met Ladan and Lelah, twenty-one-month-old twins who were joined at the head. Their parents had given them to the hospital to raise, so they spent the first part of their life there. Both eventually became lawyers. (They died, at twenty-nine, in 2003 during a fifty-hour attempt to separate them surgically in Singapore.) "I met and came to know a number of fine doctors, and was exposed to the common people who by illness or misfortune had ended up in this referral center. . . . I saw strange diseases I had only read about in textbooks."

FOCUS ON HOMETOWN

Fast-forward to 2018. Despite the far-flung medical empire, Hopkins's chief investments were in its hometown. It created a new skyline for Broadway, just as Paterakis had done along the Harbor East shoreline. One sixteen-story tower adjoining the hospital belonged to Residence Inn, which offered ninety-four studio, one- and two-bedroom suites with full kitchens to visitors to the medical institutions. Amenities included a state-of-the-art fitness center, meeting rooms, and complimentary grocery delivery service, and a roof-top restaurant featuring a seafood-focused menu. Hopkins, having learned from the Sheraton Inn disaster, this time avoided direct investment. Instead, owners included the Pyramid Hotel Group of Boston, Marriott Corporation, and a local development firm founded by Stewart Greenebaum. The latter's involvement was intriguing. He had made his philanthropic reputation at the University of Maryland where he chaired the board of the medical system's trustees and, with his wife, Marlene, donated a cancer center. Now, before his death, he branched out to the renewing Hopkins medical campus.

In addition to the hotel, Greenebaum built "townhomes" marketed with Live Near Your Work subsidies to Hopkins employees. By inner-city Baltimore standards, the houses, many with garages, were not steals—around $300,000 for new construction. "There is a bit of a premium on it, and it's an up-and-coming neighborhood," said Daniel Healy, thirty-one, a systems engineer at Hopkins, who estimated that he would cobble together more than $50,000 in incentives to make the purchase worth it. At the last moment he backed out. "It wasn't as great of an investment as I was looking for at the time, even with the incentives," he wrote in an email. The Residence Inn developers did better. Mayor Pugh gave them $800,000 in neighborhood improvement grants—out of a total pot of $1.3 million for the entire city—to compensate for the "fit-out of a mixed use building . . . and approximately 15,000 square feet of retail space."

Considering all the ups and downs in efforts to create a new image for Broadway, it was quite ironic that Bayview became the hot property. Despite an impressive collection of buildings the Hopkins ownership had erected and plenty of developable land, the old almshouse and municipal hospital site was something of an institutional stepchild. But it had location, location, location—half a mile away from I-95, the main interstate between New York and Washington. Also, the Canton shoreline was just over a mile away, and as prices there kept soaring, the magic of harbor revitalization radiated gentrification to unpretentious row-house streets across from Bayview in an area that was once known as Finntown but now was called Greektown, despite numerous Hispanics moving in.

Developers suddenly saw the Bayview vicinity as the Holy Land. Large homebuilders erected new "townhouses" there, while others set their eyes on abandoned industrial sites. One twenty-acre wreck of badly burned structures at 3501 Eastern Avenue, across from Southeastern District police station near Bayview's main entrance, was in the process of transformation. For a century, Yard 56 housed a family business that used lead to manufacture inorganic pigments and specialty glass that were used to produce porcelain enamel and ceramic glaze coatings for kitchen and bathroom appliances—and the tiles that gave Howard Johnson hotels and restaurants their distinctive orange-colored roofing.

After the company moved to Alabama, Yard 56 went vacant for a decade but now developers planned to clean up the toxins and build new destination shopping for residents and Bayview's five thousand employees. Anchored with a roughly thirty-four-thousand-square-foot LA Fitness, the complex was to house two hotels and nearly two hundred residential units, with plenty of space for future expansion. It was against this background that Hopkins in 2018 launched a further $469 million drive to modernize and expand Bayview. The market demanded an overall upgrading, including the elimination of semiprivate patient rooms.

Bayview was a quiet neighborhood at the east end of the city in generational transition. It found favor among rehabbers looking for affordable homes. I knew a twenty-seven-year-old kindergarten teacher, Alexandra Riedl, who paid $127,500 for a twenty-five-foot-wide two-story corner row house with a backyard and parking pad on a tree-lined street across from Bayview. She fixed up the 1956 vintage house, with help from her parents and friends. She opened up the kitchen by taking down the dining room wall, installing an island counter, modernizing the club basement, where one of the two full baths was located. She hunted for decorative accents like a fireplace mantel in her sun-lit living room. She could walk out of her back door and be at her school in less than two minutes. Young people like Alexandra were important. They saw possibilities, instead of problems. They were the future.

Alexandra was biracial, beautiful, and fluent in Spanish on a mostly white street, part of a generational and ethnic change; the seller family was Greek. This was the promise of Baltimore. To remain healthy, neighborhoods required more than the absolutely necessary access to conventional loans. They also needed constant rejuvenation because new homeowners brought vitality and kept the housing stock up-to-date. Even gentrified neighborhoods needed to rejuvenate. Roland Park was an example. After the 1968 riots, so many owners moved away that the garden district's population aged precipitously. Properties were hard to sell because there was little demand. Two decades later, young professionals rediscovered the old houses, mature trees, and azaleas. They replaced the remaining 1920s electrical wiring, modernized plumbing, and air-conditioned the Victorian homes. A number of Jews and blacks integrated the previously WASP streets, often attracted by proximity to private schools. The more inclusive Roland Park became, the more newcomers invested.

Neighborhood revival gained momentum in many parts of the city. When I first came to Baltimore in 1969, the front lines of renewal had recently shifted from Bolton Hill to Charles Village, near the Homewood campus, where middle-class urban pioneers fought persistent redlining in order to get mortgages and improvement loans. Slowly but steadily they increased their footprint. They reclaimed huge Victorian row houses, which some stained in a rainbow of colors—like the Painted Ladies of San Francisco. A Saturday

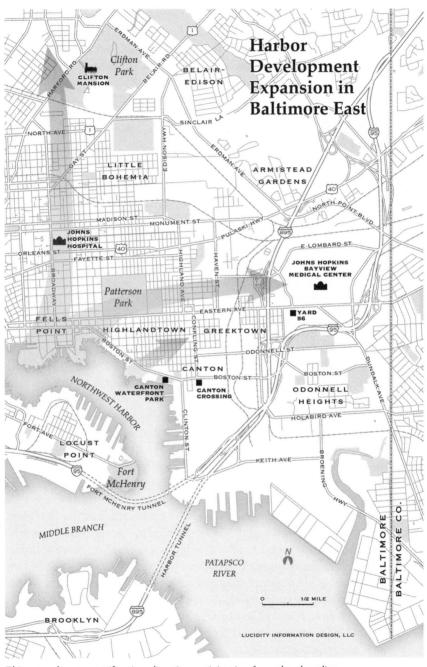

This map shows gentrification directions originating from the shoreline.
Robert Cronan. Lucidity Information Design, LLC

farmers market did brisk business. Then there was the weekend Book Thing, a huge warehouse full of used books arranged according to categories that included law, business, accounting, travel, and Judaica, in addition to several shelves of fiction and nonfiction. The books were all free; the more you took, the happier the sponsors were.

Charles Village and the adjoining Station North had once been well-to-do neighborhoods of respectable addresses. Now they regentrified. The long process of recycling was also going on in Hampden, Woodberry, and Remington. Those old blue-collar mill towns in the Jones Falls Valley were now taken over by white-collar residents; new housing was constructed. A belt of renewal stretched from there all the way to the harbor, a distance of four miles, where it connected with a rim of waterfront gentrification that extended from Fort McHenry to Canton.

There were limits to what improvers could do. Fast-speed broadband backbones ruled a world that relied on Wi-Fi to connect smart phones and computers and the evolving Internet of Things. Yet Baltimore lagged badly behind, condemned to tardy monopoly service from Verizon and Comcast. A more responsive mayoral administration would do something about bringing the city to the modern age. Wi-Fi was an economic development necessity. Hundreds of cities around the world recognized that and offered free high-speed Wi-Fi. Why not Baltimore? For the same reason why the antiquated railroad tunnels, recognized for decades as brakes on the economy, were not widened and expanded. They were not seen as a priority. A city with an unreliable transit system and inadequate railroad tunnels also had an unsatisfactory broadband. Something was seriously wrong.

LIFE AMONG RASCALS

Over nearly a century and a half, the institutions Johns Hopkins bequeathed weathered many unpredictabilities. They defied the 1889 bankruptcy of B&O Railroad, which nearly sank the university, and the 1904 Great Fire, which destroyed the hospital's fortune of Inner Harbor real estate. The university and the hospital recovered and grew. This colossus was on a solid financial footing when a double whammy hit. First, President Donald Trump discontinued U.S. visas for citizens of Iraq, Syria, Iran, Libya, Somalia, Sudan, and Yemen—many of whom lived in exile throughout the Middle East, including some rich and influential people. Although Saudi Arabia and the United Arab Emirates were among countries excluded from the "Muslim ban," the restrictions impacted Hopkins. Not only was it more difficult, if not impossible, for some Arab students and doctors to attend, but also threatened was the synergy the medical institutions had developed. Could Arab notables in flowing robes still come for treatment in Baltimore, where their families for weeks occupied whole floors of Inner Harbor luxury hotels? Or would they be offended by the restrictions and embarrassed by the attitudes?

The Trump administration also undertook to upend long-standing arrangements that had made Hopkins one of the government's top contractors in scientific and medical matters. Government intended to shift priorities. Hopkins and other big universities entered uncharted territory. So did Baltimore. The city relied on handouts. Twenty-one percent of its population lived in poverty. Any cuts in federal aid for social programs and housing would hit hard. Worse still, the city had mortgaged its future. The impressive condominium and office towers in Harbor East were built with assistance from taxpayers, but Paterakis and other developers were granted forgiveness from property taxes for decades. Meanwhile, some 40 percent of all real estate was exempt from taxes because it belonged to religious institutions like the Catholic Church or nonprofits like Hopkins. So the city's and state's largest private-sector employer paid no property taxes on nonprofit real estate. In fact, some big properties were taken off the tax rolls, when Hopkins acquired them. No one had yet made a big deal about the tax exemption but ultimately someone would, if the city's financial situation deteriorated. It was a tricky proposition. Hopkins, was the No. 1 industry, a First World anchor in a Third World city; touch it at your own peril.

The founder, Johns Hopkins, was open about his naked ambition—to make money. He even talked about selling his beloved Clifton estate because "I hate everything that does not bring in any money." He once ruminated about his boyhood days feeding pigs in Anne Arundel County—how the strongest hogs seized on the ears of corn to carry them off, while the weaker ones followed them, squeaking, and expecting scraps to fall. "I am like that strong hog," he said, "I've got the big ear of corn, and every piggish rascal in Baltimore is bound to steal it or get it from me some way if he can."[17] He then lamented: "I have a mission, and under its influence I have accumulated great wealth—but not happiness."

Such a man, such a life, such a legacy.

Notes

AUTHOR'S NOTE. MY BALTIMORE STORY QUILT

1. In the 1920s, five decades after Hopkins's death, his grandniece published a charming volume of family lore. Helen Hopkins Thom, *A Silhouette* (Johns Hopkins University Press, 2009 reprint) remains fascinating reading despite many inaccuracies.

2. Look at Harlem in New York. It began as a Native American settlement, went through Dutch, French, and British colonial periods, then became a suburb for the American-born well-off favoring fresh air. With the subway came overbuilding. Germans, Jews, Italians, and Scandinavians rotated through the area until the arrival of blacks and Puerto Ricans scared them off. Recently, whites in numbers have returned to Harlem. The Apollo Theater is the community's time capsule. It was a whites-only theater until 1934, when its white owner opened the doors for all for the first time—with a show, *Jazz a la Carte*. Today it is regarded as an African American cultural icon.

ACKNOWLEDGMENTS. WRITING THIS BOOK

1. https://books.google.com/books?id=kta8ANAuj14C&pg=PA51&dq=Noah+Davis&hl=en&sa=X&ved=0ahUKEwjMxarzl4baAhWpnOAKHfAWC8UQ6AEILDAB#v=onepage&q=Noah%20Davis&f=false.

2. I got to know Gene in 1978. I had been on the paper for nearly a decade when Jeff Price sent me to find out what had happened in a tight city council primary election between the incumbent, Mary Adams (no relation to Little Willie), and a WEBB and WEAA radio disc jockey, Kweisi Mfume. It was some kind of holiday weekend, and Raynor was alone in the election board headquarters. He told me the office was closed and no results had been certified. Price, the lead city hall reporter, called him to express his shock that a public servant was trying to keep "my man" from finding out public information. The end result was that I trudged back to the election board,

where Raynor told me he could not tell me anything—but I was free to roam around and see what I could find. I was so naive that I had to ask him to explain the outcome—just to be sure: Kweisi Mfume beat Adams by three votes, launching a career that took him to the U.S. House of Representatives and presidency of NAACP. That was my exclusive for two days.

CHAPTER 1. JOHNSIE'S BALTIMORE

1. Michael Klepper, *The Wealthy 100: From Benjamin Franklin to Bill Gates— A Ranking of the Richest Americans, Past and Present* (Carol Publishing Group, 1996), xiii.

2. Pratt Street was named for Charles Pratt, 1st Earl Camden, and not the noted Baltimorean Enoch Pratt (1808–1896).

3. *Sun*, June 20, 1999.

4. J. Reaney Kelly, *Quakers in the Founding of Anne Arundel County, Maryland* (Maryland Historical Society, 1963).

5. *Kissing the Bible: The Sun Almanac for 1899* (A. S. Abell Co., 1899), 29.

6. Sydney George Fisher, *The Quaker Colonies: A Chronicle of the Proprietors of the Delaware* (Yale University Press, 1919), 2.

7. The prophetic role of women: John M. Barry, *Roger Williams and the Creation of the American Soul: Church, State, and the Birth of Liberty* (Viking, 2012).

8. Quoted in Ezra Michener, *A Retrospective of Early Quakerism* (T. Ellwood Fell, 1860), 328.

9. Michener, 320. A state law enacted in 1664 clarified that baptism did not equal freedom.

10. Lawrence Buckley Thomas, "Genealogical Notes Containing the Pedigree of the Thomas Family of Maryland, and of the Following Connecting Families: Snowden-Buckley-Lawrence-Chew-Ellicott-Hopkins-Johnson-Rutherfurd-Fairfax -Schieffelin-Tyson (Lawrence B. Thomas, 1877), 32.

11. She kept a record of her travels 1778–1801, which was published. She described her 1780 visit to Anne Arundel County in additional material discovered by a Swarthmore College student, Albert Cook Myers, the Pennsylvania historian, which was printed by *Friends' Intelligencer and Journal*, May 5, 1897. The June 5 issue chronicled a visit one year later as well. During it, she overnighted at the house of Johns Hopkins, who by then had manumitted slaves. Also, "we went to Roger Brooke's, I having a desire to see his tender-hearted wife, who was like a prisoner, and had been for some time."

12. Miles White, *Some Colonial Ancestors of Johns Hopkins* (Harrisburg Publishing Co., 1900), 40.

13. *Friends' Intelligencer and Journal*, May 5, 1897.

14. Laura E. Holloway, *Famous American Fortunes and the Men who Have Made Them: A Series of Sketches of Many of the Notable Merchants, Manufacturers, Capitalists, Railroad Presidents, Bonanza and Cattle Kings of the Country* (J. A. Hill, 1889), 337.

15. Christopher Densmore's compilation of 1826 records pertaining to the "Disownment of Johns Hopkins by Baltimore Monthly Meeting of the Religious Society of Friends," Friends Historical Library of Swarthmore College.

16. The genealogy is detailed in Charles Henry Browning, *Americans of Royal Descent: A Collection of Genealogies of American Families Whose Lineage Is Traced to the Legitimate Issue of Kings* (Porter & Costes, 1891), 492.

17. *Baltimore: Its History and Its People*, vol. 1 (Lewis Historical Publishing Co. 1912), 14–15, 306. The earliest shipment for which records exist occurred in 1758, when Dr. John Stevenson, an Oxford-trained physician from Ireland and the city's most important merchant in those early days, exported to New York one hogshead of tobacco, fifteen barrels of flour, sixteen barrels of bread, and one barrel of beeswax. The return cargo consisted of five hundred pounds of logwood, one cask each of indigo and coffee, and twelve casks of sugar.

18. Recognizable remnants of other rolling roads may be found throughout Maryland, even though tobacco ports disappeared so long ago that hardly a trace remains.

19. In 1832 the clipper ship *John Gilpin* set a new speed record for travel. Powered by three main sails, it glided from Baltimore to Jakarta, Indonesia, in eighty-two days; proceeded to Canton, China, in eleven days, then on to Manila in five days. From the Philippines winds blew it on to Valparaiso, Chile, in another eighty-five days, and then to Lima, Peru, in six days—voyages totaling 34,920 miles at an unheard-of average speed of 183 miles a day.

20. Van Smith, "Baltimore's Narcotic History Dates Back to the 19th-Century Shipping-Driven Boom, Quietly Aided by Bringing Turkish Opium to China," *City Paper*, Oct. 21, 2014.

21. Latrobe, in a lecture at the Maryland Institute, Mar. 23, 1868. Thomas Hughes, *The Life and Times of Peter Cooper* (Macmillan & Co., 1886), 91.

22. Harris Creek, a small tributary of the Patapsco system, today runs underground through seventeen neighborhoods from Clifton to Canton. Its original penetration deep inland explains why cannons were placed in today's Patterson Park to prevent invading British from landing there in 1814. Instead, the battle took place at North Point. Eli Pousson, "Harris Creek," https://explore.baltimoreheritage.org/items/show/188.

23. J. Thomas Scharf, *The Chronicles Of Baltimore: Being A Complete History Of "Baltimore Town" And Baltimore City From The Earliest Period To The Present Time*. 710 (Turnbull Brothers, 1879). Edward A. Mueller's *The Queen of Sea Routes* offers a comprehensive history of the Merchants & Miners line. It concentrates on the role of Boston investors, even though Baltimore interests occupied three-fifths of the Merchants & Miners board.

24. *Sun*, June 28, 1871.

25. Frederick Law Olmsted, "A Journey in the Seaboard Slave States: Slavery in the Years before the American Civil War," http://docsouth.unc.edu/nc/olmsted/menu .html.

26. Peter Lesher, "A Load of Guano: Baltimore and the Fertilizer Trade in the Nineteenth Century," *Northern Mariner/le marin du nord*, XVII, no. 3–4 (July–Oct., 2008), 121–128. In 1856, deeming guano to be vital for America's interests, Congress

passed the Guano Islands Act. The measure invited U.S. citizens to claim guano islands to the American government in the Caribbean. Three years later, the United States did just that, possessing the guano-rich Navassa Island, despite protests from nearby Haiti. The island is still in U.S. hands.

27. *Sun*, Mar. 7, 1846; Aug. 17, 1867. What is an ethel? This is Baltimore architect Klaus Philipsen's interpretation: "It looks like ethels is used not as an architectural term but to describe what is depicted. I suppose it means girls or women as a rather loose plural of Ethel, the noble woman."

28. Board of Trade: *New York Times*, Jan. 15, 1874. B'nai B'rith, *Sun*, Jan. 23, 1879; Jan. 14, 1874.The building had "very defective acoustics" that made hearing "very difficult," one report complained.

29. *Sun*, Oct. 7, 1886.

30. *NYT*, Dec. 27, 1873.

31. Thom, 32–33.

32. Mame Warren's oral history interview with Samuel Hopkins, May 10, 2006, https://jscholarship.library.jhu.edu/bitstream/handle/1774.2/44571/ms404_hopkins_samuel_05-10-2006.pdf?sequence=2&isAllowed=y.

33. Wirt to daughter Catharine, Nov. 24, 1822, printed in *The Chronicles of Baltimore*, 403–404.

34. *The Chronicles of Baltimore*, 522.

35. Ralph Reppert, "Town Criers," *Sun Magazine*, July 24, 1949.

36. Stephen Schlosnagle, *Garrett County: A History of Maryland's Tableland* (McClain Printing Co., 1978), 130, quoting a 1790 traveler, Mesach Browning.

37. J. Wallace Bryan, *Transportation System and Facilities in Clayton Colman Hall, Baltimore: Its History and Its People* (Lewis Historical Publishing Co., 1912). It was possible, if one was in a hurry, wealthy, and very lucky, to reach Philadelphia from Baltimore in one long day, alternating stagecoaches with boats. But such swift connections were an exception.

38. Schlosnagle, 132.

39. J. Thomas Scharf, *History of Western Maryland* (L. H. Everts, 1862).

40. Schlosnagle, 139–140.

41. This can be ascertained from properties listed in his will. See also Letitia Stockett's delightful *Baltimore: A Not Too Serious History* (Johns Hopkins University Press, 1997), 156.

42. Each founder had a story to tell. William Patterson came penniless as a lad of fourteen from northern Ireland, spent some years in the West Indies, made a fortune in shipping and other lucrative ventures on the Canton waterfront, donated Patterson Park to the city, and had a headstrong daughter who married Jerome Bonaparte, the youngest brother of the French emperor Napoleon. Solomon Etting, American born, had recently been elected to the city council after Maryland qualified Jews to hold public office. Robert Oliver, Isaac McKim, William Lorman, George Hoffman, John B. Morris, Talbot Jones, and William Steuart may be forgotten today, but they all have streets or buildings named after them.

43. Latrobe, *Personal Recollections of the B.&O. R.R.*, 6. (Sun Printing Establishment, 1868).

44. Albert J. Churella, *The Pennsylvania Railroad*, vol. 1, "Building an Empire, 1846–1917" (University of Pennsylvania Press, 2012), 63. According to his estimate, the city's public investments represented an average per capita contribution in excess of $118—equivalent to perhaps six months' wages for a day laborer. Several books have been written about B&O. James Dilts's accounting of early years is unsurpassed in *The Great Road* (Stanford University Press, 1993).

45. "Report of the Directors of Baltimore and Ohio Rail Road Company, to the Legislature of Maryland" (Jonas Green, printer, 1831), 4–10.

46. *A Citizen of Baltimore: A History and Description of the Baltimore and Ohio Rail Road* (John Murphy, 1853), 12.

47. Cooper to William H. Brown, May 18, 1869, reprinted in *The Chronicles of Baltimore*, 455. In 1842, a newly-built steam ship, *Medorg*, exploded in The Basin. Of the eighty-two people on board, twenty-seven were killed, forty injured. *The Chronicles of Baltimore*, 506. Stone rails *Report of the Directors of the Baltimore and Ohio Rail Road Company to the Legislature of Maryland*, 39 (Jonas Green, 1831). A good description in William Henry Brown, *The History of the First Locomotives in American from Original Documents, and the Testimony of Living Witness* (D. Appleton & Co., 1871), 107–116; Thomas Hughes, *The Life and Times of Peter Cooper* (Macmillan & Co, 1886), 103. Also about the race, *American Railroad Journal*, vol. 4, 249 (1835); *Mechanic's Magazine*; and *Journal of Science, Arts & Manufactures*, vol. 23 (1835), 176.

48. Report of the Directors of Baltimore and Ohio Rail Road Company, 11–13.

49. Latrobe was a fascinating character: John Edward Semmes, *John H. B. Latrobe and His Times, 180 –1898* (Remington Co., 1917), 321. Among his inventions was the Latrobe parlor stove, an early attempt at central heating.

50. Holloway, 338.

51. Kathleen Waters Sander, *John W. Garrett and the Baltimore & Ohio Railroad* (Johns Hopkins University Press, 2017), 16.

52. Bruce William Catton, *John W. Garrett of the Baltimore and Ohio: A Study in Seaport Railroad Competition, 1820–1874*. Ph.D. dissertation, Northwestern University, 1959, 95.

53. Holloway, 22.

CHAPTER 2. THE CIVIL WAR: BLUE AND GRAY

1. E. A. Duyckick, *History of the War for the Union* (Johnson, Fry & Co.,1861), 169. Also, *Sun*, Apr. 22, 1861. That issue contained verbatim letters and telegrams between local authorities and the federal government in Washington.

2. See George L. P. Radcliffe, Thomas H. Hicks, "Maryland and the Civil War," *Johns Hopkins Studies in Historical & Political Science*, vol. XIX (1901), 7–129.

3. Tracy Matthew Melton, *Hanging Henry Gambrill: The Violent Careers of Baltimore's Plug Uglies 1854–1860* (Maryland Historical Society, 2005), 44–45.

4. Thomas Swann (1809–1883), MSA SC 3520-1464. Tracy Matthew Melton, *Hanging Henry Gambrill: The Violent Career of Baltimore's Plug Uglies* (Maryland Historical Society, 2004).

5. Sir William Howard Russell, *My Diary North and South*, vol. 2 (Bradbury & Evans, 1863), 118.

6. George William Brown, *Baltimore and the Nineteenth of April 1961: A Story of the War* (N. Murray, 1887), 47–51.

7. John Thomas Scharf, *History of Baltimore City and County, from the Earliest Period to the Present Day: Including Biographical Sketches of Their Representative Men* (L. H. Everts, 1881), 54, 130.

8. Frank R. Kent, *History of Alex. Brown & Sons 1800–1950* (Alex. Brown & Sons, 1950), 149–157.

9. Full account, *Sun*, Apr. 22, 1861.

10. Frank Towers, *The Urban South and the Coming of the Civil War* (University of Virginia Press, 2004), 166.

11. Neil A. Grauer, "Lincoln's servant + friend," an 1862 letter, *Johns Hopkins Magazine*, Summer 2003. http://hub.jhu.edu/magazine/2013/summer/johns-hopkins -lincoln-letter/.

12. Samuel Hopkins, a member of the extended family, in a 2006 oral history interview with Mame Warren, said that in the 1950s a man came to see him "who worked for the Los Angeles Times who was writing a history of Johns Hopkins, and he told me that one of the things he had found was evidence that during the Civil War Johns Hopkins had bribed members of the Maryland legislature to keep Maryland in the Union." No substantiation has been discovered for such a claim. https://jscholarship .library.jhu.edu/bitstream/handle/1774.2/44571/ms404_hopkins_samuel_05-10-2006 .pdf?sequence=2&isAllowed=y.

13. Festus Paul Summers, The Baltimore and Ohio in the Civil War (Stan Clark Military Books, 1993), 46-49: At the outset of the Civil War Garrett wanted to do business with both sides. He commanded employees that "until further orders you [are] to take all troops or munitions that offer at regular rates. Our company fully recognizes the present legal authorities State and National under which we live, and as common carriers propose to promptly and safely transport all passengers or freight that those authorities may desire. . ."

14. Summers, 27.

15. Brown, 64.

16. General Butler recounted the whole situation in a report to the Treasury Department, summarized in *NYT*, Jan. 12, 1883. He described Maryland officials' uncooperativeness, including a Naval Academy commander.

17. Brown, 99.

18. Summers, 56. Cameron had such a financial stake in a rival that the North Central Railroad was known as "Cameron's Railroad." Some scholars suggest his accusation against B&O was prompted by competitive reasons, Summers, 47, 60. B&O also transported one recorded shipment of muskets "for Southern men" in Baltimore from Harpers Ferry, where gun factories were located. Much of the railroad loot that Stonewall Jackson took proved unusable by the Confederates whose railroads, using a different gauge, did not connect with B&O. A rebel railroader, Captain Thomas R. Sharp, planned and executed the Harpers Ferry caper. After the war, Garrett controversially hired Sharp as B&O's master of transport.

19. See James Stimpert's introduction to the 2009 edition of Thom's book, ix–xviii. At an 1863 dinner Hopkins hosted for secretary of treasury Salmon P. Chase, "railroad executives, and local businessmen . . . all pledged support for emancipation and assured President Abraham Lincoln that the B. & O. Railroad would assist the government with moving troops and supplies."

20. Garrett was "as much a part of Mr. Lincoln's Cabinet as any man in it, and was often called to Cabinet counsels when questions of great moment were discussed," writes Major Theodore Lang, the West Virginia historian, in *Loyal West Virginia from 1861 to 1865* (Deutsch Publishing Co., 1895), 146.

21. *The Mayor and City Council vs. the Baltimore and Ohio Railroad Company* (John Murphy & Co., 1857), 55–105. https://books.google.com/books?id=NWU3A QAAMAAJ&printsec=frontcover&dq=B.%26O.R.R.+Papers&hl=en&sa=X&ved=0 ahUKEwiApbyh9qjaAhVG2oMKHb3QAiwQ6AEIKzAA#v=onepage&q=B.%26O .R.R.%20Papers&f=false.

22. *Sun*, Feb. 13, 1860; the private shareholders gained a board majority after the Civil War.

23. Druscilla J. Null, "Myrtilla Miner's 'School for Colored Girls': A Mirror on Antebellum Washington," *Records of the Columbia Historical Society of Washington, D.C.*, vol. 52, 252–268 (University Press of Virginia, 1989).

24. Jeffrey Brackett, *The Negro in Maryland: A Study of the Institution of Slavery* (Johns Hopkins University, 1899).

25. Jeffrey R. Brackett, "Notes on the Progress of the Colored People of Maryland since the War," *Johns Hopkins University Studies in Historical and Political Science* (1890), 8.

26. *Sun*, Mar. 26, 1860; Mar. 11, 1860. The legislature rejected a proposal that would have had sold "any free negro or slave" out of state for committing a crime that netted a prison sentence for a white man. Another defeated measure would have instituted a statewide curfew for blacks, slaves as well as free, from 9 p.m. until 5 a.m. and prescribed penalties, *Sun*, Nov. 26, 1859.

27. T. Stephen Whitman, *The Price of Slavery* (University of Kentucky Press, 1997), table 1, 10.

28. Francis E. Beirne, *The Amiable Baltimoreans* (E. P. Dutton, 1951), 272.

29. *Sun*, Nov. 9, 1837.

30. Frederick Douglass, *Narrative of the Life of Frederick Douglass, an American Slave* (Anti-Slavery Office, 1849), 32.

31. Curfew bill, *Sun*, Nov. 26, 1859. Insurance bounties: Karen Ryder, "To Realize Money Facilities": Slave Life Insurance; The Slave Trade; Credit in the Old South, in *New Directions in Slavery Studies: Commodification, Community, and Comparison* (LSU Press, 2015).

32. Ralph Clayton, *Cash for Blood* (Heritage Books, 2002), 38.

33. See *Sun*, Nov. 26, 1859.

34. Jeffrey R. Brackett, *The Negro in Maryland*, 66.

35. John H. B. Latrobe, *Maryland in Liberia: A History of the Colony Planted by the Maryland State Colonization Society under the Auspices of the State of Maryland,*

U.S. at Cape Palmas on the South-West Coast of Africa, 1833–1853 (privately published, 1885), 14–15.

36. *Maryland Colonization Journal*, April 15, 1851.

37. See Philip W. Magness, Sebastian N. Page, *Colonization after Emancipation: Lincoln and the Movement for Black Resettlement* (University of Missouri Press, 2011), 40–44, 137.

38. Latrobe's 1885 history, *Maryland in Liberia*, is the best firsthand account of the project. The 138-page book contains the colony's founding documents, https://books .google.com/books?id=e_cMAAAAYAAJ&printsec=frontcover&dq=Maryland +in+Liberia&hl=en&sa=X&ved=0ahUKEwiA-6Hu-KjaAhUH54MKHYde CNYQ6AEIKTAA#v=onepage&q=Maryland%20in%20Liberia&f=false.

39. Eugene S. Van Sickle, *A Transnational Vision: John H. B. Latrobe and Maryland's African Colonization Movement* (ProQuest, 2005). Big slave owners, including Henry Clay, the statesman from Kentucky, were among the colonization movement figureheads; some liberated their slaves, others sold them to the highest bidder.

40. Until Liberia's civil wars destroyed them in the 1980s, Liberia had an extensive collection of Southern-style mansions.

41. "Pioneer Fathers," *Sun*, May 10, 1982. This was one of several articles I wrote about Liberia as *The Sun*'s Africa correspondent.

42. Frederic Bancroft, *Slave Trading in the Old South* (Frederick Ungar Publishing Co. ,1961), 122, prints the following partial list of slavers in 1856: Allen, John, 241 Gough; Campbell, B. M. & W. L., 284 West Pratt; Casey, Thomas, 255 East Lombard; Donovan, Joseph S., 11 Camden; Goman, George, Pennsylvania Avenue extended; King, Samuel H., 36 Thames; Mitchell, John S. 105 William; Ritz, John Z., 118 Harford; Robinson, Joseph, 287 East Pratt; Wareham, James, 127 Orleans; Warfield, Caleb, 242 Conway; and Warfield, Thomas, 4 McHenry.

43. Ned Sublette, Constance Sublette, *The American Slave Coast: A History of the Slave Breeding Industry* (Chicago Review Press, 2015), 28.

44. Olmsted, *A Journey in the Seaboard Slave States* (Mason Brothers, 1861), 55: "A slaveholder writing to me with regard to my cautious statements on this subject, made in the [New York] *Daily Times*, says:—'In the States of Maryland, Virginia, North Carolina, Kentucky, Tennessee and Missouri, as much attention is paid to the breeding and growth of negroes as to that of horses and mules. Further South, we raise them both for use and for market. Planters command their girls and women (married or unmarried) to have children; and I have known a great many negro girls to be sold off, because they did not have children. A breeding woman is worth from one-sixth to one-fourth more than one that does not breed.'"

45. Bancroft, 99.

46. Douglass, 198.

47. Scharf, 440. In 1828 General Charles Ridgely, a former Maryland governor, freed all slaves older than forty-five on his Hampton plantation, but kept young males until they reached twenty-seven and women until twenty-five.

48. *Quarterly Christian Spectator* (S. Cooke, 1834), 344.

49. Wallace Shugg, *A Monument to Good Intentions: The Story of the Maryland Penitentiary, 1804–1995* (Maryland Historical Society, 2000), 43.

50. As late as 1960, contractors digging at the site of the Civic Center (later Royal Farms Arena) found a huge vaulted brick dungeon near Slatter's long-gone jail. *Sun*, Jan. 19, 1960.

51. Ned Sublette, Constance Sublette, *The American Slave Coast: A History of the Slave-Breeding Industry* (Chicago Review Press, 2015) is one of many books that deal with this subject.

52. *Niles' Weekly Register*, May 19, 1827.

53. Scott Shane, "The Secret History of City Slave Trade," *Sun*, June 20, 1999.

54. *Sun*, Sept. 28, 1866.

55. William Starr Myers, *The Self-Reconstruction of Maryland 1864–1867* (Johns Hopkins Press, 1909), 110; *Sun*, Apr. 9, 1867. Also, Dan Friedman, *The Maryland State Constitution* (Oxford University Press, 2011), 11–13.

56. *Sun*, Oct. 29, 1863.

57. Brackett, 10.

58. David D. Bogen, "The Annapolis Poll Books of 1800 and 1804: African American Voting in the Early Republic," *Maryland Historical Magazine*, Spring 1991, 57–65.

59. *Sun*, Sept. 20, 1870.

60. *NYT*, Nov. 1, 1873; Dec. 8, 1873.

61. A photo of the mansion faces page 48 in Thom's *A Silhouette*.

CHAPTER 3. A BRUSH WITH DEATH

1. John Russel Quinan, *Medical Annals of Baltimore from 1608 to 1880* (Isaac Friedenwald, 1884), 35.

2. Eugene Fauntleroy Cordell, *The Medical Annals of Maryland, 1799–1899* (Williams & Wilkins, 1903), 120.

3. Thom, 52.

4. Horatio Gates Jameson , "Cholera in Baltimore" in his *A Treatise on Epidemic Cholera* (Lindsay & Blackinston, 1855), 109.

5. Charles E. Rosenberg, *The Cholera Years: The United States in 1832, 1849, and 1866* (University of Chicago Press, 1962), 55.

6. Jameson, 110.

7. Jameson, 148.

8. Phillips, *Freedom's Port*, 139, 275.

9. Jameson, 150.

10. It may be read for free on Google Books.

11. Jameson, 152.

12. *The Ordinances of the Mayor and the City Council* (Sands & Neilson, 1835), appendix, 25.

13. Henry Orlando Marcy, "A Brief Sketch of One of Baltimore's Greatest Men, Horatio Gates Jameson, M.D." (1906), https://archive.org/details/abriefsketchone 00marcgoog.

14. *The Ordinances of the Mayor and City Council* (Sands & Neilson, 1833) offers a detailed look at Baltimore's conditions.

15. Jameson, 109.

16. Smallpox deaths in Baltimore had declined precipitously since inoculations began in 1800. John Russel Quinan, *Medical Annals of Baltimore from 1608 to 1880* (Isaac Friedenwald, 1884), 26, 254–274.

17. Report of Samuel B. Martin, health officer, appendix 21.

18. Dr. Jameson opined that the main reason for quarantine was not a belief that it was effective, but the harsh fact that had Baltimore not chosen to quarantine, other cities would have isolated it by cutting off all commercial, travel, and transport links. During earlier yellow fever epidemics Baltimore severed all contacts with Philadelphia and Annapolis.

19. Jameson, 108.

20. Cordell Medical Annals, 793. Bernard G. Steiner, *History of Education in Maryland* (Government Printing Office, 1894), 250. In 1867 a group of ex-Confederate physicians and surgeons revived the school. It was to be of service to the Lost Cause. "One student from each Congressional district of the late slave-holding States is received as a beneficiary in Washington University, precedence being given to wounded and disabled soldiers," a school catalogue stated in 1868. This is how it described Baltimore to prospective students: "This is emphatically the favored land, within whose soil no noxious political dogmas germinate, and where every *white* man, whatever his opinions or antecedents, can think and speak and act according to the dictates of his conscience, without fear of bayonets and bastiles." The school went out of business in 1877.

21. *The Ordinances of the Mayor and City Council of Baltimore* (Sands & Neilson, 1833), 19.

22. A. S. Abell profile in *Baltimore: Past and Present with Biographical Sketches of Its Representative Men* (Richardson & Bennett, 1871), 164.

23. This urban/rural divide is depicted in E. Sachse & Co.'s bird's-eye view of the city of Baltimore, 1869, a map that was painstakingly accurate.

24. *Sun*, Sept. 13, 1870.

25. *Sun*, Sept. 20, 1870.

26. The meeting was held in the shadow of city hall at a Saratoga Street educational institute named after the abolitionist Frederick Douglass. The city's black elite lived on surrounding blocks, just north of the courthouse. In 1864 St. Francis Xavier Catholic Church had dedicated a sanctuary there, and was soon followed by Bethel African Methodist Episcopal and Union Baptist. After the current city hall was constructed, the previous one was converted into Colored Primary School No. 1 in 1876. The building still stands at 225 North Holliday Street. See chapter 5.

27. See Bliss Forbush, *Moses Sheppard: Quaker Philanthropist of Baltimore* (J. B. Lippincott Co., 1968), 204; Davis S. Heisel and Trevor J. Blank, *Spring Grove State Hospital* (Arcadia Press, 2008), 14. The University of Maryland Baltimore County now occupies much of the Spring Grove Hospital's land).

28. Hopkins was elected member of the board of visitors in 1852. See Heisel and Blank.

29. Patrick Smithwick, *The Art of Healing: Union Memorial Hospital 150 Years of Caring for Patients* (Union Memorial Hospital, 2004), 4. The 1514 Division Street location was near the Immaculate Conception Catholic Church and soon

drew St. Vincent Infant Asylum and the Widows Home of the Catholic Church (*Sun*, Oct. 15, 1859).

30. *Sun*, Jan. 1, 1856.

31. His allocations to two nieces specified, in each case, that the money was for their "separate use, free from the control of any husband" they may "now, or hereafter, have."

32. Abraham Flexner, *Daniel Coit Gilman: The Creator of the American Type of University* (Harcourt, Brace & Co., 1946), 110, 220. Of the original twelve university trustees seven were Quakers, four Episcopalians, and one an independent Presbyterian.

33. He did stipulate this detail: Trustees "from time to time" were to give free education to "such candidates from Maryland, Virginia, and North Carolina, as may be most deserving of choice because of their character and intellectual promise." It was a payback for his profits from the Conestoga wagon days.

34. *Sun*, Feb. 8, 1871.

35. I am indebted to John Ciekot for much of this information. He is with Civic-Works, which is restoring Clifton.

36. Laura E. Holloway, *Famous American Fortunes and the Men who Have Made Them: A Series of Sketches of Many of the Notable Merchants, Manufacturers, Capitalists, Railroad Presidents, Bonanza and Cattle Kings of the Country* (J. A. Hill, 1889), 341.

37. An excellent overview is contained in Rudolf W. Chalfant and Charles Belfoure, *Niernsee and Neilson, Architects of Baltimore: Two Careers on the Edge of the Future* (Baltimore Architecture Foundation, 2006).

38. See Gilman entry in Jerome L. Sternstein, *Encyclopedia of American Biography* (Harper & Row, 1974) Anthony C. Sutton, *America's Secret Establishment: An Introduction to the Order of Skull & Bones* (TrineDay, 2009). Cornell's White was a fellow member.

39. See, Theodore R. McKeldin, *No Mean City* (published by the author, 1964), 14. Franklin Parker's biography, *George Peabody* (Vanderbilt University Press, 1971), gives a candid assessment of his life and times.

40. Peabody was acquired by Hopkins in 1985.

41. Holloway, 344. City now offers an International Baccalaureate diploma.

42. Florence Nightingale, *Notes on Nursing: What It Is and What It Is Not* (D. Appleton, 1860), 12.

43. Niernsee, 103–110, Chesney, 241–255, *Principles of Ventilation and Heating* (Engineering & Building Record, 1889).

44. *Sun*, Feb. 5, 1876.

45. John Russel Quinan, *Medical Annals of Baltimore from 1608 to 1880, Including Events, Men, and Literature* (Isaac Friedenwald, 1884), 6.

46. Quinan, 20.

47. John Harvey Powell, *Bring Out Your Dead: The Great Plague of Yellow Fever in Philadelphia in 1793* (University of Pennsylvania Press, 1993), xii.

48. In 2016 *Aedes aegypti* mosquitoes were identified as carriers of Zika, a virus first detected in South America that deformed pregnant women. See A. McGehee Harvey, "Johns Hopkins and Yellow Fever: A Story of Tragedy and Triumph," *Johns Hopkins Medical Journal*, July 1981, 28–39.

CHAPTER 4. AMERICA'S RICHEST SPINSTER

1. A complete account of the university's holdings was published in *The Sun*, Oct. 7, 1886. B&O would recover but, in a desperate effort to raise cash, sold its telegraph unit to Western Union.

2. A third brother, who was institutionalized, received a small amount.

3. The story is captured in Kathleen Waters Sander, *Mary Elizabeth Garrett: Society and Philanthropy in the Gilded Age* (Johns Hopkins University Press, 2011).

4. "His knowledge of Maryland history was considered to be more extensive than that of any other man in Baltimore," *The Sun* eulogized when he died 1915. Not to be confused with Mendes Israel Cohen, a banker and lottery operator, who never married.

5. Alan Mason Chesney, *The Johns Hopkins Hospital and The Johns Hopkins University School of Medicine; A Chronicle*, vol. 1, "Early Years" (Johns Hopkins Press, 1943), 298.

6. Gatling treasurer Edgar T. Welles to Garrett, Aug. 24, 1877. See Bill Barry, *The 1877 Railroad Strike in Baltimore* (CreateSpace Independent Publishing, 2014).

7. See *The Routledge Companion to Accounting History (*2009) and *The Routledge Companion to Financial Accounting Theory* (2015).

8. *NYT,* July 14, 1888.

9. Sander, 118.

10. Helen Thomas Flexner, *A Quaker Childhood* (Yale University Press, 1940), 136–137.

11. Helen Lefkowitz Horowitz, *The Power and Passion of M. Carey Thomas* (Alfred A. Knopf, 1994), 149.

12. Rosamond Randall Beirne, *Let's Pick the Daisies: The History of the Bryn Mawr School 1885–1967* (Bryn Mawr School, 1970), 8–10.

13. W. Berksdale Maynard, "More Than a Mere Student," *Johns Hopkins Magazine*, Sept. 2007.

14. Millicent Carey McIntosh in Marjorie Housepian Dobkin, *The Making of a Feminist: Early Journals and Letters of M. Carey Thomas* (Kent University Press, 1979), ix.

15. *Sun*, May 19, 1894.

16. *Sun*, May 19, 1894.

17. "Pickaninnies' Revel," *Sun*, Aug. 23, 1908. The newspaper article contained this minstrel-like description about a newcomer's parting with her father: "'Neber you mind, honey chile, don't you cry Lillian. Your old daddy is a-comin' out to see you every month. Ain't that so, ma'am?' The white-haired old darky patted affectionately the kinky hair of the little girl."

18. Edward C. Papenfuse, remarks May 19, 2016.

19. The Garrett family's holdings are captured in a Maryland Geological Survey map of northeast Baltimore, July 1913.

20. The Roland Park Company applied the same restrictions to its Guilford (1913), Homeland (1924), and Original Northwood (1930), setting the discrimination standard for other upscale neighborhoods.

21. Horowitz, 21.

22. After tensions developed over the mixing of roommates, she declared: "It is a lesson. Never again shall we put a Jew and a Christian together." Horowitz, 340.

23. Horowitz, 341–343.

24. Dobkin, 12.

25. *NYT*, Feb. 22, 1911.

26. Antero Pietila, *Not in My Neighborhood: How Bigotry Shaped a Great American City* (Ivan R. Dee, 2010), 133.

27. Neil Smith, *American Empire: Roosevelt's Geographer and the Prelude to Globalization* (University of California Press, 2004), 310.

28. Geoffrey Martin, *The Life and Thought of Isaiah Bowman* (Archon Books, 1980), 134.

29. Jason Kalman, "Dark Places around the University: The Johns Hopkins University Admissions Quota and the Jewish Community, 1945–1951," *Hebrew Union College Annual* LXXXI (2010), 2.

30. *Not in My Neighborhood*; Smith, 247.

31. *Not in My Neighborhood*, 133.

32. James Chancellor Leonhart, *One Hundred Years of the Baltimore City College* (H. G. Roebuck & Son, 1939), 220.

33. Several books discuss the racial dilemma of the Irish, including *How the Irish Became White* by Noel Ignatiev (Routledge, 2008).

34. *Sun*, Feb. 20, 1910.

35. *Not in My Neighborhood*, 177, describes efforts to change the discriminatory policies of the *Sunpapers*, Maryland's largest real-estate marketplace. Other newspapers in various parts of the country may have been similarly biased but their advertising policies have escaped scrutiny.

36. My own recollections. See *Not in My Neighborhood*, 143.

37. *Afro-American*, Nov. 18, 1939.

38. Lewis's rejection produced enough of a flap for Hopkins to quietly enroll Catherine Lane in the evening school as a non-degree student in 1942. Fair-skinned, she was a graduate of Howard University's Miner Teacher College, had a master's degree from the University of Pennsylvania, and had done further studies at Columbia. Her husband was lawyer E. Everett Lane, who would become the first black judge in Baltimore. *Afro-American*, Feb.14, 1942.

39. *Afro-American*, Aug. 31, 1929.

40. Motion of the Mount Royal Protective Association, Inc., October term, 1947.

41. Motion of the Mount Royal Protective Association, Inc., in the Supreme Court of the United States, October term, 1947.

CHAPTER 5. DOCTORS ROB GRAVES

1. Alan F. Guttmacher, *Bootlegging Bodies: A History of Body-Snatching* (Public Library of Fort Wayne and Allen County, 1955), 3. *Bulletin of the Johns Hopkins Hospital*, vol. 23, contains much valuable material about Vesalius. Particularly

fascinating is William H. Welch's essay, "The Times of Vesalius: Contributions of Vesalius Other than Anatomical," 118–133.

2. A grave robbery is part of the 1836 Gothic tale, *Berenice*, by Edgar Allan Poe. He lived near the University of Maryland medical school, but the story is not about Baltimore. In Charles Dickens's 1859 novel, *A Tale of Two Cities*, Jerry Cruncher moonlights as a "resurrection man" in addition to his work as a porter and messenger at a London bank.

3. Final illness, *Sun*, Dec. 25, 1873.

4. Other preservatives also were used. "They can be safely sent by injecting into the carotin 2 lbs chloral hydrate in 5 quarts warm water, if taken before decomposing sets in," Dr. Frank W. Daykin, of Cleveland, advised a grave robber.

5. Ronald Pilling, of Bishopville, Maryland, ruminates on the etymology (personal message): "Stiff" has several senses and the "stiff" as in "stiff drink" came by way of the "strong" (potent) branch of the "stiff" family. "Stiff" also describes a dead body—rigor mortis and all that. And "stiff drunk" fits into the dead body category—drunk, passed out cold, and stiff. The not-tipping verb usage (e.g., stiffing a waiter) also comes from the idea of treating the waiter, etc., as a corpse or as one who is so dull as to be "half-dead" anyway, which is another noun meaning of stiff. "To stiff" someone, meaning to cheat, swindle, gyp, or rob, follows this same reasoning. Also in this category is a formal or priggish person, the square, who is sometimes referred to as a "stiff."

On the History Channel, a medical school historian stated that the origin of the phrase "rotgut whiskey" came from the practice of grave robbers packing corpses into whiskey barrels to preserve and camouflage their cargo while shipping it to medical schools for dissection. The whiskey would be sold to the students after the bodies had been removed from the barrels. The Oxford English Dictionary also informs us that the word is a concatenation of the verb "rot" and the noun "gut." I'm inclined to believe it refers to what the potent potable will do to your innards.

6. *Sun*, Dec. 7, 1880.

7. *Washington Post*, Dec. 3, 1880.

8. *Sun*, Mar. 22, 1881, reprinted parts of Jensen's correspondence.

9. *Sun*, Mar. 22, 1881. Locations of graveyard from archdiocesan records. http://www.stmarys.edu/wp-content/uploads/2014/01/closed_cemeteries.pdf. Holy Cross was purchased by the city in 1959. It is now the site of Harford Heights Elementary School.

10. *Sun*, Aug. 4, 1907; May 2, 1883.

11. *Sun*, May 14, 1883; Jan. 5, 1908. AC NMAH 150.

12. *Sun*, Dec. 11, 1883.

13. *Sun*, Oct. 24, 1916.

14. *Sun*, June 6, 1887.

15. Grave robbers caught while drinking was a common theme. Newspapers of the time contain several examples of grave robbers being caught while stopping for a drink and some curious seeing the corpse. See Henry L. Boies, *History of DeKalb County, Illinois* (O. P. Bassett, 1868), 95–113.

16. *Sun*, Nov. 22, 1880.

17. *NYT*, Feb. 25, 1881.

18. George MacGregor, *The History of Burke and Hare and the Resurrectionist Times* (Thomas D. Morrison, 1884). See also, James Blake Bailey, *The Diary of a Resurrectionist, 1811–1812* (Library of Alexandria, 1896).

19. *Sun*, Sept. 10, 1887.

20. *Sun.*, Jan. 24, 1887.

21. *Sun*, Feb. 2, 1887.

22. *Sun*, Jan. 25, 1887.

23. *Sun*, Jan. 25, 1887.

24. *Sun*, Mar. 18, 1887. The College of Physicians and Surgeons eventually merged with the University of Maryland medical school.

25. Bernard C. Steiner, *History of Education in Maryland* (Government Printing Office, 1894), 292–296.

26. Charles Russell Bardeen, "Anatomy in America," *Bulletin of the University of Wisconsin*, vol. 3, no. 4 (1905), 140.

27. Lynn Morgan, *Icons of Life: A Cultural History of Human Embryos* (University of California Press, 2009), 26.

28. *Sun*, Dec. 30, 1895.

29. *Journal of Proceedings of the First Branch City Council of Baltimore* (J. Cox, 1869), 237. "We have the mortifying intelligence, that owing to the want of a suitable place, their [sic] is not even time for the Coroner to communicate to their friends the fact of death, and this, though lamentable, is not the worst. Imagine, upon proceeding with a relative of the unfortunate dead, grief stricken, and filled with painful doubts as to identify, to find worse fear more than realized, the grave desecrated, robbed, and the last earthly kindness of a christian [sic] burial denied," a memorandum said. The city built a better dead house. Unclaimed corpses were to be kept ten days in summer and thirty days in winter.

30. *Sun*, Feb. 3, 1900.

31. Baltimore Medical College existed from 1881 until 1913, when it and Maryland General Hospital were merged with the University of Maryland Medical College. The 1907/8 catalog listed 425 matriculates from twenty-two states and eight foreign countries. The Baltimore University existed from 1884 to 1894 at 21–29 North Bond Street.

32. Morgan, 42, 66. Mall was a stickler, who insisted on the integrity of research. When a Southern student of his, Robert B. Bean, attempted to show that the skulls of blacks were smaller and their brains less developed, Mall repeated the measurements on many of the same specimens. Finding out that Bean had completely distorted the dimensions and drawn the conclusions from a sample far too small to be representative, he published a devastating critique. Bean, "Some Racial Peculiarities of the Negro Brain," *American Journal of Anatomy*, September 1906, 27–432; Mall, "On Several Anatomical Characters of the Human Brain, Said to Vary According to Race and Sex, With Especial Reference to the Weight of the Frontal Lobe," *American Journal of Anatomy*, February 1909, 1–32. Gunnar Myrdal summarizes the case in *American Dilemma: The Negro Problem and Modern Democracy* (Harper & Bros, 1944), 91.

33. From Ludwig Edelstein, *The Hippocratic Oath: Text, Translation, and Interpretation* (Johns Hopkins Press, 1943).

34. The statue was at the perimeter wall at Fifth Avenue and 103rd Street until it was removed. *NYT*, Apr. 16, 2018.

35. Harriet A. Washington, *Medical Apartheid: The Dark History of Medical Experimentation on Black Americans from Colonial Times to the Present* (Knopf, 2008).

36. J. Marion Sims, *The Story of My Life* (D. Appleton, 1888), 229.

37. She was "the wife of dissipated old man, who was supposed to be of not much account, as he was gambling and leading an otherwise disreputable life." She, however, "was a respectable woman who obtained a living by washing and taking in sewing, and was much appreciated and respected among her neighbors."

38. Sims, 230.

39. *Sun*, Aug. 31, 2017.

40. *Guardian*, May 14, 2013.

41. Washington, 21.

42. Mark M. Ravich, "The Blood Bank of the Johns Hopkins University," *Journal of the American Medical Association*, July 20, 1940, 171.

43. Mencken himself lived crosstown in a row house on Union Square. His neighborhood had been prosperous once but was now being overtaken by Lithuanians and Appalachians, whom he despised, and "blackamoors" and "darkies" in alley houses. He opined in the *Evening Sun* about politics, religion, and whatever else was on his mind, edited the *American Mercury* and *Smart Set*, New York magazines that were required reading among the moderns. He catalogued the American language and wrote a stack of books. A snarky writer, he was a conflicted man. Some of his close friends were Jewish, but his private diary entries portrayed them in ways that reeked of anti-Semitism. He promoted a number of Harlem writers, including Richard Wright and James Weldon Johnson, encouraging them and finding them publishers, yet he often dismissed the African race with hurtful verbiage. His correspondence was vast, and notables from throughout the world trekked to Baltimore to see him.

44. *Sun*, July 28, 1937.

45. *The Health and Physique of the Negro American*, ed. W.E.B. Du Bois (Atlanta University Press, 1906), 99. Todd Lee Savitt, "Four African-American Proprietary Medical Colleges: 1888–1923," *Journal of the History of Medicine & Allied Sciences*, July 2000, 203–255, lists proprietary black institutions as Louisville National Medical College in 1888, followed by Hannibal Medical College (Memphis, 1889), Chattanooga National Medical College (1899), and in 1900 Knoxville Medical College, the University of West Tennessee College of Medicine and Surgery (Jackson), and the Medico-Chirurgical, Theological College and Law School of Christ's Institution, Baltimore.

46. See Phillip J. Merrill's profile of the founder, Dr. George Whittington Kennard, http://avam.org/news-and-events/pdf/press-kits/Storytelling/AVAM-TAOS-PressKit.pdf.

47. "The Forgotten History of Defunct Black Medical Schools in the 19th and 20th Centuries and the Impact of the Flexner Report," from Earl H. Harley's presentation at

the Hinton-Gladney Lecture before the Otolaryngology Section of the National Medical Association, August 6, 2006, listed the defunct institutions as Lincoln University, 1870–1874, Oxford, PA; Straight University Medical Department, 1873–1874, New Orleans, LA; Leonard Medical School Shaw University, 1882–1918, Raleigh, NC; New Orleans University Medical College (Flint Medical College), 1889–1911, New Orleans, LA; Louisville National Medical College, 1888–1912, Louisville, KY; Hannibal Medical College, 1889–1896, Memphis, TN; Knoxville College Medical Department, 1895–1900, Knoxville, TN; Knoxville Medical College, 1900–1910, Knoxville, TN; State University Medical Department, 1899–1903, Louisville, KY; Chattanooga National Medical College, 1899–1904, Chattanooga, TN; University of West Tennessee College of Physician and Surgeons, 1900–1923, Jackson, TN—1900–1907, which was relocated to Memphis, TN—1907–1923; and Medico-Chirurgical, Theological College of Christ's Institution, 1900–1908, Baltimore.

48. Katie McCabe, *Reader's Digest*, October 1989. See also the citation presenting Vivien Thomas for the degree of Doctor of Laws, in 1976.

49. Brian J. Zink, *Anyone, Anything, Anytime: A History of Emergency Medicine* (Elsevier Health Sciences, 2006), 69–71. Goldfrank was kicked out of Hopkins because of his civil rights activism. He became an important figure in the evolving field of emergency medicine.

50. See Robert L. Gamble's profile of his grandfather, *Journal of the National Medical Association*, January 1972, 85–86.

51. *Washington Post*, Feb. 24, 1976. For details of the legal case, see *Ibn-Tamas v. United States*, http://law.justia.com/cases/district-of-columbia/court-of-appeals/1979/12614-2.html.

CHAPTER 6. THE MONUMENTAL CITY

1. Cited in Abraham Flexner, *Daniel Coit Gilman: Creator of the American Type of University* (Harcourt, Brace & Co., 1946), 13. See Harris Chaiklin, "Daniel Coit Gilman's Contributions to Social Work," *The Social Welfare History Project*, http://www.socialwelfarehistory.com/social-work/daniel-coit-gilmans-contributions-to-social-work/.

2. Lance Humphries, "Who Dubbed Baltimore 'The Monumental City'?," *Sun*, Aug. 15, 2015.

3. *American Art Annual*, vol. 2 (MacMillan Co., 1899).

4. James B. Crooks, "The Baltimore Fire and Baltimore Reform," *Maryland Historical Magazine*, Spring 1970, 1–17.

5. Architectural eugenics is discussed in *The American Architect*, Dec. 11, 1918.

6. "Two-thirds of board members were at least third-generation Americans; seven were Episcopalians; and several were college graduates." (Gilman was a Congregationalist, cofounder Marburg, a Unitarian.) "The board's unity lay in its socially elite character," Crooks writes. John W. Garrett's namesake son was an original board member but soon embarked on a diplomatic career.

7. Theodore Marburg, *Baltimore News*, Sept. 25, 1910.

8. Wilson, a Virginia native, held a White House gala, with the whole Supreme Court attending, to show the controversial movie, *The Birth of a Nation*. It was based on a book penned by Thomas Dixon, another Hopkins man who had attended seminar classes with Wilson.

9. Daniel C. Gilman, *A Study in Black and White: An Address at the Opening of the Armstrong-Slater Trade School Building* (published by the Trustees, 1897), 5–14.

10. See Jean H. Baker, *The Politics of Continuity: Maryland Political Parties from 1858 to 1870* (Johns Hopkins Press, 1973).

11. Josephine D. Fisher, *Baltimore's Ethnic Building and Loan Associations 1865–1914*, Johns Hopkins graduate project, 1997, 11–12.

12. Frederick N. Rasmussen, "German Plot Hatched Here," *Sun*, Oct. 14, 2000.

13. Redwood history, *Sun*, Feb. 13, 1949. John Morris, statement, *Sun*, Mar. 12, 1895; enrollment data, *Sun*, Aug. 12, 1895; Redwood profile by Fred Rasmussen, *Sun*, Jan. 10, 2013. See also Eric L. Goldstein, *How German were "German" Jews in America in the Nineteenth Century? A View from Baltimore*, http://www.historic baltimore.org/pdf/ArnoldPrize2012.pdf.

14. Klaus G. Wust, *Zion in Baltimore 1755–1955* (Zion Church of the City of Baltimore 1955). 84. Also Julius Hofmann, *A History of Zion Church of the City of Baltimore, 1755–1897* (C. W. Scheidereith & Sons, 1905).

15. Wust, 76–78. Even though Scheib was a liberal in many matters, he sided with the Confederacy in the Civil War. It was a question of *Ordnung*, order. The Confederacy "for him was not a symbol of slavery but the manifestation of an aristocratic social order in contrast to the rowdyism so often evident on the Northern side," writes Wust. But since most of his congregants were Unionists, he rallied them to support Lincoln against the Confederacy.

16. Phillips, 125.

17. Daniel Coker, *Journal of Daniel Coker: A descendant of Africa, from the time of leaving New York, in the ship* Elizabeth, *Capt. Sebor, on a voyage for Sherbro, in Africa, in company with three agents, and about ninety persons of colour* (Edward J. Coale, 1820).

18. See also Lois Zanow, Sally Johnston, and Denny Lynch, *Monuments to Heaven: Baltimore's Historic Houses of Worship* (AuthorHouse, 2010), 7.

19. *Sun*, Feb. 19, 1855.

20. See Davis's autobiography. Also *A Christian Merchant: A Memoir of James C. Crane* (Southern Baptist Publication Society, 1858).

21. He sired two more children in freedom, bringing the total to nine.

22. Charlotte Draper, *A Free-Will Offering for the Benefit of Africa* (Frederick A. Hanzsche, Jan. 25, 1860), 38.

23. *Friends' Review*, Feb. 23, 1867.

24. *Sun*, Nov. 22, 1899.

25. Clayton Colman Hall, *Baltimore: Its History and Its People*, vol. 1 (Lewis Historical Publishing Co., 1912), 302.

26. H. L. Mencken, *Newspaper Days, 1899–1906* (Johns Hopkins University Press, 2006), 41.

27. Further controversy flared after Gilman insisted on hiring James H. Sickle, of Denver, as the superintendent. Politicians cried foul. Accustomed to running the school system and reaping the benefits of patronage, they wanted a local superintendent, familiar with Baltimore, its ways and thinking—a man they could control.

28. *Sun*, Feb. 26, 1896.

29. *Sun*, Oct. 11, 1888; June 29, 1889.

30. *Sun*, Oct. 11, 1888.

31. *Sun*, Sept. 18, 1900. The old Colored High School building on Saratoga stayed vacant for several years and then was converted into the central police station. It was reconstructed to accommodate cell blocks, a job well done, according to *Sun*, Feb. 17, 1908: "The only objection which boarders may find in the new cells is the lack of light. While those facing the alley are well lighted, those facing the interior of the building are so dark that if a negro is placed in any of them it will still look empty."

32. *Afro-American*, Nov. 7, 1903.

33. Firefighters with their equipment came by train from all over the East Coast, only to find out that Baltimore's unusual hydrant couplings would not take their hoses.

34. *Sun*, Mar. 3, 1904, published an alphabetical list of relocated businesses, with their old and new addresses.

35. *Sun*, Oct. 13, 1904; Sept. 16, 1911; Mar. 2, 1915; Mar. 21, 1917.

36. *Journal of Proceedings of the First Branch City Council of Baltimore* (J. Cox, 1904), 895–918.

37. *Sun*, Sept. 18, 1900. See Suzanne Ellery Greene, "Black Republicans on the Baltimore City Council, 1890–1931," *Maryland Historical Magazine*, September 1979.

38. When St. Francis Xavier's left, it went to Old Town. A class divide was stark: Nearly all those listed in the first annual edition of *The First Colored Professional, Clerical and Business Directory* were west side residents.

39. *Sun*, Sept. 26, 1910. The prestigious girls' school was located on McCulloh Street, just a few blocks away from the house Hawkins acquired.

40. Tuberculosis affected those in the worst living conditions, poor Jews in East Baltimore slums, and blacks in the new expansion area. There, along Biddle Street, between the Pennsylvania Avenue shopping area and Druid Hill Avenue residences, were the notorious "lung blocks," so-called because of their shockingly high death rate from tuberculosis. Curiously, many of the ill worked for white families, as laundresses, servants, or even cooks. Racial segregation was promoted as a protection for whites against infection; no thought was given to improving the housing and sanitary conditions of the blacks.

41. Welch on tuberculosis, *Sun*, Feb. 17, 1914.

42. A fuller treatment of redlining and its legacy is in *Not in My Neighborhood*.

43. At the time, even the most creditworthy white borrowers in the green category were doomed to mortgages that required at least 50 percent in down payment, with a balloon coming due in seven years and no guarantee of favorable refinancing.

44. Most high school and college biology texts from 1914 to 1948 carried the eugenics message. Steven Selden, *Inheriting Shame: The Story of Eugenics and Racism in America* (Teachers College Press, 1999). The eugenic outlook was internalized.

"It is important to repeat that none of those texts reflected over racial bias. The arguments were never made in terms of race. They were always made only in terms of biological merit," 69.

45. Homer Hoyt, *The Structure and Growth of Residential Neighborhoods in American Cities* (Federal Housing Administration, 1939), 58–71.

CHAPTER 7. GOVERNMENTS CREATE SLUMS

1. The population briefly surpassed the million mark. Because the 1940 census predated the war and 1950 came years after, they did not reflect the peak years. *Washington Post*, Sept. 28, 1942, estimated Baltimore's population at 1.2 million.

2. *Maryland in World War II: Industry and Agriculture* (Maryland Historical Society, 1951), 373–377.

3. *Sun*, May 19, 1942.

4. On Eutaw Place, once a coveted address, stately homes were stripped of their faded elegance and cut into warren-like rooming units for whites. One group of eight outwardly imposing single-family Victorian row houses—later demolished—contained ninety-three "apartments" packing in some 250 Appalachian tenants. Several stinking outhouses—"crappers"—occupied the backyard; for other basic sanitary needs tenants relied on visits to municipal public baths, where they also washed clothes. The worst was the lot of single men without friends or relatives.

5. HOLC records are stored at the National Archives at Adelphi, Maryland, Record Group 195.

6. *Sun*, May 1, 1921.

7. See Jacques Kelly, *Sun*, May 14, 2016.

8. *Sun*, Apr. 29, 1997; DeFilippo, *Sun*, Apr. 26, 1991.

9. Sabbath services: Baltimore's Hebrew Reformed Association first introduced Sabbath services on Sundays in 1854 but abandoned the experiment after six months. Twenty years later, Har Sinai adopted the practice which lasted at least until World War II. Much of the time, a regular Saturday service also was held. *Jewish Quarterly Review*, vol. 10 (Macmillan, 1898), 97. See also Kerry M. Olitzky, "The Sunday-Sabbath Movement in American Reform Judaism: Strategy or Evolution?" http://americanjewisharchives.org/publications/journal/PDF/1982_34_01_00_olitzky.pd.

10. *Sun*, Mar. 30, 1891.

11. *Sun*, Aug. 24, 1895. Thomas W. Spalding, *Premier See: A History of the Archdiocese of Baltimore, 1789–1989* (Johns Hopkins University Press, 1995), 137.

12. *The Slums of Baltimore, Chicago, New York, and Philadelphia* (Government Printing Office, 1894), 23.

13. *Sun*, Aug. 9, 10, 19, 1945.

14. http://www.drummerworld.com/drummers/Chick_Webb.html.

15. *Afro-American*, June 18, 1938.

16. Vivien Thomas, *Partners of the Heart: Vivien Thomas and His Work with Alfred Blalock* (University of Pennsylvania Press, 1998), 137.

17. *Afro-American,* Feb. 17, 1940; June 29, 1940.

18. *NYT*, July 23, 1943.

19. *Afro-American*, Apr. 14, 1928.

20. *Sun*, June 17, 1937.

21. *Sun*, Apr. 3, 1972.

22. Sinai moved from Monument Street and Rutland Avenue to Pimlico in 1959; St. Joseph's to Towson from Caroline and Oliver in 1965. Already, in 1876 St. Agnes had moved from Greenmount and North to West Baltimore.

23. David Stinson, "Belair Road and North Avenue: The First Intersection of Beer and Baseball in Baltimore," Nov. 22, 2015, http://www.davidbstinsonauthor.com/tag/henry-r-von-der-horst/. Von Der Horst also was involved in three other Oriole parks where the team played between 1883 and 1899.

24. After the Sears store closed in 1981, the art deco building, built of limestone with black marble trim, was converted into a district court.

25. *Maryland in World War II: Industry and Agriculture* contains a list of defense industry employers, their addresses and information about their workforce.

26. *Sun*, Sep. 28, 1945; Apr. 27, 1964. The new hospital was inaugurated in 1959.

27. *Sun*, Feb. 8, 1916; the Maryland Historical Trust Determination of Eligibility Form, http://msa.maryland.gov/megafile/msa/stagsere/se1/se5/043100/043182/pdf/msa_se5_43182.pdf.

28. After Little Bohemia dispersed, Czechs melted into the mainstream. At least some of Frank Novak's handiwork remained for all to see. He was an enterprising young carpenter who commanded platoons that constructed some seven thousand two-story row houses. The nicely proportioned and well-designed houses gave many a street a pleasant ambience. In 1913 a grocer named William Oktavec added an enhancement. At a time when no air-conditioning existed, he began painting ships, lighthouses, and mountains on wire-mesh window screens. The ingenious way he did it, the screens let in breezes, kept out bugs and mosquitoes, and blocked passersby from peeking in while allowing residents an unhindered view of the outside.

29. In 2005 *Thompson v. HUD*, Garbis ruled: "It is high time that HUD live up to its statutory mandate" and consider "regional approaches to promoting fair housing opportunities for African-American public housing residents in the Baltimore region. Baltimore City should not be viewed as an island reservation for use as a container for all of the poor of a contiguous region" that includes surrounding counties.

30. One of the worst. "Report of the Urban Planning Conferences under the Auspices of the Johns Hopkins University" (Johns Hopkins University Press, 1944), 51.

31. I discuss all this in *Not in My Neighborhood,* 237–240.

32. *Sun*, Aug. 18, 1943.

33. Arnold R. Hirsch, "Searching for a 'Sound Negro Policy': A Racial Agenda for the Housing Acts of 1949 and 1954," *Housing Policy Debate*, vol. 11, no. 2, 393–441; George W. Grier, "The Negro Ghettos and Federal Housing Policy," *Law and Contemporary Problems*, Summer 1967, 550–560, http://scholarship.law.duke.edu/lcp/vol32/iss3/12.

34. *Sun*, Mar. 21, 1942

35. *Sun*, Sept. 19, 1954; Jan. 23, 1941; Aug. 19, 1951. Full desegregation of Baltimore's public housing had to wait until the 1960s.

36. J. A. Stoloff, "A Brief History of Public Housing," http://reengageinc.org/research/brief_history_public_housing.pdf.

37. Martin Millspaugh in *Evening Sun*, Jan. 4, 1954.

38. Millspaugh, 9.

39. A 1945 canvass of a district bounded by Broadway, Preston, Baltimore, and Fallsway counted 22 churches, 10 public and 3 parochial schools, and 118 licensed taverns, nightclubs, and liquor goods stores.

40. The desegregation of Baltimore schools began before the *Brown* ruling. In 1952 Poly opened its advanced college preparation course to blacks. See Howell Baum, *Brown in Baltimore* (Cornell University Press), 52–55.

41. Quoted in *Not in My Neighborhood*, 168.

CHAPTER 8. MOBTOWN IN THE 1950s

1. Risky living was in the family blood. One brother was serving an eight-month term for bookmaking; another was a shop steward in a Mafia-controlled longshoremen's union on New York's Brooklyn waterfront, having escaped Baltimore when associates advised that a move would be "good for his health." *Sun*, July 22, 1952.

2. Lieutenant Joseph A. Kuda of the St. Louis Police Department testified that Liston was divided up as follows: Carbo, 52 percent; his Philadelphia sidekick, Blinky Palermo, 12; St. Louis mobster John Vitale, 12; two others, unidentified, 12 each. *Sports Illustrated*, Dec.19, 1960.

3. *Sports Illustrated*, Aug. 22, 1955; June 15, 1959.

4. Rings also were erected at other venues where big crowds could be assembled—inside the Gayety Theater, at Carlin's amusement park, the Hippodrome Theater. Tickets were cheap because the real money was made in betting and other rackets. Many boxers owned bars in neighborhoods where they plastered their moments of glory in photographs and newspaper clippings on walls, and where bets could be arranged. One such bar was Cimino's on Gay Street in Old Town. It was popular with cops.

5. Charles Whiteford, *Sun*, June 12, 1955.

6. The meticulous archives of his commission are in the special collections of the University of Baltimore.

7. The committee is usually identified by its next chairman, Senator Estes Kefauver. Full text of the Maryland section of the report is in *Sun*, Sept. 1, 1955.

8. Email exchange with Sachs. The veteran journalist Michael Olesker had another theory: "Baltimore was widely known as a rat town, where everybody ratted on everybody else to keep themselves out of jail, and the big shot mobsters figured they didn't need that kind of aggravation."

9. This description, including all verbatim quotations, are from Charles Whiteford's impressive reporting in *The Sun* in 1955, particularly March 12 and 15, May 15 and 19, June 13 and 17.

10. *Sun*, June 16, 1955. The crew was founded by the local Corbi brothers. It included Fat Benny's sibling, Nick, and son-in-law, Angelo Munafo, both owners of girlie bars on The Block.

11. FBI BA 161-279-3. BA 161-110 ("Miscellaneous information") also identified D'Alesandro as "a constant associate of John Cataneo," a Mob figure connected with Carbo and Corbi, who ran a ship-cleaning business. D'Alesandro ran for governor of Maryland in 1954, but was forced to drop out due to being implicated in receiving undeclared money from Dominic Piracci, a parking garage owner convicted of fraud, conspiracy, and conspiracy to obstruct justice. It was all in the family: D'Alesandro's son, Thomas III, who would also become a mayor, married Piracci's daughter, Margaret. The elder D'Alesandro was appointed to the parole commission in 1971. BA 161-110 contains information from Captain John R. Rollman, Western District, about how D'Alesandro protected a tavern owner there.

12. *Sun*, June 19, 1955.

13. *Sun*, June 17, 1959.

14. Fat Benny's physician testified that when he and Hepbron went to Madison Square Garden for a heavyweight championship boxing match, he recognized a Baltimore police captain and two detectives at the ringside also. They were all there courtesy of the Mob.

15. Hepbron testified that Frankie Carbo, "through [Frank] Corbi," got him and his wife tickets to fights. (When Hepbron mentioned he was unable to get tickets to the Broadway hit musical *Finian's Rainbow*, two tickets promptly appeared in his hotel mail.)

16. Captain Menasha E. Katz, "I remember—Al Capone Hiding," *Sun*, Dec. 7, 1975.

17. *Sun*, Jan. 7, 1956.

18. *Sun*, May 14, 1959.

19. *Sun*, May 16, 1959.

20. *Sun*, Sept. 6, 1913. In the early days, it seems that various sin districts operated pretty much in the open and without much need for graft. Indeed, a 1913 grand jury attacked the powerful Society for the Suppression of Vice for lobbying for the dispersal of red-light districts. The grand jury preferred to have concentrated sin areas because they were more manageable that way: "It is better to have the brothels of the city, or the majority of them, on side streets." It warned that if driven underground, graft would necessarily increase.

21. Stephen Hull, "Baltimore's Bawdy Block," *Stag*, 1952. The undated chapter is available at http://www.baltimoreorless.com/2010/08/baltimores-bawdy-block/.

22. "Named after Uncle Gerard:" Samuel Hopkins interview with Mame Warren. For detailed retail history of the area, see *Enterprising Emporiums: The Jewish Department Stores of Downtown Baltimore* (Jewish Museum of Maryland, 2001). Also books by Michael J. Lisicky, *Hutzler's: Where Baltimore Shops* (History Press; 2009) and *Baltimore's Bygone Department Stores: Many Happy Returns* (History Press, 2012).

23. Conversations with Gilbert Sandler, who knew both Mills and Bentley, and several Republican insiders who had heard the yarn from Bentley; *Sun*'s Bentley obituary, Apr. 29, 2012.

24. *Sun*, Apr. 2, 1989.

25. Cicero's had a troubled history. After the liquor board yanked the license altogether, largely due to complaints about homosexuals, it continued as an after-hours

"milk bar." Some hundred were arrested in a 3 a.m. raid in 1971. Six guns were confiscated, along with four knives, ten bags of suspected heroin, fifty-two capsules of secobarbital, whiskey, and beer. The owner's lawyer was state senator George W. Della Jr. *Sun,* Jan. 26, 1968.

26. Its landmark Gayety Theater, a fourteen hundred-seat art nouveau and baroque burlesque house, still stood in 2018.

27. *Sun,* Oct. 26, 1975.

28. In the mid-1970s, I went to hear a preacher who advertised on radio that he had seen "Uncle Mo" in the South Carolina swamps and received from his pet snake good numbers. I was the only white in the packed church. The preacher started by promising numbers for a fifty-dollar donation, and got a few takers. He eventually came down in price to five dollars, saying he wanted to help "the poor people of Baltimore." Returning to *The Sun* building, I told a security guard about my experience. "No, sir, I don't believe in any of that," Sergeant Kelly told me. When we parted, he said, "Did you get a number? They are good numbers."

29. Anthony Summers, *Official and Confidential: The Secret Life of J. Edgar Hoover* (Open Road Media, 2012), 239. It is a very readable book, and controversial. I thought it was terrific.

30. A numbers runner paid patrolmen two dollars a week, and sergeants, five dollars. If a lieutenant was involved, he was paid more. *Afro-American,* Dec. 9, 1950.

31. John D. Lawson, *American State Trials,* vol. V (F. H. Thomas Law Book, 1916), 216–329.

32. *Sun,* Oct. 22, 1914.

33. *Sun,* Oct. 5, 1922.

34. *Sun,* Sep. 10, 1955.

35. When Irv's father died, Jimmy Hoffa called Gene Raynor for directions to the shiva house.

36. Jeff Gerth, "Richard M. Nixon and Organized Crime," *Penthouse,* July 1974. Thomas B. Edsall, "White Flight and Black Rights: Decline and Fall of Baltimore's Machine," *Sun,* July 8, 1977.

37. Fred Barbash wrote a series about Mandel's money net, beginning in *Sun,* Dec. 2, 1973.

38. FBI BA 161-110. Conversations with Gene Raynor.

39. *Sports Illustrated,* Oct. 28, 1963; *Sun,* Sept. 21, 1962.

40. Gene Raynor conversations. See the acknowledgments in this book for a sketch about him.

41. BJC 938, *Washington Post,* Oct. 12, 1958; Harvey Wheeler, "Yesterday's Robin Hood: The Rise and Fall of Baltimore's Trenton Democratic Club," *American Quarterly,* Winter 1955, 332–344.

42. Source: Edgar Silver, a Pollack man who became a state delegate and circuit court judge.

43. Gene Raynor conversations. Coco had relatives living in Baltimore, including a medical doctor (under a modified last name). In an investigation published in *The Sun,* March 5, 1978, I documented how mobsters operated bingo games around Baltimore under the permits of charitable organizations, which often incurred substantial

losses while the gangsters reaped big profits and avoided paying taxes. Eddie Coco acquired several Bingo World and other halls, including one near Glen Burnie. He was dead by the time the case went to trial where several of his men were convicted. *Sun*, Apr. 8, 1992; June 9, 1993.

44. Verda F. Welcome (as told to James M. Abraham), *My Life and Times* (Henry House Publishers, 1991), 123. *Afro-American*, Apr. 18, 1964. The shooting: My conversations with Gene Raynor, the veteran elections chief, political insider, and resident of Little Italy, who knew the principals. Young was quite a guy. Once he cast a controversial vote on a raccoon bill and explained, "I did it because of self-preservation. I don't want them killing coons on the Eastern Shore."

45. *Sun*, May 2, 1903.

46. *Afro-American* printed a photo of the shrine, Sept. 10, 1938.

47. Obituary of Anna Kovens, Irv's mother, *Sun*, Nov. 13, 1993.

48. Mark R. Cheshire, *They Call Me Little Willie: The Life Story of William L. Adams* (Ellison's Books, 2016). *Not in My Neighborhood* also profiles the businessman.

49. Although Charm Centre was identified with Victorine Adams, she had no ownership stake in it. Instead, Willie held an 80 percent share and a New York dress buyer, 20 percent.

50. Conversations with Erla McKinnon, a longtime confidant of the Adamses. See Antero Pietila's *Sun* series on black powerbrokers, beginning March 18, 1979.

51. Hepbron hired a retired Scotland Yard sergeant to train the dogs.

52. This relies heavily on Charles Whiteford's reporting in *The Sun*. All the material can be easily searched online through free and commercial newspaper databases.

53. *Sun*, Oct. 31, 1957.

54. *Sun*, Oct. 29, 1959; May 3, 1961.

55. Jill Jonnes, "Everybody Must Get Stoned: The Origins of Modern Drug Culture in Baltimore," *Maryland Historical Magazine*, Summer 1996.

56. One patron, James Dean, remembered wearing a suit as he rode from the city to Carr's Beach, standing on a flatbed truck with several other men and women in their fineries who all paid a dollar. That's the way regular people traveled in the 1950s.

57. *Afro-American*, Feb. 16, 1929; May 24, 1930; Sept. 27, 1930; "interracial whoopee houses," Oct. 28, 1933 and July 20, 1940; "interracial love mart," May 13, 1944.

58. Quoted by Gilbert Sandler, *Sun*, Mar. 24, 1992.

59. Change was on the way. Just consider the evolution of today's Arch Social Club building at Pennsylvania and North, a one-time racial dividing line. The Beaux-Arts structure began as a German movie palace named Schanze, then catered to the Yiddish market until it went black as Morgan and Uptown. See Amy Davis, *Flickering Treasures: Rediscovering Baltimore's Forgotten Movie Theaters* (Johns Hopkins University Press, 2017), 56–59.

60. *Sun*, May 5, 1953.

61. *Afro-American*, Feb. 9, 1952.

62. Reminders of the glory days can still be seen in the magnificent Tiffany stained glass windows at Lovely Lane Methodist and St. Mark's Lutheran Churches

in today's Station North, and masterworks by other artists at the Episcopal St. Michael & All Angels.

63. Davis, 248. In the 1960s the Famous ballroom was the home venue of the Left Bank (originally Interracial) Jazz Society, which filled the upstairs hall with sellout crowds Sunday afternoons. John Coltrane, Duke Ellington, Dave Brubeck, Stan Getz, Chet Baker, the Modern Jazz Quartet, and Sun Ra were among those playing there. "Sometimes I think I'm in heaven," club founder Benny Kearse sighed. Racially tinged disagreements about musical tastes paralyzed the society in the 1980s, and the venue ultimately went totally dark. James D. Dilts, *Sun*, Feb. 9, 1991; Jacques Kelly, *Sun*, July 3, 1999. After the riots, Station North was home to two legendary black nightclubs, both fronts for heroin trade. Gatsby's had a see-through dance floor and three floors of entertainment that attracted an eclectic and fashionable crowd. I went there several times. Around the corner, Odells was a gangsta place and the site of several murders.

64. The writer Damon Runyon (*Guys and Dolls*) occasionally took a train from New York to visit the Club Charles, seeking inspiration for characters, according to club accountant Sidney Weinberg.

65. Two eight-story hotels overlooked the station, providing rooms for the weary. They exist today as the Henderson House student apartments on Mount Royal Avenue.

66. Her girls were white, and so were customers, including civic and political leaders. White men could hunt for black women on Pennsylvania Avenue, but black men and white women did not mix. About the only exception was the social activists' Fellowship House at 21 West Preston, around the corner from Pearl's boudoirs. For two decades after its 1938 opening, there was communal singing there, even interracial square dancing.

67. In 1953 the Lyric Theater, just around the corner, turned down a concert by the celebrated contralto Marian Anderson because she was black; the backlash "among its stockholders and patrons" was such that the Fellowship House was more or less invited to bring her to the Lyric the following year. It did, before a standing-room-only audience.

68. The hunting grounds were nicknamed Meat Rack. Mount Vernon's first gay concentration formed on Tyson Street, a picturesque narrow stretch of row houses, which became an early restoration magnet in the 1960s. Leon's corner bar was a center of gay activity. Other gay bars followed, including Mary's. The neighboring Read Street became a small-scale local version of Haight Asbury, lined with counterculture vendors.

69. *Sun*, May 1, 1952. Sidney Weinberg, who worked as an accountant for the Club Charles and several Block figures, told me that it was difficult to know who owned clubs on a particular day because they changed hands so frequently in high-stakes games. After the original Club Charles closed, Esther West acquired the name. In 1951 the Native American was able to change her Wigwam Restaurant at 1774 North Charles to the Club Charles. Over the years the bar concept has evolved; in 2016 it was a gay dive bar.

70. Blaze Starr always wanted to make love in Lincoln's bedroom. She never realized that ambition but at the height of the Cuban Missile Crisis she did manage a

tryst with Kennedy in the Oval Office, a couple of decades before Bill Clinton left his DNA on Monica Lewinsky's blue dress. Blaze wrote in an account: "After Governor Earl K. Long passed away, I renewed my friendship with then President J.F.K." They usually rendezvoused in the Georgetown home of CBS newsman Paul Nevin but one day in October 1962, the telephone rang; plans had changed. She was whisked to the White House. As she and Nevin "walked by the Oval Office the door was open," she wrote, "there was loads of people all around. Robert Kennedy stood in the open door. L.B.J. stood in the hall with his arms folded. We entered an office and J.F.K. was right behind us. As Paul left we locked the door. After a short time (very short), J.F.K. jumped up and said he was very, very sorry, but he had to leave. While he was dressing he said, 'Boy, if Fidel Castro had something like you he would think more about making love, and less about making war.'" In 2016 the framed account in her handwriting was sandwiched by pictures of Blaze Starr and JFK. It was offered for an initial price of $3,500 in an Internet auction in 2016. The memorabilia sold for $260.

71. Lisa Downing, Iain Morland, and Nikki Sullivan, *Fuckology: Critical Essays on John Money's Diagnostic Concepts* (University of Chicago Press, 2014).

72. *NYT*, Aug. 26, 1986.

CHAPTER 9. ACTIVISM BUILDS UP

1. *Sun*, Sept. 22, 1992. Many of the founder's Quaker friends and relatives also supported the YMCA, including the parents of M. Carey Thomas, the Bryn Mawr educator.

2. Jessica Elfenbein, "To 'Fit Them for Their Fight with the World': The Baltimore YMCA and the Making of a Modern City, 1852–1932," PhD diss., University of Delaware, 46.

3. That five-story Victorian castle is now home to apartments. It was designed by Niernsee and Neilson but has been since altered.

4. This draws on John W. Garrett's historical account, *Sun*, Jan. 31, 1883. See the same paper Nov. 1, 1914, and Jan. 22, 1928. George Peabody contributed to many causes. Over 150 years later, Peabody owns and manages twenty thousand properties in London, housing more than fifty-five thousand low-income people. The copper company's losses are identified in Holloway's *Famous American Fortunes*, 753.

5. In 1892 the building was pushed thirty-six feet forward, raised five feet, and repositioned along Eutaw Street. *Sun*, Nov. 26, 1892.

6. Elfenbein, 6.

7. Kelman, *Continuity and Change: My Life as a Social Psychologist*, 216–217. In A.H. Eagly, R.M. Baron, & V.L. Hamilton (Eds.), *The social psychology of group identity and social conflict: Theory, application, and practice* (American Psychological Association, 2004), 233–275.

8. The initial Baltimore sit-in involving both students and CORE was not over Howard Street but over a lunch counter and soda fountain at a store near the Morgan campus. In later years, all kinds of claims have been made about the battle over Read's Howard Street branch, near the major department stores, including a

contention that the sit-in tactic itself was pioneered there. In fact, CORE introduced sit-ins in 1943, in Washington.

9. After Gwynn Oak closed in1973, the Smithsonian bought the big carousel with sixty riding horses. It still operates on the National Mall in Washington. See Amy Nathan's incisive *Round & Round Together: Taking a Merry-Go-Round Ride into the Civil Rights Movement* (Paul Dry Books, 2011).

10. Stephen E. Ambrose and Richard H. Immerman, *Milton S. Eisenhower: Educational Statesman* (Johns Hopkins University Press, 1983), 218.

11. State Department, top secret cable from Gordon, Mar. 29, 1964. In the LBJ Presidential Library. Facsimile copy on the website of National Security Archive at George Washington University.

12. *Ramparts,* March 1967.

13. *Sun*, Jan. 31, 1971.

14. The students received legal advice from Robert B. Watts, a pioneering black judge. Among leaders was Walter S. Orlinsky, who later became a state delegate and longtime city council president. Another key figure was Ruth Fegley, who headed the Fellowship House. *Sun,* Feb. 26, 1960; *Afro-American*, Mar. 5, 1960. Harvey G. Cohen, *Duke Ellington's America* (University of Chicago, 2010), 387.Three years later, Wickwire led a panel discussion on jazz and folk music and contemporary culture and religion. The panel included Peter H. Adler, conductor of the Baltimore Symphony Orchestra; jazz pianist Dave Brubeck; the Rev. Norman O'Connor, a Catholic "jazz priest" who promoted jazz idioms in worship; and Erik Darling, who had replaced Pete Seeger on The Weavers, the legendary folk music group.

15. The University of Baltimore special collections contains oral interviews about the history of the People's Free Medical Clinic, http://cdm16352.contentdm.oclc.org/cdm/landingpage/collection/p16352coll14.

16. *Sun*, Sept. 2, 2008.

17. See Taylor Branch's Martin Luther King trilogy.

18. See Antero Pietila and Stacy Spaulding, *Race Goes to War: Ollie Stewart and the Reporting of Black Correspondents in World War II*, Kindle edition, 2015.

19. Wrote the *Afro* social columnist Lula Jones Garrett, Sept. 10, 1938: "The bride entered on the arm of her father. Her gown was made of white slipper satin with Schiapperelli sleeves, a tight basque bodice which buttoned to a heart-shaped neckline and a full skirt which drifted into sweeping train. Her veil was that of her sister, Marion, a recent bride, and was of bridal illusion attached to a coronet of tulle. She carried an arm full of white Madonna lilies. . . . Following the reception, the bride wore a tailleur of yellow shetland wool and one of the new doll hats, gloves, bag and shoes in Chateau wine."

20. *Washington Post*, Oct. 19, 1933.

21. *Afro-American*, Oct. 28, 1933. The controversy united whites in a vow of silence and galvanized blacks in protest. The newspaper had long campaigned against lynching. Now it pointed out that Armwood was a latter-day slave, plucked out of the fifth grade by a white family wanting him because he was a steady worker and cheap. Untold other blacks—feebleminded or handicapped—were condemned to similar indenture. "Negroes held in peonage, ignorance and serfdom on the Eastern Shore

of Maryland should be rounded up and placed in an institution for the sub-normal at the expense of the State," wrote the *Afro*. "White farmers should be prevented by law from 'rearing' these unbalanced Negroes which is only a polite term for slavery."

22. *Afro-American*, Oct. 6, 1934.

23. Carmichael declared at the convention that "Negroes serving in the United States armed forces in Vietnam must be regarded as black mercenaries of the Government," *NYT*, July 2, 1966.

24. *Students for a Democratic Society Bulletin*, July 1964, 6–7.

25. Dana Zakrzewski, *Students for a Democratic Society*, http://www.campus activism.org/server-new/uploads/undergrad2a-sds.htm.

26. The pen banned Muslim literature.

27. Rudolph Lewis, Walter Hall Lively (1942–1976), Civil Rights Activist & Black Liberationist, *ChickenBones: A Journal*, http://www.nathanielturner.com/walterlively.htm. See also profile by James D. Dilts, *Sun* magazine, June 16, 1968.

28. *Sun*, Oct. 4, 1967.

29. Mike Flug, *The Maryland Freedom Union: Workers Doing and Thinking*, a nine-page booklet. No date.

30. CORE would linger on, going through several metamorphoses. In 1971 it recruited fighters for Africa. I joined one such group of mercenaries who never got beyond the first day of training in Manassas, Virginia. "CORE Seeking Veterans for Service in Angola," *Sun*, Feb. 5, 1976.

CHAPTER 10. A CAT OF A DIFFERENT COLOR

1. A detailed account of the riots is contained in *Baltimore '68: Riots and Rebirth in an American City* (Temple University Press, 2011). Number of liquor stores, *Sun*, Apr. 12, 1968.

2. A recommended biography is Colin Grant, *Negro with a Hat: The Rise and Fall of Marcus Garvey* (Oxford University Press, 2008).

3. King to Scott, July 18, 1952, http://kingencyclopedia.stanford.edu/encyclopedia/documentsentry/to_coretta_scott/.

4. "Where Do We Go From Here?," SCLC Convention Atlanta, Aug. 19, 1967, http://kingencyclopedia.stanford.edu/encyclopedia/documentsentry/where_do_we_go_from_here_delivered_at_the_11th_annual_sclc_convention.1.html.

5. Judson L. Jeffries, "Black Radicalism and Political Repression in Baltimore: The Case of the Black Panther Party," *Ethnic & Racial Studies*, January 2002, 64–98.

6. The composer Leonard Bernstein famously held a cocktail fund-raiser for them in his Manhattan apartment, with leading Panthers strutting around as mannequins of armed struggle.

7. An excellent book is Charles E. Jones, *The Black Panther Party Reconsidered* (Black Classic Press, 2013).

8. Maryland CJIS Identification/index system.

9. Several conversations with A. Robert Kaufman, a dissident who migrated from one group to another.

10. Based on the author's conversations with Gibson.

11. Dec. 3, 1979, https://www.cia.gov/library/readingroom/docs/CIA-RDP83-001 56R000300020044-5.pdf; "Smuggling Arms to South Africa," *Washington Post,* Aug. 3, 1979. Poison disclosures were made in *Race Today,* in 1977 and 1978.

12. *Saturday Night,* May 27, 2000; *Ottawa Journal,* Nov. 30, 1978. A good summarization of the Royal Commission inquiry is in *Secret Service: Political Policing in Canada from the Fenians to Fortress America* by Reg Whitaker, Gregory S. Kealey, and Andrew Parnaby (University of Toronto Press, 2012). See also Steve Hewitt, *Spying 101: The RCMP's Secret Activities at Canadian Universities* (University of Toronto Press, 2002). Scott Rutherford's 2011 doctoral dissertation at Queen's University, Kingston, Ontario, "Canada's Other Red Scare: Rights, Decolonization, and Indigenous Political Protest in the Global Sixties," 191–228.

13. For good measure, his chief surveillance target, Rosie Douglas, also was expelled, separately. He was a Marxist who wanted to be his native Dominica's prime minister and in the meantime was building a nonviolent multiracial progressive coalition in Canada. Hart was his driver, a perfect cover, and confidante. All went like clockwork; "Red Rosie" became a convincing extra in a masquerade that he did not understand. On their return after a few weeks of bonding, the two were toasted by radicals. A good book on all of this is *Secret Service* about political policing in Canada (University of Toronto Press, 2012).

14. FBI response to my Freedom of Information request, Nov. 12, 2013.

15. *Miami Herald,* Feb., 16, 2001.

16. Florida Department of Corrections.

17. Levine obituary, *Sun,* July 12, 1999.

18. Frank Donner, *Protectors of Privilege: Red Squads and Police Repression in Urban America* (University of California Press, 1990); Frank J. Donner, *The Age of Surveillance: The Aims and Methods of America's Political Intelligence System* (Knopf, 1980).

19. I remember walking into the chief of patrol's office in 1970. "I see you have been with your commie friends," said the duty officer, flashing a photo of me showing my *Sun*-issued gas mask to *News American* reporter Barbara Blum at a demonstration.

20. *Sun,* Jan. 26, 1975.

21. Maryland Senate Investigating Committee Established Pursuant to Resolutions 1 and 151 (Dec. 31, 1975), 34.

22. *Evening Sun,* Nov. 26, 1980.

23. *Sun,* July 10, 1969. May 6, 8; *Washington Post,* May 8 1970.

24. Hepbron also had been a vociferous opponent of police unions.

25. *Sun,* July 20, 1920.

26. *Sun,* June 26, 1920. Nothing also came out of the grand jury recommendation that eugenic controls be imposed on marriages of all races. "Legislation requiring examination of those who would be allowed to beget and rear children would help materially in reducing feeblemindedness and degeneracy."

27. W. Marvin Dulaney, *Black Police in America* (Indiana University Press, 1996), 32–34.

28. Dan Riker, *The Blue Girl Murders: A Mystery in Turbulent Baltimore in 1966* (CreateSpace, 2015).

29. The penetration is described in the Maryland Senate report, also *Sun*, Jan. 26, 1975. Obituary in *Sun*, Feb. 13, 2003.

30. C. Fraser Smith, *William Donald Schaefer: A Political Biography* (Johns Hopkins University Press, 1999), 129. This book is a must-read, even though it does not cover Schaefer's career after he left city hall to become governor, then state comptroller.

31. When the state legalized lotteries in Maryland in 1971, many of the lucrative outlets were given to political associates of Adams, Kovens, and state senator Joseph Staszak, *Sun*, Mar. 29, 1971.

32. The turns and twists of the Jenoff case were fascinating. See *New York Daily News*, Jan. 12, 2014; *NYT*, Oct. 29, 2001.

33. Antero Pietila, "Agent Bridged Two Worlds," *Sun*, Oct. 11, 1971.

34. Roger L. Twigg was one reporter whose extension and home phone were bugged, *Sun*, Oct. 19, 1975.

35. An excellent summary of allegations in *Washington Post*, Mar. 31, 1950.

36. Mame Warren's interview with Jones, June 18, 1999, https://jscholarship .library.jhu.edu/handle/1774.2/37755.

37. *Sun*, Apr. 24, 1948. Surveillance extended to the Communist Party's New Era bookstore, on Park Avenue across from the Enoch Pratt library. It was a treasure trove of movement newspapers and radical literature. The basement was filled with dusty old works in Yiddish and Russian, and occasionally German and Finnish. Vandals repeatedly stoned New Era's display windows. Party lawyers, including Harold Buchman, were under surveillance; he defended Black Panthers in several cases.

38. At the HUAC hearing, Wertheimer was questioned by Rep. Francis Walter, a Pennsylvania Democrat. Here is how it went (*Sun*, July 13, 1951):

Walter: "We have been informed that you were denied a degree at Johns Hopkins University because of the material in the thesis on the unification of Germany on the Soviet plan."

Wertheimer: "It's a complete untruth. I'm sure you didn't call the department of history. I have not finished my thesis."

Walter: "Didn't you write a thesis on the theory of the unification of Germany?"

Wertheimer: "I did not." He then volunteered that he had written about Germany in 1848, which failed and produced an exodus of "Forty-Eighters" to the United States.

In the same hearing, Wertheimer's birth nationality prompted questions. The committee wanted to know whether he was born "in eastern or western Germany?" Gunther was born in 1926, two decades before postwar Germany was divided.

For some six years. Milton and I were part of a 7 a.m. koffee klatsch every Saturday in Fells Point to heal the world. Sometimes more than a dozen people gathered around a small table. After Milton transitioned, Gunther, who was not part of the Fells Point group, and I began meeting regularly. The Wertheimers were at the cutting edge of activism; Joan, his wife, for a time headed CORE.

39. *Sun, Evening Sun*, Jan. 14, 1966.

40. Jim Keck, People's Free Clinic oral interviews, University of Baltimore Langsdale Library special collection.

41. *Washington Post*, Feb. 10, 1923.

42. *Sun*, Nov. 28, 1978.

CHAPTER 11. A CITADEL OF HOPE

1. *Afro-American*, Aug. 10, 1895.

2. *Afro-American*, Aug. 10, 1895; Apr. 12, 1969.

3. Gregg L. Michel, "Union Power, Soul Power" Unionizing Johns Hopkins University Hospital, 1959–1974, *Labor History,* No. 1, Jan. 1966, 28–66.

4. The law would be amended to permit union activity at nonprofit hospitals in 1974. See Edmund R. Becker, Frank A. Sloan, and Bruce Steinwald, "Union Activity in Hospitals: Past, Present, and Future," *Health Care Financing Review*, June 1982.

5. *Sun*, Dec. 20, 1946.

6. After several name changes the hospital union evolved into today's Service Employees International Union (SEIU).

7. *Sun*, Aug. 13, 1969.

8. *Sun*, Dec. 3, 1974.

9. *Labor History*, 38, no. 1, 28–66.

10. *Sun*, Dec. 3, 1974.

11. *Sun*, Dec. 8, 1974.

12. In 1964 Martin Luther King, who had recently won the Nobel Peace Prize, came to Baltimore. Greeted by thousands, he drove in a motorcade on Gay Street to drum up support for the reelection of President Johnson.

13. *Post and Courier*, Sept. 30, 2013.

14. Interviews with John McClintock, and assistant managing editors John Plunkett and James Keat. *The Sun* gave extensive coverage, but labor reporter John McClintock had a terse analysis yanked out of a Sunday paper after the first edition. A top editor made the decision; the paper's publisher was a Hopkins hospital trustee. The *Afro* practically ignored the Hopkins struggle. It did not even mention Coretta King's picketing, although just months earlier it had covered the Charleston strike with news stories and editorials.

15. He backed the nationwide boycott of California lettuce and grapes declared by Cesar Chavez's United Farm Workers' Union, and also rallied behind the textile workers' union.

16. *Sun*, Aug. 26, 1969.

17. "By 1970 African-Americans occupied 95% (1188) of the non-professional employee positions at the hospital and women held approximately 88% (1100) of the jobs." *Labor History*, 34.

18. David E. Price, *Hospital Services in the 1970's*, an April 2, 1970, report in the medical archives.

19. Price.

20. Price, 15.

21. Through twists and turns over the past half century, Columbia's hospital is now part of the Hopkins empire, but the Columbia Health Plan is run by other companies.

22. James D. Dilts, *Sun*, Nov. 29, 1970.

23. When Good Samaritan was inaugurated, only physicians with an appointment at Hopkins could work there. *Sun*, May 18, 1977.

24. *Sun*, Sept. 11; Nov. 11, 1907.

25. *Sun*, July 3, 1984.

26. It is fascinating to speculate how different Maryland politics might be if Schaefer had never risen to the top. That was a distinct possibility as late as in 1967, four years before his mayoral victory. Old Tommy D'Alesandro had ended his tenure at city hall, and among those vying for the top post was former councilman Peter G. Angelos, the future asbestos litigator and Orioles owner. He had Pollack's support but could not defeat Young Tommy D'Alesandro and his city council president running mate, Schaefer, who were backed by Kovens.

27. *Sun*, May 2, 1972.

28. *Sun* profile by Michael Hill, Feb. 22, 2004.

29. Mark Reutter, email to the author.

30. Even music long was segregated. A colored park band continued until 1964.

31. Kenneth S. Clark, *Baltimore: "Cradle of Municipal Music"* (City of Baltimore, 1941).

32. *Sun*, Dec. 31, 1986.

33. *Sun*, July 8, 1946. For the whole transformation story, see Martin L. Millspaugh, "The Inner Harbor Story," *Urban Land*, April 2003.

34. H. L. Mencken, *Happy Days: Mencken's Autobiography: 1880–1892* (Johns Hopkins Press, 2006), 70.

35. That was one of the high points. The low point was not of his making: City council president Walter S. Orlinsky's imagination got the better of him. He baked the "world's largest birthday cake" for the nation's bicentennial. It was meant for visitors to enjoy, but rain melted the icing into the harbor.

36. *Sun*, June 29, 1980.

37. See Martin Millspaugh, "The Sydney Story," http://www.globalharbors.org/sydney_darling_harbor.html.

38. *Sun*, July 25, 1868.

39. *Sun*, Oct. 25, 1873.

40. *Sun*, Feb. 23, 1860.

41. *Sun*, May 24, 1944.

42. One architectural gem fortunately survives. It is the Fava iron building that was dissembled and reerected next to Carroll Mansion.

43. The downtown site that was chosen for the Baltimore Civic Center was actually not one of the many proposed to the Greater Baltimore Committee in 1955. Among nine suggested locations were three in Druid Hill Park, three at the end of the Inner Harbor, and one in Clifton Park.

44. *Sun*, Nov. 10, 1988.

45. Source: Gene Raynor.

46. *Sun* obituary, May 28, 2016.

47. *Washington Post*, Apr. 8, 1987.

48. In addition to Grasmick, a number of Kovens associates from Baltimore held shares in Caesar's Palace: Abraham Adler, Jerome Alperstein, Nathaniel Goldberg, Edward Jacobson, Nathan Jacobson, Leonard Levin, Julius Rainess, Harry Rosenberg, Ruth Schuman, and Lloyd Watner. Nevada Gaming Commission records, cited in Ed Reid's *The Grim Reapers* (Bantam, 1970), 302.

CHAPTER 12. ROUGH ROAD TO RENEWAL

1. Du liked to impress constituents by flashing wads of cash—I saw him do that at city hall and at Palmer House, a watering hole he favored near Lexington Market. But he usually gave nothing. All this time he continued to live in a modest two-story Mura Street row house that was all of fourteen feet wide.

2. *Sun*, Dec. 13, 2003.

3. *Sun*, Jan 13, 2003.

4. *Washington Post*, May 27, 1990.

5. Grenville Whitman, a former director of Man Alive methadone program: "Yes, Schmoke tried early in his administration. Reaction was strongly negative and he backed off quickly, never to mention it again. He was correct, but afraid."

6. Enterprise Foundation Annual Report, 1987, 23, 24.

7. The area was often referred to by a planning term, Sandtown-Winchester. Winchester was on the west side of Fulton Avenue behind railroad tracks, a neighborhood of row houses with porches.

8. *Sun*, Oct. 1, 1967.

9. Liz Bowie, "Dome Corp: Hopkins Humbled," *Sun*, Jan. 10, 1993.

10. Knott's business acumen was sharp. He became the board chairman and then president of the Arundel Corporation and began redeveloping its old quarries and abandoned gravel pits to marketable real estate—apartment complexes and shopping centers. Beyond Baltimore, Arundel contributed to the construction of a dam in British Columbia, a lock and power house on the Snake River in Washington State, and the underwater tunnel system in New York

11. *Sun*, Apr. 27, 1975; July 16, 1958.

12. *Sun*, Dec. 12, 1968.

13. *Sun*, May 5, 1971. Its partnership with NDC would fray in later years but the impact was seen for decades. NDC was the base of Orlinsky, who became Schaefer's first city council president. And while Joseph J. Clarke, WCBM's advertising director, failed to get elected to the state legislature, his wife, Mary Pat, became a liberal icon on the city council.

14. Email to the author.

15. *Sun*, July 29, 2005.

16. I am relying on M. William Salganik's meticulous reporting in *The Sun*.

17. "Cox Grilled on Proposed Ownership: City Panel Focuses on Investor Profits" by M. William Salganik, *Sun*, Dec. 23, 1982.

18. *Sun*, Oct. 15, 1983.

19. *Sun*, Feb. 24, March, 1984; *Washington Post*, Feb. 6, 1990. Black investors, Clarence Elder, a Baltimore businessman, and O. Patrick Scott, a Prince George's County public school art teacher, sued to get their payout. They received an immediate $8.7 million lump sum payment. In addition, United Cable transferred to them more than twenty-one hundred units, or shares, in the investment partnership that underwrote the cable system.

20. *Sun*, Jan. 8, 2005.

21. *Sun*, Nov. 29, 1970.

22. *Sun*, June 1, 1975.

23. *Sun*, July 29, 1981; Aug. 4, 1985.

24. *Sun*, May 30, 1980.

25. Sun, Mar. 20, 1979.

26. *Sun*, Dec. 14, 1896.

27. *Sun*, Feb. 7, 1980.

28. *Sun*, Aug. 18, 2008.

29. *Sun*, May 3, 1997.

30. *Sun*, Apr. 5, 2003.

31. For a benign assessment, see Richard Patrick Clinch's 2008 dissertation, "The Community Capacity Building Impact of the Baltimore Empowerment Zone," University of Maryland, https://drum.lib.umd.edu/bitstream/handle/1903/8303/umi-umd-5304.pdf?sequence=1&isAllowed=y.

32. *Sun*, Feb. 13, 2003.

33. *Sun*, Oct. 28, 2000.

34. *Sun*, June 20, 2011.

35. *Sun*, Apr. 18, 2002.

36. Philip A. Hummel, "East Side Story: The East Baltimore Development Initiative," an undated University of Maryland law school paper, http://digitalcommons.law.umaryland.edu/cgi/viewcontent.cgi?article=1010&context=mlh_pubs.

37. *Daily Record*, Jan. 31–Feb.4, 2011.

38. *Sun*, Mar. 22, 2017.

39. *Baltimore Business Journal*, Sept. 8, 2016.

CHAPTER 13. THE KNOCKERS

1. David Rocah, "When the Baltimore Police Locked Down Several Blocks of a Black Neighborhood," ACLU, Dec. 27, 2017, https://www.aclu.org/blog/criminal-law-reform/reforming-police-practices/when-baltimore-police-locked-down-several-blocks.

2. *Sun*, Dec. 9, 2017.

3. *Sun*, Oct. 27, 2017. Tim Prudente wrote how one forty-one-year-old druggie texted to tempt a nineteen-year-old woman and recovering addict with heroin she craved. He bought six grams from the police-connected ring. They binged and had sex before she died in his basement. He was sentenced to a decade in federal prison and testified hoping for an early release.

4. *Baltimore Brew*, Feb. 21, 2018.

5. Less than three months after his appointment, De Souza was charged with failure to file federal income taxes for three years. Pugh first declared she had confidence in the commissioner, but the very next day suspended him.

6. Convicted detective Momodu Gondo testified in the Gun Trace Task Force trial that he used to steal money with Detective Suiter. "You'd take money, split it among yourselves?" a lawyer asked. Gondo agreed. *Sun*, Feb. 5, 2018. The grand jury did not indict Suiter.

7. *Sun*, Oct. 24, 1873.

8. *Sun*, Aug. 12, 2004.

9. *Sun*, Jan. 9, 2016.

10. *NYT*, Oct. 2, 2017; *Sun*, Dec. 3, 2017.

11. *NYT*, Feb. 6, 2018; *Sun*, Feb. 16, 2018.

12. Burley said he thought the masked knockers were criminals trying to rob him. "I felt like I was in imminent danger and I took off," he said in a phone call with AP; WJLA television, Dec. 19, 2017. On the FBI bug, one knocker is heard suggesting that the officers alter their time sheets to show they weren't working at the time of the crash. "Hey, I was in the car just driving home," he laughed.

13. Edward Ericson Jr., *Baltimore Fishbowl*, Feb. 8, 2018.

14. *Sun*, Apr. 24, 2013.

15. *Afro-American*, Dec. 23, 1972.

16. *Washington Post*, Apr. 7, 1973.

17. *Sun*, June 9, 1908; Aug. 15, 1910.

18. *Sun*, Sept. 1, 1951.

19. Van Smith, *City Paper*, June 5, 1996.

20. Merry-Go-Round eventually crashed in the fickle retail market amid changes in young people's tastes and management mistakes in acquisitions and expansion. Wrote *Fortune*: "Human history has produced exactly one Johann Sebastian Bach, one Sir Isaac Newton, and—for better or worse—one Leonard 'Boogie' Weinglass. Weinglass is a true original—a streetwise Baltimore bad boy who grew up to be, by turns, hippie, founder of a successful retail chain, multimillionaire, jet-setting Florida playboy, unorthodox Aspen family man, and spectacular failure."

CHAPTER 14. THE PRICE OF POISON

1. Leif Michael Fredrickson, "The Age of Lead: Metropolitan Change, Environmental Health, and Inner City Underdevelopment in Baltimore," PhD diss., University of Virginia, May 2017, 20. It is a tour de force and essential reading.

2. https://www.lead.org.au/history_of_lead_poisoning_in_the_world.htm.

3. When a new water-soluble paint for general purposes, Porceline, was introduced in 1879, it had "no lead or copper or other poisonous substance in it, and can be used without injury by any person, even of the most delicate constitution." *Sun*, Aug. 16, 1879.

4. Huntington Williams's privately published autobiography for family.

5. *Sun*, Oct. 15, 1951.

6. In 1945 the Eastern Health District was used to help evaluate the new and successful treatment of syphilis by the "miracle drug" penicillin. Among universities, Hopkins at the time was the largest recipient of federal funding for research, much of it going into combatting venereal diseases.

7. *Washington Post*, Apr. 25, Apr. 29, 2015. Conversations with Stanley Sugarman.

8. *Wall Street Journal*, Sept. 8, 2015.

9. See their essay, "With the Best Intentions: Lead Research and the Challenge to Public Health," *American Journal of Public Health*, November 2012, 19–33.

10. *Sun*, Sept. 4, 1996.

11. *Sun*, Feb. 11, 2018.

12. *NYT*, Jan. 26, 2018.

13. Liz Bowie, "Baltimore Students Score Near Bottom in Reading, Math on Key National Assessment," *Sun*, Apr. 10, 2018. Channel 45, Fox News, Nov. 8, 2017.

14. *Sun*, Feb. 10, 2009.

15. *Sun*, Sept. 19, 2002.

16. Documents from 2016 mandated the recruitment of 250 to 350 additional out-of-state cases that fiscal year to reach profit targets of $5 million to $7 million.

17. Holloway, 342.

Index

About the Author

Antero Pietila's thirty-five years with the *Baltimore Sun* included coverage of the city's neighborhoods, politics, and government and also seven years reporting as a correspondent in South Africa and the Soviet Union. A native of Finland, where he graduated from Tampere's School of Social Sciences, Pietila became a student of urban racial rotations during his first visit to the United States in 1964. He later obtained a Master of Arts degree at Southern Illinois University-Carbondale. He is the author of *Not in My Neighborhood: How Bigotry Shaped a Great American City* (2010). He is a contributor to *The Life of Kings: The Baltimore Sun and the Golden Age of the American Newspaper*, as well as coauthor of an e-book, *Race Goes to War: Ollie Stewart and the Reporting of Black Correspondents in World War II*. He resides in Baltimore, Maryland.